TEXAS THROUGH WOMEN'S EYES

Book Twenty-Four
Louann Atkins Temple Women & Culture Series
Books about women and families, and their changing role in society

TEXAS THROUGH WOMEN'S EYES

The Twentieth-Century Experience

JUDITH N. MCARTHUR
AND HAROLD L. SMITH

UNIVERSITY OF TEXAS PRESS

Austin

The Louann Atkins Temple Women & Culture Series is supported by
Allison, Doug, Taylor, and Andy Bacon; Margaret, Lawrence, Will, John,
and Annie Temple; Larry Temple; the Temple-Inland Foundation; and
the National Endowment for the Humanities.

Requests for permission to reproduce material from this work should be
sent to:
Permissions
University of Texas Press
P.O. Box 7819
Austin, TX 78713-7819
www.utexas.edu/utpress/about/bpermission.html

♾ The paper used in this book meets the minimum requirements of ANSI/
NISO Z39.48-1992 (R1997) (Permanence of Paper).

LIBRARY OF CONGRESS CATALOGING-IN-PUBLICATION DATA

McArthur, Judith N.
Texas through women's eyes : the twentieth-century experience /
Judith N. McArthur and Harold L. Smith. — 1st ed.
p. cm. — (Louann Atkins Temple women & culture series ; bk. 24)
Includes bibliographical references and index.
ISBN 978-0-292-72282-8 (cloth : alk. paper)
ISBN 978-0-292-72303-0 (pbk. : alk. paper)
1. Women—Texas—History—20th century—Sources. 2. Women—
Texas—Social conditions—20th century—Sources. 3. Women's
rights—Texas—History—20th century—Sources. 4. Women—Political
activity—Texas—History—20th century—Sources. 5. Texas—Social
conditions—20th century—Sources. 6. Texas—Politics and government—
20th century—Sources. 7. Political culture—Texas—History—20th
century—Sources. I. Smith, Harold L. II. Title.
HQ1438.T4M36 2010
305.4209764'0904—dc22
2009049280

CONTENTS

Part Three   137
CONFORMITY, CIVIL RIGHTS, AND SOCIAL PROTEST, 1945–1965

Part Four   195
FEMINISM, BACKLASH, AND POLITICAL CULTURE, 1965–2000

ACKNOWLEDGMENTS

We incurred many debts of gratitude while working on this volume. At the University of Houston–Victoria, the Academic Council provided the financial support that made the research possible, and the library staff dealt efficiently with a multitude of information requests. Shirley Parkan and Lou Ellen Callarman coped with our seemingly endless flow of interlibrary loan requests over the past five years, never failing to provide superb service with a smile. Karen Locher's expert knowledge of Texas state documents was invaluable. She and the rest of the reference staff, all of whom we imposed on in turn, made our work easier.

Dozens of archivists and librarians across the state—and several from outside Texas—gave us crucial assistance. We especially thank Gerrianne Schaad at the University of Texas at San Antonio, Yu Li at the Institute of Texan Cultures, Tom Kreneck at Texas A&M University–Corpus Christi, Ruth Baker at the Austin Public Library's Austin History Center, Nancy Cott and Sarah Hambleton at the Schlesinger Library at Radcliffe Institute, and the archivists at the Sophia Smith Collection, Smith College. Dawn Letson and Ann Barton at Texas Woman's University were, as always, extraordinary. Ellen K. Brown at Baylor University graciously allowed us special access to the Texas Collection while we were refugees from Hurricane Rita, and made our time there pleasant and productive. Gary Spurr, university archivist at the University of Texas at Arlington, handled multiple requests for oral histories in the Texas Labor Archives. Richard Himmel, university archivist at the University of North Texas, stayed after-hours so that we could photocopy oral histories. Patrick Lemelle at the Institute of Texas Cultures, and John Anderson at the Texas State Library and Archives, were especially helpful in our search for photos. Claudia Rivers at the University of Texas at El Paso went out of her way to transmit a Farah strike poster in photographic format.

We are indebted to Yvonne Davis Frear and Mary Ann Villarreal for answering research queries; Caroline Castillo-Crimm and Margaret Dorsey for help with Spanish translations; Pat Stone, Denise Hulett, and John J. Leffler for supplying sources on the Texas birth control movement; and Gail

Hershatter for sharing copies of her interviews with Farah strikers. Thanks to Brenda Kennedy for an introduction to Martha and W. R. Nichols, who demonstrated the operation of a treadle sewing machine and a gasoline iron, and to Beverly Tomek and Jackie McElhaney for research assistance.

Special thanks are due to Alan Pogue for supplying a photo of Tex-Son striker Ofelia Bowers from his private archive, to Sarah Weddington for a personal photograph, and to Katie Naranjo for ensuring that we received it despite the inefficiencies of the U.S. Postal Service. Martha Cotera, who has spent a lifetime making Chicana history as well as writing it, shared a personal photograph and her insider's knowledge of Chicana participation in International Women's Year. She also kindly granted permission to publish a document from her papers in the Benson Latin American Collection at the University of Texas at Austin. Virginia Whitehill gave us by telephone an invaluable firsthand account of the early years of the abortion rights movement.

For technical assistance with document scanning we are obliged to Sheron Barnes and Greg Garcia. Kayla Sappington and Melody Vecera skillfully handled photo format conversions. We extend heartfelt gratitude to Elizabeth Hayes Turner for reading and criticizing the entire manuscript and to Bill Bishel, our sponsoring editor at the University of Texas Press, for his encouragement and astute guidance.

Our thanks to all.

INTRODUCTION

This book grew out of our frustration with the inadequate discussion of women in Texas history survey texts. As specialists in the twentieth century, we were especially disturbed by the lengthy silences regarding women's experiences between 1900 and 2000. While most texts mention the woman suffrage movement, usually without regional or analytical context, they then largely ignore women's lives except for a handful of famous individuals such as Miriam Ferguson, Emma Tenayuca, Sarah Weddington, and Ann Richards. Typically they add a paragraph at the end of discussions of the Progressive Era and the world wars to acknowledge that women were also involved, and note the feminist revival in the 1970s. Even conscientious readers can hardly avoid concluding that modern Texas women have no history to speak of, and that the twentieth century unfolded without women's labor, civic engagement, social protest, and political organizing. We offer this volume as evidence to the contrary. Our aim, in historian Anne Firor Scott's phrase, is to make the invisible woman visible.

If the nineteenth century, when women first organized to demand emancipation, was known as the "woman's century," the era after 1900 might well be called the "New Woman's century." The influx of large numbers of women into the workforce and into postsecondary education—by the 1990s female undergraduates outnumbered males on college campuses—was a new departure and marked the emergence of the modern female role. In the twentieth century, women secured the essential political and legal rights that previous generations, who could not vote, sit on a jury, or sign a contract if married, had sought unsuccessfully, and constructed new identities—in politics, sports, and the military—that were beyond imagination in 1900. A new kind of female potential unfolded in the first two decades of the century, the Progressive Era, as young women claimed personal freedom and middle-class clubwomen invented new public roles. Although voteless, they excelled at pressure-group tactics, using female networks so effectively to promote social change that historians of women have broadened the definition of politics to include the wide spectrum of women's collective efforts, both formal and informal, to shape public policy and influence government behavior. At the same time, New Women reinvigorated and expanded the woman suffrage movement and finally secured the right to vote.

Although the structured and highly visible women's movement that had won the ballot splintered in the decades after 1920, female activism persisted and assumed new forms. The extended period of prosperity that lasted from the end of World War II until the 1960s, when middle-class families could live comfortably on the income of a male breadwinner and popular culture celebrated suburban domesticity, was, despite the absence of a feminist move- ment, a time of significant social change. Women of color and working-class women, who lacked the security of the family wage, were the most publicly active, organizing civil rights and labor protests in pursuit of both economic and social justice. Notwithstanding the cultural ideal of full-time mother- hood, increasing numbers of white, married women entered the workforce. The reemergence of organized feminism coincided with the demise of the family wage system over the last third of the century, when slow economic growth and stagnant earnings for men pushed more wives into the workplace. As paid employment became the norm even for mothers with young children, and women gradually established themselves in most professions, frustration over job discrimination, wage inequality, restrictive laws, and rigid gender roles, coalesced into a new feminist movement. An equally vocal opposition quickly emerged to defend the traditional gender system and its perceived moral underpinnings. The backlash against feminism by a grassroots conser- vative women's movement, mobilized against abortion and the Equal Rights Amendment, was crucial to the emergence of the New Right in politics.

One of feminism's many goals—and one of the most challenging—was to eliminate the deeply entrenched sexual division of labor. The separation of labor into male and female jobs has invariably meant lower wages and fewer opportunities for women, while employers benefited from a cheap labor supply. Throughout the text, we emphasize the importance of labor femi- nism: the struggle of working-class women for wage justice, union recogni- tion, and an equitable share of leadership positions in workers' organizations. Although always a small proportion of unionized workers, twentieth-century Texas women have been militant and tenacious strikers, from the Houston telephone operators' walkout of 1900 to the prolonged Farah Manufacturing protest of the 1970s that resulted in a nationwide boycott of the company's slacks. After feminists coined a new term, "sex discrimination," to attack the sexual division of labor, female trade unionists not only challenged wage in- equality but also pressed for contracts with pregnancy and maternity leave that acknowledged their dual roles as wage earners and childbearers.

The themes of family and sexual life also connect with public issues that extend far beyond the workplace. In the first half of the century interracial sexual relationships could trigger community violence, and interracial marriage was prohibited. The much publicized "sexual revolution" that began in the 1960s made heterosexual cohabitation commonplace and ignited an acrimonious debate over same-sex relationships that has not abated. The impossibility of disentangling the personal and the political is nowhere more evident than in the issue of control over reproduction, which in Texas began with the birth control movement in the 1930s and continues in the aftermath of *Roe v. Wade* and abortion politics. At different times and for different reasons, women have used their maternal roles to claim public authority. Liberals and conservatives alike have organized, lobbied, and marched in the name of motherhood: to demand the vote in the 1910s and to oppose the Equal Rights Amendment in the 1970s.

In telling this story of twentieth-century Texas women, we have taken particular account of the interactions between gender and the hierarchies of race and ethnicity. Within the sex-segregated workforce, African American and Hispanic women dominated the lowest-paid and least desirable jobs. Working-class women of color were denigrated as sexually licentious and were vulnerable to sexual coercion by white men. Those of the middle class were usually denied the social privileges of whiteness, the right to be treated as "ladies," with the sexual respectability and moral authority that such status conferred. Anglo, African American, and Hispanic women had separate voluntary association traditions and agendas. White women excluded their black counterparts from the suffrage movement, and white men barred their access to the polls after the vote was won. For minority women, campaigns for gender equality have been intertwined with the pursuit of racial justice. They challenged segregation (by law for African Americans and by custom for Latinas) in the courts and on picket lines and coalesced into separate feminist movements—multiracial sisterhood was an elusive goal.

We wrote this book with two objectives: to synthesize the existing scholarship and to map the historical terrain. The Progressive Era is the best-documented period of twentieth-century Texas women's history. Historians of women, ourselves included, have brought to light an entire social justice wing of Texas Progressivism, which was dominated by middle-class women working for multiple reforms through their voluntary associations. In every major city, organized women attacked the problems of urban growth and industrial development, funding settlement houses, free public kindergartens, clean milk stations, and day nurseries for working mothers. To previous generations of historians, who defined progressivism as insurance and banking reform, prohibition, and railroad regulation, such women were invisible because they worked at the local level. Only a few scholars have investigated female grassroots activism in the post-Progressive period, although such research has the potential to reshape other narratives. Women were the foot soldiers of the civil rights movement: traveling organizers for the NAACP, administrators of local chapters, and community organizers who did the unseen work that sustained local demonstrations. As we discovered in researching this book, conservative women were likewise the ground troops in the state's Republican revolution. They did the unpaid, grassroots organizing in the 1950s and 1960s that was crucial to the growth of a two-party system in Texas and the eventual transition from Democratic to Republican dominance.

In addition to synthesis, we have done archival research to flesh out topics on which the secondary literature is thin, especially in the latter decades of the century. We began the project anticipating that Part Four, covering the period after 1965, would be shorter than any of the first three parts because so little has been written about second-wave feminism in Texas. To our surprise, we uncovered such abundant raw material—newsletters, clippings, manuscript collections, and oral histories—in the archives that it was a challenge to hold the chapter to a reasonable length. Because so much of Part Four is based on new research, we have expanded the endnotes in that section and provided extensive citations for our discussion of Anglo and Chicana feminism, antifeminist backlash and women of the New Right, and Title IX and gender equity in sports. We hope that this preliminary survey of a neglected period will encourage further scholarly investigation.

Each of the text's four parts is accompanied by a selection of primary documents, arranged in approximate chronological order (some have no precise dates) for ease of browsing. Each document is cross-referenced in the text and provides a fuller picture of the point under discussion. The majority of the documents are first-person accounts—letters, memoirs, and oral histories—that reveal what women at the time were thinking and doing. We have chosen as many as we could find that allow the reader to experience an incident or emotion with the narrator, whether campaigning for suffrage, striking for higher pay, doing stoop labor in a vegetable field, or standing up to racism. A few are amusing, many are moving, and some by women of color are disturbing, especially those that recount racially scarring childhood events. Such documents provide the visceral sense of history that is difficult to convey in an analytic text.

We intend *Texas Through Women's Eyes* for a wide audience, including college students, teachers, and anyone with an interest in Texas history and women's history. We especially hope that it will suggest research topics to young scholars. We have concluded each chapter with a list of secondary sources, grouped by subject, upon which we drew most heavily. In addition to serving as documentation, we hope these lists will function as bibliographic maps pointing to the many unexplored and barely explored avenues for future books, theses, and dissertations.

SOCIAL REFORM AND SUFFRAGE
IN THE PROGRESSIVE ERA,   *Part One*
1900–1920

In 1896, when Isadore Miner (later Callaway) became the women's editor of the *Dallas Morning News*, she christened her new domain the "Woman's Century" page to alert readers that she intended to chronicle women's achievements, not report on soirees and style changes. Social commentators often referred to the nineteenth century as the Woman's Century or the Woman's Era because women for the first time organized to demand emancipation: the right to obtain higher education, to enter the professions, to control their own property after marriage, and to vote. A few of the bravest had even abandoned their heavy, floor-sweeping dresses for short, comfortable bloomers that permitted complete freedom of movement. The bloomer experiment quickly passed, but the nineteenth century saw a series of firsts for women. They were the first generation to attend college, to campaign for suffrage, to lobby for married women's property laws, to argue collectively for women's rights. They were the first to become doctors, professors, and, like Isadore Callaway, newspaperwomen.

If the nineteenth century, the era of Elizabeth Cady Stanton and Susan B. Anthony, was the Woman's Century, the twentieth century might justly be called the New Woman's Century. The New Woman was the icon of the age. At the turn of the century she still lacked political equality, but she was defining a new ideal of white, middle-class womanhood. Liberated from crinolines and bustles, the New Woman wore a high-necked shirtwaist blouse (factory-made and easy to launder) and an ankle-length A-line skirt, an outfit for the public sphere and no impediment even to bicycling, tennis, or hiking. The New Woman was educated, perhaps even a college graduate, and productively occupied. No longer restricted to teaching, she might be a settlement house resident, a social worker, or even a stunt pilot like Katherine Stinson, one of the first women to earn an aviator's license, who with her family operated the Stinson School of Flying in San Antonio. And like Perle Penfield, a student at the University of Texas Medical Branch at Galveston who spent the summer before her 1915 graduation working as an organizer for the Texas

Woman Suffrage Association, the New Woman was likely to favor voting rights for her sex.

The new century also saw the evolution of women's voluntary associations, especially the woman's club. Study clubs originated in the nineteenth century, formed by urban middle-class women who wanted to educate themselves in literature, history, and the arts. In the twentieth century, as the conveniences of household technology, commercially processed food, and ready-made clothing freed more time for leisure activities, women's voluntary associations proliferated and joined together to form city and state federations. The Texas Federation of Women's Clubs, founded in 1897, grew rapidly, claiming ten thousand members by 1910. Club agendas expanded to include social issues such as child welfare, the problems of the poor, and city sanitation, and club members organized civic improvement associations. A newer network of mothers' clubs, which focused on child study and school improvement, became the forerunners of the Parent-Teacher Association and formed the Texas Congress of Mothers in 1909. An urban wife and mother might belong to several clubs and through them might find herself raising money to build a playground for the neighborhood school or petitioning the city council to pass a pure food ordinance.

New Women and clubwomen played a major role in shaping the language and agenda of the Progressive Era, a period of reform activism that spanned roughly the first two decades of the twentieth century. Although Texas straddled the South and the West, it was politically part of the New South, where growing urbanization and industrialization coexisted with traditional devotion to limited government and unrestricted individual liberty. Seeking to balance individual rights with the public good—parents' right to their children's labor in the cotton fields against the children's benefit of attending school, or an employer's right to maximize profits by paying as little as possible against workers' need for a living wage—put Progressives at odds with the New South's devotion to unfettered economic development. Progressive women worked for social, moral, and political reform in league with men and also through their separate female political culture of clubs and other voluntary associations. In the process, they developed a new argument for suffrage—that women needed the vote in order to protect their homes and families, and government needed female expertise. White women's commitment to social reform did not, however, include challenging racial injustice. They accepted and endorsed segregation, which grew more rigid in the early twentieth century. Black and Hispanic women had their own visions of reform, focused on local community activism. Black women worked through a network of clubs and organizations parallel to but entirely separate from those of white women, while Mexicanas were caught up in revolution on the Mexican side of the border and labor protest on the American side.

URBANIZATION AND ECONOMIC OPPORTUNITY

Women's changing roles in the early decades of the twentieth century grew out of urban expansion, the development of new technologies, and wider educational opportunity. Although Texas was still predominantly rural and agricultural, the percentage of city dwellers rose steadily. In 1890 there was no urban center in the state with a population of forty thousand; by 1920 Dallas, Fort Worth, Houston, and San Antonio all had more than one hundred thousand residents and El Paso was approaching seventy-eight thousand. The proportion of Texans in urban areas grew from 17 percent to 41 percent between 1900 and 1930. During those decades the number of women working in agriculture declined by half: for farmers' and sharecroppers' daughters, both white and black, cities were magnets. There they found urban amenities—gas, electricity, indoor plumbing—that made life easier, and others, such as telephone exchanges, department stores, and business offices, that offered new opportunities for earning daily bread.

Women in small towns had limited options for making a living. Gertrude Beasley remembered grimly how her family made ends meet in Abilene without a male breadwinner. Her mother took in boarders and, when they were scarce, asked the neighbors for sewing. Gertrude resentfully waited on the boarders' table and eventually taught in a one-room district school, where she could exert her authority over defiant adolescent boys only with a heavy switch.[1] In Dallas County, by contrast, the Texas Bureau of Labor Statistics identified significant numbers of women in half a dozen industries. Telephone operators were by far the largest category. Nelle Wooding began working for the Dallas telephone exchange in 1914, making $30 a month for a shift from 1:00 to 10:30 p.m. "That was among the lowest wages paid anywhere other than laundry workers and dime store employees," she remembered. "But I was just a teenager and I didn't have an advanced education, and that was just about the best job I was able to find at the time."[2] Cotton mill operatives were the next largest group, followed by garment workers, commercial laundry workers, and milliners (makers of women's hats). Small numbers also worked in light manufacturing, making paper boxes, envelopes, and medicines. The majority of women in the labor force worked in service or manufacturing occupations and earned half or less of what male workers were paid. "Women's jobs" were further stratified by race. The rapidly expanding "pink collar" service sector positions, whether they paid fairly well (such as stenography) or poorly (department store sales), were specifically white women's work. Women of color filled such positions only in minority-owned businesses. They were the least skilled and most poorly paid urban workers, clustered in household and hotel service, food processing, and laundry work.

Although African American women were only 18 percent of the female population in Texas, they made up 42 percent of the female labor force. Because black men were also forced into low-wage jobs, a substantial number of wives worked full- or part-time. More than 80 percent of black women in the urban labor force were personal and domestic service workers, leaving their own families for workdays that stretched from early morning until night in white households. A small number of black women were independent seamstresses and milliners, but they were excluded from garment factories. A handful owned small businesses, and the most popular was hairdressing. The number of black women working as beauticians, barbers, or manicurists quadrupled between 1910 and 1920.[3] Cosmetology did not require a high school diploma or much startup capital, and since white beauticians refused to serve black women, the clientele was extensive. Operating a successful beauty salon was a respected occupation in the black community, viewed more as a profession than a trade, and one way to rise into the middle class. Cosmetology enabled black women to earn a living independent of white employers; for their clients, professionally groomed hair and careful attention to "beauty culture" was a defense against white society's racist stereotyping.

Mexican American and Mexican-born women occupied the lowest strata of the female labor force and earned less than subsistence wages. Except in South Texas, single Mexicanas had a lower rate of labor force participation than Anglo and African American women. Married women stayed out of the urban labor market, kept at home by high birth rates and a strong cultural tradition of male dominance. Widespread poverty in Mexican *colonias* pushed daughters and single women into the workforce to supplement men's earnings. Mexicanas did low-skilled work in pecan-shelling sheds, garment factories, laundries, and small Mexican-owned stores; many others worked in Anglo homes as maids. El Paso, a Hispanic-majority city, developed one of the earliest concentrations of wage-earning Mexicanas in the United States. The majority were domestics and laundresses; they made up more than half the labor force in the city's commercial laundries. Anglo prejudice resulted in dual pay scales: "American" and "Mexican" wages for the same work. In El Paso the Mexican wage was less than half the Anglo wage, and Mexicanas who appeared before the state's Industrial Welfare Commission in 1919 affirmed that their earnings trapped them in poverty. Laundry worker Maria

Valles, who lived with her family and supported a young daughter, testified that $4.50 a week did not begin to cover expenses: "I have to make great sacrifices, some days going without food."[4] The women who spoke estimated that they would need $15 or $16 a week to live decently.

STRIKES AND LABOR ACTIVISM

The American Federation of Labor officially advocated the unionization of women but in reality did little except pass an annual resolution. Aside from locals for garment workers and telephone operators, Texas women workers were largely unorganized. A Houston Labor Council committee reported in 1911 that 55 percent of the city's male workers were organized, but only 2 percent of women were. Telephone operators, whose job straddled the line between white- and blue-collar work, were the first strikers. Operators were white and native born (unaccented speech was a requirement), often high school educated, and young. They worked in clean surroundings and dressed as department store clerks and secretaries did—the telephone companies stressed the "refined" nature of their employees. But the work itself, repetitive and fast paced, in many ways resembled a factory assembly line. Operators sat elbow to elbow before a flashing switchboard, plugging calls in and out at a rate of 200 to 250 an hour. They were monitored by female supervisors who walked back and forth behind them, and by others who listened secretly and punished slow responses or disconnects with unfavorable hours. It was nerve-wracking, low-paid work, and the turnover among operators was high.

In 1900, Houston telephone operators, who had no sick leave and worked nine or nine and one-half hours, seven days a week, for a monthly wage of $15, joined the International Brotherhood of Electrical Workers (IBEW) to get the same sickness and death benefits available to linemen (whose wage scale was $2.50 to $3.50 a *day*). Southwestern Telephone and Telegraph promptly began firing the newly unionized women, who staged a successful walkout and were rehired. Later that year San Antonio operators struck to have their eleven- and thirteen-hour shifts reduced, and operators in Dallas, Fort Worth, Galveston, and Waco walked out in sympathy; this action was less successful.

Telephone companies stressed the amenities they provided for workers: a retiring room with magazines and a Victrola or a piano for use during breaks, and sometimes a cafeteria. Such paternalism, Marguerite Weistroffer of Port Arthur wrote bitterly, did not compensate for the reality that the company paid pittance wages and "worked the sap out of the girls." Such comforts "are paid for by the profit the company makes out of the girls' low wages, and are really paid for by the girls themselves," Weistroffer pointed out. "Now wouldn't it be better if girls could draw wages that would enable them to have some of these nice things in their own homes, instead of just the privilege of using them as company property?"[5] Some of the Port Arthur operators earned as little as $18 a month and none more than $36, not enough for decent food and proper clothes. They joined the local IBEW and struck in 1916, after the Texas Long Lines Telephone Company refused to recognize the union or raise wages. When the company brought in strikebreakers from Waco (at $40 a month), the male union members struck in sympathy. But the women could not afford to stay out long, and by 1919 the Port Arthur local had disbanded.

That same year, Mexicana laundry workers in El Paso were forced into a strike, one of the earliest by Hispanic women in the United States, after they organized a local of the Laundry Workers International Union with the assistance of local Anglo labor leaders. Shortly afterward two Mexicana unionists at Acme Laundry were fired, and two hundred coworkers protested by walking out. Women from other laundries soon followed, nearly five hundred in all. The Anglo men who made up El Paso's Central Labor Union directed the strike, relegating the women to supporting roles. The laundry workers stationed themselves at the international bridge, demanding that women from Ciudad Juárez on the Mexican side of the Rio Grande not cross over as strikebreakers and denouncing those who did as *ronosas* (scabs).[6] Although the women had the moral support of the Mexican community and financial assistance from the Central Labor Union, the strike was over within weeks. The oversupply of unskilled women in El Paso and Juárez, the root cause of low wages, made it easy for the laundry owners to replace the striking workers.

The "working girl" with perhaps the highest public profile was Eva Goldsmith, one of the multitude of farm girls who migrated to Houston in search of opportunity. Goldsmith worked at various factory jobs, and by the 1910s she was president of the Texas District Council of the United Garment Workers Union. In the male-dominated Texas State Federation of Labor, she earned a reputation as an articulate and valuable advocate. The first woman appointed to the TSFL's Legislative Committee, Goldsmith was the most prominent lobbyist when the federation successfully pressed the legislature to pass a law limiting women's working hours to a maximum of nine a day or fifty-four a week in 1913. In 1915 when the statute was expanded and strengthened, Goldsmith was again a spokeswoman. Business interests, however, were strong enough to secure an exemption for cotton mills and laundries, the largest employers of female labor. Since the state had only a few labor inspectors, the law was widely violated.

EDUCATION AND PROFESSIONALISM

Both white and black girls attended high school in larger numbers than boys at the turn of the century, which is not to say that girls of both races had equal access; Texas had only sixteen "Negro" high schools in 1900. Higher female graduation rates reflected women's lack of access to the skilled trades, which boys left school to pursue, and girls' lower value as agricultural workers, which made them less essential as family farm labor. With a high school diploma young women could readily get certification to teach elementary school, a profession they had long dominated. In the decades that followed women entered college in steadily increasing numbers. In 1900 women were excluded from the Roman Catholic colleges (St. Edward's and St. Mary's), Austin College, and the Agricultural and Mechanical College of Texas (now Texas A&M University), but they made up one-third of the enrollment at the University of Texas, Southwestern University, and Baylor University. A decade later women were 40 percent of the undergraduates at the University of Texas, 34 percent at Southwestern, and 38 percent at Baylor. (The national average in both 1900 and 1910 was 35 percent.) Since the University of Texas and Baylor had grown, these percentages conceal an impressive increase in absolute numbers. Between 1900 and 1910 the number of women nearly tripled at UT (from 167 to 499) and more than tripled at Baylor (from 50 to 180).[7]

Even larger numbers attended North Texas State Normal School and Sam Houston Normal Institute, where teaching degrees could be earned in three years for modest tuition, enabling many farm girls to move into the middle class. Women heavily outnumbered men at normal schools, especially at Prairie View State Normal and Industrial College, the only state-supported institution for African Americans. There female enrollment exceeded male by two to one, the same as the ratio of female to male students in black high schools; women also outnumbered men at small private black colleges.[8] Although Prairie View was a four-year institution, the diploma that a black woman earned was not academically equivalent to the baccalaureate degree conferred on a white woman at the University of Texas. The legislature funded Prairie View far below the level for white universities; its library and laboratories were inadequate, and the curriculum was heavily vocational. The majority of students were enrolled in high school preparatory courses. African American coeds were as likely to learn sewing and dairying as mathematics and Latin, and the institution was unaccredited until 1926. Consequently, the number of black women in the professions was small, and the great majority were teachers in segregated schools.

While their numbers on campus increased, women were heavily clustered in "female" disciplines such as education, music, and home economics. They were only a small proportion of students in graduate and professional degree programs, and black women had no access to postgraduate education at all unless they could afford to leave the state. Women were a rarity in law schools — in 1910 there were only three female attorneys in the state. In medical schools they were better represented but still uncommon, a combination of deliberate exclusion and the reluctance of parents with lingering Victorian sensibilities to permit daughters to pursue a curriculum that entailed dissecting cadavers and other "immodest and unladylike" investigations. Hallie Earle had her family's support when she enrolled in Baylor University College of Medicine in 1904, even though she was a novel presence (see Document 1.3). But when Minnie Maffet, who earned her M.D. in 1915 (and later became one of the state's most prominent female physicians), decided to leave graduate school in Austin for medical school in Galveston, she made the switch in secret. For her first two weeks at the University of Texas Medical Branch she enclosed postcards to her family in letters to her former roommate, who mailed them with an Austin postmark.

Education and health care, where professional women were most heavily represented, were two-tiered fields, with women at the bottom. Texas women overtook men in the teaching profession during the Progressive Era; they were 50 percent of the field in 1900 and 80 percent by 1920. But the higher the rank, the smaller their numbers. Women were only a small proportion of college faculties and much more likely to be instructors at normal schools than at elite institutions. (In 1910 they were only 5 percent of the faculty at the University of Texas.) Ninety percent of nurses were women, but less than 2 percent of doctors were. Nursing education, an innovation of the 1890s, expanded enormously in the early twentieth century. Baylor College of Medicine joined the University of Texas Medical Branch in offering nursing degrees, and Prairie View graduated its first class of nurses in 1920. Hospitals in Fort Worth, Dallas, Austin, San Antonio, El Paso, and smaller cities instituted nurse training programs. But women physicians and pharmacists graduated from UTMB in single-digit numbers, an average of one or two every year or so. Between 1900 and 1920 thirty-three women earned medical degrees there and twenty-six completed the pharmacy program.[9]

Progressive women also pursued professional status for women's traditional domestic roles. In the new "scientific" approaches to homemaking and child-rearing that emerged in the 1890s, middle-class women saw potential for expanding their still-limited career options. The early household economists incorporated the new germ theory of disease into the practice of "sanitary science," which applied equally to public health and private homes. Although the end result was ultimately somewhat different, the pioneers of the field envisioned new careers for single women in urban food inspection and water analysis. For wives and mothers in an era before nutritional labels, antiseptic household cleansers, pediatricians, and antibiotics, home economics held out the promise of healthier families and lower infant mortality. Mothers, not doctors, were responsible for keeping families well; the medical profession had not yet embraced preventive care, and physicians did not do pediatric check-ups. Women held life and health in their hands, Isadore Callaway pointed out in her newspaper column, yet homemaking and motherhood were "classed with the unskilled trades, to be learned only by hard experience."[10]

Seeking to elevate "women's work" to a respected profession, women's voluntary associations, led by the Woman's Christian Temperance Union and the Texas Federation of Women's Clubs (TFWC), lobbied the state legislature to create a vocational college for white women with household economics as the centerpiece of the curriculum. In 1901 they secured reluctant authorization for their Girls' Industrial College (now Texas Woman's University) as a counterpart to the Agricultural and Mechanical College of Texas, from which women were excluded. Three of the seven regents' positions were earmarked for women (although the institution would not have a woman president until more than seventy years later). The Girls' Industrial College opened in 1903, and the TFWC almost immediately began a campaign to persuade the University of Texas to establish a home economics program. When the university, no more enthusiastic than the legislature had been, claimed that no money was available, the clubwomen persuaded a wealthy regent to donate it. The School of Domestic Economy, which women regarded as a beachhead in a male preserve, offered its first classes in 1912. Its director, Mary Edna Gearing, was the first woman to chair a department at the University of Texas.

MOTHERHOOD AND SOCIAL HOUSEKEEPING

The New Woman notwithstanding, the primary occupation for the majority of women was still marriage and motherhood. Pregnancy and childbirth were health risks that women faced with apprehension. They worried over their own and their doctors' ignorance of infant care and feeding and sought expert guidance from the U.S. Children's Bureau, established in 1912 after years of pressure from women reformers outraged at the nation's high infant mortality rate. Women from every social background, including the poor, wrote to the Children's Bureau seeking medical guidance. Their letters articulated the anxiety of childbirth without skilled medical attendants and the frustration of caring for sick children on their own (see Document 1.5). Most women continued to give birth at home, but rural women, especially African Americans and Mexicanas, were more likely to be assisted by a midwife than by a physician. Midwives were usually respected older women who had borne children themselves and developed their skill through experience. They provided emotional support and used massage, herbs, and folk remedies to ease pain and "help nature." At the turn of the century midwives attended up to 75 percent of births, but over the next twenty-five years their presence declined steadily, especially in urban areas. In Galveston, for example, midwife-assisted deliveries, which occurred primarily among the working-class and immigrant populations, dropped from 37 percent in 1910 to 4 percent in 1920.[11]

Progressive Era women bore fewer children than their grandmothers: in 1910 the birthrate for Texas women was 4.6 children, slightly higher than the national average. Rural women had more children than urban ones, and foreign-born had more than native-born. The decline in the birthrate was most pronounced among urban middle-class women, who sought smaller families and more widely spaced births through contraceptive techniques such as douching and male withdrawal. Rejecting the tradition that women had a social duty to endure a prolonged cycle of childbearing, they advocated "voluntary motherhood." To male criticism that limiting births was unnatural and selfish, a prominent clubwoman retorted that women needed not more children but "fewer and better ones."[12] By "better children," women meant healthier ones; mortality was high, and even middle-class mothers worried about losing babies during the summer "sickly season" when bacteria multiplied in milk and water supplies. They studied the new literature on sanitary housekeeping, infant feeding, and child development in women's and mothers' clubs and applied the knowledge not only to their own homes and children but also to the larger problems of urban living.

Women reformers frequently described their activities as municipal or social housekeeping, a tactic that helped deflect criticism of their new undertakings. The private household was so dependent on city services and urban markets, they argued, that women could not fulfill their traditional homemaking responsibilities without pure water, food, and milk supplies; sanitary sewage disposal; garbage-free streets; and fully equipped schools—all of which the men who ran city and state government had failed to provide. "Our schools are in a deplorable condition because women, who are more alive to their needs than men, have no voice in their management," Isadore Callaway complained in the regular column she wrote as "Pauline Periwinkle."[13] Denton clubwoman Mary Brown Work lamented that one-third of the nation's children died during their first two years of life, an epidemic that men ignored, yet when the boll weevil destroyed one-tenth of the cotton crop, "recall how prompt was legislative action, how generous the rewards offered for remedies." No government ever investigated the infant death rate, she observed, "because men have charge over the cotton; women, the babies."[14] Mary Work expressed a rationale for Progressive women's public activism that historians have termed "maternalism." They analyzed social problems from the perspective of motherhood and mobilized as mothers to lobby for change.

Female social housekeeping took varied forms and emphasized public health, public education, child welfare, and moral reform. Women's organizations sponsored citywide cleanup campaigns and established baby clinics, day nurseries, and milk stations where poor women could get certified clean milk. In Dallas the Federation of Women's Clubs and the Woman's Forum campaigned for five years for a bond issue to build a water filtration plant. Women's voluntary associations raised money to construct public libraries and playgrounds and persuaded municipal authorities to take over their operation. School mothers' clubs raised money for everything from sanitary drinking fountains (to replace the germ-infested bucket and dipper) to visiting nurses and hot lunch programs. Clubwomen pressed for the creation of a separate juvenile court system to prevent children from being jailed with adult criminals, paid the salaries of the first city police matrons, and joined the Woman's Christian Temperance Union in demanding the abolition of prostitution districts.

PUBLIC HEALTH: CLEANING UP THE FOOD SUPPLY

Consumers, usually women, had to beware of both careless contamination of the food they bought—grocery stores with unscreened windows that let in flies, and dairy wagons that sold milk from open containers—and deliberate adulteration. Some adulterants, such as cheap bran in ground coffee or dyed and flavored apple pulp laced with grass seed and sold as raspberry jam, merely cheated the buyer. Others, like formaldehyde in milk or rancid butter rechurned with fresh were potentially dangerous (see Document 1.2). The sins of the commercial food processing industry prompted Congress to pass the Pure Food and Drug Act of 1906, and within weeks the Dallas Woman's Forum began pressing city commissioners for a municipal pure food law and a city chemist to test samples. A Woman's Forum committee wrote the ordinance and outlobbied the grocers, dairymen, and druggists who sought to delay implementation. It went into effect in March 1907.

At the same time, the Texas Federation of Women's Clubs and the

Woman's Christian Temperance Union began a campaign for a state pure food law. Mary Brown Work, chair of the TFWC's Household Economics Committee, took the lead and sought out the state representative who had unsuccessfully sponsored a pure food bill in the previous legislative session. She offered to put the lobbying power of the TFWC behind him in return for a provision requiring that the enforcement office be located at the College of Industrial Arts (the new name of the Girls' Industrial College), where it would be safe from political influence, rather than in the state health department in Austin. With the help of a statewide network of local clubs publicizing the issue and pressuring their legislative representatives, plus a lobbying delegation at the capitol led by Mary Work, the Texas Pure Food and Drug Act passed in 1907.

The state legislature authorized the appointment of a dairy and food commissioner but gave him only a small budget and no investigative staff, so women from local clubs stepped in to help enforce the new law. The commissioner deputized volunteers and supplied them with guidelines and scorecards; the women collected food samples for analysis, and the commissioner's office reimbursed them for the purchase price. In small communities the pure food committee of the local women's club substituted for a health department. In large cities, women's organizations exposed low standards and lax enforcement. The Houston Housewives' League divided the city into districts and made regular bakery and dairy inspections. The league's sanitation committee also accompanied the Houston health inspector on his regular dairy inspection rounds. While he scored the dairies according to the city health code, the committeewomen evaluated them according to the Housewives' League's considerably higher standards, which most failed to meet. The women posted the scores in the exhibit hall at City Auditorium, where the league, which had fifteen hundred members, met each week.

In Galveston the Women's Health Protective Association, which organized after the devastating hurricane of 1900, had an even higher profile. The WHPA pressured the city to enforce the municipal and state pure food laws and to hire more inspectors; it did its own sanitary inspections of grocery stores, bakeries, and meat markets, and the reports were published in the newspapers. Citizens frustrated by uncollected garbage and trash in the alleys took their complaints to the WHPA and asked the women to prod the health department. Beginning in 1912, the WHPA waged a five-year campaign against Galveston's dirty and dangerous milk supply, a source of typhoid fever and infant cholera. The chairwoman of the association's dairy committee examined the lab reports from the city's inspections and found that nearly all of the dairies had visible dirt and sand in the milk bottles and that half of the establishments exceeded the permitted bacterial safety count, yet none of the operators had been fined or had their licenses revoked. The WHPA subjected the dairymen to public exposure, lawsuits, and boycotts, all the while lobbying city hall, and finally secured a pure milk ordinance with stringent enforcement provisions in 1917.

MATERNALIST LEGISLATION: CHILD LABOR, COMPULSORY EDUCATION, AND MOTHERS' PENSIONS

Like other southern states, Texas had high rates of child labor and low school attendance. Cotton was the culprit: children helped cultivate, harvest, and spin it into cloth in textile factories while attending school sporadically, sometimes only a few weeks a year. Children started picking cotton at age six or younger, using special sacks scaled to their small size, and landowners preferred tenant farmers and sharecroppers with large families who could help with the crop. Cotton mills employed children as young as eight for twelve-hour shifts in spinning rooms. An owner told the *Dallas Morning News* with complete sincerity that "one advantage a man has at a mill over the farm tenant is that he can get employment for the whole family every day in the year at the mill, and at the same time educate his children, provided he will work half of them at a time, sending the other half to school."[15] When children were part of a family labor force, education took second place to economic survival.

In 1903, organized labor lobbied the state's first child labor law through the legislature; it set the minimum age for factory work at twelve and the minimum for mines and quarries at fifteen. Clubwomen were just beginning to investigate child labor (see Document 1.1), and the Texas Federation of Women's Clubs endorsed the restriction. But the legislature did not create an enforcement agency until 1909, and the law was widely ignored. In 1910 the leaders of the Texas Congress of Mothers, the state federation of mothers' clubs, convened the state's first child welfare conference. The meeting drew delegates from a dozen organizations concerned with children and led to the formation of a new organization, the Child Welfare Conference of Texas, to plan legislative goals. Adella Kelsey Turner, a past president of the TFWC and one of the first women elected to the Dallas school board, was chosen as president. A new child labor law was one of three measures for which the conference worked in the 1911 legislative session, and the only one that passed. The 1911 law extended the age limit for working in factories and mills to fifteen (the highest limit of any southern state at that time) and the minimum age for dangerous occupations like mining and quarrying to seventeen.

The Child Welfare Conference spawned another new organization, the Texas Child Labor Committee, in which women's organizations were prominently represented; Adella Turner served as secretary. In 1913 the committee brought an investigator from the National Child Labor Committee to Texas for undercover work, which resulted in the discovery that messenger boys as young as eleven and twelve regularly delivered telegrams and drugstore items to brothels. With this evidence, the child labor reformers were able to get the age-fifteen limit extended to messenger services, theaters, and workshops. Strong opposition from businessmen and manufacturers, however, consistently defeated their efforts to limit child workers to an eight-hour day, prevent them from working at night, or require documentary proof of age.

Clubwomen considered a compulsory education law the best deterrent of all to child labor, and the only one that could get children out of the cotton fields, since agriculture was exempt from labor statutes. The overwhelming majority of working children were employed outside of factories in agriculture (nearly seven out of eight), domestic service, news vending, and street trades. School attendance was voluntary, and in 1910 Texas ranked forty-second in the number of school days (fifty-six) per child; it was one of only six states— all in the South—without a compulsory education law. Conservative legislators claimed that requiring children to be in school would intrude on parents' rights and force the state to spend money educating "Negroes and Mexicans." The Child Welfare Conference of Texas pressed unsuccessfully for a compulsory education law in 1911. The Texas Federation of Women's Clubs, which had been advocating the cause for a decade, then took the lead. With support from other reform organizations, it lobbied a bill through the legislature in 1915 that required children from eight to fourteen to attend school for a minimum of sixty days annually, beginning in 1916. The law automatically extended the requirement to eighty days in 1917 and one hundred days (five months) in 1919. As usual, the legislature made no provision for enforcement, and the TFWC's Education Committee tackled the job itself. The chairwoman directed each club in the federation to contact the superintendent of its local school district and offer assistance. Just as clubwomen had filled in as voluntary inspectors for the pure food law, they volunteered themselves as truant officers, performing for free the work that the state refused to fund.

Concern for child welfare also turned clubwomen's attention to the "problem" of mothers raising children alone. Unwed motherhood was uncommon and divorce rare; the majority of single mothers were widowed or separated ("deserted," in the language of the time). There was no state or federal assistance for such women, who depended on relatives, private charity, and their own earnings. Single mothers had difficulty earning a living wage; their children were often unsupervised or forced into wage work also. The most desperate cases became "half orphans," surrendered by destitute mothers to orphanages or foster care.

Progressives advocated state aid to struggling single mothers in the form of stipends, called mothers' pensions, for children under designated ages; thirty-nine states had enacted them by 1919. The National Congress of Mothers and the General Federation of Women's Clubs and their state affiliates were among the most outspoken proponents of mothers' aid, and in Texas the Public Welfare Committee of the Dallas Woman's Forum drafted the mothers' pension bill introduced in the state legislature in 1917. The first Texas public welfare measure, it provoked an outcry of "creeping socialism" and a "handout to Negroes" from conservative lawmakers, words that would echo for the next two decades in every attempt of the women's lobby to expand state responsibility for maternal and child welfare. An amendment excluding African American women from assistance failed, but conservatives achieved the same effect by specifying that the boards of county commissioners, who were responsible for authorizing the pensions, would have the power to deny applications and that their decisions were final and not subject to review. Narrow eligibility requirements and strict supervisory authority were also added; nevertheless, one of the nay voters indignantly recorded his conviction that "all negroes and Mexicans would be entitled to pensions" and that the bill was "Socialism gone to seed."[16]

Although clubwomen had envisioned mothers' pensions as a way for poor women to stay home with their children, keep them in school, and hold families together, the law as passed was only a slight improvement on private charity. Since no county was *required* to provide mothers' aid, most did not. Black women, who had higher rates of single motherhood, got nothing. Neither did women whose husbands were absent, in prison, or physically or mentally incapacitated. The law restricted application to widows who had resided in the state for five years and in the county for two, while requirements for producing family documentation effectively excluded non-English speakers and the illiterate. If the commissioners then chose to grant a pension, the widow was subject to a home inspection, and the county could terminate the aid at any time if she failed to provide "proper" care. Despite clubwomen's good intentions, single mothers who were not white, English-speaking, sexually abstinent widows able to meet middle-class standards of housekeeping and child care were on their own.

CLAIMING URBAN SPACE: SETTLEMENT HOUSES
AND PROSTITUTION DISTRICTS

Settlement houses, middle-class women's attempt to provide social services in poor urban neighborhoods, came later to Texas than to the North but depended even more heavily than their northern models on female initiative. Nationally, women made up an estimated 60 percent of settlement house residents; in Texas they were 92 percent of residents and volunteers. Settlements such as the Neighborhood Houses in Dallas (founded in 1903) and Fort Worth (1908) and Houston's Rusk Settlement (1909) were collaborative projects between New Women, who oversaw them, and clubwomen, who raised the operating funds. Secular settlements formed around the nuclei of public kindergartens, which Progressive women founded and championed in much the same way that liberal women fifty years later would promote Head Start and other "early intervention" programs. They believed that kindergartens (which they wanted to see introduced into the schools also) enhanced intelligence, socialized immigrant children, and prevented future juvenile delinquency. The kindergarten teacher, who added the role of home visitor to her duties, was the opening wedge into working-class neighborhoods, encouraging the mothers to visit the settlement and sample its programs. Neighborhood House in Dallas established two branch kindergartens, one of them in the cotton mill district, where the settlement association also operated a day nursery for the employed mothers.

Although settlement houses served the whole community, concern for children and mothers was especially evident. They offered domestic science and sewing classes and organized mothers' clubs; public health nurses demonstrated how to sterilize milk and prepare food that babies could digest. Rusk Settlement in Houston evolved directly from concern over child welfare. Sybil Campbell, a teacher at Rusk Elementary School, discovered a preschool sibling of one of her students sleeping on the schoolhouse steps one morning. The mother was at work and the older child was responsible for the younger one, a situation that Campbell discovered was not uncommon. She persuaded the Houston Woman's Club to build a free kindergarten and day nursery, and when demand outgrew the facilities, the women formed the Houston Settlement Association. In addition to the kindergarten and nursery, Rusk Settlement included a library, recreation facilities, clubs for children and adults, a medical dispensary, and a visiting nurses department. Campbell became the settlement's second head resident.

Another group of settlement houses owed their existence to churchwomen. Waco's Evangelia Settlement (1906), which grew out of the initiative of two young women who began a day nursery near the woolen mills for children of working mothers, evolved into a full-service settlement overseen by a board of women from the city's Protestant denominations. In El Paso the Rose Gregory Houchen Settlement was run by Methodist deaconesses in the Segundo Barrio. Methodist women dominated the mission settlement movement, which combined social services with evangelism. Their city mission boards served the same fundraising and administrative functions for Methodism's Wesley Houses that clubwomen exercised in secular settlements. The Dallas Woman's Board of City Missions opened the first Wesley House in Texas in 1903; by 1913 there were Wesley Houses in Galveston, Houston, Fort Worth, and San Antonio. With the aim of "Americanizing and Christianizing" immigrants, especially Hispanics, the houses were staffed by women who made careers in church work. They ministered to bodies as well as souls, erecting female-run medical and social service centers in barrio neighborhoods. San Antonio's Wesley House operated the city's only free dental clinic. The deaconesses persuaded doctors to donate their services to the medical dispensary and borrowed staff nurses from the city health department.

In every major Texas city and many smaller ones, prostitutes lived and worked in legally sanctioned vice districts, a consequence of the double standard of morality that approved sexual freedom for men but not for women. Prostitution pitted reformers against municipal regulators in a contentious debate that was not resolved until World War I. Regulators argued that male access to prostitutes helped protect "virtuous" women from seduction. It was a problem as old as the ages and best handled, they claimed, by confining it to a few blocks and requiring the women to be licensed and to submit to regular medical inspections. Reformers included middle-class women's organizations, such as the Woman's Christian Temperance Union, which had been protesting the double standard since the nineteenth century, the Texas Federation of Women's Clubs, and the Texas Congress of Mothers. They contended that young men contracted venereal disease in brothels and passed it to their unsuspecting brides when they married. Citing statistics from a state board of health physician, who attributed high rates of gynecological surgery in wives and 80 percent of blindness in newborns to venereal transmission from husbands, the Congress of Mothers demanded a law abolishing red-light districts. When the reformers were vociferous enough, municipal authorities temporarily cracked down on prostitution (see Document 1.8). Protest forced Dallas, Austin, and Amarillo to close their districts by 1914. Others stayed in business because the system of licensing and fines brought the cities so much revenue and kept local taxes low. When El Paso temporarily closed its district in 1913, the city lost more than $15,000 a month.

For most of the women, however, prostitution was only superficially lucrative. At a time when most "female" jobs in El Paso paid $3 to $6 a week, prostitutes earned $30 to $50, but license fees, fines, rent, medical care, and clothes consumed most of the profits. Despite the required medical inspection, many prostitutes were infected with venereal disease. One woman told a grand jury that the city physician "comes down here twice each month and puts an instrument in us, washes it . . . writes out a certificate and goes on to the next house." She continued, "He must be making lots of money for there are, I think, 367 girls on the line at present. . . . I go to another doctor every two weeks to be examined carefully for I do not think [he] is careful enough."[17] Alcohol and drugs took a further toll on health. Their use was common enough that the madam of a brothel in San Antonio included among her rules: "Girls getting drunk outside must not come in the parlor" and "No dope fiends or whiskey heads allowed in this house as life is too short to be troubled with them."[18] For men—absentee landlords, saloonkeepers, police, doctors, and lawyers—reservation districts were business enterprises that generated large returns. For the prostitute herself, they were a losing proposition.

THE BOUNDARIES OF RACE

Progressivism is commonly described as "for whites only," and the era itself as the nadir of race relations. Although Texas had the smallest proportion of African Americans of all the former Confederate states—17 percent in 1910—it followed the rest of the South in separating blacks and whites through statutory law and social custom, a system of segregation colloquially called Jim Crow. Its roots reached well back into the nineteenth century, but urban growth prompted new restrictions during the Progressive Era. In 1903, Houston and San Antonio enacted ordinances confining African Americans to the rear seats of streetcars, prompting long boycotts; when Austin followed in 1906, black domestics threatened to quit their jobs rather than ride in segregated transportation. State laws passed in 1910 and 1911 required separate waiting rooms at railroad stations. The trains themselves had been segregated since 1891; white women rode in the smoke-free, first-class "ladies' car," while black women were restricted to the dirty Jim Crow coach that lacked flush toilets, soap and washbasins, and running water. The legislature in 1907 authorized theaters and amusement parks to segregate or deny admittance to blacks, putting legal force behind common practice. Segregation functioned to remind blacks of their inferior "place" in society, and learning to safely negotiate the norms of Jim Crow was part of every black child's upbringing (see Document 1.4).

Segregation, and the violence against black men justified in its name, asserted both racial and gender dominance. White supremacy was in reality white male supremacy, with sexual control of women at its heart. By falsely portraying black men as bestial sexual predators who lusted after white women, white men kept a tight grip on patriarchal authority. Segregation privileged white women but kept them fearful and dependent on men as protectors; it stripped black women of the same security and left them truly vulnerable to sexual coercion. Unlike the public brutality of lynching, the sexual oppression of black women by white men was private and unacknowledged, and the victim bore the blame. Refusing to believe that their own men could be sexual predators across the color line, white women attributed the mulatto children in their communities to black women's immorality and promiscuity.

An antimiscegenation law that dated from the nineteenth century forbidding marriages (but not sexual relations) between blacks and whites prevented interracial love affairs, usually between white men and black women, from being regularized. In such instances an African American woman who cohabited with a white man in a long-term relationship and bore his children was deprived of the social status of a wife and of a widow's guaranteed share of the couple's estate after his death. Beginning in the Progressive Era and continuing over the next decade, several cities passed ordinances with hefty fines attached prohibiting interracial sex itself. Fort Worth imposed the first in 1915. Minnie Strauss challenged the Fort Worth ordinance in the Court of Criminal Appeals after she and her white partner were arrested; she won reversal on a procedural technicality, but the appellate court upheld the legality of the statute.[19] (In enforcing these laws the courts defined Hispanics as white, thereby criminalizing Hispanic–African American liaisons as well.) Until the U.S. Supreme Court ruled such legislation unconstitutional in 1967, interracial couples masked or hid their relationships in order to avoid legal punishment. When a white woman was known to have chosen a black man the result could be violent and tragic, as in the 1919 Longview race riot that followed the lynching of a Kilgore woman's lover.

Keeping African American men from feeling entitled to "social equality," the code word for interracial relationships, was part of the motivation for denying them political power. A 1902 voter-approved state law requiring payment of a poll tax in order to vote removed the majority of black men from the electorate, but it had consequences for black women as well. Although neither white nor black women were allowed to vote, disfranchisement by sex bore harder on black women. White women were supposedly able, in part, to compensate for their inability to cast a ballot by exerting "indirect influence" on their husbands' and sons' voting behavior. When black men were deprived of the ballot, black women lost even this weak and theoretical political voice. And without the threat of male voters standing behind them, black women reformers could not expect, as white women could, to lobby city officials and state legislators to any effect.

For black women, the first generation born in freedom, the Progressive Era marked the beginning rather than the zenith of a female public culture. Excluded from white women's organizations, middle-class black women founded a parallel network of clubs and civic associations. Unlike their white counterparts, many African American clubwomen worked full- or part-time, usually as teachers; only a minority were married to men financially able to support leisured wives. Often light-skinned, they were an economically privileged class, the wives and daughters of the black community's professional and business men, and many were graduates of black colleges. Their study clubs dated only to the late 1890s; a state federation, the Texas Association of Colored Women's Clubs formed in 1905. Because the African American middle class was tiny, the black federation was always much smaller than its white counterpart. Thirty-one clubs sent delegations to the TACWC convention in 1911; by contrast, the white federation counted ten thousand members in hundreds of clubs and was still growing rapidly. While white clubwomen held their annual state convention in first-class hotels, segregation forced the TACWC to meet in African American churches and the attendees to stay in private homes.

Despite being ignored by white clubwomen, black women participated in Progressive reforms, focusing on community improvement and racial uplift for the black underclass. African American clubwomen founded kindergartens and old-age homes and raised funds for the separate and unequal "colored" schools, which received only about one-third of the revenue expended on white schools and lacked libraries, playgrounds, and connections to sewer lines. Always striving to counter the white perception of black womanhood as promiscuous, thriftless, and slovenly, they assigned women the responsibility for "improving" the race, urging working-class mothers to study the domestic arts and keep themselves and their daughters morally irreproachable. Like white clubwomen, they endured male criticism for stepping out of women's "sphere," and they criticized black men in return for failing to provide strong racial leadership. "Our men have never given us the support and encouragement we so well deserve," the TACWC noted in an annual report.[20] African American clubwomen did settlement work, but they could not afford to found houses. Houston's black Bethlehem Settlement, established in 1917, was a social service project of the Texas Conference of Charities and Correction. Located between the city dump and the vice district, the building was a firetrap and lacked a playground, but it had an interracial board, a small crack in the wall of separation.

IMMIGRATION AND REVOLUTION IN THE BORDERLANDS

Between 1900 and 1920 the official count of Mexican-born residents in Texas increased from 71,062 to 251,827, with an unknown number of undocumented arrivals. Before 1910 the immigrants were largely peasants pushed off their communal landholdings by the growth of large agricultural estates in Mexico. They were pulled into South Texas by the rapid expansion of commercial farming, which created a demand for low-wage labor. Mexican women usually arrived in Texas as part of a family group and often made the journey after the male head had gone ahead to secure employment. Mexicanas who picked cotton, vegetables, and melons labored as part of a family unit; husbands and fathers collected and controlled their wages.

Some women also did laundry and sewing for Anglo families. In Crystal City, Irene Castaneda's mother washed, starched, and ironed clothes for a dollar a load, teaching her children to read in Spanish while she worked, because Mexicans were excluded from Anglo schools. Medical care was inadequate, and women and their children suffered most; child mortality was higher among Hispanics than Anglos and highest among the immigrant generation. Castaneda's mother "learned as best she could to deliver babies," her daughter remembered, "sometimes on the floor with just a small blanket. . . . Sometimes she would bring pillows or blankets from home. Many of the women had not eaten—she would bring them rice from home and feed them by spoonfuls." She made tea of hot peppers "to give the baby strength to be born." No doctor was available—"the only one had to travel to several towns and when he arrived it was too late."[21]

Immigrants and Texas-born Hispanics were part of a transborder culture, which historian Gabriela Gonzalez has defined as "a region where the political and cultural systems of the United States and Mexico overlapped."[22] With the approach of revolution in Mexico, the Rio Grande became an arbitrary political boundary that restrained neither Mexican nationals nor Texas Mexicans. Years before the outbreak of violence in 1910 the leaders of the Partido Liberal Mexicano (PLM), whose goal was overthrowing the dictator Porfirio Díaz, escaped to the north and established headquarters in exile in Laredo and San Antonio. Calling for a radical transformation of Mexico's semifeudal society and advocating working-class revolution—including the emancipation of women—the PLM established a network of liberal clubs in Texas and the Southwest.

Although men predominated, some urban groups were entirely female, and women transborder activists, or *fronterizas*, were outspoken opponents of the Díaz regime. Journalists Andrea and Teresa Villarreal fled Coahuila for San Antonio, where they helped establish El Club Liberal de Señoras y Señoritas, Leona Vicario y Antonio Nava in 1904; it raised money for the PLM and assumed a leading role when male activists went underground to evade arrest. Mexican-born Sara Estela Ramírez, who arrived in Laredo as a young teacher, was one of the earliest supporters of the PLM and a confidante of its cofounders, Ricardo and Enrique Flores Magón. A poet as well as a political activist, Ramírez was a spokesperson for the party in Laredo, calling for an egalitarian society in Mexico governed by just laws and based on cooperative ideals rather than capitalism.

Ricardo Flores Magón addressed a special message to women, deploring that they were "humiliated, degraded, bound by chains of tradition to an irrational authority," and exploited as cheap labor.[23] Mexicanas who supported the socialist resistance movement likewise advocated an expanded role for women. The Villarreal sisters established a newspaper, *La Mujer Moderna* (*The Modern Woman*), which promoted women's emancipation. Teresa also served as president of Regeneración, a group of San Antonio Mexicanas who wanted the revolution to liberate women. In 1911 it sent a statement to the PLM newspaper denouncing the "enslavement" of women to men and concluding: "It is now time for women to become independent and for men to stop considering themselves the center of the universe, and to stop oppressing her and to give her in daily life the position of comrade and companion that corresponds to her."[24]

Resistance, intertwined with maternalist feminism, motivated the activism of Jovita Idar, a Laredo teacher and journalist. Idar wrote for her father's weekly paper, *La Crónica* (*The Chronicle*), which she ran after his death in 1914, and for *El Progreso* (*Progress*). Her articles exposed the separate, substandard schools for Mexican American children and denounced the racist brutality of the Texas Rangers. She also praised self-sufficient women and "women who put social conventions aside to dedicate themselves to work for something worthwhile." "The times of humiliation have passed," she announced in *La Crónica*: "Women are no longer slaves sold for a few coins. They are no longer men's servants but their equals, their partners."[25] In 1911, Idar and her brother joined their father in organizing El Congreso Mexicanista, a conference to discuss the multiple grievances of Mexican Americans—discrimination, loss of land, labor exploitation, maltreatment by law enforcement—and to consider how the Mexicano community might unify and protect itself. After a female delegate pointed out that women needed more education and economic opportunity, the Congreso authorized a separate organization, La Liga Femenil Mexicanista (Mexican Feminine League). Idar became the first president.

La Liga Femenil, like Anglo women's voluntary associations, applied maternalist principles to public work. The league's primary mission was extending free education to poor children; many of the members were teachers, and those who operated their own schools accepted such children without charge. At the same time, La Liga Femenil functioned as a benevolent association, distributing food and clothing with funds that members raised by staging theatrical productions and literary evenings. Jovita Idar combined her maternalist work for the league, which used her parents' home as one of its meeting places, with radical journalism. A 1914 piece for *El Progreso*, criticizing President Woodrow Wilson for sending troops to the border, resulted in a confrontation with the Texas Rangers. Idar stood in the doorway of the newspaper building and faced them down, but in a subsequent nocturnal attack they silenced the paper by smashing the presses and everything in the office.

By then Mexico had been convulsed by revolution for more than three years, and *fronterizas* participated from the beginning. Flores de Andrade founded a women's organization in Chihuahua that worked against the Díaz regime, and she established another in El Paso after she relocated to Texas. She moved back and forth between El Paso and Juárez, collecting ammunition and supplies, and helped Francisco Madero, the leader of the opposition, and his entourage hide in El Paso. When Madero was ready to launch the uprising of November 1910, she smuggled them back into Mexico (see Document 1.6). Another Madero supporter, the wealthy, convent-educated Leonor Villegas de Magnón, worked with a pro-revolution group in Laredo and sheltered Mexican political refugees in her home. In 1913 she persuaded Jovita Idar and four other women to cross the border and nurse wounded soldiers in the opposition forces; the group quickly grew into a medical aid society, La Cruz Blanca (the White Cross). After Nuevo Laredo was attacked in 1914, Villegas de Magnón turned her home into a hospital for Constitutionalist soldiers and outwitted American authorities who sought to take them into custody (see Document 1.7). That same year she took La Cruz Blanca into Mexico to travel with Venustiano Carranza's army.

To escape the fighting in Mexico, hundreds of thousands of refugees poured into the United States, which reacted by rescinding its relatively open border policy. Tighter entry restrictions disadvantaged women more than men, whose labor was in demand. Mexicanas who arrived at the Santa Fe Street bridge between Ciudad Juárez and El Paso alone or as single mothers were routinely stopped by authorities, who perceived them as potentially dependent on public assistance. Beginning in 1917, nearly all immigrants who entered through El Paso were required to undergo a draconian cleansing and medical inspection at the disinfection plant operated by the U.S. Public Health Service. Men and women were separated and required to strip naked; while their clothing went through a chemical laundering, their scalps were examined for lice. Women were deloused with an application of kerosene and vinegar to the scalp (men had their heads shaved) and then sent to the showers, which sprayed them with soap and water mixed with kerosene.

Ciudad Juárez residents who crossed daily to work in El Paso had to undergo this humiliating process not once but weekly and to carry a certificate specifying when their next cleansing was due. When the policy was implemented, seventeen-year-old Carmelita Torres, a maid, led a crowd of women that the *El Paso Times* described as "consisting in large part of servant girls employed in El Paso" in a protest on the Santa Fe Street bridge. They hurled stones, mud, and insults at Americans and attacked automobiles. As the demonstration wore on, men joined, the crowd seized streetcars, and women detached the controls to use as weapons.[26] The "bathhouse riots" had no effect on the disinfection policy, which continued until the late 1930s; a similar plant operated at Laredo's international bridge. Professional and middle-class Mexicans (or those who dressed to pass above their class) were not required to undergo the quarantine; it was imposed only on the campesino and working-class majority, whose dark skin and Indian features made them racially inferior in Anglo eyes.

The trauma of being classed as "dirty" stayed with some women for a lifetime, Yolanda Chávez Leyva discovered. Her mother had left Mexico during the revolution, and Leyva described what her mother experienced when she was elderly and dying and no longer able to distinguish between past and present: "She returned to the landscape that had made her who she was. She relived crossing the border as a child almost eighty years earlier. . . . For days she experienced anxiety. Frequently she asked me if we were still in Juárez, wanting some assurance that we were still on familiar ground. . . . Suddenly one day my mother's mood changed dramatically. The worry was replaced with relief and self-assurance. 'Ellos saben que somos gente buena' [They know that we are good people], she announced. I asked why. 'They didn't make us take a bath when we crossed.'"[27]

VOTES FOR WOMEN

Before the 1910s, Texas and other southern states shared a common pat-tern of sporadic and short-lived suffrage activity. A small state organization, the Texas Equal Rights Association, existed briefly in the 1890s, and a sec-ond organizing attempt early in the new century was likewise unsuccessful. Annette Finnigan of Houston, a Wellesley College graduate, and her sisters established the Texas Woman Suffrage Association in 1903, but it was able to organize only three local chapters. The TWSA ceased functioning in 1905 when the Finnigans left the state, and it did not revive until 1913. Between the 1890s and the 1910s few women were willing to declare themselves in favor of suffrage, and the movement appeared to be in the doldrums. But the dramatic growth of women's voluntary associations, especially women's and mothers' clubs, during those decades laid the foundation for a revival and pro-duced the women who became the rank and file of a mass suffrage movement after 1913. Through voluntary associations and their municipal housekeeping and child welfare projects, middle-class women developed a political agenda, and by the 1910s the idea of votes for women had ceased to be a radical ab-straction. Years of working for pure food, safe milk and water, decent public schools, an end to child labor, the elimination of legal prostitution districts, and other reforms had shown clubwomen what they might do with the ballot. Moreover, significant numbers were becoming impatient and frustrated with begging politicians for reforms that they could achieve with far less effort by direct action at the polls.

Perhaps most important of all, through their voluntary associations middle-class women had developed a maternalist rationale for public activism that had wide appeal and did not contradict the cultural definition of womanliness. They had been lobbying for civic improvement and social welfare reforms as public housekeepers and concerned mothers, contending that because indus-trialization had taken over so much of women's traditional work, they needed to follow it out of doors: streets and schools were an extension of the home. It was hardly "unwomanly" (the favorite epithet of suffrage opponents) to argue that wives and mothers needed the ballot to exercise the oversight that men had neglected. Perle Penfield, the TWSA's first organizer, stressed this theme repeatedly in speeches: "It is no more than right that the mother should have a voice in stating what should be done to protect her home, her family's food, and her family's surroundings."[28] The suffrage movement that emerged in the 1910s endured because it grew spontaneously, from the bottom up rather than the top down. The impulse came from the grassroots, as women in San

Antonio, Houston, Galveston, and Dallas who had been politicized through voluntary associations formed municipal suffrage societies in 1912 and 1913. Minnie Fisher Cunningham of Galveston voiced the concern that motivated many, wishing that if more leisured women "could go to Fort Worth and Dallas and Houston, and while there *think* about children[,] they would notice all of the poor little fellows on the street at night and how pitiful their condition is." She concluded, "Woman suffrage is the only thing that will ever reach this state of affairs."[29]

The revived suffrage movement was as modern as the growing cities in which it flourished. The slogan "Votes for Women" (which fit neatly on shoulder sashes and placards) replaced the nineteenth-century demand for "women's rights." Progressive Era suffragists spoke more often of a woman's responsibilities, civic and maternal, than of her rights. They stressed what they could do for others with the ballot and how much the homemaker's input was needed in public policy. Adopting commercial advertising techniques, suffragists distributed cartoons and broadsides that featured appealing images and succinct, persuasive reasoning—in effect, "selling" suffrage (see Document 1.11). They also integrated their activities into popular culture. Suffragists in Dallas organized "Suffrage Day" annually at the State Fair of Texas, and those in Galveston did the same at the city's yearly Cotton Carnival. Local societies put on suffrage-themed plays and entertainments and decorated department store windows. They held public rallies, spoke from open cars, and, in San Antonio, persuaded a minister to preach a pro-suffrage sermon on Mother's Day. The Galveston Equal Suffrage Association held its monthly meetings outdoors in summer, decorating a shady lot with flags and "Votes for Women" banners; the close of business was followed by public speaking.

At the same time that clubwomen were transforming the suffrage movement, they also mounted a legislative campaign for married women's property rights. Under English common law, the doctrine of coverture stripped a woman of her separate legal identity when she married and gave her husband ownership of her property and earnings. Texas had modified coverture with a community property statute, which recognized a wife's right to own property but denied her control of it (see Document 1.9). The husband had the sole right to manage community property acquired during marriage and any separate property that the wife owned before marriage or received afterward as a gift, such as a bequest from relatives. Only the husband had the right to sell community property, but creditors could seize his wife's share to pay *his* debts.

Working separately, both the Texas Federation of Women's Clubs and the Texas Congress of Mothers focused their lobbying in the 1913 legislative session on a married women's property bill, using the same maternalist rhetoric that was transforming the suffrage movement. Hortense Ward, the Congress of Mothers' vice chair for legislation, marshaled examples of the victims of coverture: the deserted wife working to support a small child who was left penniless when the derelict husband assigned her wages to one of his creditors; the middle-class wife with her own bank account, who discovered when one of her checks bounced that "her husband had withdrawn the money and spent it on drinking and gambling."[30] The Married Women's Property Act that women's voluntary associations obtained in 1913 gave wives control of their separate personal property and excluded a married woman's personal earnings and the income from her rental property and stocks from her husband's management. The wife's separate property and the portion of community property that she managed were exempted from her husband's debts.

THE POLITICS OF WOMAN SUFFRAGE

The parallels between legal coverture and its political equivalent, disfranchisement, were obvious: if a woman was entitled to control her own property, she should likewise be able to cast her own ballot instead of being "represented" at the polls by her menfolk, whose actions often disappointed her. At the instigation of local suffrage societies, the Texas Woman Suffrage Association revived in 1913 and held its first state convention since 1904. In 1914, Annette Finnigan, who had returned to Houston, was elected president and began the process of shaping the TWSA into a serious working organization with a lobbying presence in the legislature. She also appointed Minnie Fisher Cunningham, president of the Galveston Equal Suffrage Association, as state organizer. Cunningham was one of the first women to earn a pharmacy degree from the University of Texas Medical Branch at Galveston, but she had followed social convention and given up practicing her profession when she married. One of the corps of Progressive women who put suffrage above every other cause, she undertook the job of organizer with energy and enthusiasm (see Document 1.10). By 1915 twenty-one local suffrage societies belonged to the TWSA. At its convention that year Finnigan declined consideration for another presidential term, and Cunningham was elected to lead the organization. The name was changed to Texas Equal Suffrage Association (TESA) in 1916 to indicate that men were welcome, and Cunningham was reelected president annually for the remainder of the decade.

Under Cunningham's leadership the TESA grew to 9,500 members, organized in ninety-eight local societies spread across the state. For guidance and strategy it looked to the National American Woman Suffrage Association, with which it was affiliated, and Cunningham worked closely with NAWSA president Carrie Chapman Catt. In order to build a suffrage "machine" capable of successful pressure group politics, Cunningham appointed a chairwoman for each of the state's senatorial districts, who then directed suffrage organizing at the county and town level. Suffragists in each district supported the lobbying effort that Cunningham led in Austin by sending their legislative representatives letters, telegrams, and petitions. The women also kept steady pressure on the state's congressional delegation in Washington, D.C., to vote for the federal suffrage amendment to the U.S. Constitution.

At both levels, the odds were heavily against them. Texas lacked a functioning two-party system and the bargaining leverage that went with it. Democrats, the party of secession and Civil War, controlled all levels of government; the small and weak Republican Party offered only token opposition. The dominant political issue was prohibition, championed by the Progressives, which had split the Democrats into "wet" and "dry" factions. Women tended to be strongly prohibitionist, and their votes could have advanced the cause, but the prohibition faction was home to both Progressives and religious conservatives, and the latter opposed suffrage. The anti-prohibitionists, led by Governor James Ferguson, strongly opposed woman suffrage. In short, the suffragists had too few allies in the prohibitionist wing, and none at all in the anti-prohibitionist wing. But politicians on both sides were united in claiming that woman suffrage would mean the downfall of white supremacy. Hordes of Negro women would flock to the polls, the argument went, and the federal government would intervene to enforce their claim to the ballot.

Suffragists called this contention the "Negro bogey" because it was obviously untrue. Few African Americans could meet the discriminatory voting requirements that the southern states had imposed, and the federal government had ignored black disfranchisement for years; in fact, it would continue to turn a blind eye to racial discrimination in voting until the 1960s. Racial repression was justified by the fiction of "protecting" white women, and southern politicians wanted them voiceless and voteless in order to maintain the status quo. Southern resistance to suffrage was so adamant that in 1916 NAWSA decided that continuing to pursue state constitutional amendments below the Mason-Dixon Line was simply wasting energy and money. Minnie Fisher Cunningham and other southern presidents agreed to work only for partial suffrage measures that could be won without a voter referendum: the right to vote in party primaries and for presidential electors. The TESA lobbied unsuccessfully for both measures in the 1917 legislative session.

After the United States entered World War I in April 1917, suffragists, without relaxing their campaign for the ballot, joined other women in home-front war work. They sold Liberty bonds and thrift stamps to raise money for the government, distributed food conservation pledge cards, helped run recreational canteens for soldiers, and volunteered for the Red Cross. Minnie Fisher Cunningham initiated one of the most ambitious projects, the Texas Women's Anti-Vice Committee. Fifteen women's voluntary associations joined the TESA in the new organization, which formed in response to re-ports of high rates of venereal infection in the state's military training camps. The Selective Service Act authorized the secretary of war to ban prostitu-tion within five miles of a military establishment and prohibited the sale of alcohol to soldiers in uniform, but both regulations were widely ignored. The Anti-Vice Committee mobilized local women to monitor conditions around the camps and pressure officials to enforce the prohibitions against brothels and saloons; Cunningham sent regular reports of the committee's findings to Washington, D.C.

War work gave suffragists an opportunity to attract positive publicity, and patriotic service enhanced their public image. The war also provided them with new arguments for the vote. Suffragists were quick to point out the contradiction of fighting for democracy abroad while half the population was disfranchised at home. African Americans noted that the same inconsistency applied to the black community, but the presence of black men in uniform worsened rather than improved race relations. A race riot erupted in Houston in August 1917 after an off-duty African American guard from Camp Logan intervened in police harassment of a black woman (see Document 1.13). In a racially polarized society white suffragists did not dare make common cause with black ones. In El Paso, the cordial relations between the local suffrage society and the Colored Women's Club led the suffrage president to suggest that the club apply for affiliation with the TESA. Fearing the political conse-quences, the TESA leadership consulted with Carrie Chapman Catt at NAWSA and followed her advice to tell the black clubwomen "that you will be able to get the vote for women more easily if they do not embarrass you by asking for membership."[31]

Although public sentiment against woman suffrage remained steadfast, the TESA did become one of the few southern suffrage associations to fulfill NAWSA's goal of winning partial voting rights. In March 1918 the Texas Legis-lature passed a bill authorizing women to vote in primary elections, which in a one-party state was nearly the equivalent of full suffrage. Primary suffrage was not a reward for women's war work (the politicians' public excuse) but a concession to suffragists' political astuteness and skillful lobbying. Working behind the scenes, Minnie Fisher Cunningham convinced the leaders of the prohibitionist wing of the Democratic Party that they needed women's votes in order to win the gubernatorial election. Acting Governor William P. Hobby was running for the office in his own right against former governor James Ferguson, an anti-suffragist who had been impeached on multiple counts of misusing public funds, and several prohibitionist candidates. Ferguson, a skilled demagogic campaigner, was enormously popular with poor farmers and had the financial backing of the brewing industry. Hobby was young and inexperienced, a former anti-prohibitionist who had finally endorsed banning alcohol as a wartime necessity to conserve grain and sugar. TESA leaders saw what was likely to happen: Hobby and the prohibitionist challengers would split the dry vote, enabling Ferguson to regain the governor's office.

The suffragists also realized that if women, who tended to be prohibitionists and advocates of "good government" were enfranchised, they could provide enough votes to defeat Ferguson. The TESA executive board offered Hobby the organization's backing if he would ask the legislature, which was scheduled to convene a special wartime session, to pass a primary suffrage bill. Fearing that he would lose more votes than he would gain by endorsing the ballot for women, Hobby declined to act. Cunningham then privately made the case to Representative Charles Metcalfe, a suffrage ally who was supporting Hobby's candidacy. In return for Cunningham's promise to turn out the women's vote for Hobby, Metcalfe lined up support to pass the primary suffrage bill. Hobby signed it on March 26, 1918, and the suffragists immediately launched a massive drive to register women voters. Proving themselves adept at message manipulation, or "spin," they mounted an enthusiastic campaign for Hobby that completely reshaped his public image. Obscuring his late, reluctant endorsement of suffrage, they presented him as a champion of progressive women's causes, "the man whom good women want." To help draw women to the polls, Cunningham persuaded Annie Webb Blanton, a professor at North Texas State Normal College and the first female president of the Texas State Teachers Association, to run for state superintendent of public instruction. Hobby won the primary by a landslide, and Blanton became the first woman in Texas elected to a statewide office.

Women secured primary suffrage only because the Democratic Party was divided, and they were able to show one faction a direct political advantage to enfranchising women. (They never revealed their behind-the-scenes bargaining and publicly supported the men's assertion that the ballot was a reward

for women's war work.) After the women's Hobby campaign clearly demonstrated female voters' usefulness, the legislature in 1919 passed a constitutional
amendment authorizing full suffrage, subject to a voter referendum. Suffrage
leaders tried in vain to prevent this unwanted gift, knowing that it would be
nearly impossible to persuade Texas men to vote yes—no southern association
had ever won a constitutional referendum for full suffrage. Short of money
and womanpower, the TESA nevertheless campaigned hard. The antis, however, mounted a vicious race-baiting attack, and the amendment was defeated
at the polls in May 1919. Less than two weeks later Congress passed the Nineteenth Amendment to the U.S. Constitution, giving all women the right to
vote, and sent it to the states for ratification. The defeated state amendment
enabled the antis to claim that Texans had rejected suffrage, making the suffragists' task of persuading the legislature to ratify the federal amendment
that much harder. They succeeded by shrewd politicking and by stationing
watchers at the train station to apprehend anti-suffragist senators who attempted to break the quorum by sneaking out of town (see Document 1.12).
On June 28, 1919, Texas became the ninth state in the nation and the first in
the South to ratify the Nineteenth Amendment.

SUFFRAGE IN BLACK AND WHITE

"With what high hopes and enthusiasms women stepped forth into a world
in which they were citizens at last!" wrote Austin suffragist Jane McCallum, the TESA's historian.[32] In reality, not all women achieved political citizenship. While sex had been removed as a barrier to voting, inequalities of
class and race kept many women disenfranchised. The poll tax, which had
been imposed at the beginning of the century to discourage blacks and poor
whites from voting, was a disproportionate burden on women of both races
because of their economic inequality relative to men. Jane McCallum, married to Austin's superintendent of schools, could pay her tax as casually as
she ordered groceries, but to the wife of a tenant farmer, who saw little cash
from year to year, the required $1.50 was a significant sum. A poor farmer who
could barely scrape together the money to pay his own poll tax annually was
likely to conclude that his wife didn't "need" to vote.

African American women were twice disadvantaged: if they could afford
the poll tax, they were still excluded from the whites-only primary. (The Republican Party was so small that it did not hold primaries.) During the drive
to register women voters in the 1918 gubernatorial campaign, black women
who tried to sign up met varying responses. In some counties party officials
refused them entirely; in others they were allowed to register but told they

would not be permitted to vote in the primary. In Houston the tax collector refused to register black women until the newly chartered branch of the National Association for the Advancement of Colored People threatened to prepare a protest; two hundred women were ultimately registered at a separate table from whites. Black clubwomen were at the forefront of organizing several of the thirty-one branches of the NAACP that formed in Texas in 1918–1919, and in some branches they were more than 40 percent of the membership. The NAACP pushed for the abolition of the white primary, but as long as it stood (until 1944), black women's political citizenship was limited to paying a poll tax for the privilege of voting in the general election for either a Democrat already selected by white voters in the primary or a Republican who was certain to lose. White women, as teacher Christia Adair discovered in 1919, were not willing to champion black women's political rights, and the Republican Party barely tolerated them (see Document 1.14). Adair became a prominent NAACP activist, and she and other African American women had to work decades longer to become political "citizens" at last.

Middle-class women, through their network of voluntary associations, dominated the social welfare side of Texas Progressivism. Redefining the community as an extended household, they invented new female public roles and asserted a claim to shared governance based on their expertise as housewives and mothers. Positioning themselves in opposition to essential tenets of southern political culture such as cheap, limited government and low-wage capitalism, they pressed for restraints on the power of business and industry to exploit consumers, children, and workers and for expanded social welfare spending. Turning themselves into social investigators and lobbyists, clubwomen put the weight of their organizations behind campaigns for a pure food law, minimum wage and maximum hours legislation for working women, restrictions on child labor, compulsory education, and mothers' pensions. In every major city they attacked the problems of urban growth and industrial development, founding settlement houses, free public kindergartens, clean milk stations, and day nurseries for working mothers and pressuring municipal governments to appoint food inspectors and clean up the water supply.

Progressive women's most radical challenge to the established order was the campaign for female suffrage, a direct assault on the southern tradition of restricted democracy and white male supremacy, and their chances of success were small. Northern suffragists had the merely difficult task of persuading men to take the final steps in the century-long progress toward universal suffrage by enfranchising women; southern suffragists shouldered the nearly impossible burden of expanding an electorate that had been pared down to a core of males who could afford poll taxes. The door to suffrage, ajar in the North, had been purposely closed and locked in the South. Texas suffragists, like those in other southern states, were scourged by racial politics, but they were among the few who found a strategy that forced the closed door partially open. Most who walked through were white; the racial order was one aspect of the southern status quo that reformist women declined to challenge. Throughout the Progressive decades white and black women worked through parallel but separate voluntary associations, with few interracial contacts, a pattern that would persist after 1920 and for decades to come.

SUGGESTED REFERENCES

GENERAL WORKS

The period between 1900 and 1920 has generated the most abundant scholarship in Texas women's history. For a general overview of women and the Progressive Era, see Judith N. McArthur, *Creating the New Woman: The Rise of Southern Women's Progressive Culture in Texas, 1893–1918* (Urbana: University of Illinois Press, 1998).

WOMEN WORKERS

The growth of the Hispanic female labor force is detailed in Barbara J. Rozek, "The Entry of Mexican Women into Urban Based Industries: Experiences in Texas during the Twentieth Century," in *Women and Texas History: Selected Essays,* ed. Fane Downs and Nancy Baker Jones (Austin: Texas State Historical Association, 1993). Irene Ledesma, "Unlikely Strikers: Mexican American Women in Strike Activity in Texas, 1919–1974" (Ph.D. diss., Ohio State University, 1992), is the definitive work on Mexicana labor protest, while Mario T. Garcia, "The Chicana in American History: The Mexican Women of El Paso, 1880–1920—A Case Study," *Pacific Historical Review* 49:2 (May 1980), explores workplace discrimination and labor activism in a Hispanic-majority city. Ruthe Winegarten, *Black Texas Women: 150 Years of Trial and Triumph* (Austin: University of Texas Press, 1995), contains a substantial discussion of both professional and working-class African Americans. Julia Kirk Blackwelder's *Styling Jim Crow: African American Beauty Training during Segregation* (College Station: Texas A&M University Press, 2003), includes the history of Houston's Franklin School of Beauty. On telephone operators, see Nancy Hadley, "The 'Hello Girls' of Houston," *Houston Review* 9:2 (1987).

SOCIAL HOUSEKEEPING

Jacquelyn Masur McElhaney's *Pauline Periwinkle and Progressive Reform in Dallas* (College Station: Texas A&M University Press, 1998), combines a biography of the "voice" of clubwomen reformers with reprints of selected Periwinkle columns. The most exhaustive survey of the women's club movement is Megan Seaholm, "Earnest Women: The White Women's Club Movement in Progressive Era Texas" (Ph.D. diss., Rice University, 1988). Winegarten, *Black Texas Women*, includes a discussion of clubwomen; see in addition Audrey Crawford, "'To Protect, to Feed, and to Give Momentum to Every Effort': African American Clubwomen in Houston, 1880–1910," *Houston Review of History and Culture* 1:1 (Fall 2003). The activities of Dallas clubwomen are described in Elizabeth York Enstam, *Women and the Creation of Urban Life: Dallas, Texas, 1843–1920* (College Station: Texas A&M University Press, 1998); see also her "They Called It 'Motherhood': Dallas Women and Public Life, 1895–1918," in *Hidden Histories of Women in the New South*, ed. Virginia Bernhard, Betty Brandon, Elizabeth Fox-Genovese, Theda Purdue, and Elizabeth H. Turner (Columbia: University of Missouri Press, 1994), and "The Forgotten Frontier: Dallas Women and Social Caring, 1895–1920," *Legacies: A History Journal for Dallas and North Central Texas* 1:1 (Spring 1989). Jackie McElhaney, "Save the Babies: Blanche Greenberg and the Milk Stations," *Legacies* 13:2 (Fall 2001), also focuses on Dallas. Elizabeth Hayes Turner, *Women, Culture, and Community: Religion and Reform in Galveston, 1880–1920* (New York: Oxford University Press, 1997), covers both clubwomen and churchwomen. Judith N. McArthur, "Saving the Children: The Clubwomen's Crusade against Child Labor, 1902–1918," in *Women and Texas History*, is the most detailed account of women's initiative. On settlement houses, see Vicki Ruiz, "Dead Ends or Gold Mines? Using Missionary Records in Mexican-American Women's History," *Frontiers* 12:1 (1991), which analyzes the Rose Gregory Houchen Settlement, and Maria Cristina Garcia, "Agents of Americanization: Rusk Settlement and the Houston Mexicano Community, 1907–1950," in *Mexican Americans in Texas History: Selected Essays*, ed. Emilio Zamora, Cynthia Orozco, and Rodolfo Rocha (Austin: Texas State Historical Association Press, 2000). Studies of prostitution include David C. Humphrey, "Prostitution in Texas: From the 1830s to the 1960s," *East Texas Historical Journal* 33:1 (1995); Humphrey, "Prostitution and Public Policy in Austin, Texas, 1870–1915," *Southwestern Historical Quarterly* 86 (April 1983); and Ann R. Gabbert, "Prostitution and Moral Reform in the Borderlands: El Paso, 1890–1920," *Journal of the History of Sexuality* 12:4 (October 2003).

SUFFRAGE

Citizens at Last: The Woman Suffrage Movement in Texas, ed. Ruthe Winegarten and Judith N. McArthur (Austin: Ellen C. Temple, 1987), reprints A. Elizabeth Taylor's foundational 1951 essay "The Woman Suffrage Movement in Texas," originally published in the *Journal of Southern History*, with a selection of primary documents. Judith N. McArthur documents the political bargain that produced primary suffrage in "Minnie Fisher Cunningham's Back Door Lobby in Texas: Political Maneuvering in a One-Party State," in *One Woman, One Vote: Rediscovering the Woman Suffrage Movement*, ed. Marjorie Spruill Wheeler (Troutdale, Ore.: NewSage Press, 1995), and "How Did Texas Women Win Partial Suffrage in a One-Party Southern State in 1918?" *Women and Social Movements in the United States, 1600–2000*, http://www .alexanderstreet6.com/wasm. Judith N. McArthur and Harold L. Smith, *Minnie Fisher Cunningham: A Suffragist's Life in Politics* (New York: Oxford University Press,

2003), and Janet G. Humphrey, *A Texas Suffragist: Diaries and Writings of Jane Y. Mc-Callum* (Austin: Ellen C. Temple, 1988), profile two leaders. Studies of local movements include Elizabeth York Enstam, "The Dallas Equal Suffrage Association, Political Style, and Popular Culture: Grassroots Strategies of the Woman Suffrage Movement, 1913–1919," *Journal of Southern History* 68:4 (November 2002); Elizabeth Hayes Turner, "'White-Gloved Ladies' and 'New Women' in the Texas Woman Suffrage Movement," in *Southern Women: Histories and Identities,* ed. Virginia Bernhard, Betty Brandon, Elizabeth Fox-Genovese, and Theda Purdue (Columbia: University of Missouri Press, 1992); Janelle D. Scott, "Local Leadership in the Woman Suffrage Movement: Houston's Campaign for the Vote, 1917–1918," *Houston Review* 12:1 (1990); and Larry J. Wygant, "'A Municipal Broom': The Woman Suffrage Campaign in Galveston, Texas," *Houston Review* 6:3 (1984). Annie Webb Blanton's campaign for state superintendent of public instruction is discussed in Debbie Mauldin Cottrell, *Pioneer Woman Educator: The Progressive Spirit of Annie Webb Blanton* (College Station: Texas A&M University Press, 1993).

THE BORDER

Teresa Palomo Acosta and Ruthe Winegarten's *Las Tejanas: 300 Years of History* (Austin: University of Texas Press, 2003) offers a general overview of female border activism during the Mexican Revolution, while Clara Lomas, "Transborder Discourse: The Articulation of Gender in the Borderlands in the Early Twentieth Century," *Frontiers* 24:2–3 (June–September 2003), focuses on Mexicanas' pro-revolutionary journalism. Gabriela Gonzalez, "Two Flags Entwined: Transborder Activists and the Politics of Race, Ethnicity, Class, and Gender in South Texas, 1900–1950" (Ph.D. diss., Stanford University, 2005), analyzes women's participation within the framework of transnationalism. Alexandra Minna Stern has written extensively on medical inspection of immigrants; see especially "Buildings, Boundaries, and Blood: Medicalization and Nation-Building on the U.S.-Mexico Border, 1910–1930," *Hispanic American Historical Review* 79:1 (1999), and *Eugenic Nation: Faults and Frontiers of Better Breeding in America* (Berkeley: University of California Press, 2005). There are references to Texas in Amy L. Fairchild, *Science at the Borders: Immigrant Medical Inspection and the Shaping of the Modern Industrial Labor Force* (Baltimore: Johns Hopkins University Press, 2003). Ann R. Gabbert, "Defining the Boundaries of Care: Local Responses to Global Concerns in El Paso Public Health Policy, 1881–1941" (Ph.D. diss., University of Texas at El Paso, 2006), is definitive on prostitution, medical inspection of Mexicanas, and prenatal surveillance of Mexican mothers. David Dorado Romo, *Ringside Seat to a Revolution: An Underground Cultural History of El Paso and Juarez: 1893–1923* (El Paso: Cinco Puntos Press, 2005), includes a chapter on the "bathhouse riot."

1.1. CLUBWOMEN INVESTIGATE CHILD LABOR
IN THE DALLAS COTTON MILLS (1902)

When the Texas Federation of Women's Clubs added the child labor problem to its agenda in 1902, the state had no law restricting children from working or requiring them to attend school. Since no one knew how many children worked in factories, mines, and street trades, the clubwomen assigned themselves the job of investigating child labor in their local communities. They used the statistics they gathered to pressure the Texas Legislature to pass a law in 1903 prohibiting the employment of children younger than twelve. Mrs. J. C. Roberts, who was married to a Dallas attorney, belonged to the Quaero Club of Oak Cliff, which was a member of the Dallas Federation of Women's Clubs. Here she reports to Anna J. H. Pennybacker, president of the Texas Federation of Women's Clubs, on the Dallas Federation's efforts to find out how many children were at work in the city's cotton mills. When the owners refused to cooperate, the clubwomen, all refined middle-class ladies, resorted to spying. Roberts was also a member of the Dallas Federation's committee that drafted a child labor bill that was presented to the legislature.

Dallas, June 24, 1902
My Dear Mrs. Pennybacker—

I beg pardon for delaying so long a reply to your letter. . . . You ask me for statistics concerning the number of children at work in the Mills, what abuses they suffer and what has been done in Dallas to ameliorate these conditions. I spent many months at the most discouraging labor before I discovered that there were no statistics on the subject from the fact that statistics could only come from an inspector. We have no law regulating the labor of children, therefore no inspector to see that the law is enforced. Visitors are peremptorily denied admission to the Mills on the ground that they might become entangled in the machinery. The only way to discover the number of children employed in any Mill is to employ the disagreeable tactics of Mary's lamb and "linger near" until work hours are over and count the children as they pass out on the way home.

Unpleasant as this espionage is it has been resorted to in Dallas with the result that sixty-five (I quote from memory) children varying from five to thirteen years were counted on one day. These children work from six in the morning until six in the afternoon with only forty-five minutes intermission for lunch.

The day-shift is then relieved by the night-shift, who work in their turn until six in the morning. There are nearly as many children in the night-shift as work during the day.

These little victims not only suffer from the close confinement, unsanitary conditions and long hours, but are almost entirely cut off from all opportunities for the acquirement of an education. On Sunday they sleep the lethargic slumber born of physical exhaustion and the whole family usually remain in bed all day. Knowing, as you do, how ignorance and vice go hand in hand, there is no need to picture to you the sequel to lives begun in that way.

You ask what we have done: Since the first note of protest was uttered at the meeting at the State Federation [of Women's Clubs] last May this whole abuse has been checked as regards Dallas. The Quaero Club of Oak Cliff, of which I am a member was the first club to take up the work. I was sent as delegate to the City Federation to push this reform. Almost at once matters began to improve in the Mills district. It was like the clearing away of suffocating fogs at the blowing of the fairy Prince's silver horn. A free kindergarten was established for the children of that part of the city whose mothers were for the most part at work in the looms. For the support of this kindergarten the management of the Mills subscribed a room, a piano, and ten dollars per month. About one month ago the Superintendent discharged every child in the Mills under twelve years of age, which is the age specified in our bill.

Within the last week the Public School Board has voted to establish a night school in that district which is another step forward. A discouraging fact recently encountered is that the children dismissed from the Mills here have been sent to other places and re-employed at the same work. Thus you see how much we are in need of a State law such as they have in all the northern and New England States. I had five hundred of the enclosed bills struck off and our City Federation is having one mailed to every club in the [State] Federation. We hope to begin a broad and wide agitation which shall reach its fiercest point during the coming meeting of the Legislature and we shall leave no stone unturned to get this bill passed. You can give us so much help, and you will I am sure!

Yr friend

Mrs. J. C. Roberts

225 Holmes St.

Source: Records of the Texas Federation of Women's Clubs, Blagg-Huey Library, Texas Woman's University.

1.2. PAULINE PERIWINKLE, "WAY TO A MAN'S HEART . . ." (1905)

After business interests defeated a pure food bill in the 1905 legislative session, women's organizations, with the Texas Federation of Women's Clubs in the lead, launched a pure food publicity campaign. Isadore Calloway, a prominent clubwoman and editor of the Woman's Century page of the *Dallas Morning News*, used her journalistic voice, "Pauline Periwinkle," to especially good effect. Her columns castigated the dishonest food processors and the legislators who passed laws forbidding the adulteration of food for livestock but not for humans. Mothers, she frequently pointed out, had no way to protect their children, because women lacked the vote and, while babies died, the male population did nothing. In the following exasperated column she recommended, tongue in cheek, a kitchen table strategy for getting men's attention and stirring them to action. Thanks in part to the Progressive women's lobby, the pure food bill passed in 1907.

When all appeals to the heart fail, let us by all means appeal to the stomach. Those who have been working for pure food laws in Texas have evidently overlooked the mighty factor of the sensitive stomach in the anxious search for a possible heart. They have told pathetic stories of the babies whose pinched faces and tiny graves were eloquent though mute indictments of milk embalmed by formalin. They have pointed out that the poor man, the man driven by necessity to patronize the cheapest products, was being systematically robbed by rich manufacturers; that the poverty of the poor was being enhanced by a system of cheating that enabled the manufacturer to palm off anywhere from 10 to 50 per cent of non-nutritious adulterants in all such staples as flour, bread, coffee, syrups, jams, spices, baking powders, etc.

Little has been accomplished by this means. Few if any cities have official chemists or food inspectors, and graft flourishes accordingly. True, a law has been passed whereby horses and cows and other live stock are protected in getting sufficient nutriment in their feed, by excluding ground corn cobs and hulls, but the human animal must continue to suffer, that greed may be satisfied. And yet the advocates of pure food laws ask no more than do the cattle interests. They ask only that the labels on sacks and boxes and packages and bottles that contain alleged foods shall state exactly the ingredients and proportions that go to make up its contents. "Let the label tell" is their slogan. In this way the housekeeper to whom economy is the consideration may have opportunity to figure out whether when she buys 25 cents worth of ground coffee, it is wise to pay 20 cents of it for parched bran, etc., that at most costs 2 cents. Why not give the poor woman, instead of the rich manufacturer, the opportunity to make money by adulterating at home the 5 cents worth of coffee? Dr. Wiley, the Government food expert, says that $375,000,000 is made off the American public every year. Dr. Abbott of the Massachusetts Health Board puts the figures up to $750,000,000. . . .

The housewife, naturally, is the one to whom the vital necessity of proper food values chiefly appeals. Alas, she has no way of making her protest score, unless she can touch the men with similar perception. Let her try "the stomach route" of sending her shafts home, since other means have failed. For instance, good housewife, when the head of the house has broken open one of those flaky biscuits for which your cuisine is justly famous, when he is liberally applying to the piping surface a layer of golden butter, suppose you casually remark: "Dear did you read what the recent report of the Pure Food Commission said about the manufacture of butter. It's positively startling. Out of fifty-eight kinds of butter sold in one city not a single one was genuine. They say that most of the butter we buy is renovated. Wait just a minute, I cut the report out of the paper because I knew you'd be so interested. Here it is." (Reads)

"Butter renovating factories have agents in all the large markets who buy up the refuse from the commission men and retailers, take the stale, rancid, dirty and unsuitable butter in various degrees of putrefaction. This refuse is put through a process of boiling, straining, filtering and renovating and is finally churned with sweet milk, giving it a more salable appearance. The effect is only temporary, however, as in a few days the stuff becomes rancid, and the odor it gives off is something frightful. It is usually sold to people having a large trade who will dispose of it quickly, for if it is not consumed at once, it can not be used at all without being further renovated."

A few readings of this sort, well timed, would be apt to produce effects of some kind or other than "going in one ear and out of the other." He would begin to view with distrust those neat square packages for which we pay a round price, and evince a willingness to "put up" toward paying for a chemical analysis. And if that doesn't fetch him tell him about the London chemist who has discovered how to make a very good "commercial" butter out of ordinary city sewage. If the trust gets hold of the invention they will drive every cow into the pens of their fellow plotters, the beef trust, in order to force a monopoly of their revenue-making product.

Milk is, of course, one of the grossest forms of food adulteration, since it affects helpless infancy and childhood. Unlike adults, the young child is limited in diet, and if the milk lacks in nutrition or has been "doctored" to prevent souring the effects are at once seriously manifested. There are some adulterations of adult food that are comparatively harmless. Nevertheless, the purchaser has a right to know what he is buying with his money. Ground white rock, bone dust and starch are cheaper than baking powders, and some of the latter are fully one-third composed of these cheap white dusts.

Then there are the syrups, jams and jellies. The basis of all the cheaper grades of fruit products are the same—apple pulp, gelatine, glucose—flavored and dyed to suit by chemical aids. "But," exclaimed one purchaser of raspberry jam, "I'm sure this is all right, because it's got just lots of seeds in it." The experienced inspector smiled and finally succeeded in convincing her that the seeds were seeds indeed, but extracted from the "head" of timothy grass, and not from a luscious raspberry. . . .

Some of the acid flavors and vinegars are very unwholesome. They are calculated to eat the bottom out of a copper kettle, then what must they do to the sensitive stomach? . . . Wood alcohol, aniline dyes, formaldehyde, salicylic acid, even arsenic and strychnine have been found in colored and preserved "sham food."

Source: Pauline Periwinkle, "Way to a Man's Heart . . . Need of Food Inspectors," *Dallas Morning News*, July 31, 1905.

1.3. HALLIE EARLE WRITES HOME FROM
MEDICAL SCHOOL (1904–1906)

The New Woman of the unfolding century was likely to be a college graduate who expected to earn her own living, at least until marriage. A few New Women, like Hallie
Earle, sought careers in traditionally male professions. Earle, who grew up in rural
McLennan County, graduated from Baylor University in 1901 and earned an M.S.
degree the following year. An advanced degree may have helped ensure her success
at Baylor University College of Medicine in Dallas, which she entered in 1904. "The
boys are all nice to me," she reported in one of her letters home, and her scholastic
ability impressed her professors. Earle was not the only woman in her class, but she
was the only one who finished; she became the medical school's first woman graduate
in 1907.

October 22, 1904
Dearest Mother,
    . . . Yesterday Prof. Brooks of Waco was in Dallas and came around to Baylor.
What do you think Dr Cary told him—that it would be a chase between a red
headed boy and myself as to who would be leader in the sophomore class. I was perfectly thunder struck. He also told Brooks that I was working nicely. . . .

October 25, 1904
Dearest Mother,
    . . . I went to school in the afternoon—at night a crowd of us went out to the
circus. Dr Farar chaperoned the crowd. . . . By the way in one of the lecture classes
to day Dr Wells (the lecturer and one of my favorites) call[ed] on one of the young
men: and asked him to answer some questions for him which Miss Earle had told
them yesterday. Well the man could not do it. Then Dr Wells said—yes that is
it—Miss Earle will be practicing medicine, and making $20,000 a yr. when you all
are chewing paper bags! . . . Dr Johnson, one of the instructors in anatomy . . . was
jollying me up good to day about being at the circus. Then he quizzed me on the
dissection, and when I answered all of his questions he said well I certainly did well
even if I did go to the show. . . .

April 12, 1906
My Dear Mother,
    We have had two examinations to day. The one we had this morning under Dr
Becton on surgical pathology was oral and he told me that I had made a hundred.
We had one yesterday in regional anatomy, and I am sure that I made a good grade
and we had one in Electro-therapeutics this afternoon—had 100 hundred [sic] questions—I think I will make a passing grade, and that is a good deal more than most
of the class will do. . . .
    I want to take the state medical board which meets in Dallas June the 12–13–

14. . . . I need to review up if I go before the board . . . and may be able to pass the board—but it will take $15 to go before the board, and so tell Mary to sell lots of Turkey eggs so she can lend me the money to face the board. Then if I pass I will give her the certificate as a security note.

Source: Courtesy Graves-Earle Family Papers, The Texas Collection, Baylor University, Waco, Texas.

1.4. ADA DEBLANC LEARNS HER "PLACE" UNDER JIM CROW (1914)

Ada DeBlanc Simond was born in southern Louisiana in 1903 to a light-skinned, French-speaking family. "To be born a girl child—the fourth in a family where boys were very important—was to be born handicapped," she recalled. To be born black in a racist society was even worse, she discovered abruptly at age eleven, when the family moved to the Texas coast.

Port O'Conner [*sic*] was a strange place. We were accustomed to the bayou but Matagorda Bay was altogether different. The hardest thing of all to understand was that we were in Texas now. One of the younger boys could not learn to leave off the Louisiana part. He would say I am in Texas Louisiana.

Papa had a nice cottage for us to live in. We did not mind that it was small and crowded. It was summer and we spent most of the time outside. Within a few days we were all employed except for the two youngest boys. Mama had washings from the guests at the Port O'Conner Hotel. The boys ran errands for some guests who lived in nearby cabins. I had a job helping a lady who lived in one of the cabins. I helped tidy up the house and played with the three small children, one a baby.

It was this woman who introduced me to my second handicap—the blackness I had never known.

Papa had explained to us that all these people lived in cities someplace else. They came to this place to rest from their work. They could fish and do other things for fun. Some stayed only a few days, some for a week and more. The family I worked for had been there several weeks. During the day the man was home only at dinnertime. I went home after the dinner dishes were washed and put away. I took the soiled clothes with me, washed them with Mama's help, and returned them the next day. It was a very good job and I had never known about a job before. I had always done these things, but we never used the term job.

One day the woman seemed very unnerved. She was preparing a spread for the raw greens she had in a bowl. We had never used the term salad. I had seen Mama break an egg in a bowl, beat it a little while with a fork, add a little olive oil, beat a little more, add a little vinegar, beat a little more (Mama always beat it hard and fast), add more olive oil, then beat and repeat until she had enough thick and creamy spread for the vegetables. This woman would break an egg in the bowl, beat with the beater, add lemon juice, and with great anger pour it all in the trash. She did this three times before I told her I could show her how Mama did it. She seemed to be relieved and with deliberation wiped her hands on her apron and took the baby from my arms. Then with great anger in her face and in a harsh tone told me she did not need a "nigger" to show her how to do anything and to get out of her house. I could not for the life of me figure her out, but I was sure I had done a terrible thing. "Nigger" had no meaning, for I had never heard the word before. When I told Mama she looked as if she had suddenly become very ill.

Mama rounded up all five of us and told us a long story, some of which I don't think I ever heard. But she made us understand that some people are white, some are colored, and that some white people hate colored people. The point that she made sure we understood was that in the sight of God we were exactly like Him in every way except perfection. God is perfect: further that we were all beautiful, good, and smart; and that God loved us more than anyone could ever hate us. She assured us that we were such precious things to her and to Papa that they would never let anything ever happen to us, nor would they ever let anyone harm us. She wanted us to understand we must never go around any white people until they had talked with her or Papa. I was not permitted to help anyone else. Mama said she needed me to take care of things at our house. If someone wanted one of my brothers to play with a child or run an errand, that person had to talk with Mama. When Papa came home that evening, he had some special things to say to my brothers about white people. The boys stood tall, saying, "Yes sir, Papa." But we were very frightened. From that day I knew what it was to be different, to be black.

Source: Adah [*sic*] DeBlanc Simond, "The Discovery of Being Black: A Recollection," *Southwestern Historical Quarterly* 76:4 (April 1973). Courtesy of Texas State Historical Association, Denton.

I.5. A TEXAS MOTHER SEEKS ADVICE FROM THE CHILDREN'S BUREAU (1916)

The New Woman notwithstanding, most women's occupation was raising a family. Infant mortality was high, and worried mothers like Mrs. N.W. wrote to the female-staffed U.S. Children's Bureau from every part of the country, asking for literature and personal advice. The free pamphlets *Prenatal Care* (1913) and *Infant Care* (1914) that Mrs. N.W. requested were enormously popular; by 1920 the bureau had distributed more than one million copies of the latter. As these two letters reveal, women who struggled with difficult pregnancies and sickly children often felt isolated and overwhelmed, frustrated by their own ignorance and by inadequate medical care.

Mrs. N.W., Texas (February 2, 1916)
Dear Sir:
Please send me your book "Infant Care." I would appreciate very much if you could advise me in regard to my 28 months old baby boy. As we live in the extreme Southwest we do not always get fresh vegetables, with the exception of cabbage, onions

and lettuce, nor do we always get fresh fruit. He is very sallow looking, tongue is always coated, sometimes constipated, although I give him castor oil and castoria; these help temporarily. His ears are yellow looking, no blood seems to be in them. He looks to be anaemic but I really don't know what to feed him.

I cannot always get a chicken when I need one for him and nothing in beef except round steak which isn't always fresh. The doctor here told me he'd outgrow his anaemia and coated tongue but I doubt it, as I never got over my anaemia and have a very weak stomach. If it is possible for you to send me a prescription for a good tonic to build him up and give him an appetite I would be very thankful to you for same. Thanking you in advance for any favors you may give.

Mrs. N.W., Texas (February 18, 1916)

Dear Madam:

Although I haven't heard from you regarding my boy who is past two years old, I am anxiously awaiting your reply to my letter and take the liberty of writing you again in regard to his eyes.

Last March he was bitten in the forehead by a dog making a very deep hole directly over his right eye. The dog's head was sent to the Pasteur Institute, Austin, and they wired back the dog had no rabies. It had become intensely hot in June when I noticed a small knot in his left eye. I consulted an eye doctor here who prescribed several kinds of eye drops and pastes but his eyes grew worse, both became inflamed, and a film form[ed] around the iris of both eyes.

After paying the doctor $12 for services which made the eyes worse, I began treating them myself. I purchased [a] dozen small towels, boiled them thoroughly and used them for his eyes exclusively, never using the towel more than once. Used boric acid in eyes, but when this didn't relieve inflammation, [I] tried hot applications and baking soda in water instead of boric acid, which relieved them somewhat.

When cold weather came, I noticed an improvement and finally the inflammation disappeared. One day last week, I noticed a small film again on the iris of his left eye and up to the present time both eyes are again inflamed and the film has spread around the iris of both eyes, making his eyes look weak.

He always had clear, bright, pretty brown eyes with long thick lashes. Now the lashes are falling out, and he always rubs his eyes. The eyelids and around the lashes look to be in healthy condition, no redness whatever. A good many Mexicans live here and the doctor thought his eyes may have become infected from them. Or do you think it has something to do with the dog bite?

Any advice you could give would be so appreciated. There is no other doctor here who can advise me and I feel so helpless and like a prisoner who can't escape from this hole.

Please send me the book "Prenatal Care." Last June I gave birth to an 8 mos. baby girl who died 16 hrs. later. I became very weak, [with] pains in both side continually. In Dec. I determined to undergo an operation. The surgeon said I had [the] beginning of appendix trouble (I had frequent dull pains around the navel), [and] retroversion of the womb. He'd scrape [the] womb, sew up laceration (was torn when my boy came two years ago and never sewed), and heal ulceration of womb, and he might have to cut a little off of an ovary. I had dreadful cramps. I was treated for bowel trouble, and it wasn't until my baby came prematurely that I found out it was my womb cramping and the doctors didn't know what was the matter with me. They gave me hypodermics which made me sicker than ever but didn't relieve my cramps. So I am begging you to help my boy and myself, if in your power. I don't want to lose this baby, which, God willing, I expect in August. I am very constipated; pills don't help me much, except an enema. [I] have a heavy bearing down feeling, vomit a great deal, and every now and then pains at mouth of womb, slight pains in right side occasionally. I had my last period on Nov. 21st.

Anxiously awaiting your letter, and again thanking you for any advice you can give me. I beg to remain, very sincerely yours.

P.S. I forgot to state that in the last two weeks I have been cramping again. My just beginning to cramp again reminded me.

Source: Molly Ladd-Taylor, *Raising a Baby the Government Way: Mothers' Letters to the Children's Bureau, 1915–1932* (New Brunswick, N.J.: Rutgers University Press, 1986).

1.6. FLORES DE ANDRADE ORGANIZES WOMEN IN SUPPORT OF REVOLUTION (1909–1911)

In the decade before the Mexican Revolution, the Partido Liberal Mexicano (PLM), founded by Ricardo and Enrique Magón (who fled to Texas in 1904), organized opposition to the dictatorship of Porfirio Díaz. The PLM had chapters as far north as San Antonio and encouraged women's participation. Flores de Andrade organized women in northern Mexico and El Paso, working clandestinely because the U.S. government considered PLM activity in Texas a violation of American neutrality. She describes hiding Francisco de Madero, who issued the call to take up arms in 1910, in an El Paso safe house operated by her PLM women's club. When preparations for the uprising were complete, she escorted Madero and his entourage across the border. She narrowly escaped being shot by Díaz's troops in Mexico and was arrested by American military authorities on her return to El Paso.

I . . . decided to go to Chihuahua, that is to say, to the capital of the state, and there, a widow and with six children, I began to fight for liberal ideals, organizing a women's club which was called the "Daughters of Cuauhtemoc," a semi-secret organization which worked with the Liberal Party of the Flores Magón brothers in fighting the dictatorship of Don Porfirio Díaz. We were able to establish branches of the woman's club in all parts of the state by carrying on an intense propaganda. . . .

[A]fter four-years stay in Chihuahua, I decided to come to El Paso, Texas. I came in the first place to see if I could better my economic condition and secondly to continue fighting in that region in favor of the Liberal ideals, that is to say, to plot against the dictatorship of Don Porfirio. I came to El Paso in 1906, together with my children and comrade Pedro Mendoza, who was coming to take part in the Liberal propaganda work. . . .

In 1909 a group of comrades founded in El Paso a Liberal women's club. They made me president of that group, and soon afterwards I began to carry on the propaganda work in El Paso and in Ciudad Juárez. My house from about that time was turned into a conspiratory center against the dictatorship. Messengers came there from the Flores Magón band and from Madero bringing me instructions. I took charge of collecting money, clothes, medicines and even ammunition and arms to begin to prepare for the revolutionary movement, for the uprisings were already starting in some places.

The American police and the Department of Justice began to suspect our activities and soon began to watch out for me, but they were never able to find either in my house or in the offices of the club documents or arms or anything which would compromise me or those who were plotting. I was able to get houses of men or women comrades to hide our war equipment and also some farms. . . .

In 1911, a little before the revolutionary Sr. Madero became general, he came to El Paso, pursued by the Mexican and American authorities. He came to my house with some others. I couldn't hide them in my house, but got a little house for them which was somewhat secluded and had a number of rooms, and put them there. . . . I put a rug on the floor and then got some quilts and bed clothes so that they could sleep in comfort. So that no one would suspect who was there, I put three of the women of the club there, who washed for them, and took them their food which was also prepared by some of the women.

Don Francisco and his companions were hidden in that house for three months. One day Don Francisco Madero entrusted my husband to go to a Mexican farm on the shore of the Bravo River so as to bring two men who were coming to reach an agreement concerning the movement. My husband got drunk and didn't go. Then I offered my services to Sr. Madero and I went for the two men who were on this side of the border, that is to say in Texas territory, at a wedding. Two Texan rangers who had followed me asked me where I was going, and I told them to a festival and they asked me to invite them. I took them to the festival and there managed to get them drunk; then I took away the two men and brought them to Don Francisco. Then I went back to the farm and brought the Rangers to El Paso where I took them drunk to the City Hall and left them there.

Later when everything was ready for the revolutionary movement against the dictatorship, Don Francisco and all those who accompanied him decided to pass over to Mexican territory. I prepared an afternoon party so as to disguise the movement. They all dressed in masked costumes as if for a festival and then we went towards the border. The river was very high and it was necessary to cross over without hesitating, for the American authorities were already following us, and on the Mexican side there was a group of armed men who were ready to take care of Don Francisco. Finally, mounting a horse barebacked, I took charge of taking those who were accompanying Don Francisco over two by two. They crossed over to a farm and there they remounted for the mountains.

A woman companion and I came back to the American side, for I received instructions to go on with the campaign. This happened the 18 of May, 1911. We slept there in the house of the owner of the ranch and on the next day when we were getting ready to leave, the Colonel came with a picket of soldiers. I told the owner of the ranch to tell him that he didn't know me and that another woman and I had come to sleep there. When the authorities came up that was what he did; the owner of the ranch said that he didn't know me and I said that I didn't know him. They then asked me for my name and I gave it to them. They asked me what I was doing there and I said that I had been hunting and showed them two rabbits that I had shot. They then took away my 30-30 rifle and my pistol and told me that they had orders to shoot me because I had been conspiring against Don Porfirio. I told them that was true and that they should shoot me right away because otherwise I was going to lose courage. The Colonel, however, sent for instructions from his general, who was exploring the mountains. He sent orders that I should be shot at once.

This occurred almost on the shores of the Rio Grande and my family already had received a notice of what was happening to me and went to make pleas to the American authorities, especially my husband. They were already making up the squad to shoot me when the American Consul arrived and asked me if I could show that I was an American citizen so that they couldn't shoot, but I didn't want to do that. . . .

The Colonel was trying to stave off my execution so that he could save me, he said. An officer then came and said that the General was approaching. The Colonel said that it would be well to wait until the chief came so that he could decide concerning my life, but a corporal told him that they should shoot me at once for if the general came and they had not executed me then they would be blamed. They then told me that they were going to blindfold me but I asked them if their mothers weren't Mexicans, for a Mexican isn't afraid of dying. I didn't want them to blindfold me. The corporal who was interested in having me shot was going to fire when I took the colonel's rifle away from him and menaced him; he then ordered the soldiers to throw their rifles at the feet of the Mexican woman and throw themselves into the river, for the troops of the General were already coming. I gathered up the rifles and crossed the river in my little buggy. There the American authorities arrested me and took me to Fort Bliss. They did the same thing with the soldiers, gathering up the arms, etc. On the next day the authorities at Fort Bliss received a telegram from President Taft in which he ordered me to be put at liberty, and they sent me home, a negro military band accompanying me through the streets.

Source: Manuel Gamio, *The Mexican Immigrant: His Life Story* (Chicago: University of Chicago Press, 1931).

1.7. LEONOR VILLEGAS DE MAGNÓN AND LA CRUZ
BLANCA NURSE WOUNDED MEXICAN REVOLUTIONARIES
IN LAREDO (1914)

Leonor Villegas de Magnón was born in Nuevo Laredo, Mexico, to a wealthy family that later moved to Laredo and became American citizens. After the Mexican Revolution unsettled the Rio Grande border, Villegas de Magnón founded La Cruz Blanca (the White Cross) in 1913. She turned her home and the bilingual kindergarten she had established in Laredo into a volunteer hospital and cared for the wounded Carrancistas—followers of Jesús Carranza, the leader of the Constitutionalists. Writing in the third person and referring to herself as the Rebel, Villegas de Magnón describes how Cruz Blanca nurses smuggled soldiers back into Mexico as they recovered, under the suspicious gaze of the American military deployed on the border.

On January 1, 1914, at daybreak, the Carrancistas attacked Nuevo Laredo and were repulsed with heavy losses. The battle was one of the fiercest ever fought in Northern Mexico. . . . After days of fighting, the Carrancistas retreated several miles south to await reinforcements from Matamoros, making Camargo their headquarters.

Meanwhile, on the American side, there was great alarm. An embargo had been declared and the international bridge was closed. When American Consul Garret wired Washington, explaining the situation of Mexican citizens in the war-torn town, they were allowed to cross the river and take refuge on American soil. . . .

Arriving home, the Rebel found friends awaiting her; the newsboys told her that wounded soldiers were being brought to her place for care.

"Go to the river for help," she told them. "On your way tell the volunteer nurses, Marie, Bessie Moore, and Lily Long, all of them, to come."

Quickly, the kindergarten tables were made into comfortable beds with bed clothes available from her own linens, and those that the Rebel raided from her brother's home. As the wounded were brought in, they were immediately taken to the operating room. The Rebel's little living room was stripped of furniture, equipping an operating room in less than twenty-four hours.

The temporary hospital was soon filled to capacity. Leopold came to his sister's aid, offering her a large building just across the street from her house on his property. By night, the wounded numbered a hundred. . . . Soon three emergency hospitals were in use on American soil, all under the supervision of the Rebel and the Constitutionalist White Cross. . . .

Public sentiment in Laredo sided with the Constitutionalists. When news spread that the wounded were being taken to the Rebel's house, neighbors, friends, and sympathizers came bringing mattresses, bed linens, food, dressing, and medicines. . . . American doctors were working side by side with Mexican doctors. . . . The four doctors from Mexico made their headquarters at the Rebel's house. . . .

In the heat of enthusiasm, no regard of violation of international law was thought of by the people of Laredo, but trouble again arose. The Federals protested at so much care and leniency for the Carrancistas. In Presidio and Marfa, 3,000 Federal soldiers were being held prisoners in American camps, having fled across the border when 6,500 rebels had attacked Ojinaga. The Federals had taken refuge in the United States, carrying arms. The Rebel wondered how long she could keep her Mexican wounded. The hospital was surrounded by American soldiers. But . . . the problem had to be faced. The men could not leave the hospital and go about on American soil; they would be arrested. . . . So it was planned to spirit them out.

To the American soldiers they all looked alike, these natives of Laredo and the Mexican soldiers. So the hospital traded a milkman or two who came to deliver cans of milk for a soldier or two, sending them out past the guards. It was hours before the escape was discovered. But when it was, the Rebel was reprimanded. The wounded were counted ever so many times a day. When five poor fellows actually died, many more were reported dead. . . . Towards evening the dead were carried out, their bodies wrapped in sheets. No one looked at the dead. One day, however, one of the guards did open a coffin.

"Why put in this man's shoes?" he asked.

"It is a Spanish custom," the Rebel replied feebly. But that was the end of the coffin escapes. . . .

"If another man leaves this place, I'll shoot every one of you," the [American] captain shouted down at the crying Rebel. . . .

When available influences failed, the Rebel . . . got a lawyer, Mr. Otto Weffing, who called personally on the governor of Texas and wrote letters to Washington, pointing out that the Ojinaga Federal prisoners had crossed over with arms, while the Laredo soldiers had been brought over unconscious and wounded into a private home. Hospitality had been violated by imprisoning these men. . . .

It was the latter part of March when the Rebel received the first letter from General Pablo González, of the Constitutionalist northeastern military sector, thanking her for her care of his soldiers and her efforts to secure their release. Though she was not personally acquainted with him, the brave young commander had become an idol to her. She spoke of him so often that the hospital staff always saluted his photograph that hung in the tiny entry.

Source: Leonor Villegas de Magnón, *The Rebel*, edited by Clara Lomas (Houston: Arte Público Press, 1994).

1.8. THE CITY OF EL PASO SETS REGULATIONS FOR ITS PROSTITUTION DISTRICT (1913)

From the late nineteenth century until World War I, prostitution districts, called "reservations" or "segregated districts," were common in American cities. Municipal authorities contended that men would always seek prostitutes and that regulating the trade kept it geographically contained. Middle-class women, by contrast, denounced the sexual double standard and advocated abolishing reservation districts. Periodic crackdowns such as this one in El Paso restricted prostitutes' personal freedom and their civil liberties, as authorities tried to make prostitution less visible without giving up the revenue that licensing fees generated. A grand jury investigation in 1913 identified 367 prostitutes in El Paso, about 1 percent of the population.

Rules for Reservation [1913]
El Paso, Texas

Women must keep screen doors fastened on inside and keep curtain on lower half of screen door.

Must sit back from doors and windows and not sit with legs crossed in a vulgar manner and must keep skirts down.

Must remain in rooms until after twelve o'clock, and when they come out on the street after twelve o'clock they must not be loud or boisterous or be playing with each other or with men. They must not be hugging men or women around the street or be trying to pull men into their cribs.[1]

Must not sit in windows with screens down, or stand in doors at any time.

Must never leave curtains up with men in their rooms.

Must not cross street in middle of block, but must go to Second or Third Street and cross over when crossing street.

Must not yell or scream from one room to another, or use loud, vulgar language.

Must not leave line and remain away all night. Must not solicit off the reservation, on public streets or in the public parks.

Must not wear gaudy clothes or commit any act of flirtation or other act that will attract unusual attention on the streets.

Must not go to supper on the reservation with men or remain around restaurants flirting or joking with men.

Must not encourage men to hang around their doors.

No minor will be allowed to frequent or loiter on the reservation.

Women must not banter or quarrel with each other in front of cribs or on streets.

When women claim men are diseased they must refund money when men furnish doctor's certificate showing them to be free from disease. If men are diseased the woman should be allowed to keep the money given her for the examination.

Women should not take in drunken men and demand pay for their time.

Must not work with light out.

When women are on street must be in full dress and not wear "kimonos."

Must not solicit at back doors.

No curious people allowed on street.

Officers will not show partiality to any one and must not take sides in any factional row or dispute. When women are having a dispute and will not obey officer send them all to the station.

Officers must not drink or mingle with women in any manner. They must be disinterested at all times.

Source: Howard B. Woolston, *Prostitution in the United States prior to the En-*

trance of the United States into the World War (Appleton-Century Co., 1921; reprint Montclair, N.J.: Patterson Smith, 1969).

1.9. HORTENSE WARD CALLS FOR EQUAL PROPERTY RIGHTS FOR WIVES (1911)

Texas was one of a handful of states in which wives remained under coverture in the twentieth century. Under the law, when a woman married, she lost her separate legal identity, and everything she owned became her husband's property. Houston attorney Hortense Ward explained the unfairness of wives' legal status, as part of a campaign to persuade the legislature to grant married women control of their property and earnings. Published in the *Houston Chronicle* in 1911, Ward's essay was reprinted as a document for the Texas Federation of Women's Clubs in 1912. Intense publicity and skilled lobbying by a broad coalition of women's groups led to the Married Women's Property Act in 1913.

When a woman marries in Texas, her husband has the sole management of all her separate property and all her interest in the community property. All her money, earnings, notes, securities, and even her wearing apparel, are absolutely under his control. He has the management of them without her consent, and even against her will. He can draw out every cent of her money from the bank, and do with it as he pleases. . . . She cannot even exercise any right of control over her separate property without his permission, and then only as his agent, which permission and agency may be withdrawn at any time. He can lease or rent her real property and collect all rents therefor, and dispose of such rents as he sees fit. . . . He may even mortgage or sell every piece of furniture in the home, and she is helpless to prevent, even if her earnings have paid for every piece. He has the right to sell her dresses if he wishes, and she cannot prevent. He may sell all the community property except the home, though she has earned every dollar by her own labor. . . .

If she goes out into the world to earn a livelihood, the husband alone can collect her wages. In case of suit, he can prevent her employer paying the wages to her instead of himself . . .; and having obtained her wages he can spend them for what he chooses; they are at all times subject to his debts—even ante-nuptial debts—and she cannot collect them against his wishes.

When a woman marries, whether her husband is honest and capable or not, the law turns over to him the absolute control and management of all her property, and no corresponding responsibility is asked of him. He may lose it all, and she cannot ask for an accounting. . . .

So much for his rights. Now as to his responsibilities.

You might suppose that the law, having given him all this, would at least exact of him that he support his wife; but . . . in the case of Treveno vs. Treveno . . . the plaintiff was in poor health, without funds and unable to support herself. She prayed for an order requiring her husband to support her. . . . The Supreme Court held she had no remedy and dismissed the suit.

The husband, even though he has deserted his wife absolutely, and ceases to discharge his duties, and contributes nothing to the support of her and his children, does not forfeit his right to sell the community property or otherwise dispose of it. . . . In other words, though the husband had deserted his family, and the wife by her exertions may have bought a cow to provide milk for the children, a horse to plow the garden to provide food, and household furniture for their needs, [she] is not protected against the sale by the husband of these necessities—though he may have deserted her—and without her knowledge he may sell all these things and the buyer can come into her home and take them and she has no legal recourse.

. . . Being unable to choose your daughter's husband—don't you think it might be wise to limit his authority—don't you think it might be kind to protect your child? Don't you think you can trust your daughter—at least nearly as well as her husband—with the property you may leave her? Don't you think your daughter is entitled to spend on her children and herself the wages she earns? The curse pronounced on the sons of Adam is made, by the laws of Texas, a deeper curse on the daughters of Eve. They may not even earn their bread—it may be snatched from their children's mouths by the law of the land and placed in the hands of idle and brutal husbands and fathers.

The mere fact that a woman marries should not put her in the class with minors and idiots—and yet this is what the present law does. Until a woman assumes the duties of wife and mother, she has exactly the same property rights as a man—when death or the divorce court severs the bonds of matrimony, she enjoys all the legal rights enjoyed by her brother—does it not seem a trifle absurd to say that during coverture she is incompetent to manage her own estate?

Source: Hortense Ward, "The Legal Status of Married Women in Texas," Anna Pennybacker Papers, Center for American History, University of Texas at Austin.

I.IO. MINNIE FISHER CUNNINGHAM ORGANIZES LOCAL CHAPTERS FOR THE TEXAS WOMAN SUFFRAGE ASSOCIATION (1915)

The campaign for woman suffrage was the most controversial and labor-intensive Progressive Era reform. Suffragists had two difficult tasks: organizing a network of local suffrage societies across the state and lobbying the legislature to pass a bill. These letters from suffrage organizer Minnie Fisher Cunningham to Annette Finnigan, president of the Texas Woman Suffrage Association, show how the two activities were interrelated. The grassroots societies that Cunningham was organizing helped generate pro-suffrage publicity by sponsoring a lecture tour by Helen Todd of California, a national suffrage speaker. Equally important, the suffragists in each community were asked to gather signatures from prominent male citizens for telegrams endorsing woman suffrage and urging their legislative representatives to vote yes. Cunningham's enthusiasm for this work, despite being caught in a train wreck and running out of money, shines through these reports.

Jacksonville
Friday afternoon [1915]
My dear Miss Finnigan:

I've just digested the pleasing fact that my train is three hours and a half late, which will put me into Dallas something after twelve and make it impossible for me to get to Ft Worth tonight at all, so I thought I'd while away a few minutes telling you about Nacadoches [*sic*] and Palestine. We had splendid meetings in both places[,] rather larger in Nac, but very much in earnest in Palestine. The membership of both organizations curiously enough is the same. Twelve. Miss Kate Hunter, 209 S. Sycamore St, is the Palestine President and she promises to be a wonder. Please send her *lots* of literature as she intends to make a house to house and office to office canvas to invite people to hear Miss Todd.[2] And let me tell you you *must* send them Miss Todd or I'll never dare to show my head in East Texas again. They'll *kill* me! They'd really *like* to have her *tomorrow*! I never saw anything like the way they hunger and thirst for her coming and read every scrap in the papers about her. . . .

Miss Hunter says if they can have Miss Todd they will make their chapter "the best chapter of the State organization"—and I believe she can come very near to doing it within the necessary limitations of size. Her spirit is wonderful. . . .

I wish I had some Jacksonville names. I'd certainly get out & try to stir up something here. The "next time" you send me out you'll have to send along with me somebody to talk to. I'm simply perishing with ingrowing conversation—meeting all of these splendid women and never a chance to "talk it over" as I go. . . .

Truly Yours
Minnie F. Cunningham

Sulphur Springs
Wednesday 1915
My dear Miss Finnigan:

Arrived here in the midst of perfectly awful weather[,] cold & pouring rain. I've made every effort to get a meeting to organize. But there seems no hope with this weather. However I managed to locate a very clever woman—very much interested in Suffrage who will see to the telegrams to Mr. Wynn—Mrs. Polk. I don't know her initials but the only Polk here. She gets the signatures and I pay for the telegram—one I mean. In addition to this she says she will take up the work of organizing later. So you might regard her as a chairman.

I had to pay some cab fares to trail around and see these women and so I am completely out of money. . . . I've telegraphed Mrs. Walker [treasurer of the Texas Woman Suffrage Association] to wire me ten more and I cant leave here until it comes because I cant pay my hotel bill!

. . . I think I accomplished results in Mineola, but I dont expect it will effect

M. because they had already petitioned him to vote for the Amendment. Sent him between a hundred and seventy five and two hundred names, all done up with pink silk tassels and things they told me. But they are perfect *trumps,* and promised to sally forth to day & have the telegrams—I paid for one—sent. Did not entertain me however—In fact they were in *bed* & I had to get them up & out for a conference. Werent they good to do it?

Hoping to hear from you in Bonham.

M. F. C.

Source: McCallum (Jane Y.) Papers (AR.E.004), box 88, Austin History Center, Austin Public Library, Austin.

I.II. TEXAS EQUAL SUFFRAGE ASSOCIATION: ISN'T IT TRUE [THAT HOMEMAKERS NEED THE VOTE]?

One of the most appealing arguments for woman suffrage took the anti-suffragist claim that women's business was housekeeping and reversed it. Suffragists contended that women needed the vote precisely because they were responsible for homemaking and child rearing. They pointed out that private and public housekeeping were intertwined: women could not keep germs out of their homes if city officials did nothing about filthy streets, uncollected garbage, and contaminated water supplies. This broadside, published by the National American Woman Suffrage Association and distributed by the Texas Equal Suffrage Association, was one of a number that stressed the housekeeper's need to help elect the men who ran city government—and government's need for women's input.[3]

Isn't It True?

Isn't It True

That a **man's success** in business depends not only on himself but on the men he helps elect **to office?**

Isn't It True

That housekeeping is a woman's business and that her success depends not only on herself but on **the way** her town is governed?

Isn't It True

That the control of **food, air, light, water, health, education, morals and all living conditions is to-day** in the hands of the officials of the town?

Isn't It True

That it is only **common justice** and **common sense** to let the woman in the home share in electing the man on whom the comfort of the home depends?

Isn't It True

That a man **does not** neglect his business because he votes, and that a woman **will not** neglect her home because she votes?

Isn't It True

That the happiness of a home **does not** depend on the woman **always** being in it, but on the **kind** of woman she is?
Isn't It True
That in the right kind of a home BOTH the man's AND the woman's points of view are needed?

Votes for Women

National Woman Suffrage Publishing Company, Inc.
505 Fifth Avenue, New York City
    Source: McCallum (Jane Y.) Papers (AR.E.004), box 54, Austin History Center, Austin Public Library, Austin.

1.12. SUFFRAGISTS PUSH RATIFICATION THROUGH A DIVIDED LEGISLATURE (1919)

After the U.S. Senate passed the Nineteenth Amendment conceding women the right to vote on June 4, 1919, suffragists still had to secure ratification by three-fourths (thirty-six) of the states. Minnie Fisher Cunningham, who had become president of the state suffrage association in 1915, was in an especially difficult position because Texas voters had just defeated a state suffrage amendment. The anti-suffragists in the legislature therefore argued that "the people" didn't want woman suffrage. The antis demanded a public referendum (which presumably would also be negative) on the ratification question.

    Contrary to expectation, on June 28, 1919, Texas became the ninth state in the nation and the first in the generally hostile South to ratify the Nineteenth Amendment. Suffragists always portrayed themselves as outsiders who persuaded men to grant them justice, but this letter from Cunningham to Carrie Chapman Catt, president of the National American Woman Suffrage Association, shows the reality behind the public image. Suffrage leaders were sophisticated politicians, intimately familiar with the legislative process, who knew how to count votes and line up support as well as their opponents. They outmaneuvered the anti-suffragists at every step of the process, securing pro-suffrage pledges before the special session convened and patrolling the railroad station to prevent diehard senators from breaking the quorum by slipping out of Austin.

July 2, 1919
Mrs. Carrie Chapman Catt
171 Madison Ave.
New York
My Dear Mrs. Catt:
    Enclosed please find a copy of the Ratification Resolution passed by the Texas Legislature; in the House by 96 to 20, in the Senate 19 to 10.

It was a hot battle with the advantage on our side from the start because we went to work the day after we knew we had lost our referendum, whereas the Antis were too busy counting up a great big majority against us so we wouldn't contest the election and expose their cheating.[4] They depended too much on that majority, and it very properly failed them.

The Legislature met Monday, June 23rd. Our Resolution was No. One in both House and Senate. We were strongest in the House, so we planned to rush it there to help the morale of the Senate. It was committed at once, at the noon recess the committee met and brought out a unanimously favorable report.

The Antis had arranged a big convention here for Monday morning so they were attending that while we were getting the Resolution thru Committee; as we came down from the Capitol at noon we met their Chairman (ex-Congressman R. L. Henry) going up to arrange a hearing before the Committee! They say his face was a picture when he was told the Committee had met and reported unanimously favorable. . . .

In the Senate things were more difficult. We had a sufficient number of signers to the Resolution to put us thru but the Dallas Senator went back on his pledge. Two nights before the Legislature met one of our Senators was shot and killed leaving us with a tie vote 15 to 15 with the Lieutenant Governor pledged to vote it off on our side, and three of the other side certain to vote for ratification if it could be put to them straight, but certain also to vote for a referendum if that ever came to a vote first, while there were constant rumors that two of our signers also favored the Referendum. . . .

Because we had to hold up, the Antis were able to arrange a hearing before the Committee, which was staged Wednesday afternoon at four. Miss Charlotte Rowe,[5] and Mr. Henry spoke for the Antis. . . . The hearing lasted four long hot hours, but our bill was reported out favorably and the substitute which the Antis were fighting for had to come out on a minority report.

The matter coming up the next day (Thursday) the House Bill was substituted for the Senate Bill, and the Antis offered their referendum resolution as a substitute. Our side raised the point of order that this was a special session and nothing could be considered except as submitted by the Governor; that a referendum required legislation, and the Governor had not submitted it, therefore it could not be considered and was out of order. The chair ruled the point of order well taken; they appealed from the chair; the chair was sustained by a vote of 14 to 13! That was our real test vote, and we knew that we were safe by a hairs breadth.

. . . Friday was consumed in oratory and an effort to break the quorum, first by getting ten Senators to resign and run over again on this issue. We openly rejoiced at the idea, and urged them to do it, pledging then that there would be ten new faces in their places at the end of the necessary twenty days and we would still have time to ratify this session. They realized the truth of our statement and tried to get enough of them to leave town to break the quorum, but couldn't manage it, as our people policed the Railroad stations.

We finally lived thru the oratory, and came to the vote on Friday afternoon, with the result . . . 19 to 10 with one absent. . . .

I lived [a] million years while they were voting on the appeal from the decision of the Chair. If we had ever had to vote on that referendum idea we were in for trouble. . . . We could have killed it in the House if the Senate adopted it, but we did not want to have to fight that fight unless we were forced to.

Our men were wonderful. I've never seen such splendid team work, and they did every thing we asked or even suggested. . . . The women were wonderful too. They rose to this battle as tho they were just home from long cool vacations instead of worn to a frazzle with our campaign. There was more than one case of real heroism in the work they did.

Very Sincerely Yours,

[Minnie Fisher Cunningham]

President

Source: McCallum (Jane Y.) Papers (AR.E.004), part II, box 3, Austin History Center, Austin Public Library, Austin.

1.13. SARA TRAVERS IS ASSAULTED BY HOUSTON POLICE OFFICERS AND A RACE RIOT ERUPTS (1917)

World War I brought military training camps to Texas cities, and the presence of African American men from the North in uniform on the streets added another dimension to racial tensions. Black soldiers resented segregation and racism; white citizens were even more bitterly determined to keep African Americans "in their place." On August 23, 1917, two off-duty soldiers from an unarmed Illinois black guard regiment at Fort Logan in Houston were badly beaten when they protested the rough handling of Sara Travers, a black housewife, by police officers. An angry group marched out of camp and into downtown that night, and sixteen whites and four blacks were killed in the riot that ensued. Sara Travers's account, told to an investigator for the National Association for the Advancement of Colored People, makes clear that police brutality was common in African American neighborhoods. Anyone, even a woman ironing, could be a target.

On the afternoon of August 23, two policemen, Lee Sparks and Rufe Daniels—the former known to the colored people as a brutal bully—entered the house of a respectable colored woman in an alleged search for a colored fugitive accused of crap-shooting. Failing to find him, they arrested the woman, striking and cursing her and forcing her out into the street only partly clad. While they were waiting for a patrol wagon a crowd gathered about the weeping woman who had become hysterical and was begging to know why she was being arrested. In this crowd was a colored soldier, Private Edwards. Edwards seems to have questioned the police officers or remonstrated with them. Accounts differ on this point, but they all agree that the officers immediately set upon him and beat him to the ground with the butts of their six-shooters, continuing to beat and kick him while he was on the ground, and arrested him. In the words of Sparks himself: "I beat that nigger until his heart got right. He was a good nigger when I got through with him." Later Corporal Baltimore, a member of the military police, approached the officers and inquired for Edwards, as it was his duty to do. Sparks immediately opened fire, and Baltimore, being unarmed, fled with the two policemen in pursuit shooting as they ran. Baltimore entered a house in the neighborhood and hid under a bed. They followed, dragged him out, beat him up and arrested him. It was this outrage which infuriated the men of the 24th Infantry to the point of revolt. Following is the story of the arrest as given by its victim, Mrs. [Sara] Travers, and by eyewitnesses whose names are in the possession of the Association, but are withheld for their protection.

Mrs. Travers, an evidently respectable, hardworking colored woman, said:

"I was in my house ironing. I got five children. I heard shooting and I'd run out in my yard to see what was happening. Sparks he came into my house and said, 'Did you see a nigger jumping over that yard?' and I said, 'No, sir.' He came in the house and looked all around. Went in back. Then Daniels, the other policeman, he came around the corner on his horse. I called to Mrs. Williams, my friend that lives across the street, and asked her what was the matter. She said, 'I don't know; I think they were shooting at crap-shooters.'

"He (Sparks) came in again just then and said, 'You're a God damn liar; I shot down in the ground.' I looked at her and she looked at me and he said, 'You all God damn nigger bitches. Since these God damn sons of bitches of nigger soldiers come here you are trying to take the town.' He came into the bedroom then and into the kitchen and I ask him what he want. He replied to me, 'Don't you ask an officer what he want in your house.' He say 'I'm from Fort Ben [Bend] and we don't allow niggers to talk back to us. We generally whip them down there.' Then he hauled off and slapped me. I hollered and the big one—this Daniels—he ran in, and then Sparks said to him, 'I slapped her and what shall we do about it?' Daniels says, 'Take and give her ninety days on the Pea Farm [Prison Farm] 'cause she's one of these biggety nigger women.' Then they both took me by the arm and commenced dragging me out. I asked them to let me put some clothes on and Sparks says, 'No, we'll take you just as you are. If you was naked we'd take you.' Then I take the baby in my arms and asked him to let me take it. He took it out of my arms and threw it down on the sidewalk. Took me with my arms behind my back and Daniels, he says, if I didn't come he'd break them. They took me out on Tempson Street. He rung up the Police Department. Whilst I was standing crowd began a-coming (all I had on was this old dress-skirt and a pair panties and a ol' raggedy [shirt]waist. No shoes or nothing)—crowd and a colored soldier man came. [Private Edwards.] Sparks, he says to me, 'YOU STAND HERE,' and I did and a lady friend brought me shoes and a bonnet and apron and he (Sparks) says, 'Stay here,' and went over, and before the soldier could say a word he said, 'What you got to do with this,' and he raised his six-shooter and he beat him—beat him *good*. He didn't do a thing but just raise his hand to ward them off. Didn't even tell them to quit, nor nothing. Then another soldier, this Sergeant Somebody, came, and the first one called to him and the policeman said to him, 'If you come here, we'll give you the same.' Edwards said, 'Must I go with them?' and the second one says, 'Yes, go with them and we'll come along after you.' I hear they shot that second soldier but I didn't see it, for they took me away. They take me to the Police Department and locked me up for using 'abusive language'—but they dismissed the case today.

"I ain't never been before no court of inquiry, no ma'am. Only just to the court when they dismissed the case against me, and there ain't no generals nor no one been out to see me or ask anything. I don't know why they don't come to me. They been to most everyone else around here, and I could tell them the truth. Seems like they might ask me, when I'm the one it happened to, and I'm not afraid to tell, even if Sparks do come back afterwards and do some more to me, but you're the only one yet that's come to ask me."

When interviewed a second time, Mrs. Travers added the following to her statement:

"I been down to the Prosecutor's office today. He asked me what did I know about the riot. I said, 'I don't know nothing about it. I was in bed with my children when it happened." . . . I told him . . . I could tell him what happened before the riot to make it happen, and I started to tell him that Sparks came into my house and hit me. He say he didn't want to hear anything more about that and he sent me home."

Source: Martha Gruening, "Houston: An N.A.A.C.P. Investigation," *The Crisis* 15 (November 1917): 14–16.

I.14. CHRISTIA ADAIR FACES RACIAL DISCRIMINATION FROM BOTH POLITICAL PARTIES (1920)

Christia Adair, a clubwoman, a former teacher, and a future civil rights worker, spent her early married life in Kingsville. Unlike Sara Travers in the previous document, Adair was part of the tiny black middle class, but politically the two shared the same status. The 1918 law that allowed "women" to vote in primary elections was in reality restricted to white women. Excluding African Americans from primary voting kept power in the hands of white Democrats. The state's small and weak Republican Party was active only in general elections. Most blacks were still loyal to the party of Lincoln, which tolerated rather than welcomed them, as Warren G. Harding's 1920 campaign snub painfully demonstrated to Adair.

Now, we did not know in those days the value of what it [woman suffrage] meant to us, that we couldn't vote in the primaries. We knew we could vote in presidential elections and were satisfied, but we just figured we were not supposed to and didn't try. But these women told us about this effort being made to pass a bill where women would be able to vote like men. Well, we still didn't know that that didn't mean us, but we helped make contacts and excite public opinion and worked on people about it. And the bill did pass.

And so the first election that they had after the bill passed, the white women were going to vote. And we dressed up and went to vote, and when we got down there, well, we couldn't vote. They gave us all different kinds of excuses why, but we just stayed. We stayed, we asked, "We want to know why we couldn't vote." The answers to the questions were so invalid, we were not satisfied. So finally one woman, a Mrs. Simmons said, "Are you saying that we can't vote because we're Negroes?" And he said, "Yes, Negroes don't vote in primary in Texas." So that just hurt our hearts real bad and we went on. There was nothing we could do about that but just take it as it was. . . .

When Harding was running for President, the railroad company always sent special trains to bring special people down into that section. Because of my husband's seniority, he was always one of the brakemen that was on the train that would go to bring these home seekers and officials. . . . And so my husband went on the train that went to bring Mr. Harding down.

Somewhere between Washington [and] . . . Kingsville, my husband observed that people were bringing school children to the train to shake hands with the candidate. And so he called me long distance and told me what was going on. I went over to the school and asked the teachers if they would take their children. And when they didn't have time . . . I asked them . . . could I take some of their children? And I did have 11 or 12 children, and I took them to the train. Well . . . I knew just about how the trains stopped and where the location of cars would be so I knew where to place my children to get the best attention. And when the train stopped, well, my husband was the rear brakeman, and he came out to open the observation gates so the candidate could get out to talk with the people. And so my children were right at the steps. And some white children were there by white teachers or parents, and he—Mr. Harding—reached over my children's heads to shake hands with the white children and never did pay any attention to my children. And I pulled my children out, hurt, disappointed and sorry for the children. But in my own heart, I said, "If that's what Republicans do, I cannot be a Republican. I'll have to change parties. From here on out I'll have to work for Democrat presidents."

Source: Black Women Oral History Project, Arthur and Elizabeth Schlesinger Library on the History of Women in America, Radcliffe College.

Southwestern Telephone switchboard operators in Houston, ca. 1900. Courtesy of the Houston Metropolitan Research Center, Houston Public Library.

Women's Progressive Club of San Antonio, founded ca. 1910. UTSA's Institute of Texan Cultures, #081-0097. Courtesy of Lillian W. Sutton-Taylor.

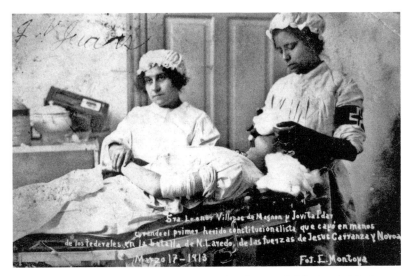

Leonor Villegas de Magnón and Jovita Idar nursing the wounded during the Mexican Revolution, 1913. UTSA's Institute of Texan Cultures, #084-0597. Courtesy of A. Ike Idar.

Basketball players, ca. 1915, College of Industrial Arts, Denton, Texas. Courtesy of the Woman's Collection, Texas Woman's University.

Austin women on Travis County Courthouse steps registering to vote, 1918. PICA A11669, *Austin History Center, Austin Public Library.*

Family picking cotton, Wharton County, 1930. UTSA's *Institute of Texan Cultures, #082-0201, Courtesy of the Wharton County Historical Museum.*

Charlotte Duncan Graham, Jessie Burgett with son Roy, and Mary Sealey in Dallas jail, 1935, during the International Ladies' Garment Workers' Union strike. Courtesy of Charlotte Graham Papers, Special Collections, the University of Texas at Arlington Library.

Emma Tenayuca (fist raised) speaking at a Workers' Alliance demonstration on San Antonio City Hall steps, April 1937. San Antonio Light Collection, UTSA's Institute of Texan Cultures, #1-541-D. Courtesy of the Hearst Corporation.

Hispanic women workers at the Southern Pecan Shelling Company, San Antonio, 1938. Women and girls were paid by the pound for picking the nuts out of the crushed shells, earning below-subsistence wages. San Antonio Light *Collection,* UTSA's *Institute of Texan Cultures, #L-1759-B. Courtesy of the Hearst Corporation.*

Woman doing laundry with a washtub and hand wringer on her farm in El Indio, 1939. Library of Congress, Prints and Photographs Division, FSA-OWI *Collection (Russell Lee, photographer),* LC-USF33-012098-M2 DLC.

Drilling on a Liberator Bomber, Consolidated Aircraft Corporation, Fort Worth, 1942. Library of Congress, Prints and Photographs Division, FSA-OWI Collection, LC-USW36-434.

Col. Oveta Culp Hobby (right) talks with Women's Army Auxiliary Corps (WAAC) members Margaret Peterson and Capt. Elizabeth Gilbert at Mitchel Field, 1943. Library of Congress, Prints and Photographs Division, New York World-Telegram *and the* Sun *Newspaper Photograph Collection (Al Aumuller, photographer), LC-USZ62-118263.*

Jane Straughan, Women Airforce Service Pilot, with an AT-6 at Houston Municipal Airport during World War II. Courtesy of the Woman's Collection, Texas Woman's University.

Juanita Craft with state and national NAACP leaders (including Thurgood Marshall, top right), Dallas, 1948. Dolph Briscoe Center for American History, the University of Texas at Austin, Juanita Jewel Shanks Craft Collection, CN 00674.

NAACP pickets at the Texas State Fair in 1955. Dolph Briscoe Center for American History, the University of Texas at Austin, R. C. Hickman Photographic Archive, DI number 01666.

Ofelia Bowers being arrested during Tex-Son strike in San Antonio, March 1959. San Antonio Light Archive. Courtesy of Alan Pogue.

Austin antisegregation demonstration, early 1960s. PICA *AS-65-50025-4, Austin History Center, Austin Public Library.*

Casey Hayden, Student Nonviolent Coordinating Committee staff member, in Hattiesburg, Mississippi, in July 1964 during Mississippi Freedom Summer. M351 Randall (Herbert) Freedom Summer Photographs. Courtesy of the McCain Library and Archives, University of Southern Mississippi.

Chicano and Chicana students picketing Crystal City High School with signs that read: "Viva la Causa," "Viva la Raza," and "We Want Our Rights." The strike began on December 9, 1969, and lasted nearly a month. San Antonio Express-News Collection, UTSA's Institute of Texan Cultures, #E-0018-201-A-1. Courtesy of the Hearst Corporation.

During the 1972–1974 strike against Farah Manufacturing Company plants in Texas and New Mexico, thousands of copies of this poster were distributed by local Farah Strike Support Committees. Chicanas were a majority of the strikers. Courtesy, Chicano Services Section collection (MS191), Special Collections Department, University of Texas at El Paso Library.

Sarah Weddington, surrounded by her campaign staff, following her election to the Texas House of Representatives in 1972. Campaign manager Ann Richards is at the far left. Courtesy of Sarah Weddington.

Pro-ERA demonstration in Austin, 1975. PICA W5100 PIC A09932, Austin History Center, Austin Public Library.

Martha Cotera speaking at the International Women's Year Conference, Houston, 1977. Courtesy of Martha Cotera.

Barbara Jordan delivering the keynote address at the International Women's Year Conference, Houston, 1977. Courtesy of the Houston Metropolitan Research Center, Houston Public Library.

Coach Jody Conradt and the Lady Longhorns basketball team, University of Texas at Austin. Photo by Susan Sigmon, University of Texas at Austin.

Governor Ann Richards, Inauguration Day, January 15, 1991. Courtesy of the Texas State Library and Archives Commission.

RURAL LIFE

The New Woman notwithstanding, most Texas women still lived in the countryside and filled traditional roles; one-third of all wage-earning women worked in agriculture. In 1920, rural dwellers were 68 percent of the population, and 40 percent of them lived in counties that had no urban centers. The state was in transition from a rural to an urban society, but rural people would outnumber city dwellers until World War II. While urban women enjoyed expanded educational and employment opportunities, a rising standard of living, and leisure time for clubs and civic work, rural women continued to have limited choices and small social networks. Some of them were truly isolated. In order to exercise her new right to vote, Helen Sewell, a young teacher at a one-room ranch school in Jim Hogg County, had to ride horseback thirty miles to Hebbronville.[1]

Although the heyday of cattle ranching was long over and the number of beef cattle and horses declining, ranch culture was deeply embedded in the western and southern parts of the state. Young women raised on ranches grew up on horseback and learned to brand and vaccinate cattle, break colts, and perform many other tasks for which competence mattered more than sex. The most athletic showed off their riding and roping skills in local rodeos. There were no "women's jobs" in working cattle; when wives and daughters were part of a family labor force, they worked in tandem with men. Big Bend rancher Hallie Stillwell described her part in a fall roundup with her husband and son: "After we got a string of calves tied down . . . Guy did the branding, with a hot iron, Roy did the ear marking and castrating, while I did the vaccinating for blackleg. Then we all three did the dehorning, which is the most tedious job of all. . . . Then all the calves had to be untied and 'turned up' as we call it. Some of them got up fighting mad, especially the bulls which had just been made into steers. Sometimes they charged and we had to climb the fence."[2]

Many more women got their livelihoods from agriculture. Cotton farming, entrenched in the eastern portion of the state since the nineteenth century, had spread to Central Texas, the High Plains and Panhandle, and the Rio Grande Valley, but the agricultural economy was far from healthy. Cotton prices were depressed throughout the otherwise prosperous 1920s, and by the start of the next decade 61 percent of farm families—half of whites and nearly three-fourths of blacks—were tenants working land owned by some-one else. The structure of a farm woman's life was determined by her race and her family's relationship to land. At the top of the economic hierarchy were large landowners with several hundred acres and substantial homes, whose wives were full-time homemakers and whose children went to school all year. Smaller landowners had adequate housing, wives who did some field work, and children who went to school but were expected to work as well. The land-less majority divided into three groups: tenant farmers, sharecroppers, and wage laborers. Tenant farmers, who owned their mule teams and farm imple-ments, and sharecroppers, who owned nothing, were trapped in the crop lien system. They lived in two-room shacks, borrowed every year for expenses, and paid the landowner a portion of the crop after the fall harvest. In the crop lien system wives and children (who stayed out of school until the end of cotton picking in December) were part of a family labor force that struggled—and often failed—just to break even, moving every few years in search of better land. Blacks and Mexicans were clustered in tenant and cropper peonage and made up the majority of wage laborers as well.

The landlord who asserted "that he never rented a farm to any man who did not have at least eight children and a wife who worked in the field like a man" unwittingly acknowledged the extent to which cotton farming de-pended on women.[3] Rural women married young, and the number of chil-dren they bore—six to ten was common for whites and more than ten not uncommon for blacks—determined how much acreage a family could farm. Women of all races did field work, but tenant and nonwhite women did the most. Labor economist Ruth Allen, who surveyed cotton-farming women in Central Texas in 1930, reported that 46 percent of white women, 65 percent of Mexican women, and 87 percent of African American women labored in the fields. The majority worked for their own families rather than for wages, although for black women the majority was slim—nearly half chopped and picked cotton for pay. Allen calculated that the value of wives' and daughters' unpaid field labor was equal to one-thirtieth of the crop for white women and one-eighth for black women, who worked more months. She concluded that only unpaid female labor, especially that of teenaged daughters, enabled cotton producers to make a profit.

In East and Central Texas, cotton farming was largely unmechanized;

families planted and plowed with mules, cleared weeds with hoes, and picked cotton by hand. Women most commonly did chopping and picking, but at least one in ten white women plowed, and one in three black women. Picking cotton required sunup-to-sundown stoop labor in the broiling sun, dragging a long sack by a shoulder strap. "If you bent over and picked, then you had a sore back after the first day," one woman remembered of her childhood, "and if you crawled on your knees, then your knees was sore. Oh, that second day, you couldn't hardly get out of bed!" Mothers with small children took them along and improvised care, bedding babies down under the shade of cotton wagons or pulling them along on the end of the cotton sack (which weighed 70 pounds by the time it was full). Women left the field a little early to prepare the noon meal. "I guess she cooked beans the night before, and she'd fix corn-bread," a Bell County woman remembered of her mother. "We had a swing on the porch, and Daddy would lay down [after eating] and take him about a five-minute nap. And she'd be in there washing dishes!"[4]

Farm life, as even a child could see, assigned more work to women. Farm-wives did field work, child care, and household labor simultaneously, which stretched their working day to between twelve and fourteen hours. While women and girls were called upon to "help" in the fields, they had no re-ciprocal claim on male labor; men and boys did not assist with "women's work" beyond lending a hand carrying wood and water into the house. In 1930 only 5 percent of farms had electricity and 8 percent had indoor plumb-ing, making housework as hard and hot as field work for most women. Ruth Allen reported that 57 percent of white women in Central Texas cooked on woodstoves, 89 percent did laundry with tubs and washboards, and 62 percent ironed with flatirons, as did nearly all black women. Some Mexican women lacked even these bare basics: 40 percent did laundry in creeks and rivers, and 4 percent cooked over open fires. Allen found that only 1 percent of African American women had piped water and no Mexican women did. Among white women, 36 percent (the wives of landowners) had water piped as far as an outdoor spigot, and only 16 percent had it piped *into* the house to the kitchen and bathroom.[5]

Even the simplest tasks, like making coffee, required carrying in water (often from several hundred feet or more away and after straining to pull up a heavy bucket from the bottom of a well) and kindling a fire in a stove. Cook-ing on a woodstove with no mechanism to regulate the temperature or keep it steady was a chore, but laundry, which for a large family consumed several hundred gallons of water, was an all-day misery of bending and lifting over outdoor tubs. "By the time you got done washing, your back was broke," one Hill Country woman remembered.[6] Ironing the next day with a set of six-pound flatirons called "sad irons" required more stooping and lifting over a hot stove. Each iron held heat for only a few minutes, so that the woman was continually slinging one back on the stove and hefting another, stopping periodically to clean off soot buildup on the bottom that could smudge the clean clothes. In Allen's sample, about one quarter of white women reported using gasoline irons, which had a complex mechanism: combustion necessitated pumping air with a plunger into a gas tank the size of an orange and lighting the flame while regulating the flow of the air and gas mixture. Gas irons were much more expensive and only a little lighter, but they stayed clean on the bottom and didn't require standing over a blazing stove.

Women's labor also clothed and fed their families. The great majority of white women had treadle sewing machines, which were operated by forward and backward pressure on a cast-iron footplate attached to a belt. Often squinting to see by the light of a kerosene lamp, farmwives sewed nearly everything they and their families used or wore, including cotton sacks and kneepads. Lengths of fabric were much cheaper than ready-made clothes, and muslin feed and flour sacks were free and at hand. Wives' success or failure as food producers determined family health. Men provided the common southern poverty staples of pork, cornmeal, and sorghum syrup, a vitamin-deficient diet that led to diseases such as pellagra, which was widespread in the 1920s. If there were vegetables, eggs, milk, and butter on the dinner table, it was because the wife tended a garden, fed a flock of chickens, milked a cow, and churned regularly.

The meager standard of living of so many rural families was a primary concern of home demonstration agents (also called home extension agents), a new profession for women that had emerged after Congress created the Agricultural Extension Service in 1914. Agents introduced the new technology of water bath canning and encouraged farmwives to improve their families' diets by planting large gardens and canning the surplus. Home demonstration was an attractive career for college-educated women, and especially for African American women, whose access to the professions was severely restricted; by 1940 there were thirty-six black home demonstration agents in Texas. White and black agents worked in separate divisions (Hispanics were largely ignored) and approached the job from different perspectives. Mary Evelyn V. Hunter, the first coordinator (1915–1931) of home demonstration for the black extension service, taught canning, poultry raising, and craft skills as a means of helping African American families pull themselves out of poverty. White home demonstration agents, whose clientele included a much larger proportion of landowners, wanted to get women out of the fields and in control of their own labor. They encouraged farmwives to put their energy into home industries and moneymaking projects such as selling eggs and butter and to use the income for indoor labor-saving devices and domestic comforts.

Even women like Hallie Stillwell, who took pride in their outdoor skills, resented the double standard by which men invested in technology to make their outdoor work easier—installing running water in the barn, for example—while rejecting women's requests for indoor improvements as luxuries (see Document 2.1). Mary Gearing, head of the School of Domestic Economy at the University of Texas, claimed to know a farm family in which the husband dismissed the wife and daughters' repeated requests for running water in the kitchen as too expensive, until the women were called away to care for a sick relative and left the domestic chores, including toting water, to the men for several weeks. When the women returned, they found running water in the house. Gearing suggested, semiseriously, that country women should go on general strike for a month.[7] Not a strike but the New Deal finally brought technology to overworked rural women. Power companies had long refused to run electric lines into the countryside, claiming that the return on the investment would be too small. The Rural Electrification Administration, set up in 1935 in President Franklin Roosevelt's first term, enabled country people to form rural electric cooperatives and borrow money from the federal government to bring power to farms and ranches. With it came the potential for wringer washing machines, electric irons, hot water at the sink, and refrigerators. When electricity came to the farm, rural women finally entered the twentieth century.

THE NEW WOMAN IN POLITICS

Texas women had already undergone their political baptism by 1920, when the ratification of the Nineteenth Amendment conferred full voting rights on all American women. After the successful and highly publicized 1918 campaign that helped elect William Hobby governor and Annie Webb Blanton secretary of public instruction, suffragists optimistically expected that women's new voting power would be an instrument for both social change and the "improvement," as they phrased it, of the political process itself. The Texas Equal Suffrage Association transformed itself into the Texas League of Women Voters (TLWV) in 1919; former TESA treasurer Jessie Daniel Ames was elected president. Its goals were to train women to exercise their new voting power and to continue lobbying for the social reform agenda that women's voluntary associations had sought throughout the Progressive Era. The TLWV encouraged women to join political parties but committed itself to nonpartisanship. The new organization also sought to remove the remaining legal discriminations against women, but its first attempt, a bill permitting women to serve on juries, died in the 1921 legislative session.

The TLWV encouraged women to run for office (although it made no endorsements), and nine women won election to the legislature between 1922 and 1939. Two were one-term widows who succeeded husbands who died in office, and the majority served only one or two terms. Exceptions were former newspaper editor Margie Neal (1927–1935), the first woman elected to the state senate and a serious party activist, and Helen Moore (1929–1933, 1935–1937), a former TESA vice president and a former president of the TLWV. Women with higher ambitions were stymied: Annie Webb Blanton was reelected superintendent of public instruction in 1920 but lost a race for Congress in 1922; Edith Wilmans, the first woman elected to the state legislature (1922) was defeated for governor in 1926 and 1928. Former TESA president Minnie Fisher Cunningham campaigned hard for the U.S. Senate but lost badly and concluded that gender was an almost insurmountable handicap.[8]

The prevailing attitude was that women should have modest political aspirations, and some men were openly hostile to female candidates. Sarah T. Hughes, a Dallas attorney, won the first of two terms in the legislature (1931–1935) by defeating an opponent who declared that she should have her face slapped and be sent back to the kitchen. Women were appointed to state offices that had little power, such as secretary of state (Emma Meharg, 1925–1927, and Jane McCallum, 1927–1931), or that were perceived as "female" areas. Ethel Frances Hilton, the first assistant attorney general (1927–1931), was tapped to concentrate on laws pertaining to women and children in industry. An exception was Sarah Hughes, appointed the first female district court judge by Governor James Allred as a reward for supporting him in the legislature. Women had more success in winning local offices. In 1929 more than 40 percent of county treasurers were female, and several dozen women served as county school superintendents and county and district clerks.[9]

Men were more than willing for women to do political volunteer work such as fund-raising and election-year campaigning, but they firmly resisted admitting them to the inner party councils. The 1920 Democratic state convention tabled Jessie Daniel Ames's resolution to require equal representation for women on the state executive committee. A "50-50" bill backed by the TLWV, the Texas Congress of Mothers, and the Texas Federation of Women's Clubs that required equal representation on county and state executive committees failed in the next two legislative sessions, and a senator who had been a suffrage supporter told the lobbying women that they were trying his patience. After organized women helped put Dan Moody in the governor's mansion in 1926, Ames bluntly informed the state convention that women wanted to "get into the heart of the Democratic Party": "We do not want empty honors thrust on us in the last twenty-four hours of the state convention, and then have the men say they have recognized us. . . . We want on the executive committee of the State Democratic Party. We want [to be] where we can help shape the policies of government."[10] But the women failed to get a resolution from the convention, and they failed another attempt to get a 50-50 bill through the legislature in 1927.

A desire for more than token representation in party offices was one of the few things that united women in the post-suffrage decades. Winning the vote removed the common goal that had held women of diverse backgrounds together in the Progressive Era; with that objective achieved, the women's movement fractured along lines of ideology, class, and age. While liberal women remained committed to social reform, the rise of the second Ku Klux Klan, which appeared in Texas late in 1920, produced a countervailing force of right-wing women. Unlike its nineteenth-century predecessor, the KKK of the 1920s was not focused exclusively on repressing African Americans. The new Klan's targets also included immigrants, Catholics, and Jews, and it was as powerful in the Midwest as in the South. Its rise was a reaction to urban growth, to a perceived increase in lawlessness due to widespread flouting of prohibition, and especially to what it regarded as the moral decay of modernism. Championing patriotism ("100 Per Cent Americanism"), law and order, and biblical morality, the KKK was endorsed by Protestant ministers and leading citizens. It recruited members heavily from the white middle class, including law enforcement officials and judges. Texas had more than one hundred Klan chapters in the 1920s; the Dallas chapter, with thirteen thousand members, was the largest in the nation.

Klansmen administered extralegal "justice" with nighttime floggings or tar and feathers. Clandestine liquor traffickers were favorite targets, along with gamblers, pimps, prostitutes, and divorce lawyers. Sexual behavior—both violation of biblical shibboleths and the embrace of new sexual mores—was a prime concern. Rumored adultery drew Klan whippings for both partners but additional humiliation for the woman, whose hair (symbolic of the temptress) would be hacked off. Audrey Harrison of Goose Creek and Beulah Johnson of Tenaha suffered such punishment; Johnson, accused of bigamy, was tarred and feathered and dumped in the public square as well. In its desire to control female sexuality and impose moral conformity, the KKK expressed traditionalists' anxiety over the changing image of women in postwar popular culture. Skirts, which had revealed only ankles in 1915, rose to the knees and were worn with the new, equally revealing, flesh-colored stockings. Following the example of movie actresses, who projected sex appeal rather than modesty, the "modern" girl bobbed her hair and rouged her lips and cheeks, obliterating a traditional distinction between "nice girls" and "loose women." Young urban women smoked cigarettes, visited jazz clubs, and invented dances that shocked their elders. Courtship rituals moved out of middle-class homes, where they had been overseen by parents, to public amusements (where working-class youth had always courted) and parked cars. "Petting" and "necking" sparked worried magazine articles (see Document 2.2) and provoked intense Klan disapproval. Hooded figures materialized out of the darkness at notorious parking spots to intimidate "auto spooners."

Thousands of Texas women joined the women's branch of the Klan, even before the national organization, Women of the Invisible Empire of America, began recruiting in the state in 1923. Unofficial associations of Klanswomen formed in Dallas and Fort Worth in the summer of 1922, and a state organization was chartered with Agnes B. Cloud as Imperial Kaliph and commander of the Texas realm. Fifteen hundred masked and robed Fort Worth Klanswomen staged the first official women's Klan parade in the nation in June 1923. The following year one thousand Dallas Klanswomen paraded with two thousand men. At the annual convention in Dallas in 1924, three hundred Klanswomen planned a recruitment campaign and appointed ten organizers.

The women's KKK (WKKK) was a study in contradiction: a right-wing movement grounded in bigotry but with tinges of Progressive coloration. There was a notable overlap between the membership of the WKKK and the Woman's Christian Temperance Union (WCTU); both militantly supported prohibition and drew their memberships from Protestant churches. Gertrude Bloodworth, the state Democratic national committeewoman from 1924 to 1928, an officer in the WCTU, and Excellent Commander of the Fort Worth Women of the Ku Klux Klan, was the most high-profile dual affiliate. The WKKK's opposition to liquor and vice echoed the moral reform strand of Progressivism, and its emphasis on law enforcement, good government, and "Americanism" appealed to the kind of civic-mindedness that also drew women to the Texas League of Women Voters (TLWV). Some of the elite Klanswomen, such as Florence Sterling, sister of a future Texas governor, had backgrounds in Progressive Era politics. Before 1920 Sterling had been well known for suffrage, club, and civic work; afterward she was president of both the Houston LWV and the Houston WKKK and led a majority of the city's TLWV members into the Houston Klan.

Not surprisingly, then, women failed to vote as a bloc after suffrage. The Klan's entrance into politics complicated electoral choices, as did the reemergence of Progressive women's old nemesis, James Ferguson, the ethically challenged, anti-suffrage former governor. Refusing to accept the ban against holding state office that had been handed down with his impeachment, Ferguson reemerged in the 1920s as a KKK opponent. In 1924, after failing to get on the state ballot, he put forward his wife, Miriam, as a candidate for governor against a Klan-backed judge, Felix Robertson. Thus the first woman to run for governor with a real chance of winning was a former anti-suffragist whose willingness to serve as her disgraced husband's proxy made a mockery of suffragists' hopes that enfranchised women would clean up politics. James Ferguson was his wife's campaign manager and strategist and made most of her speeches. Since Miriam Ferguson (unlike her husband) was a firm prohibitionist, as dry as Robertson, the WCTU vote was divided. Many former suffragists, including Jessie Daniel Ames and the new TLWV president, Helen Moore, voted reluctantly for the Fergusons as the only choice against the Klan (see Document 2.3). Others, including Jane McCallum and Minnie Fisher Cunningham, bolted the Democratic Party and joined the anti-Ferguson men in forming the Good Government Democratic League of Texas, which supported the Republican candidate.

Miriam Ferguson's victory in the general election was a decisive defeat for the Ku Klux Klan but hardly a triumph for women. She allowed her husband a hand in government, with which he exercised his talent for taking payoffs; the governor herself came under fire for granting thousands of pardons. When she ran for reelection in 1926, Miriam Ferguson did her own campaigning and, without a trace of irony, asked everyone who believed in woman suffrage to turn out for her and cast a ballot for women's rights. As in the Hobby campaign of 1918, Progressive women united behind a reform candidate, the crusading young attorney general, Dan Moody, and against "Fergusonism." Jane McCallum and Jessie Daniel Ames established and ran a women's campaign committee to do grassroots organizing for Moody; he won handily and appointed McCallum secretary of state. By the end of women's first decade of enfranchisement three things were clear: women, contrary to predictions, did not form a voting bloc; they were shut out of real influence in party structures; and, as a consequence, they had small success in winning elective office above the local level.

"FEMALE" POLITICS AND THE "PETTICOAT" LOBBY

Despite women's relative lack of success in winning elective office and securing party influence, they did have an impact on the practice of politics. Conservative Democratic Party leaders had worked for decades to shrink the voter pool; the TLWV and its local chapters immediately set out to expand it. They publicized the deadline for poll tax payment and mounted voter mobilization drives to encourage every registered voter to turn out on Election Day. To lessen the possibility of disqualified ballots—Texas required voters to scratch through the names of candidates they *didn't* support—local LWVs held classes for the public and demonstrated the process of marking a valid ballot. Rejecting the male model of politics that relied on urban machines and courthouse rings to control and deliver the vote, the TLWV urged voters to put issues above party loyalty. Local leagues distributed questionnaires to candidates and used the answers to compile voter information guides, urging both sexes to choose the best-qualified candidates, regardless of party affiliation. The effect, as in the 1924 gubernatorial election, was an upward nudge in Republican numbers.

Organized women also persisted in the voluntary association pressure-group politics that they had practiced effectively in the Progressive Era. After the ratification of the Nineteenth Amendment in 1920, ten national women's organizations created an umbrella organization, the Women's Joint Congressional Committee, to lobby Congress for their social welfare initiatives. In some states, including Texas, organized women formed legislative lobbies modeled on the WJCC, confident that demands backed by their new voting power would get affirmative votes. Five organizations—the Texas Federation of Women's Clubs, the Texas Congress of Mothers, the Woman's Christian Temperance Union, the Texas League of Women Voters, and Texas Business and Professional Women's Clubs—created the Women's Joint Legislative Council (WJLC) in 1922 to coordinate their lobbying efforts; the Texas Graduate Nurses Association joined in 1924. Under executive secretary Jane McCallum the WJLC was active during the 1923, 1925, and 1927 legislative sessions, carrying forward the female pressure-group politics of the Progressive Era and earning the nickname "Petticoat Lobby" from legislators who would have preferred not to be troubled by it.

The WJLC scored most of its victories in 1923 and 1925. It secured a supplemental appropriation for the public schools, surveys of the education and prison systems to pinpoint the need for reform legislation, and bills to strengthen prohibition enforcement and the child labor law. Its most important and difficult achievement was persuading lawmakers to authorize the state's participation in the federal Sheppard-Towner Maternity and Infancy Act, which the WJCC had lobbied through a reluctant Congress in 1921. The first federal social welfare program in the United States, Sheppard-Towner was designed to combat high maternal and infant mortality rates by offering grants-in-aid to the states to set up prenatal and infant care education programs. In order to benefit, a state had to formally accept the act, appropriate matching funds, and submit a plan of work to the federal Children's Bureau.

Texas legislators responded predictably to the WJLC's lobbying for the Sheppard-Towner Act. It was denounced as "Bolshevism," a "pernicious federal snooping bill," and an insult to southern racial mores: "the federal government would send 'Nigger' women down here to run over our white women."[11] After they succeeded in getting Texas to participate, the women's coalition, with the League of Women Voters, the Congress of Mothers, and the Federation of Women's Clubs in the lead, engaged in a prolonged power struggle with the doctors who ran the Texas Department of Health and its Bureau of Child Hygiene. The men's interpretation of the permissible uses of Sheppard-Towner funds differed from the guidelines set up by the Children's Bureau and its director, Grace Abbott. By keeping in close communication with Abbott in Washington, D.C., and pressuring Governor Pat Neff to replace the obstructionist leadership in the health department, the women eventually got a cooperative director of the child hygiene bureau. A volunteer female advisory council worked with him; it was composed of two members from each of the WJLC member organizations and headed by Ina Caddell Marrs, president of the Congress of Mothers.

The Sheppard-Towner Act, which was renewed until 1927 and expired in 1929, funded a health education service for rural mothers that was run almost entirely by women. A corps of nurses, including two African Americans and one Mexicana, traveled from county to county, holding prenatal and child health conferences at which they diagnosed health problems. Local women's and mothers' clubs provided advance publicity to ensure good attendance. In 1925, for example, the state Bureau of Child Hygiene reported 469 child health conferences, at which 10,146 children were examined, and 350 prenatal conferences. In addition, Sheppard-Towner nurses visited women in their homes and signed them up to receive free prenatal and infant care pamphlets. Sheppard-Towner money also paid for a survey to identify midwives who, because they were not required to be licensed, practiced without supervision; nearly four thousand were located in counties with large African American and Mexican American populations. A full-time midwife supervisor coordinated midwife outreach, offering classes and individual instruction to improve the birthing skills of these practitioners, who delivered 50 percent of the babies born to poor women of color.

ATHLETICS: HOOP DREAMS AND RODEO QUEENS

The 1920s and 1930s were the first golden age of sports, for women as well as men. Women's athletics, however, still struggled with issues carried over from its nineteenth-century beginnings. The female physical education instructors who developed women's collegiate programs nationally in the 1890s designed them to avoid what they regarded as the evils of men's athletics. Instead of being public entertainment, women's college teams initially played without spectators, and female coaches stressed participation for everyone rather than cultivating standout players and varsity teams. The focus was on building health and strength and on training every girl in at least one sport she could enjoy for life.

Despite the emphasis on intramural and interclass play, some women's athletic programs, of which basketball was by far the most popular, took on varying degrees of male coloration. In Texas, Southwestern University, the College of Industrial Arts, Baylor College at Belton, and Southwest Texas State University formed a Women's Intercollegiate Association. The University of Texas also played intercollegiate basketball but required the other teams to come to its court. The University Interscholastic League sponsored a program for Texas high school girls beginning in 1918, which played at the county level, without a state championship. Similar patterns unfolded in other states, and by the 1920s national associations of women physical education professionals were speaking out to reclaim the original vision of female athletics. Insisting that intercollegiate competition was too physically and emotionally stressful for young women, they pushed female athletics largely back to intramural and interclass play. Anna Hiss, director of women's physical education at the University of Texas, formed a Texas chapter of the Athletic Conference of American College Women, which condemned intercollegiate play, and the University Interscholastic League dropped girls' basketball in 1928.

But the public enthusiasm for women's sports, especially basketball, was undampened. High school girls continued to play basketball in three leagues sponsored by the Texas High School Basketball Coaches Association, the *San Antonio Light,* and the Amateur Athletic Union (AAU). Churches, playgrounds, and businesses sponsored leagues for adult women. The latter, called industrial leagues, promoted competitive amateurism for women and attracted skilled players by offering jobs or job training combined with an opportunity to shine as players. Coached by male former athletes, industrial leagues were both good advertising for businesses and good for employee morale. Dallas newspapers covered forty-eight regional women's basketball teams, college and semiprofessional, in 1930. Among the most outstanding industrial teams between 1925 and 1932 were the Sunoco Oil Company Oilers and the Employers Casualty Company Golden Cyclones. The Oilers won the Amateur Athletic Union National Championship three years in a row, beginning in 1928.

The Golden Cyclones competed in track and field as well as basketball. Employers Casualty recruited all-American athletes and star high school players, including future Olympian Babe Didrikson (Zaharias), who joined its team in 1930 (see Document 2.4). Cyclones games drew upwards of four thousand spectators and were broadcast live on radio. The only team in the United States that held national records in both basketball and track, the Golden Cyclones made the AAU National Championship semifinals or finals every year between 1927 and 1932 and won the championship in 1931. Retrenchment during the Depression hastened the demise of company-financed teams, but women continued to play competitive ball in business-sponsored commercial and recreational teams.

Rodeo, like basketball, had roots that reached back to the late nineteenth century, and the earliest rodeo cowgirls competed in the same events that men did. As rodeos grew in size after World War I, they began to feature cowgirl events in trick riding, bronc riding, and relay racing. In the 1920s and 1930s roughly one-third of rodeos included cowgirl contests, although women continued to compete against men in events such as steer roping. Sports historian Mary Lou LeCompte has identified more than 250 professional rodeo cowgirls on the circuit between 1929 and 1947. The most celebrated was Nebraska-born Barbara "Tad" Lucas, who settled in Fort Worth as a young woman and dominated women's rodeoing from the mid-1920s to World War II. Her specialty was trick riding, but Lucas won prizes in all categories, including the $10,000 MGM trophy for all-around cowgirl at Madison Square Garden three times. In general, however, women had fewer opportunities for lucrative careers than men. Purses for cowgirls were only 60 to 70 percent of those for men's contests, and rodeos usually had no more than three events for women, while men competed in eight to ten.

After steer roping was banned and replaced with calf roping, cowgirl calf roping became a popular event both on the professional circuit and at small local rodeos. But women's position began to erode by the late 1930s, when Texas rodeos introduced sponsor contests, inviting businesses and large ranches to send attractive young women to participate in a riding competition but mainly to be judged on their appearance and outfits. Within a few years real cowgirl contests that tested athletic ability had nearly disappeared. The trend began to reverse slowly after World War II, following an all-cowgirl rodeo at Amarillo organized by Thena Mae Farr and Nancy Binford in 1947 as an alternative to sponsor contests. In 1948 they formed the Girls Rodeo Association (now the Women's Professional Rodeo Association) in San Angelo to organize professional cowgirls and raise the standards of cowgirl contests.

EDUCATION AND WORK

By 1935 Texas women had caught up with men in college attendance, but they remained clustered in a few fields, with education, business, and home economics leading the choice of majors. The female presence in professional schools was growing but still tiny: that year thirty-seven women were pursing degrees in medicine, forty in theology, and seventy in law. Although women earned more master's degrees (primarily in education) than men, few pursued doctorates. Women made up only 32 percent of the state's college and university faculty, and the more elite the institution, the smaller their numbers. They also earned less than male faculty, and at black colleges the pay disparity was even greater.[12] Some academic women, however, made notable careers. Ruth A. Allen joined the economics faculty at the University of Texas in 1923, at a time when the proportion of women faculty there had barely reached double digits and women were a rarity in the field of economics. Allen earned her Ph.D. from the University of Chicago a decade later; her dissertation, "The Labor of Women in the Production of Cotton," was one of the first Texas field studies of women's living and working conditions. During her thirty-six years at the University of Texas, Allen published pioneering studies of the Texas labor movement and eventually chaired the all-male economics department. Mary Elizabeth Branch took over as president of Tillotson College, a historically black institution in Austin, in 1930, when it was struggling to survive. In the depths of the Depression, she brought it back to stability, upgrading and expanding the physical plant, more than tripling enrollment, and restoring its senior college standing.

Two-thirds of professional women were teachers, and they outnumbered men by four to one. Not all entered the field willingly. Elizabeth Stroud Shelton remembered: "It was all right for a woman to get a college education as long as she was planning to be a teacher. But if it was any other profession it wasn't. . . . I wanted to be a lawyer. Pop wouldn't hear of it."[13] Women teachers were paid, on average, roughly two-thirds of what men earned. They had fewer advancement opportunities: in 1937 white women were less than 3 percent of the state's school superintendents and only 4 percent of high school principals.[14] Female teachers, moreover, were subject to special scrutiny and restrictions in dress and deportment. When Elizabeth Shelton began teaching in Medina County in 1922, she refused to conform to the district rule that teachers wear two petticoats and skirts no more than two inches from the floor, arguing that not even her father had been so strict. Contracts commonly regulated conduct outside the classroom as well; many women remembered being forbidden to dance, for example. "If you were a teacher, you just shouldn't go off on night parties," one recalled. "Of course you couldn't drink."[15] Especially in small towns, teachers complained of limited social life and tyrannical male school boards. In the 1940s a South Texas teacher who was seen kissing her boyfriend was called before her board and accused of immorality. Another board member made it plain to new hires that they should patronize his store and his wife's beauty parlor if they expected to have their contracts renewed.[16]

African American women struggled against both sexism and Jim Crow. Few held administrative positions, and they were the lowest paid of all teachers, earning less than black men and much less than white women.[17] The state deliberately underfunded black schools—in 1930 they received only 85 percent of the amount allotted for white schools—and districts often spent much less than the appropriation. As a consequence, African American teachers coped with large class sizes, short terms, and substandard facilities (see Document 2.5). Everything a black teacher had to work with, from textbooks to the building itself, was likely to be a worn-out discard from the white school system. Most of the schools were without libraries or playgrounds, and many had no books or toilets. School terms could end abruptly and without notice when funds ran out. In small rural schools black teachers operated with little or no oversight, as Dorothy Robinson discovered when she began teaching in 1929. She surmised that the relative autonomy stemmed from white indifference to what went on in African American classrooms; black children's education, or lack of it, did not matter.[18]

WOMEN OF COLOR: DISCRIMINATION AND PROTEST

Maggie Lanham Washington, who grew up in Waco in the 1930s, described for an interviewer what a girl's life was like on the black side of the color line. She attended shabby segregated schools and drank from separate water fountains—"I don't care how thirsty you are or were, unless it said 'colored' you don't drink." She bought clothes and hats without being permitted to try them on and did not even attempt to enter the big department stores, where blacks could be menial employees but not customers. Most galling of all, when Washington enlisted in the U.S. Army during World War II, she and the other African American women inducted with her were still second-class citizens. On the morning of their departure, escorted by a white female officer, they had to eat breakfast in the kitchen of a downtown restaurant and then board a segregated train car.[19]

The customs of Jim Crow were calculated denials of dignity. "You couldn't come in [white] people's house[s]—just had to eat outdoors when you workin' for 'em, just like cats and dogs," a rural woman remembered.[20] No black woman could expect to be addressed as "Mrs." or "Miss," which would have been an acknowledgment of ladyhood, and adult women had to endure being called "girl." In stores a black woman was automatically last in line, never waited on until white customers had been helped, and she never knew when she might be insulted or refused service. If she went to the movies, she would be required to enter by a side door and sit in the balcony. By far the worst consequence of segregation for black women was sexual harassment and aggression by white men, which inflicted lasting psychological damage (see Document 2.6). In rural areas there were virtually no restraints on the power of white landowners. Annie Mae Hunt never forgot one of them, "Old Man Morrett" of Navasota, who "liked to rape black women," including Hunt's married sister: "Oh, my sister like to went into hysterics. She never did get over that."[21]

Physical resistance to white aggression was dangerous. Eleila Upshaw of Nacogdoches County, who fired a double-barreled shotgun at two white men who tried to take her calf after she declined to sell it, was the one who ended up in sheriff's custody. A safer strategy was accommodation-activism—asserting dignity by boycotting stores that discriminated, as teacher Dorothy Robinson did after being refused a ticket for a lottery drawing even though she had bought more than the minimum required purchase. Historian Bernadette Pruitt argues that the migration of thousands of blacks from the countryside to urban centers, where they were less subject to white control, was also a form of resistance to racism. In 1910 the state's black population was 74 percent rural; by 1940 it was nearly 46 percent urban and steadily increasing. Unmarried African American women were especially likely to migrate to the cities, where they were much more likely to be heads of households than Anglo or Mexicana women.

A handful of middle-class white and black women willing to speak out on racial issues helped found the Texas Commission on Interracial Cooperation in 1920. Integration was beyond anyone's imagination, and both the men's and women's divisions of the commission were subdivided by race. Many of the white women were active in church work, and some belonged to the state's Federated Council of Church Women, which had denounced lynching and was on record in favor of genuinely equal (though separate) railroad coaches for African Americans and racially inclusive child welfare assistance. The black women were drawn from the elite network of clubwomen and professionals. Jennie Belle Murphy Covington, the second president of the Negro Women's Division, had a typical record of achievement: she belonged to two Houston clubs and had helped found the city's Bethlehem Settlement and its Blue Triangle [Negro] Branch of the YWCA. Jessie Daniel Ames served as executive director of the Women's Division from 1924 until 1929, when she moved to Atlanta to take over as director of women's work for the national Commission on Interracial Cooperation. Ames's sensitivity to racial issues developed out of her revulsion against the Ku Klux Klan and the realization, through her work with the Joint Legislative Council, that racism impeded women's efforts for social reform. She spoke against mob violence, lobbied for an anti-lynching law, and mobilized white women's organizations to help the Texas Association of Colored Women's Clubs pry funds for a training school for delinquent black girls from the legislature.

It was racial confrontation by organized African Americans, however, that over the course of decades dismantled the structures of segregation. The process of chipping away at the foundation of Jim Crow began when delegates from the five city branches of the National Association for the Advancement of Colored People met in Dallas in 1937 to form the Texas State Conference of Branches, NAACP. The organization grew slowly before World War II but committed itself to a long-range program of challenging segregation and disfranchisement in the courts. Houston and Dallas had the largest and most influential chapters in the state conference, in part due to the efforts of Lulu B. White and Juanita Craft, who were also highly influential in the statewide movement. White, a graduate of Prairie View A&M and a former teacher, became executive secretary of the Houston branch in 1943 and launched a drive that more than doubled the membership in two years. By 1945 she had built enrollment to twelve thousand, making the Houston NAACP the largest in the South. Married to a successful nightclub owner and businessman, White had the leisure and resources to work full time investigating grievances and seeking plaintiffs for lawsuits. Close ties with national NAACP leaders made her second in influence only to the state executive secretary. Lulu White's example influenced Juanita Craft of Dallas, who went to Houston to meet and learn from her. In 1945 Craft led the Dallas chapter's ambitious recruitment campaign, which boosted membership to seven thousand by 1946.

Two successful legal challenges to racial discrimination before 1945 were especially significant for women. On behalf of a Houston plaintiff, the Texas NAACP filed a voting rights lawsuit that eventually reached the U.S. Supreme Court. The 1944 decision in *Smith v. Allright* declared the white primary unconstitutional. By closing its primary to blacks (contending that political parties were private organizations), the Democratic Party, without flagrantly violating the Fifteenth Amendment, had kept them from voting. Lulu White hailed the Court's rejection of this subterfuge as "the second emancipation of the Negro"; it gave black women the same right that white women had won from the state legislature in 1918. (In Dallas County, Juanita Craft became the first African American woman to vote in the Democratic primary.) During the same period, black teachers, who in 1940 earned approximately 61 percent of what their white counterparts were paid, demanded and won pay equalization. Since three-quarters of African American professional women were teachers, the issue was a gender victory as well as a racial one. The Dallas Negro Teachers Alliance filed the first suit, with Thelma Paige as plaintiff. Represented by an NAACP lawyer, Paige won a judgment in federal district court in 1943. In Houston, Lulu White served as a consultant to the Negro Committee of the Teachers Association and accompanied its representatives to the school board to demand pay equalization, which was conceded without going to court.[22] In Galveston, Jessie McGuire Dent's lawsuit brought an end to differential salaries, and by 1945 many other cities had ceased to discriminate.

Mexican-born and Mexican American women occupied, in historian Neil Foley's words, "the ethnoracial middle ground between Anglo Americans and African Americans, not white enough to claim equality with Anglos and yet, in many cases, white enough to escape the worst features of the Jim Crow South."[23] Anglos drew the line of racial separation according to how "white" a Hispanic individual appeared; light skin and higher social class made a difference in social acceptability for Mexicanas, as it did not for African American women. Mexicanas whose heritage was largely Spanish experienced relatively little discrimination; the "No Mexicans" signs in store and restaurant windows were aimed at the mestizo majority with dark skin and Indian features. Unlike African Americans, Mexicans were Jim Crowed by custom rather than by legislation, and social separation was less rigid. No law prevented Mexicans from intermarrying with Anglos, and Mexican males were not demonized as sexual threats to white women. Nor did the law require separate school systems. Some Mexicans attended school with Anglo children; many others, especially if poor and not fluent in English, were segregated in "Mexican schools" and tracked into vocational courses.

Mexicana schoolgirls were doubly deprived. Forced, as African Americans were, into segregated, shabby facilities but without the positive role models black girls found in their teachers, they were far less likely even to reach high school, much less graduate. Teachers and administrators in "Mexican schools" were white and condescending, belittling the children's heritage and punishing them for speaking Spanish. Aurora Orozco of Mercedes remembered how she hated her teacher: "With a red rubber band, she would hit my poor hands until they nearly bled. But she never broke my spirit and determination to speak my native language." The principal, Mrs. Day, began every Monday with verbal abuse that reduced some to tears: "You Mexicans come from very ignorant people without ambition, dirty, and full of lice. You will never amount to anything in your lives." Maria Sanchez dreaded the beginning of the week at her school for another reason: "Every Monday morning they would line us up and use two pencils to search for head lice. I can still remember the feeling of embarrassment.[24] If a child was found to have lice, the entire class would have kerosene sprayed on their heads (see Document 2.7).

Heavy immigration from Mexico continued throughout the 1920s—the number of people of Mexican origin nearly tripled between 1920 and 1930—and cities far north of the border acquired significant Hispanic communities. In Houston the Mexican-origin population jumped from six thousand to fifteen thousand, and Dallas by 1930 had a barrio of six thousand. With urban growth, a small middle class emerged, but with few opportunities for advancement for women; in heavily Hispanic San Antonio the census counted only 120 Tejana professional women. Teaching, the most common career of Anglo and African American women, was largely closed to Tejanas; the pool of high school graduates was small, and college graduates rare. In South and Central Texas especially, teachers trained in Mexico operated *escuelitas*, private schools that offered elementary and secondary instruction in Spanish, but the public schools resisted hiring Mexican-origin women. Only after pressure from the Council of PTAs did Austin hire its first Tejana teacher, Consuelo Herrera Mendez, as an instructor in a barrio school in 1927.

Urban life did, however, encourage the growth of female voluntary association culture. Working-class Tejanas contributed to mutual aid societies—*sociedades mutualistas*—which provided sickness and burial insurance, while wealthier women formed benevolent associations such as La Cruz Azul Mexicana (Mexican Blue Cross) to provide individual relief and community services. In middle-class voluntary associations Mexican-origin women combined a primary goal—maternalism or charity or self-development—with a mission to defend and preserve Mexican identity. Young women's social clubs sought to counter stereotypes of unassimilated Mexicans by celebrating biculturalism. Almost half of the founders of the Club Chapultepec had Anglo surnames, but they named the organization for a noted site of resistance to the U.S. invasion of Mexico in 1847. In the secretary's words, "we wanted to keep our own culture, not lose it," but at the same time the members "wanted to show the Anglo American community that we could be good Americans, not just Mexican girls."[25] Meetings were conducted alternately in English and Spanish and held at the Houston YWCA—unlike black women, Hispanics were not forced into a separate Y. As "Mexican girls," however, Club Femenino Chapultepec members were turned away when they tried to rent downtown ballrooms for their dances. In 1937, six years after its founding, the club issued a public letter condemning discrimination and racism against Mexicans in Houston (see Document 2.8).

The Mexican community also founded voluntary associations to fight discrimination. Local women's groups started the Spanish-Speaking PTA in 1923 in response to second-class treatment of their children in the public schools. Insufficient English-language skills kept many Mexicana mothers from attending mixed PTAs, and the Texas Congress of Mothers and PTAs excluded from membership those attached to "Mexican" schools. Like the "Anglo" PTA, the Spanish-Speaking PTA undertook school improvement projects, raising money to provide what the state did not: shade trees for playgrounds, musical instruments, encyclopedias, supplies. Carolina Munguía organized the Spanish-Speaking PTA for San Antonio's Crockett Elementary, a mixed school, after she went to her first PTA meeting and found herself the only Mexicana mother present. Under her direction the Crockett chapter added social services to its mission; it set up a free-lunch kitchen and bathing facilities and organized a sewing circle to supply clothing. María L. de Hernández, one of San Antonio's most prominent Mexicana activists, cofounded La Liga de Defensa Pro-Escolar (School Improvement League) with her husband, Pablo, to draw attention to the inadequate schools on the city's impoverished West Side.

Discrimination by Anglos was not the only burden borne by Mexican-origin women; they also faced sexism within the voluntary association established to fight for Hispanic civil rights. While African American women were integral to the functioning of the NAACP, Tejanas were not included when the all-male League of United Latin American Citizens (LULAC) was founded in 1929 in Corpus Christi. LULAC reflected the rise of a middle-class, bilingual, and bicultural generation that saw itself as Mexican American rather than Mexican. As English-speaking American citizens, not aliens, they resented being denigrated as "Meskins" and established LULAC to mount legal challenges to discrimination in schools and other public places. Membership was restricted to U.S. citizens, and although LULAC conducted bilingual activities, English was its official operating language. Initially, women were permitted to join only as honorary members, without voting rights.

Both cultural factors and practical reality worked against female inclusion. Catholic, patriarchal Hispanic society defined women's place as home and church, with politics as a male-only activity. Relatively few Mexican American women had the education, income, or leisure to pursue civic culture. There was no Tejana corps of teachers or federation of women's clubs, and as historian Cynthia Orozco has observed, "there was no Mexican-origin 'woman citizen' in the 1920s."[26] Within a few years, however, women had gained a foothold in LULAC. Several "ladies' auxiliaries" had attached themselves to local chapters by 1932, and in 1933 the annual convention authorized women to organize on the same basis as men: Ladies LULAC was born. Until World War II the association had a "ladies organizer general," and eighteen chapters had been established by 1940. Women's and men's chapters worked separately, and not all women were satisfied with their role in LULAC (see Document 2.9).

SURVIVING THE GREAT DEPRESSION

For all women, regardless of race or ethnicity, the 1930s were hard times. Four months after the New York stock market crashed in October 1929, the economic depression that ensued picked May Eccles's pocket. Eccles, a fifty-four-year-old title clerk at the Bexar County courthouse in San Antonio, learned on Valentine's Day 1930 that a 15 percent pay cut would be imposed on everyone making more than $125 per month. In September, salaries were reduced by another 20 percent, "but I guess we should be thankful for a job at all," she noted in her diary. She and her sister Buzzie rented out one of their spare bedrooms, but even so, they had to take out a bank loan at the beginning of 1932 to pay their taxes, and Buzzie's salary was cut six weeks later. Eccles was "knocked cold" in 1933 to learn that her salary would be reduced yet again.[27] For single mother Vera Bosanko the 1930s were truly grim. Widowed at twenty-four while pregnant with her fifth child, Bosanko raised a garden and got milk for her brood by doing laundry for a neighbor with a cow. As a destitute head of household she was certified for a federal Works Progress Administration relief job, working first at a canning plant and later at a high school library in Fort Worth for $42 per month. "But about every few months they'd come in and say they just didn't have no more money for this project," she recalled. "I never knowed where the job was going. Maybe that's the reason why I turned whiteheaded when I was a young age."[28]

Family composition, ethnicity, and socioeconomic class affected women's experience of the Depression. Middle-class urbanites like the Eccles sisters economized and "made do" (and forced their Mexican maid to do likewise by cutting her wages to $3 per week). Rural wives improvised strategies to generate supplemental cash; Jewel Babb of Langtry found her opportunity in half a dozen skinny cows (see Document 2.10). The poor, like Vera Bosanko, struggled for subsistence and had to accept government help. Self-employed women often found that their customers had no cash; beautician Amy Horton accepted vegetables and quilts as payment for haircuts and permanent waves. Because occupational segregation confined women to lower-paying jobs, the Depression bit deeper into their incomes, and Texas women industrial workers were the worst paid in the nation; the median weekly wage was $8.75 for white women, $5.95 for black women, and $5.85 for Mexicanas.[29] Sympathy for the "forgotten man" did not extend to women. Employers and government relief agencies regarded women as temporary or secondary earners who worked for luxuries and didn't "need" jobs, overlooking the significant percentage of families that had always required the income of more than one wage earner to make ends meet.

Nevertheless, the percentage of women in the labor force actually increased in the 1930s. Middle-class white women accounted for the rise: the clerical work sector which they dominated continued to grow steadily. Minority women, however, faced extra hardship. Hispanic women, hit hard by the decline in manufacturing, were forced to accept wretchedly low wages for industrial home work in the garment industry, picking up bundles of unfinished infants' and children's clothing at factories and sewing the garments at home. The pay averaged five cents an hour, a weekly wage of about $2.50. Black women suffered the highest unemployment rates because of the contraction of domestic service and the prejudice that kept them out of most other jobs (see Document 2.11). In Houston, which had the state's largest urban African American population, the unemployment rate for black women in 1931 was 46 percent, higher than for black men, and three and one-half times higher than for white women.

The percentage of married women in the Texas labor force (11.5 in 1930, virtually the same as the national average) continued to inch upward during the Depression, despite efforts to push wives out of the workplace because of fear that they competed with men for scarce jobs. In reality the labor market was so gender-segregated that women did not displace men—firing a secretary did not open a job for a construction worker—but public opinion strongly opposed a wife working if the husband had a job. This "marriage bar" targeted mainly middle-class women. Section 213 of the Economy Act passed by Congress in 1932 prohibited a husband and wife from working for the government at the same time, and since men generally earned more, it was usually the wife who had to resign or was terminated.

Gussie Lee Howell, who worked for the Railway Mail Service, was one of them, and the consequences of her firing were dire; she and her husband could not meet their mortgage payments and lost their house. Howell's salary had also been supporting her elderly father and her widowed sister, who had two children. Howell appealed without success to her congressman; Section 213, she concluded bitterly, was "a most unjust piece of legislation."[30] The Texas Legislature deliberated a more restrictive measure that would have prohibited state government from employing anyone with a working spouse, even one with a job in the private sector. The Texas Federation of Business and Professional Women's Clubs, led by Sarah Hughes, mobilized women's organizations in protest and secured a less onerous clause that, like the Economy Act, forbade employment by the state for both halves of a married couple. Although the language was not gender specific, women were clearly the target. The *San Antonio Weekly Dispatch* editorialized: "Probably no laws could or should be enacted to bar married women from jobs. But business and industry, by agreement, could establish rules under which a married woman would be employed [only] in exceptional cases, the first of which would be that the husband was not able to provide a living for the family."[31] In Bexar County, married women had already been dismissed from the courthouse, and the San Antonio school district had terminated all married teachers whose husbands earned $2,000 or more per year.

Across the state, teachers suffered more than any other group from the marriage bar. A 1932 sampling of school districts of between 2,500 and 50,000 in population found that 31 percent had a formal marriage bar, but in practice 62 percent discriminated. Seven years later a larger survey that subdivided districts more finely by size, reported prohibitions ranging steadily upward from 32.6 percent in districts of 2,500 to 5,000 (which could least afford to be choosy) to 72.7 percent in districts of 25,000 to 100,000.[32] Some women in districts with marriage bars represented themselves as separated on their applications or kept their marriages secret.

Mexican women, along with their menfolk, were also unwanted in the depressed labor market. In the 1930s as many as 250,000 Texas Mexicans repatriated under the combined pressure of economic crisis and resentment of immigrants; they were seen as competitors for scarce jobs and a burden on the relief rolls. The collapse of the agricultural economy displaced Mexican tenant farmers and laborers, and urban dwellers who lost jobs in labor-intensive industries were denied work relief if they could not prove citizenship. At the same time the U.S. Immigration Service began deportation sweeps against illegal aliens in the countryside and at urban job sites. Women were deported both as workers and as dependent wives, and authorities were careless of civil rights. Señora X, an alien afraid to reveal her name, shared her story with an oral history interviewer decades later. She and her husband repatriated voluntarily in the early 1930s, when he could no longer find work. The X family stayed four years in Mexico before crossing again into Texas without papers. When immigration authorities raided her husband's job site during the Christmas holidays in 1939 and arrested the undocumented workers, Sra. X and the baby she was nursing were jailed along with the husband. Neighbors cared for the couple's older children until a judge ordered her release a month later. While her husband awaited processing, Sra. X earned money to feed the children by cleaning houses. Then the couple and their five American-born children—U.S. citizens—were deported.[33]

THE NEW DEAL AND WOMEN

The legislation that President Franklin D. Roosevelt pushed through Congress in the 1930s to create relief programs—"a New Deal"—for the needy was bold and innovative in many respects, but most programs treated women as second-class citizens. The National Industrial Recovery Act of 1933 (NIRA) created the National Recovery Administration (NRA) to establish voluntary Codes of Fair Competition for manufacturers, fixing minimum wages and maximum hours and price controls. The NRA codes reinforced job segregation by sex, and a quarter of them authorized lower pay scales for women even when both sexes did substantially the same work. Half of the women in the workforce were left out: most clerical workers, as well as all farm and domestic workers. (The latter two categories were a calculated exclusion of African Americans.) A Houston domestic lamented the injustice to FDR: "The prices we are getting run from $3.50 to about $6.00 per week, [and] we have to pay transportation out [of] that. We can't make a living. . . . Please Mr. Roosevelt do something for the cooks and maids. Please cut our hour [sic] and raise our wages."[34]

Women in manufacturing, however, did benefit. The NIRA guaranteed the right to collective bargaining, which sparked the growth of labor unions. The NRA codes also provided the first minimum wage guarantee Texas women had ever experienced. In 1919 the legislature had yielded to pressure from women's groups and the labor lobby and authorized a minimum wage for women, which a wage commission subsequently set at $12 per week. But the next legislature, in 1921, repealed the law before the provisions went into effect. In 1931 the median wage for Texas garment-factory workers, almost all of whom were female, was less than $6 for a week of forty-four to fifty-four hours. The NRA-mandated code for Dallas, the center of the state's small garment industry, was $14, and the work week was set at thirty-five hours for silk dress manufacturing and forty hours for cotton dress manufacturing. It was an enormous advance—on paper. In reality, the factory owners, who could not be compelled to adopt the codes, used them as window dressing and subverted both the wage and hour guarantees. Under the dress manufacturing code owners were permitted to pay a three-quarters salary—$9—during the first six weeks, a worker's learning or apprenticeship period. Manufacturers used this loophole to fire workers before they put in the full six weeks and rehire them later at the learner rate. To evade the forty-hour week maximum, they forced workers to clock out and leave the building, then reenter through the rear entrance and go back to work.

In response to these code violations and to pent-up grievances over working conditions, a dozen women, led by Charlotte Duncan Graham, began organizing. (Graham was particularly angry that workers were forbidden to use the lavatory except during the thirty-minute lunch hour or fifteen-minute afternoon break. After one of her coworkers had an accident in her seat, Graham marched into the restroom and stayed for half an hour, daring the manager to fire her.) The women requested and received charters from the International Ladies' Garment Workers' Union (ILGWU), and in March 1935 the Dallas locals voted overwhelmingly for a general strike of the dress industry. The walkout lasted for months, with frequent bouts of violence between strikers, the scabs who crossed their picket lines, and the police (see Document 2.12). The Dallas workers were up against intransigent factory owners and hostile public opinion, and the strike eventually failed when the union ran out of funds. The strikers were blacklisted and many, including Graham, were forced to look for jobs out of state.

Other garment strikes were more successful. The prolonged and costly Dallas strike convinced five women's wear manufacturers in Houston to negotiate with the ILGWU. The union got contracts with all in 1935 for a $12, forty-hour week. In San Antonio, where the majority of garment workers were Mexicanas, the ILGWU struck three plants: Dorothy Frocks in 1936, Shirlee Frocks in 1937, and Texas Infants Dress Company in 1937–1938. Bitter animosity between the strikers and scab workers escorted into the plants by police and company officials characterized all three walkouts. Picketers punched, grabbed hair, and tore off clothing, sometimes completely stripping strikebreaking women. Mexicanas also vented scorn for scabs in mocking songs that denounced their collusion with the owners. Two of the strikes were outright successes—Texas Infants Dress Company and Shirlee Frocks agreed to recognize the union. By then the Supreme Court had ruled the NRA and wage codes unconstitutional, however, and the pay increase at Shirlee to $8 minimum for a week of forty-eight hours was clearly still a "Mexican" wage (pay was not in dispute at Infants Dress). The owner of Dorothy Frocks decided to relocate to the resolutely anti-union city of Dallas.

The garment strikes were bracketed by two other labor protests in San Antonio. In 1933, 1934, and 1935 Tejana cigar rollers at Finck Cigar Company walked out to protest harsh rules, unhealthful working conditions, and wages far below the NRA minimum. The leader, Sra. W. H. "Refugio" Ernst, summed up their grievances in one sentence: "We don't want to be treated like slaves."[35] The first strike was brief, and the women went out again the following year when Finck reneged on his promise to implement NRA codes and improve sanitation. In 1934 the strikers were joined on the picket line by sixteen-year-old Emma Tenayuca, an articulate, politically aware high school senior who was outraged that the sheriff had had his photo taken wearing new boots that he bragged he was going to use on the strikers. When sheriff's deputies broke up the picket line and arrested the strikers, Tenayuca was jailed too. A third strike in 1935 erupted in violence between strikers and scab workers. The intervention of a U.S. Department of Labor negotiator secured some of the cigar rollers' demands but not a salary increase, and Ernst and the strike leadership were never rehired.

Emma Tenayuca, however, had been radicalized, and during the next few years she became a labor organizer and the voice of Tejano labor protest in San Antonio. Tenayuca attended Socialist Party meetings, served as secretary of the West Side Unemployed Council, and joined the Workers' Alliance of America, which was formed by Socialist-led groups and the Unemployed Leagues and later included the Communist-led Unemployment Councils. The Workers' Alliance championed the interests of the unemployed and those who labored on the federal government's public relief projects. Tenayuca served on the alliance's national executive council and led the organization's San Antonio branch. She organized demonstrations to protest the layoff of Works Progress Administration (WPA) workers and tried to get WPA officials in Washington to investigate the Texas Relief Commission, which frequently turned down Tejano applicants and dispatched them to field labor at below subsistence wages. In 1937 she also joined the Communist Party because, she recalled years later, "Communists were at the forefront of the struggles" and they defended the rights of Hispanics and African Americans to organize. The following year she married Homer Brooks, the party's head in Texas. Tenayuca's priority, however, was not Communism but the working poor of the vast West Side barrio, one of the worst slums in the nation. She wanted labor organizing to deliver social services as well as economic relief: "I had visions of a huge hall on the West Side, possibly maintained by several unions—pecan, laundry, ironworkers—which would become a center where you could help people become citizens, where you could have classes in English."[36] Admiring Tejanos nicknamed the charismatic and eloquent Tenayuca "La Pasionaria."

When San Antonio pecan shellers walked out in 1938 to protest a cut in their already abysmal wages, they asked Tenayuca to be the strike spokeswoman. Pecan shelling, a winter job for many Mexicans and Tejanos who spent the rest of the year as migrant field workers, was one of the least desirable, poorest-paid industrial occupations. The average wage was $2 to $3 a week, and women were the majority of the workforce. In the 1920s the industry had mechanized, but in San Antonio the influx of Mexican immigrants depressed wages so severely that hand shelling became cheaper, and the owners stopped investing in machinery. As always, women had the least-skilled, lowest-paid tasks. "Crackers," who broke shells with a hammer were usually men and paid by the hour; female "pickers" separated the nuts from the shells and were paid by the pound. They worked elbow to elbow in unheated rooms thick with fine pecan dust, fingers swollen and sometimes infected from handling broken shells. A reduction in rates for this piecework prompted the walkout of some eight thousand workers, the largest strike in San Antonio history.

Tenayuca was jailed briefly, as was Minnie Rendon, the secretary of the International Pecan Shellers Union. The strikers were teargassed on multiple occasions, and hundreds were arrested, including women whose children were incarcerated with them. The most potent weapon, however, was red-baiting, in which the press, city officials, and the Catholic Church also joined. Tenayuca's Communist Party affiliation became so controversial that the leadership of the Congress of Industrial Organizations (CIO), which was organizing a union, pressed her to step down as strike chairman. She continued to work behind the scenes, meeting with the picket captains and writing all the strike circulars. Six weeks into the strike, one of the larger owners agreed to arbitration, and eventually industry-wide negotiations conceded the strikers their major demand, a recision of the pay cut. Despite Tenayuca's remarkable achievement in mobilizing the West Side, the strikers' victory was soon undercut. Congress passed the country's first minimum wage law, twenty-five cents an hour, which the pecan producers subverted by closing the shelling sheds and selling pecans to the workers to shell at home, then buying them back. Ultimately, the industry mechanized again, eliminating thousands of jobs.

DISCRIMINATION IN THE NEW DEAL

New Deal programs treated women and men differently: men got jobs (and the dignity that accompanied them), while women were more likely to get direct relief or welfare. Work relief programs such as the Federal Emergency Relief Administration (1933–1935) and its successor, the Works Progress Administration (1935–1941), overtly discriminated against women, who were automatically considered auxiliary workers. Nationally, less than 20 percent of all WPA workers were female. The agency allowed one job per destitute family—for the household head, who was presumed to be the husband. Women whose husbands were physically able to work but jobless had great difficulty securing WPA jobs, as did single women. Most WPA funding in Texas was for construction jobs for men; women were segregated into low-paying, stereotypical service jobs or those related to household skills. The largest number of women on federal work relief were employed in sewing rooms, producing clothing that was distributed to destitute families. San Antonio, for example, had 2,300 women in sewing projects in 1936. Women also worked in canning plants, housekeeping aid programs, matron services, preschool child care, and library service.

Government programs also institutionalized racial and ethnic discrimination (see Document 2.13). Hispanic women (and men) not American-born or naturalized were ineligible for either work relief or public assistance. African American women made up only 3 percent nationally of WPA workers, and local officials routinely turned down their applications or gave them short hours to force them to take domestic service jobs. Many such women wrote in frustration to Eleanor Roosevelt, a civil rights sympathizer and advocate for blacks in FDR's administration. The president and vice president of the Workers' Alliance of America, Colored Local 3, San Antonio, complained, "They treat us very bad at the W.P.A. offices, minor clerks tell us that there are no jobs for Negroes. There are [jobs] for white people and Mexicans." Two other San Antonio women wrote to protest the layoffs of most of the black women in the sewing projects in 1940; a supervisor had claimed that Washington "told us not to hire you Nigger women any more, get out and get you a job or take the maid training that is for you all." When black women were hired in the sewing rooms, they were segregated and "so abused that we can hardly stay on the job."[37]

For rural women the most significant New Deal agency was the Agricultural Adjustment Administration (AAA), which inadvertently widened the gap between landowners and tenant farmers. The AAA sought to raise the price of crops by paying farmers to take land out of production, thereby reducing harvests and curbing the oversupply of commodities. For daughters in landowning white families, cotton crop reduction unexpectedly made possible a previously unaffordable luxury: store-bought dresses. Each acre of land left unplanted was worth a certain number of cotton stamps, good solely for the purchase of cotton goods such as clothing. Before cotton stamps, remembered Mary Cimarolli of Hopkins County, all of her dresses, nightgowns, and underwear had been made from empty cloth flour sacks and livestock feed sacks (many of which were printed with flowers or other patterns). "Mama could turn those sacks into very pretty dresses, but to have a ready-made dress was such a treat. . . . I was in heaven helping to select my dresses from the retail store."[38] For many tenant and sharecropping families, however, the AAA made hard times worse. Tenants were supposed to receive a portion of the payment for land taken out of production, but landowners often kept all of it. They also invested government payments in farm machinery, evicting renters and forcing them to become wage laborers. Women whose families managed to stay on the land sometimes did without necessities (see Document 2.14), and those who were displaced lacked even feed and flour sacks to make school dresses (see Document 2.15).

The enduring legacy of the New Deal, the Social Security Act of 1935, set up a federal pension system that institutionalized gender and racial inequality. Structured on the family wage ideology, which assumed that men were breadwinners and women were dependents who stayed at home, the act also left out many women who worked in poorly paid female-dominated fields. Teachers, nurses, religious workers, and social welfare workers were excluded. Texas teachers, three-quarters of them women, thus had no pensions until the state set up a retirement system for educators in 1941. Farmworkers and domestic servants were excluded from Social Security at the insistence of southern congressmen, in order to protect the region's access to low-wage black labor; as a result most rural dwellers, white as well as black, were outside the safety net. Taken together, the Social Security provisions excluded three-fifths of women and nearly all black women. Thus while men benefited from a federally administered entitlement program, women, who earned less during their working lives and were more in need of old-age insurance, were left to the vagaries of state welfare systems.

Amendments to the Social Security Act in 1939 gave wives and widows of covered male workers benefits with a number of attached conditions: a wife was entitled to one-half of her husband's benefit, a widow to three-fourths (provided that she didn't remarry). Divorced and deserted wives, who have always fared poorly financially, were excluded. For this group, the Social Security Act created Aid to Dependent Children (ADC), a federal-state collaboration that treated widowed and divorced mothers as charity cases rather than household heads. As ADC passed through Congress, southerners and other conservatives shaped it to give states rather than the federal government control of eligibility requirements and assistance levels. Needy women were subjected to demeaning scrutiny of their moral character and of the "suitability" of their homes. States set benefits very low and adopted rules that disqualified black women, even though they were a higher proportion of single mothers than white women.

Aid to Dependent Children supplanted the Progressive Era mothers' pensions, which proved inadequate to cope with the increased need for relief during the Depression. In Texas, as in most states, mothers' pensions had been funded by county governments, which were overwhelmed by the expanding number of needy families during the 1930s. Coverage was spotty because mothers' pension laws permitted, but did not require, a state or county to act. In 1933 only 20 of 254 Texas counties offered mothers' aid, and the number dropped as the Depression deepened—to 8 by 1935. Fewer than two families per ten thousand were being assisted, and the average monthly grant of $12.07 was only half the national average and below even the average ($14.06) for the southern states. In 1935, with 24,400 female-headed families supporting at least one dependent child, the Texas Federation of Women's Clubs petitioned the legislature without success for state supplementation for mothers' pensions. After the Social Security Act passed, the clubwomen urged the state to submit a plan for accepting ADC. Texas, however, was one of the last states to sign up. The enabling legislation was finally passed in 1939, but no funds were appropriated until 1941. Moreover, the state limited its contribution to not more than $8 for one child or $12 per family and set the cutoff age at fourteen, even though the federal government, which contributed one-third of ADC grants, permitted a maximum of $18 for the first child and $12 for each additional child under sixteen. Thus, while coverage was broader than under the mothers' pension law, it was still stingy—and Texas was the only state that required the dependent child to be a citizen.

During the Depression the national birthrate dropped below replacement level for the first time, as economic distress prompted a desire for smaller families. While middle-class women had been controlling their fertility for decades, working-class and immigrant wives lacked—and often desperately wanted—reliable information on spacing and limiting births (see Document 2.16). In 1932 twenty-seven states, including Texas, had no birth control clinics, but as the decade progressed, the American Birth Control League opened hundreds across the nation. Texas's first clinic, however, was not part of the ABCL network; it was founded in Dallas in 1935 by clubwoman Kate Ripley and initially funded by her husband, who owned a shirt manufacturing company. Because the federal Comstock Law of 1873 prohibited the distribution of obscene materials, including contraceptives, through the mail, diaphragms—the most effective contraceptive at the time—were posted to Dallas from New York concealed in Ripley Company shirt boxes.[39] During the next four years clinics also opened in Houston, Austin, El Paso, Fort Worth, San Angelo, San Antonio, and Waco. Agnese Nelms, who founded the Houston clinic, was the prime mover in forming a state organization, the Birth Control League of Texas, in 1936, and she became its first president.

Opponents of birth control had always contended that it would encourage illicit sexuality. Birth control advocates of the 1930s, many of whom belonged to women's clubs or the Junior League, countered by presenting clinics as a means of safeguarding maternal and infant health, reducing the abortion rate, and helping poor families. Texas's maternal mortality rate (7.3 per 1,000 live births) was higher than the national average and higher than most of the other southern states; birth controllers claimed that this was partly due to high rates of self-induced abortion, which women were more likely to attempt after having several children and unsuccessfully trying to prevent additional pregnancies. Thirty-five percent of the women who sought contraceptives from the Maternal Health Center of Houston reported having had one or more previous abortions, according to statistics compiled for the years 1936 to 1939. "The choice is not between birth control and no birth control," Kate Ripley asserted, "it is between amateur, unreliable back-fence gossip and advice, and safe, harmless, medically prescribed instructions."[40]

Agnese Nelms pointed out that safe and reliable contraception was a class privilege, unavailable to women who could not afford a private physician, and that birth control clinics filled the gap. A high proportion of clinic patients were on public relief or receiving aid from local welfare agencies, and the majority were white. Racial separation was observed, usually by having whites, blacks, and Hispanics come on different days. All clinics limited their services to married women. For single women, accidental pregnancy was a social disgrace. An eighteen-year-old girl recalled desperately trying to solve the problem by taking ergot, a drug that induced strong muscular contractions; popularly believed to induce abortion, it was only sporadically successful. She finally resorted to a midwife-abortionist, "a dreadful quack who just butchered me on a kitchen table." She concluded, "I guess I was lucky I didn't die, but for a few weeks I remember wishing I would."[41]

WORLD WAR II: THE HOME FRONT

The innovations of the New Deal notwithstanding, the Great Depression ended only when World War II and defense production revitalized the economy. Even before the Japanese attack on Pearl Harbor, Hawaii, in December 1941 brought the United States into the war, President Franklin Roosevelt had pledged the country to increase defense production and become an "arsenal of democracy" for the Allies. By mid-1942, as the military draft pulled men out of the workforce, an increasingly acute labor shortage created a dramatic, if temporary, increase in well-paid jobs for women. The war crisis smothered disapproval of working wives; women who had been unwanted in the labor force a decade earlier were sought after. School districts, facing a labor shortage as teachers left for higher-wage defense work, lifted marriage bars. The federal government likewise did a dramatic about-face. The National Youth Administration, which during the Depression had employed young women only in such traditional jobs as seamstresses, office workers, and hospital and cafeteria assistants, recruited them to learn welding, sheet metal, and other trades needed by the defense industries. An intensive government propaganda campaign urged women everywhere to become "soldiers without guns" by taking "war jobs" in defense industries. Rosie the Riveter, a fictional icon, flexed a bicep and proclaimed, "We Can Do It!" in government-commissioned posters. Nationally, the female labor force increased to 37 percent by 1944, and the majority of the new workers were older, married women. But even as women were exhorted to take up positions that men had vacated, they were constantly reminded to preserve their femininity (Rosie wore lipstick and nail polish with her coveralls) and that their new roles were only for the duration of the war.

In Texas 310,000 women entered the workforce during the war years. While some were motivated by a desire to help defeat the Axis powers and bring husbands and boyfriends home more quickly, others were attracted by high wages. Women already in the labor force left low-skilled, low-paid "women's" jobs to sign up for defense training. The war temporarily disrupted the gender segregation of the labor force: women for the first time became machinists, welders, riveters, tool and die makers, electricians, and quality control inspectors. Consolidated Aircraft's Fort Worth plant had eight training schools for women workers in operation within five months after Pearl Harbor; by November 1943 women were 38 percent of its employees and worked in almost all departments. At Hughes Tool Company in Houston the percentage of female employees rose from 1.4 in May 1942 to 26.6 in September 1943. At Houston Shipbuilding Corporation women began as welders and burners and eventually filled most jobs, constituting as much as 12 percent of the workforce. Humble Oil in Baytown hired women to work in the instrument department of the refinery, which produced aviation fuel, and recruited new college graduates as lab testers in its butyl plant, which made synthetic rubber.

Small-town industries likewise converted to war production and hired women for formerly male jobs. In East Texas, Lufkin Foundry put women to work operating drill presses, cutting and filing tank gears, machining transmissions, and making guns. Margaret Osborn Hayley, a former bridal shop buyer, was much happier working on Howitzers, although she had to dodge her grandfather when she returned home at night, dirty and scorched: "He just couldn't stand to see me in those clothes. You'd just burn everything up."[42] Southland Paper Mills hired women as lab technicians to test wet pulp, training them on the job. Lufkin's box factories converted from making beer boxes and vegetable crates to making ammunition boxes, with female operators at the machine saws. Women worked full shifts outdoors, stacking and loading lumber, and did every job in the timber industry except felling trees.

While women workers were sought after in industry, they were not always welcomed by male co-workers or treated equally by bosses. Men frequently resented female newcomers and tried to make them uncomfortable (see Document 2.17). Supervisors were always male, women were often concentrated in a few job classifications, and employers resisted promoting them. Equal pay was the exception rather than the rule, especially in the aircraft and shipbuilding industries. Humble's Baytown Refinery, for example, hired women for the instrument department, not at the regular apprentice rate, but at the lower, regular labor rate. When women did get equal pay, as at the butyl plant, it was at the union's insistence—not out of fairness to women workers but to preserve the pay rate for men when they returned from overseas. For African American women, job discrimination eased only slightly. They were most likely to be hired as cafeteria workers and cleaners and for unskilled outdoor work, such as washing locomotives. At the Diboll box factory they worked alongside white women stacking and loading lumber but had a separate bathroom and lunchroom. White and black women also worked together at Texas Foundries in Lufkin, but most of the black women were in the core room, the dirtiest part of the plant, making sand-impression molds for castings from the wooden master patterns that skill-trained white women had fabricated.

As white women took jobs in defense industries, more black women were able to move into food processing, textiles, and other light industry. A sample of African American families in rural East Texas found that the percentage of black women in domestic and personal service jobs declined from 47 percent in 1941 to 17 percent in 1944. In Dallas a shortage of garment workers induced the Nordis Company to hire black women. The owner "took the Negro woman out of the kitchen and put her on the power machines in the city and it paid off for him," recalled Olivia Rawlston, who was hired in 1942. The black women worked in a separate shop, under white forewomen, and black women were also hired as pressers in the white shop. In addition to earning "lovely money," the African American women organized their own ILGWU local, Nordis No. 2, with Rawlston as the first president. Becoming a union leader changed the shape of Olivia Rawlston's world. Despite formal segregation, she formed cordial relationships with her white counterparts — "we knew it was in our interest to really pull together and we did" — and entertained Charlotte Graham in her home. Rawlston was the first black woman from the South to be a delegate to an ILGWU convention. Most important, she acquired the standing to complain about a white forewoman to a white manager; when he fired Rawlston after a heated argument, the union got her promptly reinstated and there was no recurrence.[43]

One group of women had their lives turned upside down by the war. The bombing of Pearl Harbor unleashed suspicion and hostility toward the country's Japanese population. The FBI targeted every Japanese household in Texas for search and interrogation. Beatrice Akagi, who operated a vegetable farm near Sheldon with her husband, described her family's ordeal, which began when federal agents and local police ransacked the house. They confiscated a radio and a camera, smashed a small Buddhist altar, and took her husband and his brother and father to Houston for interrogation. The younger men were subsequently released, but Akagi's father-in-law, who had been born in Japan, was jailed as an enemy alien for three months, while she made repeated visits to the district attorney's office, seeking assistance. Akagi gathered statements from neighbors attesting to her father-in-law's loyalty, which persuaded the enemy alien hearing board to release him. In San Antonio, widow Alice Miyoshi Jingu and her children were forced out of their living quarters in the Japanese Tea Garden in Brackenridge Park; for the next forty-two years it was called the Chinese Tea Garden.

The Immigration and Naturalization Service sited three of its internment camps in Texas, at Kenedy, Seagoville, and Crystal City, where thousands of Japanese, mostly from outside the state, were confined until the end of the war. Crystal City was the only camp that did not fracture family life by separating men from wives and children. Joyce Nozaki described it: "We had one-fourth of a barrack, went to a common bathroom and showers, and our eating area also served as a living room. . . . But later arrivals had it worse. They got housing called 'Victory Huts,' a small squarish space built with a minimum expenditure of lumber, that offered shelter from wind and rain but not much from heat and cold."[44] None of the internees had been charged with sabotage or disloyalty, and American-born Japanese, who were citizens, were swept up along with immigrants.

WOMEN IN UNIFORM

Twelve thousand Texas women served in the military during World War II, but in the immediate aftermath of Pearl Harbor they could volunteer only for the Army Nurse Corps and Navy Nurse Corps because none of the services accepted women as regular enlistees. The presence of nurses, who had "relative rank" (i.e., no command authority), caused no controversy; as a traditional female profession, nursing did not challenge gender roles or threaten male supremacy. Nurses volunteered in great numbers and served in every theater of combat, including North Africa and the Pacific. They staffed field hospitals close to the front lines, and some were taken prisoner by the Japanese in the Philippines; others narrowly escaped capture (see Document 2.18). In Europe, Texas flight nurse Dolly Vinsant was killed in action when the medical evacuation plane she was serving on crashed. In 1944 nurses in both the army and the navy were given full military rank and thereby command over the enlisted men who served as medical corpsmen. Because nurses themselves were nearly always subordinate to higher-ranking doctors, this important role reversal went unremarked.

While nurses were welcomed, none of the services initially wanted to admit women as regular enlistees. Only military necessity, combined with pressure from prominent women in government, finally persuaded the generals and admirals to support legislation that created the Women's Army Auxiliary Corps (WAAC), the Navy's Women Accepted for Voluntary Emergency Service (WAVES), the Coast Guard Women's Reserve (SPARS), and the Marine Corps Women's Reserve. (The marine women had no acronym, but Janie Sheppard of Midlothian remembered that the men "called us BAMS, for broad-ass Marines, so we called them HAMS, half-ass Marines.")[45] To enhance their prestige, the services chose highly educated professional women as corps commanders, who served at the rank of colonel. The WAAC (later the WAC) was led by Houston's Oveta Culp Hobby, a Houston newspaper executive and former parliamentarian of the Texas House of Representatives who had been serving as chief of the Women's Interest Section of the War Department's Bureau of Public Relations. The women's services were not intended for combat duty, and the WAVES were not even allowed overseas until 1944. The armed services were segregated, and the women's services likewise followed a "Jane Crow" policy. The WAC authorized a "Negro" quota of 10 percent but never reached more than 6 percent; four graduates of Prairie View A&M were among the first inductees. The WAVES did not admit African Americans until late in 1944; the SPARS, not until 1945. The Marines never opened up to black women.

Women were integrated into the armed forces with as little disruption as possible to the prewar sexual order and were in fact less likely to do non-traditional work than the civilian women who took war jobs. Janie Sheppard, who was given a six-week electrician training course in the Marines and put to work wiring Quonset huts, was in the minority; most military women worked in the clerical and administrative sectors, communications, and food service. Like Rosie the Riveter in the civilian labor force, the function of women in uniform was to free a man to fight—in this case to liberate him from a desk job and send him to the front. The public relations campaign to encourage women to enlist struck the same themes as the effort to persuade civilian women to take defense jobs. Posters of attractive women in crisp uniforms urged them to "Join the WAC Now!" and "Free a Man to Fight." The heads of the women's services stressed that women were not usurping men's roles. Colonel Hobby assured critics that the WACs were "only performing the duties that women would ordinarily do in civilian life" and that military service would not undermine their femininity.[46] Nevertheless, the WAC had to counter a slander campaign started by male enlistees—many of whom did not want to be freed to become cannon fodder—that claimed that women in the military were sexually promiscuous.

The only group of volunteers not performing ordinary civilian duties was the Women Airforce Service Pilots (WASPS). Authorized in August 1943, the WASP attracted 25,000 applicants, all licensed pilots, for training at Avenger Field in Sweetwater, Texas; more than 1,800 were accepted, and 1,074 graduated. WASPS ferried military aircraft from factories to airfields, towed targets for gunnery practice, and tested planes (see Document 2.19). They flew dozens of types of aircraft, including heavy long-range bombers, and logged more than sixty million miles, but they were never given military status. The thirty-eight WASPS who were killed in service received neither death benefits nor military funerals. Women filling high-status military roles appeared to threaten male prerogatives, and resentment of WASPS ranged from the absurd—the commander at Love Field for a while refused to let them fly during their menstrual periods—to outright hostility. Male pilots led the opposition to legislation in 1944 that would have given the WASP military instead of civil service status, arguing that female pilots would take assignments away from men. As the pilot shortage eased, the WASPS were deactivated in

December 1944, before the war ended; they were not granted veteran status and benefits until 1977.

Most of the advances women made during World War II turned out to be temporary. In 1948, three years after the war ended, Congress passed the Women's Armed Services Integration Act, which gave women regular, permanent status in the military but not equality. The range of occupations was scaled back to "feminine" work in all of the services, including the Air Force; the 121 former WASPs who accepted commissions were restricted to administration and support. The armed services established a quota of 2 percent for women, prohibited them from rising beyond the rank of lieutenant colonel or commander, and refused to accept married women unless they were veterans. Janie Sheppard enlisted for an additional year in the marines in order to get an extra stripe and then went to college on the GI Bill to get teacher certification, because "nobody was going to hire a woman electrician."[47]

The civilian labor force began shedding women even before 1945. Airplane mechanic Josephine Ledesma, the only Latina at Randolph Air Force Base in San Antonio, had to go back to her old job as a sales clerk. She had loved working on planes, but "after the war there was not anything like that."[48] Despite a propaganda campaign urging women to return to full-time homemaking, a survey by the U.S. Women's Bureau found that three out of four women wanted to keep working after the war. As the government canceled defense contracts, women were fired at a higher rate than men; the *Houston Post* reported in September 1945 that 11 percent of the city's female war workers had been terminated, but only 5 percent of males had been. As men returned home from the armed services, women lost the better-paid, higher-skilled jobs that the war had temporarily made available, but some were able to move a rung up the ladder. Single mother Anna Dunavent had been a waitress before being hired as a riveter at Consolidated Aircraft in Fort Worth. By the time she was terminated, she had earned enough for a down payment on a farm for her parents and cosmetology school for herself; after the war she became the proprietor of her own beauty shop. Elsie Summers, who had struggled to raise five children with cannery and cafeteria jobs, called her hiring as a laborer at Texas Foundries in 1942 "the luckiest day of my life, I guess"; she learned to make patterns and retired thirty-eight years later at a skilled laborer's pay.[49] War did not permanently affect sex segregation of the workplace nor seriously undermine the cultural assumption that women's primary role was in the home. Within a few years, however, female labor force participation began to rise again, especially among married women.

CONCLUSION: NEW WOMEN, LABOR WOMEN, AND RACE WOMEN

There is no simple answer to the question of how much Texas women's lives changed in the two and one-half decades after 1920. From the perspective of the former suffragists, there were disappointments. The woman's ballot proved less revolutionary than they had hoped and their opponents had feared. Only four women served in the state legislature in 1945, and none had made it to Congress. The first woman governor had been a profound disappointment. Women were still excluded from jury service and lacked power in the political parties. The middle-class women's lobby had achieved some of its social welfare goals, but by the 1930s a female community committed to public activism based on maternalist values no longer flourished. Enfranchised women's inability to transform the political system did not, however, mean that they had no effect. The League of Women Voters' labor to expand the electorate through campaigns to encourage poll tax payment and increase voter turnout undermined the disfranchising efforts of conservative Democratic Party leaders. Its voter information guides and emphasis on nonpartisanship encouraged voters to focus on issues rather than party loyalty, helping to increase Republican voting strength.

For women of color these were years of incremental progress in the face of enduring racism. Among Mexican-origin women, urbanization and the growth of a small middle class enabled female voluntary association culture to expand and address social welfare and school improvement issues. In Ladies LULAC they took formal first steps in organizing against discrimination. African American women, who had been instrumental in establishing NAACP chapters in the Progressive Era, moved to the next level, helping to found a state organization and doing essential work as organizers to build membership. Those who could afford to pay a poll tax, and were willing to assert themselves against unwelcoming election officials, claimed a long-denied right to cast a vote that actually mattered after the Supreme Court invalidated the white primary.

Wage-earning women seeking economic justice made significant strides in unionizing. The 1930s were an unprecedented decade of female labor activism, organizing, and strikes. Women worked outside the home in greater numbers, and more wives and mothers entered paid labor, but racial and ethnic discrimination held firm: black women were excluded from most industrial jobs, and both they and Mexican-origin women were paid less than white women. The stubbornly persistent sex segregation of the labor force temporarily broke down during World War II, when industry desperately needed women's labor, but lacking a movement to criticize gender discrimination, women could mount no effective resistance as they were forced out of well-paid war jobs during the reconversion. The pressure to return to domesticity at a time when suburbs were spreading over empty landscapes foreshadowed a new kind of female isolation within the family. In the repressive political climate of the 1950s, simmering discontent with domesticity would eventually prompt some women to a new critique of women's proper place, and Hispanic and African American women would dramatically escalate their separate civil rights crusades.

SUGGESTED REFERENCES

GENERAL WORKS

A variety of scholarship covers topics that span the period 1920–1945. For rural women, the groundbreaking work is Ruth Allen's *The Labor of Women in the Production of Cotton*, University of Texas Bulletin 3134, September 1931. Rebecca Sharpless, *Fertile Ground, Narrow Choices: Women on Texas Cotton Farms, 1900–1940* (Chapel Hill: University of North Carolina Press, 1999), makes extensive use of oral histories, while Debra Ann Reid, *Reaping a Greater Harvest: The Extension Service and Rural Reform in Jim Crow Texas* (College Station: Texas A&M University Press, 2008), discusses the roles of both sexes. On sports, see Mary Lou LeCompte, *Cowgirls of the Rodeo: Pioneer Professional Athletes* (Urbana: University of Illinois Press, 1993), and "Home on the Range: Women in Professional Rodeo, 1929–1947," *Journal of Sport History* 17:3 (Winter 1990); Roxanne M. Albertson, "Basketball Texas Style, 1910–1933: School to Industrial League Competition," in *A Century of Women's Basketball: From Frailty to Final Four*, ed. Joan S. Hult and Marianna Treckell (Reston, Va.: National Association for Girls and Women in Sport, 1991); and Susan E. Cayliff, *Babe: The Life and Legend of Babe Didrikson Zaharias* (Urbana: University of Illinois Press, 1995). Comprehensive surveys of African American and Hispanic women are Ruthe Winegarten, *Black Texas Women: 150 Years of Trial and Triumph* (Austin: University of Texas Press, 1995), and Teresa Palomo Acosta and Ruthe Winegarten, *Las Tejanas: 300 Years of History* (Austin: University of Texas Press, 2003). Irene Ledesma covers labor activism in "Unlikely Strikers: Mexican American Women in Strike Activity in Texas, 1919–1974" (Ph.D. diss., Ohio State University, 1992), as does Sonia Hernandez in "Mexicanos and Mexicanas in a Transitional Borderland, 1880–1940" (Ph.D. diss., University of Houston, 2006). Biographies of women active during this period include Judith N. McArthur and Harold L. Smith, *Minnie Fisher Cunningham: A Suffragist's Life in Politics* (New York: Oxford University Press, 2003); Merline Pitre, *In Struggle against Jim Crow: Lulu B. White and the NAACP, 1900–1957* (College Station: Texas A&M University Press, 1999); and Darwin Payne, *Indomitable Sarah: The Life of Judge Sarah T. Hughes* (Dallas: Southern Methodist University Press, 2004).

1920S

Emma Louise Jackson Moyer surveys the post-suffrage decade in "'Petticoat Politics': Political Activism among Texas Women in the 1920's" (Ph.D. diss., University of Texas at Austin, 1980). More detail on the state's first woman governor appears in Shelley Sallee, "'The Woman of It': Governor Miriam Ferguson's 1924 Election," *Southwestern Historical Quarterly* (July 1996), and Nancy Beck Young, "'Me for Ma': Miriam Ferguson and Texas Politics in the 1920s," in *We Have Come to Stay: American Women and Political Parties, 1880–1960*, ed. Melanie Gustafson, Kristie Miller, and Elisabeth Israels Perry (Albuquerque: University of New Mexico Press, 1999). Studies that focus specifically on Hispanic women include Julie Leininger Pycior, "Tejanas Navigating the 1920s," in *Tejano Epic*, ed. Arnoldo De León (Austin: Texas State Historical Association Press, 2005); Cynthia A. Morales, "A Survey of Leadership, Activism, and Community Involvement of Mexican American Women in San Antonio, 1920–1940," *Journal of South Texas* 13:2 (Fall 2000); and Gabriela Gonzalez, "Carolina Munguía and Emma Tenayuca: The Politics of Benevolence and Radical Reform," *Frontiers* 24:2–3 (June–September 2003).

1930S

The only book-length study of the Depression is Julia Kirk Blackwelder, *Women of the Depression: Caste and Culture in San Antonio, 1929–1939* (College Station: Texas A&M University Press, 1984). See also Rebecca Sharpless, "Women and Work during the Great Depression in Texas," in *Invisible Texans: Women and Minorities in Texas History*, ed. Donald Willett and Stephen Curley (New York: McGraw Hill, 2005); Yolanda Chávez Leyva, "'Faithful Hard-Working Mexican Hands': Mexicana Workers during the Great Depression," in *Mexican American Women: Changing Images*, ed. John R. Garcia and Thomas Gelsinon (Tucson: Mexican American Studies and Research Center, University of Arizona, 1995); and Marilyn D. Rhinehart and Thomas H. Kreneck, "'In the Shadow of Uncertainty': Texas Mexicans and Repatriation in Houston during the Great Depression," *Houston Review* 10 (1988). Studies that focus on labor activism include Melissa Hield, "'Union-Minded': Women in the Texas ILGWU, 1933–1950," *Frontiers* 4:2 (Summer 1979); Robert S. Shelton, "Yankee Devils in Paradise? Unionizing Efforts among Dallas Garment Workers, 1933–1935," *Legacies* 6:2 (1994); and Patricia Everidge Hill, "Real Women and True Womanhood: Grassroots Organizing among Dallas Dressmakers in 1935," *Labor's Heritage* 5 (Spring 1994). Emma Tenayuca and the pecan shellers are featured in Richard Croxdale, "The 1938 San Antonio Pecan Shellers Strike," in *Women in the Texas Workforce: Yesterday and Today*, ed. Richard Croxdale and Melissa Hield (Austin: People's History in Texas, 1979); Roberto R. Calderón and Emilio Zamora, "Manuela Solis Sager and Emma Tenayuca: A Tribute," in *Chicana Voices: Intersections of Class, Race, and Gender*, ed. Teresa Cordova, Norma Elia Cantú, Gilberto Cardenas, Juan García, and Christine M. Sierra (Center for Mexican American Studies, University of Texas, 1986); Zaragosa Vargas, "Tejana

Radical: Emma Tenayuca and the San Antonio Labor Movement during the Great Depression," *Pacific Historical Review* 66 (1997); and Julia Kirk Blackwelder, "Emma Tenayuca: Vision and Courage," in *The Human Tradition in Texas,* ed. Ty Cashion and Jesús F. de la Teja (Wilmington, Del.: Scholarly Resources, 2001). There are chapters on women in Carol A. Weisenberger, *Dollars and Dreams: The National Youth Administration in Texas* (New York: Peter Lang, 1994), and Evan McCarty Arendell, "Crossing into Bounty: Blacks, Women, Mexicans, and the Texas NYA" (M.A. thesis, Tarleton State University, 1994). On Social Security, see Kendall P. Cochran, "The Aid to Dependent Children Program in Texas" (M.A. thesis, University of Texas, 1950).

1940s

Studies that consider various aspects of women's work in defense industries include Donna Bonin, "Baytown's Rosie the Riveter," in *From Humble Beginnings: Exxon Baytown Seventy-fifth Anniversary, 1920–1995* (Baytown, Tex: Exxon, 1995); Gary J. Rabalais, "Humble Women at War: The Case of Humble's Baytown Refinery, 1942–1945," *Houston Review* 2:2 (Spring 2005); and Mary Potchernick Cook, "Angelina's Rosies: Women at War in World War II East Texas" (M.A. thesis, Stephen F. Austin University, 1998). Kelli Cardenas Walsh, "Oveta Culp Hobby: A Transformational Leader from the Texas Legislature to Washington, D.C." (Ph.D. diss., University of South Carolina, 2006), focuses on Hobby's leadership of the Women's Army Corps, and Robert Pando, "Oveta Culp Hobby: A Study of Power and Control" (Ph.D. diss., Florida State University, 2008), also addresses the subject. There are a number of books on the Women Airforce Service Pilots; see especially Molly Merriman, *Clipped Wings: The Rise and Fall of the Women Airforce Service Pilots (WASPs) of World War II* (New York: New York University Press, 1991), and Jean Hascall Cole, *Women Pilots of World War II* (Provo: University of Utah Press, 2002). See also Kathleen Cornelson, "Women Airforce Service Pilots of World War II: Military Aviation, Encountering Discrimination, and Exchanging Traditional Roles in Service to America," *Journal of Women's History* 17:4 (Winter 2005). The Woman's Collection at Texas Woman's University maintains a collection of WASP oral histories; see http://www.twu.edu/wasp/. Published oral histories of servicewomen include Clarice F. Pollard, "WAACs in Texas during the Second World War," *Southwestern Historical Quarterly* 93 (July 1989); Lucy Wilson Jopling, *Warrior in White* (San Antonio: Watercress Press, 1990); and Cindy Weigand, *Texas Women in World War II* (Lanham, Md.: Republic of Texas Press, 2003).

2.1. HALLIE CRAWFORD STILLWELL GETS A
SINK AND BUILDS A BATHROOM

Hallie Crawford Stillwell (1897–1997) lived most of her long life in the Big Bend. She was a young teacher when she married a much older rancher, Roy Stillwell, in 1918. Like many rural women, she was expected to "make a hand" outdoors while doing all the indoor work without "luxuries" such as indoor plumbing. In this excerpt from the first volume of her memoirs, she describes the couple's ongoing battle of wills over piped-in water and a bathroom.

My way of thinking—wanting more conveniences in our home—did not coincide with Roy's view of life. My friend, Margaret Hess, gave me her discarded kitchen sink when her family remodeled their home in Marathon. When Roy saw me unload the sink at the ranch, he exploded. "We're not going to put that thing in! We don't need a kitchen sink. I've piped water from the well here to the arbor, which is handy for you, and besides that, a sink is always stopping up, and I don't want to have to be cleaning out pipes all the time!"

"All right," I said. I hid the sink under the house. Every once in a while, I would drag the sink out in full view without saying a word to Roy. I was just mean enough to remind Roy that I still had the sink. One day while visiting Tom Henderson of Marathon, Roy's great-nephew, I told him about the sink and my conflict with Roy. He just laughed. Then, a year or so later, Roy's nephew Gus Rountree from Beeville, who had come to visit Tom, heard about my sink. Tom told him, "Aunt Hallie has a kitchen sink and Uncle Roy won't have it put in her kitchen. She still has to carry water from a hydrant under the arbor into the kitchen."

Gus muttered as he smoked on his cigar, and then calmly said, "I'll put the sink in for Hallie." . . .

Roy even enjoyed the kitchen sink as much as I did, and the drain pipe never did stop up or need cleaning. Once I had water in the kitchen, another thought cropped up. I said to Roy, "Save me some of those two-by-fours and lumber out of that old barn you tore down. I want to build a bathroom."

Roy staunchly replied, "I'm going to use that lumber to build a big corral. You've been complaining and wanted a bigger and better corral, so now I'm going to build it!" I accepted Roy's attitude and dropped the subject.

Finally, though, Roy began to see things my way and let me have the material I needed to build the bathroom I so desperately wanted. What a job it was, too. The lumber was old and hard, my saw was dull, and the days were hot. However, I sawed, I nailed, I sweated. Not a soul would help me. Sometimes I would need a specific board and wouldn't have it. I would go to the new corral, while the men were out in the pasture, and take a good board off the new corral and replace it with a bad one that Roy had pawned off on me. I would never tell what I had done, but Roy knew. He didn't say a word. He would just let me have my way.

By summer's end, my bathroom was finished. What a luxury! Shower, inside toilet, and hot water heated from a little potbellied wood water heater. You never saw a better-bathed family than the Stillwells. Roy took two showers to my one, and all again became quiet on the western front.

Source: Hallie Crawford Stillwell, *I'll Gather My Geese* (College Station: Texas A&M University Press, 1991).

2.2. EDITH JOHNSON, "PETTING PARTIES"

Changing sexual mores among young urban women worried their elders, who discussed the "problem" at length in print. Among the middle class, traditional courtship rituals were being supplanted by the modern dating system. Traditional courtship had been controlled by mothers and daughters: a young man requested permission to "call on" a girl and was received at her home. Dating, which emerged in the 1910s and was accelerated by the growth of automobile culture, was controlled by men, who paid for an evening's unchaperoned entertainment. Since working-class families lacked parlors and privacy, young men and women from this class had always courted in public, but as dating became the norm for middle-class girls, social observers lamented the decline of propriety and the loss of female modesty. This article was part of a series of commentaries by Edith Johnson (who appears in her photo to be of an earlier generation) with titles such as "The Flapper" and "Fashions in Love-Making." It appeared in a short-lived magazine published by Florence Sterling, a Houston businesswoman and former suffragist active in female voluntary association politics.

The petting party is as modern as the radio or the airplane. It differs as strikingly from the courtship of our parents and grand-parents as bobbed hair does from the pompadour of 1895. It boasts of more than one modern feature, such as parking by the road-side, and it differs from earlier fashions in courting in manner, in spirit and in human effect.

Twenty-five or thirty-five years ago a young man carried on his courting with ceremony. He might telephone, but he might also send a note. A social engagement was a more or less important event with him, for a man in those days had to assume the burden of the courting—a girl did not meet him more than halfway.

Now instead of telephoning or writing ceremoniously to beg the honor of Miss Smith's company, a young swain dashes up in his motor, honks the horn to give warning of his arrival, bounds up to the door and accosts the daughter of the house with a casual "Let's go."

. . . The spirit of the petting party is light and frivolous. Its object is not marriage—only a momentary thrill. It completely gives the lie to those sweet, old phrases, "the only man" and "the only girl." For where there used to be only one girl there may be a score of them now. The old time beau with his charming gallantries too often has become the accomplished philanderer. . . .

The tendency of the petting party is to kill romance and to dispel enchantment. How could it be otherwise when it parks boldly at the roadside, or sometimes even flaunts itself in the bright light of day? . . .

Promiscuous petting parties destroy that most perfect of gifts, the capacity to sincerely love. While they satisfy a craving for excitement, they kill fineness of feeling and they impoverish the heart and the soul.

The petting party is a product of the jazz age. It comes easier because lovemaking no longer is mysterious to young people—what child of twelve has not seen innumerable love situations enacted on the screen? It lacks chivalry on the man's part and modesty on the girl's. All in all, is it not a violation of the law of the true, romantic love?

Source: *Woman's Viewpoint* 2:10 (November 1924): 20.

2.3. JESSIE DANIEL AMES URGES WOMEN TO VOTE AGAINST THE KU KLUX KLAN

In the 1924 gubernatorial campaign the former suffragists faced an unsavory choice. Because no candidate had won a majority in the first Democratic primary, the top two vote-getters, Felix Robertson and Miriam Ferguson, faced each other in a runoff. Judge Robertson was a Ku Klux Klan member and had the organization's backing; Miriam Ferguson was a proxy for her husband, James Ferguson, the anti-suffragist, anti-prohibitionist former governor whose impeachment the suffragists had cheered. Jessie Daniel Ames, a former TESA officer and the immediate past president of the Texas League of Women Voters, wrote this letter to the numerous women who so disliked both candidates that they were considering not voting at all. In it, Ames urges women not to be taken in by the argument of men from the old Progressive-prohibitionist coalition, including the Anti-Saloon League, that prohibition enforcement was the overriding issue and Robertson the "drier" candidate. The larger issue was the threat of allowing a Klansman to seize the governor's office, for which women would bear responsibility if they abstain from voting.

Letters from Readers, Dallas News—14 August—1924
KLAN, NOT PROHIBITION
REAL ISSUE IN CAMPAIGN
To the News:

Judge Felix Robertson calls himself the "praying Judge."[1] . . . If he can inspire enough voters to stay at home on Aug. 23 his prayer will be answered. Certainly we do not want to help answer his prayer.

Women of Texas have two political traditions, one of which is the "anti-Ferguson" tradition. The question which confronts many of us is whether or not we can ever be justified in voting against this tradition. We have taught ourselves to look askance at anyone who has ever voted for Ferguson and now that we are torn between convictions and tradition, we are weakly considering a compromise by not voting at all. We would disfranchise ourselves at a time when our State and Nation need most all its liberty-loving citizens. We would assume by this course greater responsibility for the domination of the Ku Klux Klan than those who actively espouse it. There is no middle-ground that we can occupy. Those who choose to think so will find after the election is over that they are without standing among their own people.

There are those who reason that there is no choice between candidates. Being no choice, they can't choose. But there is a wide difference between the principles back of these candidates and it is between these principles we must choose. Prohibition is not the principle. Whoever tries to reason that it is merely tries to create a shelter for herself under which to hide. Judge Robertson is calling to mind in a most touching manner that his defeat means the victory of the anti-prohibitionists. He reviews at length Mr. Ferguson's prohibition record, all of which every child over 12 years old knows. But he does not know something that we women do. The Woman's Christian Temperance Union of Texas fought desperately against Judge Robertson and the saloon druggists in the first campaign.[2] Now that the Woman's Christian Temperance Union is silent in this second campaign it is clear that its leaders realize that there is no danger to prohibition in Mrs. Ferguson greater than that in Judge Robertson. Certainly the Woman's Christian Temperance Union, but not the Anti-Saloon League, would be fighting Mrs. Ferguson if Judge Robertson were less dangerous. So we know that the issue is not prohibition.

The Ku Klux Klan is alone the issue. I could write at length on the reasons why I am supporting Mrs. Ferguson for Governor. Many of them have been given by others who have helped to build our anti-Ferguson tradition. But there is one angle to this issue that none has spoken of. There is only one answer we can give to the hisses and boos accorded our great State in the convention of States in New York.[3] Texas can repudiate the reputation gained at the national Democratic convention only by repudiating the Ku Klux Klan on Aug. 23. The defeat of the Klan in Texas under the peculiar conditions which confront us means the speedy dissolution of that organization as a political power throughout the Nation. It means a better chance for the Democratic party and John W. Davis in November.[4] So soon as Texas stands forth free, so soon will the voters in the doubtful States cease to fear the domination of the party which holds its greatest single strength in us.

Jessie Daniel Ames
Georgetown, Texas
Source: *Dallas Morning News*, August 14, 1924.

2.4. BABE DIDRIKSON STARS IN BASKETBALL
AND TRACK AND FIELD

Mildred "Babe" Didrikson (Zaharias), the daughter of Norwegian immigrants, was born in Port Arthur in 1911 and grew up in Beaumont. A natural athlete, she was an exuberant competitor from childhood—she hurdled the hedges on her street, racing her sister, who sprinted on the pavement alongside. Didrikson won three medals in track and field at the 1932 Olympic Games and went on to become a professional golfer, the best-known woman athlete of her era, and helped found the Ladies' Professional Golf Association in 1947. In this selection from her autobiography she recounts her experience as a star attraction of the Golden Cyclones, the women's athletic team developed by Employers Casualty Company of Dallas. Between 1930 and 1932 Didrikson led the Cyclones to two finals and a national championship in basketball and was voted all-American each season. At the Amateur Athletics Union Championships and Olympic Trials in 1932, Employers Casualty entered her as a one-woman track and field team in eight events; she placed in seven, breaking four world records and amassing more points than the entire second-place team.

I was a junior before they finally gave me a chance on the Beaumont High girls' team. And I was the high scorer from the start. We went to different towns to play girls at other high schools, and we beat them all. I got my first newspaper write-up—a little item headed, BEAUMONT GIRL STARS IN BASKETBALL GAME. Then it was, BEAUMONT GIRL STARS AGAIN. I became all-city and all-state in basketball. Down in Dallas, Col. M. J. McCombs saw those write-ups and decided to take a look at me. . . . He was the boss of a department in an insurance firm, the Employers Casualty Company, and he also was director of the women's athletic program. He put in a lot of time on it after the regular office hours. He read about me scoring thirty and forty points in these high-school games, and he wanted to see if I was good enough to help their basketball team, which had finished second the year before in the women's national A.A.U. tournament. . . .

After the game Colonel McCombs came around and introduced himself, and asked if I'd like to play on a real big basketball team.

I said, "Boy, would I! Where?"

. . . It was arranged that I should play out the season with the Employers Casualty Company, then come back to Beaumont and finish up at high school. The school let me take three weeks out there to play basketball because my marks were good.

Colonel McCombs introduced me to all the girls. One of them, Lalia Warren, said, "What position do you think you're going to play?"

So I got a little pepped up there, and I said, "What do *you* play?"

She said, "I'm the star forward."

I said, "Well, that's what I want to be." And that's how it worked out, too.

Colonel McCombs asked me what kind of office work I could do. I told him I knew typing and shorthand. I'd taken that in high school. I wanted to be an athlete, but I didn't suppose then that I could make a living out of it, except maybe in physical education. I thought I might wind up being a secretary. I won a gold medal in school for hitting the best speed on the typewriter. . . .

Anyway, Colonel McCombs asked if I could work a slide rule. I said, "No, but if it's numbers I can learn it quick." And they wound up assigning me to a job where I used a slide rule. . . .

I went right into a game that first night. We played the Oil Company girls, the defending national champions, in a pre-tournament game. They had some pretty tough guards. They'd heard about me, and they weren't going to let this little kid from Beaumont do any shooting at all. They started hitting me that night, and they kept it up the whole season. If one guard fouled out against me, they'd send in another one.

But I broke away for my share of shots. We beat them that first night by a pretty good score. I was the high scorer. I got four or five points more than the whole Sun Oilers' team did. From that night on I had it made.

Colonel McCombs would drive me to and from work, and any of the other girls that wanted to go, to save us carfare. One Saturday morning at the office early that first summer he said to me, "Babe, what are you doing to occupy yourself now that the basketball season's over?" I told him I wasn't doing anything much. He said, "Well, how would you like to go out to Lakeside Park with me this afternoon and watch a track meet?"

Here I'd been thinking about the Olympic Games since 1928, and yet I never had seen a track meet. So I went out there with him, and we stood around watching. . . .

By the time we left, Colonel McCombs was agreeing with me that it would be a good idea if Employers Casualty had a women's track and field team, so the girls would have some athletics during the summer. I'm sure that's what he'd had in mind all along. He said he'd take it up with Homer R. Mitchell, the president of the company.

I told him I was going to talk to Mr. Mitchell too. Monday morning I went in and made my pitch, and Mr. Mitchell said, "Babe, whatever you all want you can have."

So we all got together and started talking about this track team we were going to organize. One girl said, "I'm going to throw the javelin." Another said, "I'm going to throw the discus." Another girl thought she'd like to do the hurdles.

When it came around to me, I said, "Colonel, how many events are there in this track and field?" He said, "Why, Babe, I think there are about nine or ten."

I said, "Well, I'm going to do them all."

Everybody nearly died laughing. I talked like that in those days, and some people thought I was just popping off. But I was serious. I said it because I thought I could do it. And in one meet we had, competing for the Texas state championship against the Bowen Air Lines girls of Fort Worth, I entered all ten events and won eight of them.

. . . But 1932 was the summer when I was really keyed up about track and field. That was an Olympic year. The national championships and the Olympic tryouts were being combined. So the ones who came out ahead in the nationals would also get to be in the Olympics. There were a lot of different events that I wanted to compete in. . . .

So I went into [McCombs's] office. I said, "Colonel, will I get to go up to Chicago for the nationals this year?"

He said, "Yes. That's what I wanted to talk to you about. I've been studying the records of the girls on the other teams that will be in the meet. I think if you enter enough different events, and give your regular performance, you can do something that's never been done before. I believe we can send you up there to represent the Employers Casualty Company, and you can win the national championship for us all by yourself." . . .

Colonel McCombs had that track meet doped out just about right. Of the eight events I entered, I placed in seven. I won five of them outright, and tied for first in a sixth. I scored a total of thirty points, which was plenty to win the national championship for Employers Casualty. The Illinois Women's Athletic Club was second with twenty-two points.

Source: Babe Didrikson Zaharias, *This Life I've Led* (New York: A. S. Barnes, 1955).

2.5. DOROTHY REDUS ROBINSON TEACHES AT MARKHAM COLORED SCHOOL (1929–1930)

Dorothy Redus Robinson was born in Cuero (DeWitt County) and taught public school for thirty-six years, the last four of which she also served as principal of a desegregated elementary school. Robinson battled Jim Crow most of her life. When her father attempted to transfer her and her brother to a school district with a "Negro" high school, the county superintendent responded that "niggers don't need any education." Robinson graduated from Prairie View College, and, because no graduate school in Texas admitted African Americans, she did graduate work during summer sessions in California. By the time she earned a master's degree from San Francisco State Teachers College, she recalled, she "had driven more than ten thousand miles by automobile, traveling all night on three or four occasions; had been denied motel accommodations in Nevada, breakfast in Salt Lake City, and had been refused a cup of coffee at two o'clock in the morning in a Wyoming coffee shop."

Robinsons' first teaching post was in Wellersberg; in this selection she recounts her second job, in Matagorda County, for $50 a month. The teacher who had previously signed the contract failed to appear, and the white school trustee who "interviewed" Robinson in his store asked only if she had a teaching certificate. Her experience at Markham Colored School was typical: in 1929 two-thirds of the state's black teachers taught in one-room, one-teacher schools.

. . . The following day about noon papa and I appeared again at Mr. Barber's store and were told that the other teacher had not honored the contract, so the job was mine. He gave me a zinc water bucket, a dipper, and a box of chalk and said, "We'll get you some wood down there before the first norther comes." While I have never heard these exact words repeated by a school official, they are significant because that quick transaction was typical of the measures used to provide the needs of the Negro schools of that day and for many years afterward. Indeed, this approach had not completely disappeared as late as the mid-1960s.

Materials, supplies, and equipment for Negro schools were inadequate or non-existent, the lack justified by declaring insufficient funds. The belief was held by many, and expressed by some, that money spent on the education of Negroes was a waste, or that educated Negroes "got out of their places" and proved to be bad influences among others.

Facility-wise, the Markham school did not differ greatly from the Wellersberg school. It too, was a one-room affair, but it had six windows and two doors and had once received a coat of white paint. This paint had long since yielded to the ravages of the coastal area's salt air and, with the attitude about education for Negroes and the tight money situation of the depression, I don't suppose anyone ever gave any thought to a new paint job. I know I did not. Here too, the campus was bare with no plantings and no playground equipment. Unlike the Wellersberg school, the Markham school boasted two surface toilets. There was a hand pump that usually had to be primed before any water poured forth. Sometimes even the priming was fruitless, and water had to be carried from a nearby private well. There was no storage facility of any kind. A small, rickety table served as the teacher's desk. Pupils' desks were commercial products with metal supports of intricate design resembling the fretwork of the New Orleans French Quarter. Even when new, this furniture probably was more beautiful than practical. Anyway, by the time I inherited the desks, they already had seen years of use in the white school (I was told). Ink stains, carved initials, missing nuts and bolts, and a general dilapidated condition gave strong testimony of long prior use somewhere.

Some of the desks were absolutely beyond use and, in the interest of physical safety, I relegated several to the only storage place I could find—an area underneath the building which was accessible because there was no underpinning. I kept enough to accommodate my thirty-odd pupils, but there was little I could do to enhance their adequacy. Frequently the order of my classroom was disrupted when the slight movement of a small body brought desk and occupant down in a heap of rusty metal, splintered wood, and howling humanity.

Like the desks, the textbooks bespoke prior use and abuse. While the number of books was sufficient, missing sections and torn pages presented problems.

Little was said and less was done about the limited budget the school officials allocated for the operation of the Negro school. This is not to say that there was not a general awareness of the inequity. Somehow I learned what the state per-capita appropriation was for that school year. I do not recall the exact amount, but I multiplied the per-capita figure by the number of children I had enrolled. The result confirmed what I already knew. There was a grave disparity between the state allocation and the actual expenditures. Absolutely nothing was spent on that school during the year except the $300 for my salary and the insignificant cost of two or three cords of wood, and two or three boxes of chalk.

One day I mentioned this to the trustee with whom I did all my official transactions. He turned a violent red and retorted very sternly, "Dorothy, are you accusing someone of misappropriation of funds? That is a serious accusation." I replied, perhaps not with equal sternness, "I am accusing no one of anything. I am simply saying that the money is not being received by the school where I work." The matter was pursued no further, but the following year, I received a five-dollar-a-month raise, a matter of particular significance when salaries were being slashed and work forces reduced throughout the nation.

Early in the school year, I called a meeting of all citizens, and we organized a Parent-Teacher Association (PTA). This organization became a vital social force in the community, and it enjoyed the support of parents and nonparents alike. The group decided upon a project that was to have tremendous impact upon the educational endeavors of Negroes in Matagorda County. I still regard it as the most rewarding accomplishment of my Markham years. I do not recall how the idea was born, nor who the promoters were, but at some point it was decided that the PTA would raise fifty dollars and pay me to teach an extra month.

The money was raised by various and ingenious means. One event used to further the cause remains vividly in my memory: a box supper. To conduct this affair, young ladies brought beautifully decorated boxes filled with assorted delicacies. Young men then bought the boxes and each dined with the lady whose box he had purchased. Sometimes, to add to the drama of the occasion, the boxes were not identified and the purchaser could only hope that he had chosen the box he wanted. At other times the boxes bore identifications. Suspense on these occasions was assured if more than one young man had a strong desire to dine with a particular young lady. Then, if the contents of their pocketbooks matched the intensity of their longing, frantic bidding ensued. This was the situation that maintained on the night of our PTA box supper. When the bidding ended, my box had brought the magnificent sum of three dollars. Our receipts that night totaled slightly more than thirteen dollars, which was more than one-fourth of the ultimate goal.

Certainly the success of this financial effort provided the necessary motivation. I taught the seventh month and, at the end of April, a representative of the PTA brought me fifty dollars in coins and one-dollar bills tied in a man's soiled handkerchief. So the Negro youngsters of Markham had a seven-month school term in 1929–1930. It was, I was told, the first time in the history of the school that the term had extended beyond six months. When I was asked by my trustee if I wanted the school for the next year, I replied with ill-concealed eagerness, "Yes, thank you."

The next year the PTA chose to repeat its previous project but, alas, the grip of the depression was so severe, raising a sum of fifty dollars proved to be an unrealistic goal. Only thirty dollars was raised, and I worked a seventh month for that sum.

Source: Dorothy Redus Robinson, *The Bell Rings at Four: A Black Teacher's Chronicle of Change* (Austin, Tex.: Madrona Press, 1978).

2.6. WHITE POLICEMEN SEXUALLY HARASS FERDIE WALKER

The most vicious aspect of Jim Crow was the sexual stereotyping and scapegoating of African Americans—men as bestial rapists and women as lustful temptresses. A black man dared not brush against a white woman on the sidewalk, but nothing restrained white men (including those who wore the uniform of law enforcement) from harassing and assaulting black women. Ferdie Walker, born in 1928, describes the terror she felt as a child when two Fort Worth policemen made a sadistic game of repeatedly exposing themselves to her.

I tell you this one thing that really sticks in my mind, one really harassing kind of thing that I went through at that time. I was 11 years old, and I will never forget it. I used to go back and forth to church on Sunday afternoons to the United Methodist youth group, and I always rode the bus. You had to stand on the corner, which was about two blocks from my house, to catch the bus. In those days, all police people were white, and all bus drivers were white, and these policemen would harass me as I was standing on this corner waiting for the bus to come. Sometimes the two of them would drive up. The bus stop was up high and the street was down low. They'd drive up under there and then they'd expose themselves while I was standing there, and it just really scared me to death. And the only reason I did not go home at that time was because if I had gone home, my mother would have made me stay. So I just stepped back from the corner, and because I rode that way all the time, the bus driver didn't [have to] see me standing there at the corner. He'd always stop and I'd get on the bus.

But it was these *same cops*. So I had a morbid fear of policemen all of my life and it has not completely gone away. This was in the broad open daylight with the sun shining. But I will *never forget* it, and it always comes back to me every time I get into a really tight experience. That was really bad and it was bad for *all black girls*, you know.

It was really hard for me to tell my children that [policemen] were helping people. It was really hard. I really prayed a lot over that, and I said, "Well, this is something that you got to do." I had a job as public health nurse at Topeka, Kansas, and we had a lot of child abuse even then and that was in the fifties. My supervisor gave me a situation. She said, "Now when you go to a house and a man is beating his wife, what are you going to do?" I said "Call the minister." And she said, "Ferdie, you're an intelligent person. You know that's not right." I told her. She's a wonderful person. I said, "Alice Jensen, I know that's not the right answer. I should call the police but I don't believe in the police." And that was after my third child was born.

So it has taken a long time for me to have any kind of trust in policemen as a group even when I tried to say to myself, "It's one person and everybody is not like everybody else." But it's really very difficult for me. That has stayed with me.

Source: William H. Chafe et al., eds., *Remembering Jim Crow: African Americans Tell About Life in the Segregated South* (New York: New Press, 2001).

2.7. GLORIA LÓPEZ-STAFFORD AND HER CLASSMATES ARE SPRAYED FOR LICE

In the eyes of Anglo teachers and school administrators, all Mexican children were "dirty," and *piojo* line is a frequent painful memory in Mexicana oral histories. Martha Cotera, who attended a mixed Anglo and Mexican school, recalled: "Once a week the school nurse would come and line up all the Chicanos—and only the Chicanos—and look for lice in their hair. And then, whether you had them or not, they put kerosene on your hair. . . . And this you know had a very bad effect, even on the strongest children. It had a very humiliating, repressive effect."[5]

In this selection Gloria López-Stafford, who, like Cotera, was a child in El Paso in the 1940s but attended a "Mexican" school, describes the indignity of the kerosene treatment and the outrage of her Anglo godfather, who had adopted her.

That fall some of the children had lice, often a guest of poverty. The teacher would yell and say disgusting things to those children found with the uninvited parasites. I had had lice when I lived in the Second Ward with Maria, but she handled the problem and after a while I was free of them.

One cool morning, I remember because I had on my favorite navy blue sweater—the teacher told us to line up against the blackboard. We lined up like *borregitos*, like little lambs. Trusting our teacher, we laughed. and just waited to see what the surprise was going to be. A few minutes later, someone came in with spray guns like those used on trees or dogs. The person moved up and down the line of children against the blackboard, spraying our hair. Some children started crying but I was scared tearless. When they got to me, I objected, saying that I didn't have lice. That didn't matter, I was sprayed anyway. When it was over we went outside and were allowed to stay longer for recess that morning. At lunch, I went home and by this time my eyes were almost swollen shut. My godparents, whom I now called my parents, were beside themselves.

"What happened to you?" my father asked. His ruddy complexion became redder. "What is wrong with your eyes."

"They sprayed us because some children had lice," I answered very sad. I told them the whole story and how they hadn't cared if we protested.

My father rushed to the telephone book and looked up the number of the school. He asked for the principal, a very unpleasant man, and wanted to know why they had sprayed me. I watched as he listened to the response. Then my father told them that they had no right to spray me or any other child. He talked back and forth with the principal and then hung up. Martha immediately wanted to know what he had said. The principal had said that there were several children with lice and because lice jump from person to person, they had to spray us all. The principal said that lice posed a health problem because they could enter a child's brain and cause harm. My father insisted he had no right to spray, but the principal said he did. Fred wanted to do something about it but Martha told him to let it go. That didn't make me feel very good. The reason they got away with it, Fred said, was they knew the poor Mexicans wouldn't do anything about it. Nevertheless, it wouldn't do any good to complain, Martha added. I was proud that my father had stood up to the principal.

Source: Gloria López-Stafford, *A Place in the Sun: A Mexican-American Childhood in El Paso* (Albuquerque: University of New Mexico Press, 1996).

2.8. THE CHAPULTEPEC CLUB ADDRESSES DISCRIMINATION AGAINST MEXICAN AMERICANS

The Club Femenino Chapultepec was founded in 1931 by twenty-one young Mexican-origin working women in Houston. Sponsored by the Business and Professional Department of the Houston YWCA, the club formed for recreation and socializing; it was not a civic organization. But as the Great Depression deepened and hostility toward "unwanted" Mexicans rose, the members also turned their attention to the hardships and discrimination Mexicanas encountered. They composed this ten-point letter of grievances a week after two Houston policemen were acquitted of murdering a Mexican national (referred to obliquely in grievance 9). Although the "Letter from Chapultepec" was an attempt at outreach and not an angry manifesto, it caused controversy in both the Anglo and Mexican communities. Olive Lewis, the YWCA sponsor who also signed the letter, was fired.

June 11, 1937
Miss Leona B. Hendrix[6]
2219 Tracy Street
Kansas City, Missouri
My dear Miss Hendrix:

The Chapultepec Club of the Houston Y.W.C.A. has the following to offer as findings from their study of minorities. Here in Texas they [the club members] happen to constitute a minority group themselves and are called Mexicans. Some of the group were born in Mexico and have not taken out citizenship papers. [The] reason [is as] follows: Many were born in Texas and are therefore American citizens but are still called Mexicans. The group is made up of an excellent cross section of the Mexican colony in Houston. There are several high school graduates in the group and of course every year more Mexicans are staying in school until graduation.

These are the problems which these young Mexican girls and women face in Texas and they wonder what the future will be for them and their children. From this study they hope sincerely for recommendations from the National

B. & P. Council on action they can take to better understanding, respect and opportunity. They recognize that minority groups elsewhere in the United States face
some, though not all, of the same problems.

1. Texas is next door to Mexico and there are border town problems to be considered, historically as well as at present.
       Texas history is founded on troubles, oft created by Texans, to get land and
   cattle from the Mexican people. [N]ow the problem of stolen automobiles is
   causing the same problem and also the water power of the Rio Grande River is
   causing hard feelings.
2. Texas cannot, due to Chamber of Commerce and patriotic society activities,
   forget that Texas lost a tragic battle at the [A]lamo in San Antonio and won
   a battle at San Jacinto. This causes teachers to preach a patriotism not kind to
   Mexican children. Mexicans have been known to stay out of school [in Hous-
   ton] when that part of history was being taught because of abuses inflicted by
   pupils and even teachers.
3. Mexicans in [a] desire to get ahead have at times denied their nationality calling themselves French, Italian, and Spanish. This induces the Mexican colony's
   disfavor. Nationalistic spirit [is] being cultured at present [and] this of course
   can be as dangerous an attitude as the denial [of] one.
       If they should move back to Mexico they are considered traitors for having
   lived in Texas.
4. They do not take out citizenship papers because those who have are still called
   Mexicans and treated as such.
5. The Mexican people find it impossible to rent or buy in any decent section of
   town and are forced to live in dirty crowded conditions in houses out of which
   Americans have moved.
6. Playgrounds and parks show distinct distaste to their presence on them and in
   some cases they are ordered off or forbidden on. This problem is caused by the
   youth and not the recreation leaders.
7. Falsely accused of many crimes in the city and because of some difficulty with
   the English language they are taken advantage of frequently.
8. Mexican people are paid less in wages on all jobs and a great many jobs and
   industries are closed to them.
9. Mexican lawyers receive no respect from other lawyers nor even from our
   judges. It is a well known fact that a case is practically lost if a Mexican lawyer
   handles it. Justice is very one-sided, and they have had some rather serious cases
   recently.
10. They are called "brown people," "greasers," et cetera and of course want to be
    called white.

This letter is also going to Beatrice Langley and at the same time the group is also
sending a letter to the American Youth Congress protesting certain movies which
have been shown in Texas portraying the Mexicans in a very bad light.

Very truly yours,
Stella Quintenella
Carmen Cortez
Olive Lewis
P.S. These statements were verified by outstanding men in the Mexican colony, such as the consul, doctors, and teachers.
Source: *Houston Review* 3:2 (Summer 1981): 269–271. Original document in MSS 135, the Melesio Gomez Family Collection, Houston Metropolitan Research Center, Houston Public Library.

2.9. ALICE DICKERSON MONTEMAYOR, "SON MUY HOMBRES(?)"

Alice Dickerson Montemayor, born in 1902 and a social worker in Webb County, joined the Hispanic civil rights organization LULAC in 1936, three years after its Ladies Councils were authorized. She was a charter member of the Ladies LULAC chapter in Laredo, serving successively as secretary and president. In 1937 Montemayor was elected second vice president general of national LULAC, the first woman to win the post. She subsequently became associate editor of *LULAC News* and founding director general of Junior LULAC, a coed youth group.

Long before there was a feminist movement among Mexican-origin women, Montemayor was an outspoken critic of gender discrimination and machismo. The editorial that she wrote in 1938 for the *LULAC News,* with the sarcastic title "Son Muy Hombres(?)" (Are They Real Men?), suggested that the sexism of the LULAC leadership reflected insecurity, not male superiority. *Real* men, she asserted, were not threatened by sharing power with women. Decades later Montemayor told an interviewer, "Many men didn't want any ladies involved in LULAC. The men just hated me."[7]

Subsequent to the last Annual Convention there has been some talk about suppressing the Ladies Councils of our League or at least to relegate them to the category of auxiliaries. . . . Those who are inclined to favor the move base their contention on the pretext that the Ladies Councils of our League have been a source of trouble, friction and discontent. That out of the seventeen Ladies Councils that have been installed only about four are really active. That means that a little less than 25 per cent of the Ladies Councils are active. Assuming that their contention is correct as to the activity of the Ladies Councils, yet those in favor of the move seem to forget that most of the serious trouble, friction and discontent which has been experienced by our League, since its existence, can be easily traced to our Men's Councils' activities. . . .

Using LULAC NEWS as a barometer and taking the League as a whole, we can safely state that out of nearly eighty Men's Councils that have been duly installed only about EIGHT of them are—in the full sense of the word—really active. That means that about 10 per cent of our Men's Councils are active. At this writing one half per cent of the Men's Councils have paid up their indebtedness to LULAC

NEWS, while nearly 30 per cent of the Ladies Councils are in good standing and are taking care of their credit. Food for thought and for comparison. Some of these General Officers and members who think they are MUY HOMBRES (?) and who are the vain possessors of a superiority complex should look around and investigate their own councils and determine whether their own local councils are really active, instead of finding fault with councils other than their own. The majority of our Men's Councils get active just about Convention time. Once that is over, they forget about our aims and purposes and civic activities in their communities until Convention time rolls around again.

. . . The real cause of the apprehension among those who favor the move, is the aggressive attitude which some of our women members have adopted and shown in the conduct of our League's affairs. The contributing causes for this state of mind among our MUY HOMBRES (?) is the fear that our women will take a leading part in the evolution of our League; that our women might make a name for themselves in their activities; that our MUY HOMBRES (?) might be shouldered from their position as arbiters of our League; and the fact that some of our would-be leaders and members can not get over that Latin way of thinking that in civic affairs and administrative fields men are superior to women.

A statement was made to us, in writing, by one of our high officials which reflects the attitude assumed by our MUY HOMBRES (?). We cannot doubt this General Officer's sincerity, because the statement came to us unsolicited and it was made spontaneously. "I hope that President Longoria will get well soon. I understand he wanted to resign. Only being told of Vice-President Chavez's continued illness and his removal to Mayo Brothers Clinic at Rochester, Minnesota, deterred him. There are those of us, who hate to be under a woman [Second Vice President Montemayor], and taking this into account, and the fact that his illness is no fault of his own, he decided to make one supreme effort to get well."

. . . My honest opinion of those who think in that line, is that they are cowardly and unfair, ignorant and narrow minded. Both our Federal and Lulac Constitutions grant our women equal rights and representation. If a woman is qualified to fill a general office and some of our membership draw the line on her just because of her sex, then they are not true Lulackers and are not complying with that which is provided for in our Constitution. It is cowardly and unfair to have our women organize councils and contribute their share of the expense of administering the League, and then slap their face by barring them from becoming the ranking officer of our organization.

. . . [W]e hold that those General Officers and members who are the exponents or who are in favor of suppressing our Ladies Councils or of denying them equal rights, the equal protection of our laws and equal opportunities and privileges, SON MUY HOMBRES (?).

Source: *LULAC News* 5:2 (March 1938).

2.10. JEWEL BABB WEATHERS THE DEPRESSION
BY SELLING MILK

To compensate for reduced income during the 1930s, women "made do." They sewed children's clothes from cut-down adult garments, raised gardens and canned the surplus, and bought day-old bread and cheaper cuts of meat. Wives and mothers like Jewel Babb, who ranched with her husband in Val Verde County, also used their domestic skills to earn cash. Babb sold pies to a restaurant and took in ironing, but her most lucrative venture was the dairy business she improvised from six underfed cows that her husband had resisted buying. After the banks failed in Langtry, Babb's animals literally became cash cows, providing money that helped the couple keep up the payments on their truck.

I always liked milk cows. So one evening Walter came in, and he was mad. He said, "You know what? One of our friends wanted to sell me some old poor Jersey cows." And he said, "I don't want no Jersey cows!" Ranchers don't like Jersey cows. He said, "I told him I wouldn't want Jersey cows—just six of them for $150.00."

I said, "Well, you go right over and tell him we'll take those cows." And then he really got mad. He said, "We don't want them cows."

I said, "Get them, because there's money in them."

Well, I wore him down. So he went to the phone and told that man we'd take the cows. So a few days later, here come George out at the ranch with the scrawniest looking Jersey cows you ever seen. They didn't hardly look worth anything. Only one of them was giving milk. So we fed her up and milked her because she was giving milk. Then a month or so later, we went into Langtry and rented this little house because it was time for the kids to go to school. And so every time I milked this cow, there was an old woman who come to the back door holding this little pan out, and she says, "I want a dime's worth milk." Every morning, every time I milked, she wanted a dime's worth. So most every time I'd give her about this much milk, and she'd give a dime. Milk was selling for a dime a quart in those days. So that was about all the milk I was selling about then.

Anyhow, we had bought a new bobtailed truck, a big one, and we didn't pay any money because all you had to do was give a check. Everything was easy. But we got up the next morning, and everything was closed. We couldn't get no money nowhere. So I told my husband, "You go to the ranch." It must've been about twelve months since we first got the cows, and by that time they were in better shape, and one or two of them had calves. And I said, "You bring me another cow, and I'll sell milk. I'll milk them and sell milk." Well, I did. And it kept on. We couldn't get no money nowhere. Things had all closed. And Walter didn't have a salary, being a rancher, so he brought another cow in. And by that time, I was milking two cows, selling milk a dime a quart. And the little boys, Irvin and Dixie, would deliver. They'd walk on down the street carrying it to the houses, and they'd always make it pretty good unless they stopped and shot marbles in the middle of the street or have a fight. But finally they'd get there.

So about that time, a big construction outfit came into Langtry, and they began to need milk. I said, "Bring some more cows." Kept on til I was milking seven twice a day. So I don't know how much I was getting, but maybe I was making three or four dollars a day at the time, because they was better milk cows than we thought they was. And the boys delivering it and helping me. And Mr. Babb [father-in-law] had a farm with lots of cane hay, so we hauled this hay in for the cows. And Walter went out on the weekend and chopped wood and sold it to the people. . . . Wood and that [winning dice games] and milk, and we'd save up enough every month to make payments on that truck. Payments were a hundred dollars probably. A family right close to us said, "Well, I think she's crazy milking them ol' cows." And they had bought a big fine car, and they lost it. But we didn't lose the truck.

Source: Jewel Babb, *Border Healing Woman: The Story of Jewel Babb*, as told to Pat Ellis Taylor (Austin: University of Texas Press, 1981). Copyright © the University of Texas Press 1981, 1994.

2.11. ANNA MAE DICKSON WORKS AS A MAID

Anna Mae Dickson grew up in rural Grimes County and dropped out of Navasota's "colored" high school in tenth grade to work because she knew that her choices with or without a diploma were exactly the same: domestic service or farm labor. In a racist society, the challenge for African American women was economic survival without sacrificing dignity. Dickson chose households with more possibilities to leverage her position, and if she was disrespected, she walked out. "You learn to be two persons," she told an oral history interviewer, maintaining a demeanor acceptable to white employers while preserving an independent inner self.

"I had wanted to be a secretary for a long time because once I saw the secretary to the high school principal and that seemed to be the most important job I saw a black woman have. But if you lived where I did you did domestic work or farming, even if you finished high school. If you married you worked for a chance to get on somebody's place that had real good land that you could farm and make good crops. For a black girl there wasn't anything like working at the stores. They weren't open to us at that time, in the late thirties. And I don't remember any registered nurses that was colored working in the hospital then. The only nursing that you did was taking care of people's children. It was easy to find a job baby-sitting, or somebody to cook for and houseclean. So that's what I did. And I didn't leave Navasota because I was scared to go to a big place like Houston. I worked for $2.50 and $3 a week back then in 1938. And by the end of the 1950s I was making $10 to $12 a week.

"I learned to take what opportunities I had. For a long time, for example, I wouldn't work for families that didn't have children because I found out there was more opportunity working in homes where there were children. If you were real good to the children and took care of them well you could do more things and the people would help you; I first got to know Houston because I worked for a family that had a little boy that took sick. They carried him to Houston to stay with his relatives and that little boy didn't want to leave me. So I went, too. The relatives saw how well I looked after that boy, and one day, to my surprise—because I wasn't getting very much from them—they took me to a big store and bought me some real fine underwear. It was the first time I ever had good underclothes.

"You could learn a lot about cooking in some homes. I'll never forget the first time I had to cook and serve a dinner by myself. I was thirteen. It was my first steady job—working summers between school. The lady was having fifteen people for Sunday dinner. She was having these little birds they call quail. I had never seen them before. Well, she showed me the recipe book, explained it to me, and said to have it ready when they came back from church. I was so scared I must have cried the whole time I cooked those birds. But I served them. And that lady didn't let anyone say anything bad about the food or the way I was serving it. I'll never forget that day. That lady taught me everything I know about cooking for white people.

". . . Conditions changed from family to family. I've worked for people I would go back and work for anytime because they treated me as a member of the family. They didn't treat me like a servant. You'd try to find the people who seemed like they'd help you get ahead. But actually people chose us most of the time rather than we choosing them. You'd get jobs by somebody recommending you. So I've had to work for people that treated you like they didn't have any feelings for you. Some people, I don't care what you did, it was never right.

"Like this banker's wife, one day I was serving a lunch for her. She had all the bankers there, and she was the only woman. She had her meals served in courses. We had got to the dessert and coffee. I came in with the coffee cups—I used to be able to tote twelve cups of coffee on one hand and serve with the other. Well, I went in this day and it's a wonder I didn't scald two of those men and scald them good! When I set the first cup of coffee down, Mrs. Thompson hollered, 'Anna Mae, goddamnit, you're serving that coffee on the wrong side!' Boy, I just started to shake. One of the men just caught the tray and set it on the table.

"I went back in her kitchen, and I looked at the dishes stacked from one end of that room to the other. I took off her dainty little apron and her dainty little hat piece and folded them up in the drawer. Then I put on my old straw hat, and I walked out.

"When I went into a family I'd tell them the children had to obey me. One family I worked for had a little boy, and I guess he just hated black folks. He would spit on us and do things like that. I said to the lady, 'Now I want to tell you there's one thing I cannot tolerate: I cannot stand for anybody to spit on me. If he does that you may hate me for the rest of your life, but I will whip him good.'

"Well, one day I went to work, and I was wearing one of those blue uniforms. And, girl, when I ironed one I thought it shouldn't have a wrinkle in it anywhere!

So I thought I was looking pretty cool that day. The lady was sick when I got to work, and she asked me to dress the little boy for school. I dressed him and brushed his hair. When I turned around he spit on the back of my dress. I grabbed him down in that bathtub and whipped him good with a rough towel he had there. His mother started yelling, 'Are you whipping him?' I said, 'I sure am!' She started to say something, and I said, 'Don't bother, I'm leaving anyway.' I left and never went back.

"Another time I was called a thief. You know that is something you never want on your record. Stealing is one thing I never did. I never even wanted to break anything.

"Well, I was working for this schoolteacher, Mrs. Reagon, and she had some beautiful pocket handkerchiefs. One Sunday she went to church and later on she couldn't find the handkerchief she took with her. She said, 'I know I came home with that handkerchief, Anna Mae. I know you got it.'

"Oh, my God, I just flipped! I started yelling at her, telling her what I thought, and you could hear me down the road! 'If I were stealing and I had to take a pocket handkerchief, I'd be a pretty poor thief,' I told her. 'What in the world would I do with one of your pretty little handkerchiefs, other than wipe my sweat with it? If I were stealing I certainly wouldn't take something that you'd miss right away.' I quit right then and there and walked out.

"Her daughter came up to the house before I left and said she would look for it because she didn't believe I took it. Sure enough they found it the next day in Mrs. Reagon's coat sleeve. Mrs. Reagon called me at home and said she and her husband would like me to come back to work. I said, 'I'm glad you have cleared my record but you'll have to find yourself another Anna Mae, because this one won't be back.'

"When you grow up into something all your life, you don't always think about the negative side. Like coming in the door—all our lives we'd been going to the back door, so I never fretted much about it. But some things did bother me. Why could I go out the front door to sweep the porch but couldn't go through that front door for any other reason?

"Or you would go in the kitchen and make biscuits and rolls for people because they weren't buying bread in those days. Now you know you got to put your hands in it to make it. All right you'd make the bread and then after it would get brown and ready to eat, but they wouldn't want you to put your hands on it. And it was the same thing with meat. You could touch the meat before it was cooked but after it was done, don't touch it! Oh, that would get me mad!

"But you'd go on because you needed the work. There were mornings I hated to go to work. I'd be saying to myself, 'Why don't they do their own work? I do mine, why don't they do theirs?' Then I'd get angry with myself—thinking about dropping out of school, thinking if I had gone on to school maybe I wouldn't have to be doing this kind of work. Wouldn't have to be going to the back doors to work.

"You did what you had to and didn't feel sorry for yourself. We just had to make a living and that was the only way to do it."

Source: Wendy Watriss, "It's Something Inside You," in *Speaking for Ourselves: Women of the South*, edited by Maxine Alexander (New York: Pantheon Books, 1977), copyright © 1984 by Institute for Southern Studies. Used by permission of Pantheon Books, a division of Random House, Inc.

2.12. CHARLOTTE GRAHAM LEADS THE DALLAS GARMENT WORKERS STRIKE OF 1935

Charlotte Duncan Graham was just out of high school when she went to work at a Dallas dress factory in 1929. Four years later she and eleven other women organized a union that affiliated with the International Ladies' Garment Workers' Union and staged a walkout in 1935. During the long and bitter strike, which spread to all fifteen Dallas factories in the Texas Dress Manufacturing Association, Graham was arrested fifty-four times. The strike ultimately failed because the union ran out of money, and the strikers were blacklisted.

In this oral history, taken in the 1970s, Graham describes the confrontations between picketers and strikebreakers, including a stripping riot that made national news. Lester Lorch, the president of the Texas Dress Manufacturing Association, promised that the owners would negotiate if the picketers would withdraw during Market Week, when buyers arrived to look over the new season's fashions. The union complied, but the owners reneged. The picketers, who had been dispersed in front of the various plants before the moratorium, then gathered en masse at Lorch's factory. They rushed the police line that protected the arriving strikebreakers and ripped the clothing from ten of the scab workers.

They [the owners] didn't care as much about the people that worked for them as they did the machines because when a machine broke down, they had to hire it fixed, [but] when you broke down, they'd just put somebody else in your place. There was no loyalty, no care. It just didn't matter if you got hurt in the shop. I ran a needle in my finger, and it broke off with thread hanging from the top side and the bottom side. It took me about an hour and a half to see a doctor and get the needle out. But they didn't care about that. You lost this all on your own time. They really felt you were less than human and cared much more about the machines than they did people. Maybe once a year some of them would give a picnic, but that was just their idea of being a good boss. . . .

. . . We would meet in secret. Then, of course, those of us who had the courage would talk in the shop. At least twelve people were fired.

. . . We made housecalls—we'd go to see people—and talk to them at night in their homes. Actually, I think that was really when the companies got worried because it was after we started making night calls on people that I think the company thought maybe we were getting somewhere. I don't think they worried too much when we were just talking in the shop, but once we started going out in pairs or threes and fours at night asking people to sign cards, then they got worried. That's when the firings started.

. . . How did we call the strike that morning? Those of us who were real active went down at 6:30 that morning with our handbills with the general strike call. I think a good many people even didn't know—they stood around in groups outside—they really didn't know whether to go in or stay out. They wanted to be with the union, and they were afraid because they had been told they'd never spend another day in a shop in Dallas and that was their home . . . they were just frightened and hungry.

[Management] called the cops. We had more cops around the shop than we had pickets. Of course, the cops were given liquor, and we know this for a fact. We saw it. They were, I'm sure, given extra checks to come out to curse the people and say ugly things. They even used their billy clubs on people, hauled us to jail. I guess the fight was [more] bitter with the cops than it was even with management because they were having a good time. They didn't want to get off the picket line either. And then the company would hire cabs. The same company who wouldn't pay a decent salary would haul the scabs to work in cabs. I'm positive that a good many of those people had never been in a cab before in their lives. It was a big deal, but they would bring them in cabs. Then the cops would line up shoulder to shoulder or hold hands and make an aisle for the cabs. They'd be lined up for blocks and they'd run 'em through like cattle to get them into the shop, and then the cabs would pick them up to take them home. Now they didn't take them all the way home. They'd take them far enough away and then dump 'em.

. . . We stopped some of them for the moment. Then a lot of bitterness was built up, so it became a battle then between the people. Of course, if you stopped them for one day, they came back the next day. There was fights on both sides and then the people inside the shops would stand up in the windows and dump wave set—the girls used to set their hair in the shops at noon and that slick, flax stuff they'd use—they'd stand up and throw it out on the pickets. And they'd dump boxes of pins out on the pickets. And they'd empty the trash cans out on the pickets. The pickets in turn would try to get even with them when they would be passing through.

. . . Lester Lorch, who was the spokesman for the Manufacturers' Association, called and said that if we would call off the pickets during Market Week that they would meet with us to try to come to an agreement. We knew he was not sincere. We knew he was lying the way he'd always done, but we couldn't afford not to say that we cooperated, so we called off the pickets for the week. And when Mr. Perlstein [the ILGWU national organizer] called him for an appointment, he [Lorch] told him to go to hell. So we had a mass picket line around his shop that morning. In other words, instead of distributing the pickets around five or six shops, we concentrated on Lester Lorch's shop. Quite by accident—the police actually caused it—all of a sudden one of the scabs was left without any clothes on, and the police were having a ball. But we got international publicity on the so-called stripping party.

Once things got started on both sides, there was a lot of people left without clothes that morning, and the police were having so much fun that when they grabbed us, they'd take us around the corner and they'd say, "Go back and get another one, but I'll take you to jail when it's over."

. . . It was kind of hard to tell whether the police grabbed them first or you did because the police were having a good time. Lester Lorch went upstairs—he made a line of uniforms, I think they were nurses' uniforms. They were white (they could have been restaurant uniforms), but anyway they were uniforms. And he brought stacks and stacks of them down, and he'd stand inside the door and wrap them up in a uniform when they'd finally get in the door. I understand—I can't swear this to my own knowledge—he made them pay for those uniforms after they'd lost their own clothes trying to get into his shop. We'd tell Lorch that if he'd come out and face us we'd leave his people alone, but he never would come out the door. He later told one of our manufacturers in St. Louis that he'd rather fifty men would get hold of him than those four women.

Source: Glenn Scott, oral history interview with Charlotte Graham, Talkin' Union Interviews, Texas Labor Archives Oral Histories, University of Texas–Arlington.

2.13. NICO RODRIGUEZ DEMANDS A JOB FROM THE WORKS PROGRESS ADMINISTRATION

Like many Tejanas, Nico Rodriguez married young, had a large family, and did seasonal agricultural labor. Families like hers were especially hard hit by the Depression and faced hiring discrimination in New Deal relief programs. Rodriguez's husband, as a Mexican national, was ineligible for a WPA job, and local officials initially lied to her about her own eligibility. The Cable Act, passed by Congress in 1922, had given married women independent citizenship—that is, a woman who married an alien no longer lost her American citizenship. Here Rodriquez describes how she refused to be intimidated, even though she did not know the law.

I'm born in San Angelo, Texas, and raised in Brownwood. I work in the field, picking cotton, cutting wood, shearing sheep. My brother used to shear the stomach of the sheep, tie him up, and I finish, because we were six girls and my father have only three boys. The boys, soon as they grown up they leave—fly and go—and so it was six girls and my father. I am oldest girl. You name it—I did it.

Almost nineteen, I get married. I marry because I was working too hard. I get mad. I'm not going to work like a man the rest of my life, I says to my father. I am gonna marry the first one that asks me. So here comes one, and I see him.

I got married on Sunday by the Catholic church and I went to work on Monday, and up to this day I haven't rest! I can tell you that much. I get married on Sunday and on Monday I'm chopping cotton.

I am strong and healthy. The first doctor I see in my life was when my first baby come. I am so embarrassed. But I never have headache, never have backache, and I used to work from dawn 'til dark.

Five babies come—two boys and three girls, and when they are so big, I try to get work with WPA. My husband can't find work because of the Depression.

They won't let me work on WPA. I have to fight. The place where I went to put my application, they tell me that I cannot work because I'm not citizen. I say, "How come I not citizen? I born and raised here and my father and mother. What else do you want?"

The lady call a man who say, "But you lost your citizenship when you married your husband. He is a citizen of Mexico."

I ask him, "You mean I get job only if I divorce him? What am I to be, and what are my kids to be? Give me paper to explain it to the judge why I divorce this man, because he is not citizen."

And the man says: "I can't do that."

I am mad and I say back to him: "Then explain it to me how my kids gonna eat? How I'm gonna feed them?"

So he said he'd think about it. "No time to think about it," I told him. "I want answer quick, because I'm not gonna let my kids starve to death."

Then—two, three days later—they send me a card to report to work. He wrote to Dallas or something, and they send papers for me to sign. I go to work in the sewing room and get thirty dollars a month, and I make so many pants that they give me a raise to forty dollars a month.

When that WPA stop we go back to the fields until I press my foot down. I tell my husband, "This is it. No more field work. We have to educate the kids. We have to stay in one place and think about them now. . . ."

We have big fight, but I win. I told him if he wanted to go on the field, to go. I stay with the kids.

And that's when I start to work in the houses, you know. I have to do housework, have to do whatever come in. They pay one dollar a day, practically nothing . . . but it is enough. And I settled down on the town and since my oldest son go to school, I don't go back to the fields ever. I know my kids need the education.

My husband used to say it cost too much, but I didn't pay any attention to him. I say, "The door is open. You can walk out and walk in whenever you want, but *I am not going to the fields.*"

Every lady seems to like me—except one. I mean she wasn't nasty or anything, but I didn't like it the way she act. She says, "Well, Nico, I want you to clean the whole house, iron and wash and do the windows and clean the cupboards and put in new paper. . . ." I just look at her and I say, "You a woman . . . I a woman. Do you think you could do all that in eight hours?"

Source: Reprinted from *Making Do: How Women Survived the '30s* (Chicago: Follett Publishing Co., 1976), by Jeane Westin. Copyright © 1976 Jeane Westin.

2.14. LAQUATA LANDRY DOES WITHOUT ON A COTTON FARM

The old saying, "Use it up, wear it out, make it do, or do without" was a refrain that many women lived by in the 1930s. For Laquata Landry in Shelby County, doing without included underwear and lunch. With cotton selling for only five cents a pound, tenant families like hers made a bare subsistence. Even in the hard times, women and girls tried to maintain the new beauty culture standards introduced in the previous decade. Before World War I a few daring young women had cut their hair; in the 1920s short ("bobbed") hair became a fad, prompting an enormous nationwide expansion in the number of beauty shops. Short hair was kept in place with the new tight-gripping bobby pins and curled with a hot curling iron or a beauty shop permanent wave. Both methods were beyond Landry's financial means; she used a heated nail as an improvised curling iron, and even a cheap permanent kit was a major outlay.

We lived on a farm about twelve miles out in the country from Timpson. We were real poor—poor-poor. I've eaten flour and water gravy with water biscuit for breakfast—or either fried potatoes. We didn't have a icebox. Didn't have a toilet—just nothing. And trying to go to school and didn't have a penny. Really, you wouldn't believe this and you'll probably think I'm lying, but didn't even hardly have a penny to buy a pencil and a Big Chief [note]Book.

I chopped cotton for twenty-five cents a day, and I wanted me a pair of high-heel shoes. I was about eleven, twelve, or thirteen I guess. I had to work all week, five days, to buy those ninety-eight cent shoes—which I did. I started high school, and I had one pair of drawers—well, two or three pair of flour-sack drawers—Light Crust or [Beulah's] Best—with a drawstring. I'd bought one pair of panties that cost a dime, and I'd wear 'em and wash 'em out and wear 'em the next day. I had one pair of socks. I didn't have a brassiere. Mother had made a band that would hold the breasts down—not hold 'em up—and we pinned it with two big pins and then had straps on it. We thought it served the purpose.

I played basketball when I was going to high school. [Since] we didn't have brassieres, the breasts were bopping up and down and would rub [and] make our breasts sore, and you wouldn't believe it, the nipples would be raw. We'd have to put Vick salve or something on 'em, 'cause the basketball uniforms were gabardine. Finally, I think about the ninth or tenth grade they did come out with some brassieres. I think they was about fifteen cents, maybe a quarter. I did manage around to clean [a house], and she paid me a dollar a week. And I did get me a bra, but that wasn't up till about the ninth grade.

Well, we didn't have any shampoo and no make-up. We'd use [moistened red] crepe paper, and we'd use flour for face powder. Now, this was like in the eighth grade. And I had to wear overalls. No deodorant. We just scrubbed with lye soap. We could put vanilla extract on, but mostly it was lye soap. We'd take vanilla extract and we'd put it under our arms—or ether alcohol. We washed our hair with that lye soap, or maybe we might accidentally in Timpson, in the showers, wash it with bar soap that the school furnished. We would take a pencil and roll [our hair]—or either we would take a big spike nail. We had lamps burnt with coal oil, and we'd put this nail up on top of this lamp and let it get hot. Then we'd have us an ol' rag holding it, and we'd roll our hair and that nail will curl and frizz that hair. So that made our curls around our face. And then the pencil, we rolled it and we had bobby pins. I don't know how we got the bobby pins. Evidently, they must not have been over two or three cents a pack.

Now, the first perm that I ever got I guess I must have been about fifteen or sixteen, and it was a Shirley Temple when she came out with a Shirley Temple perm. It was the whole amount of fifty-nine cents. Fifty-nine cents, and I got one. My God, I don't know how I got fifty-nine cents. I guess maybe that was one of the dollars I'd worked for.

We never got bread. We had canned food, but we didn't have any meat or anything to go with it. Then we had the ol' home-cooked lard which nowadays would be [high] cholesterol. I don't know why they all didn't die back in them days. A hot dog was a nickel and a cold drink was a nickel, and we couldn't even afford a dime for us to eat, so I'd have to do without [noon] dinner. Well, we'd eat breakfast, catch the bus, and we wouldn't get anything to eat till we got back that afternoon. Now, that's not just me. It was everybody out in that community. A lot of 'em carried biscuit and scrambled egg or a biscuit and syrup, but now I didn't. I had too much pride.

Source: Laquata Landry, "I Just Thought It Was the Bright Lights," in Louis Fairchild, ed., *They Called It the War Effort: Oral Histories from Orange, Texas* (Austin, Tex.: Eakin Press, 1993).

2.15. A FARM GIRL ASKS ELEANOR ROOSEVELT FOR SCHOOL CLOTHES

Eleanor Roosevelt was the New Deal's most public and sympathetic face, known to Americans through her daily newspaper column, "My Day"; her articles in popular women's magazines; and her tireless fact-finding travels around the country. Citizens wrote the First Lady by the tens of thousands, asking for assistance or intervention, and even children recognized her as an advocate for the underprivileged. The daughter of a school bus driver in Santa Rosa, one of a family of eleven, wrote a businesslike appeal: "I would like to borrow enough money to go to school for four years at a nice college." Others were humble. A sixteen-year-old in Royce City doing day labor with her family and living in a shack with a few pieces of borrowed furniture, asked for "some old clothes, coats, and shoes or any kind of clothing you could send to us" and added, "I have read so much about your kindness I know if you have any you will send them." The letter below, an appeal for school clothes, combines a child's hopefulness with practical initiative.

Comanche, Texas

[received Sept. 3, 1940]

Dear Mrs. Roosevelt.

I am a thirteen (13) year old Farm girl from down in Comanche Texas. School will start this next Monday Sept. 2.

And I have no clothes or shoes to wear to school. My Father (G. C. P.) is seventy two years of age and gets on Old Age pension of $14 a month, but there are eight (8) of us so it takes All that to live on.

I am the oldest child of our Family.

My mother is sick all time, and can't work. And Oh, Mrs. Roosevelt I do want to go to school. I will be in the seventh grade when school starts. I would have been in the eighth grade but I did not get to go to school last term. I always make exilent grades on all my work in school when I can go, and this is the reason. Every time I get to start I always stay in after school and at recess for fear I will have to stop school and wont get to make all my grades. And while I am trying so hard to go to school, Others are being made go to school and are wishing they would not have to go. Mrs. Roosevelt why is it that way?

Why can't I find a way to get me some clothes and shoes. Mrs. Roosevelt can you help me? I have written an order to Sears RoeBuck and Co. Dallas Texas for clothes and shoes and I am sending it to you. And if you will help me you can send the order on to Sears RoeBuck and Comapany [*sic*]. Mrs. Roosevelt if you have a kind heart (which I'm sure you do) you will help me. Its hard to write this, with tears rolling down ones cheeks. But this was my only chanch Mrs Roosevelt, I am wondering if Monday morning will be a happy day for a little girl who is now sad. And I have great Faith in you helping me. If you send the Order (which I'm sure you will) all you have to do is send the money and your name and address. But have the order sent to me.

Mrs Roosevelt I can't believe you will fail me.

Please, Mrs Roosevelt help me.

I'm not wanting much just what I think you can afford.

May God Bless You

GP

Source: Robert Cohen, ed., *Dear Mrs. Roosevelt: Letters from Children of the Great Depression* (Chapel Hill: University of North Carolina Press, 2002). Copyright © 2002 by the University of North Carolina Press.

2.16. WOMEN ASK MARGARET SANGER FOR CONTRACEPTIVE INFORMATION

Margaret Sanger, a New York City nurse, opened the first American birth control clinic in Brooklyn in 1916, moved by the desperation of immigrant women who wanted respite from constant childbearing but did not know how to prevent pregnancy. Sanger was promptly arrested for violating the federal Comstock Act (1873), which prohibited the distribution of obscene material, including contraceptive information. She founded the American Birth Control League in 1921 and devoted her life to the cause. Letters like the two below, published in Sanger's *Birth Control Review* in 1925, poured into the league's headquarters. Both writers were frustrated by the ineffectiveness of birth control "remedies" and their own ignorance. The most popular commercial contraceptives—douches, vaginal jellies, foaming tablets, and suppositories—were marketed as "feminine hygiene" products in order to evade the Comstock Law and various state restrictions. Completely unregulated, many were useless, dangerous, or both. Antiseptic douche powders and liquids (including Lysol) were the cheapest and most popular commercial preparations. They were also the least effective, with a failure rate reported at 70 percent. The "method which I know is not healthful to either of us," to which the second writer refers, is probably coitus interruptus.

FIVE LIVING AND THREE DEAD
TEXAS.

I have been looking for help for many years, but I have failed to get the right kind of help. I am the mother of eight children, five living and three dead. My eldest one is twelve years and there isn't one of my children strong. Have had one set of twins that died at two months and oh, I had a hard time trying to take care of these babies. I am not strong, a small woman, weigh 107 pounds, have been so weak at times I couldn't hardly stay up and carry my load. I have done all in this world that anyone told me a woman could do to control birth, but nothing I have ever done helped me along this line. A doctor told me something but another baby came just the same. We are poor people, no place to call home and can't do a good part by the little children. My baby is only eight months old and I have been going to the field picking cotton and putting it on my sack as I picked. My husband gets only two dollars a day. I won't write any more on this subject, but help is what I want.

REMEDIES
TEXAS.

I was only a high school girl at the age of fifteen when I married the man of my choice who was twenty-one. He being older than I, I thought that he knew how to prevent children coming too fast, so we tried a "remedy" and at the end of two months and a half I was pregnant, at eleven months we were the proud parents of a girl. At the advice of a sister-in-law I now tried another "remedy." My baby was only ten months old when I again became pregnant. At seven and a half months another girl was born, but with careful nursing she is now two years old. Since she was born we have been using another method which I know is not healthful to either of us. My oldest baby is three years and five months of age, the other one will be two June 18th and I'll be twenty in September. I had an operation for appendicitis last September so I would like to put off child bearing a few years. My husband is good and true to me, and has never visited questionable places even when he was single.

We are renters and are of the working class of people you speak of in your book who are absolutely ignorant in a way.

Source: *The Margaret Sanger Papers,* edited by Esther Katz, Kathy Moran Hajo, and Peter Engleman (Bethesda, Md.: University Publications of America, 1996), microform, reel C3, frames 602 and 766.

2.17. JULIA WINGATE BACOM TAKES A WAR JOB IN ORANGE

Julia Wingate was twenty years old when the United States entered World War II. She watched the population of her hometown, Orange (7,500), triple within months as the defense industry swung into high gear. Rural people from Texas and Louisiana poured into town to take jobs at the naval shipyards and the new Consolidated Steel plant, precipitating a housing shortage so severe that families lived in tents and even converted chicken coops. Before Pearl Harbor, Wingate had been employed registering people for defense work training schools; afterward she took a job at Consolidated Steel. The war "changed us," she recalled. "I think we found out we were worth something, because we felt that the work we did was important and we were doing it well. We took pride in it."

I went to work for Consolidated Steel, and I was the first girl to work out in the yard. No girls had ever worked out in the yard before. They worked in the administration building. They decided they needed secretarial skills out in the warehouse, where all of the materials were coming in for building and equipping the ships. I was a little leery about that. I went out there for the interview and talked to the superintendent on the night shift. I was very hesitant about it, and then I saw a cousin of mine working there. I thought, well, if Johnny's here it'll be okay. I had somebody who'd look after me.

Johnny had warned me that these men liked to play jokes, and being the only girl out there they were going to play jokes on me, like don't type up a report for left-handed monkey wrenches or a sky hook or anything. So sometime later we got a report turned in on a bunch of steam strainers. Well, I knew you didn't strain steam, so I just set it back. I didn't pay any attention to it, and about three days later everybody was looking for steam strainers. They came and asked me for them, and I said, "Oh, you can't fool me. You don't strain steam." The top guy over the warehouse division said, "You take her out there and show her some steam strainers." I came in and I typed 'em up and sent the report through.

As young as I was, my job was to see that every ship that left here had every spare part it needed. We had to list every spare part they would need, and I had to see that when those ships were commissioned those spare parts were on there. It was a tremendous responsibility. One time on those spare parts I typed an order for a dozen winches to put aboard the *Newell,* and I spelled it "wenches." That was a typographical error. I knew better. The next morning I had a dictionary on my desk, and I had complaints from the crew of the ship—they liked it the way I had it.

One thing that I ran into there that I did not like was telling dirty jokes. As other girls came out into the yard they found some girls who laughed at their jokes. I didn't. I didn't think they were funny. I resented being told them, because I felt they had no respect for me if they were telling me off-colored jokes, and some of them were pretty raunchy. And to tell the truth, a lot of them I didn't really understand, but I wasn't about to say [so]. . . .

It wasn't too long down at Consolidated that they started having women work out in the yards as welders and Rosie the Riveter and all that stuff. I remember one time they had a problem with the restrooms out in the yard. In the past they had all been men, and they had signs—MEN—everywhere. So they took one of the restroom areas and put a "wo" in front of it. One day somebody laid a piece of tin across that "wo," and some men walked in there. It was pandemonium because the men were not accustomed to it. Now the men resented the women being out in the yard. They resented it. They had all kinds of jokes. They were very condescending, and when a woman could do the job as well as they could they didn't like it. They were threatened. Their superiority was threatened.

We were accustomed to calling the doctor and within an hour having something. Now we had to wait five or six hours in the waiting room to see a doctor. The men were always taken first 'cause they had to go to work. But by now the women were working, and they were beginning to resent having to wait while the men were taken care of. By now women's time was beginning to be worth something, and they didn't like having to wait while the men went through first. Maybe he did cut his finger on the job and had to get back to work. But okay, I had blood poisoning in my face, but I had to get back to work, too. And that was another thing—you didn't miss work for a hangnail. Your job was important. You didn't lay around.

Source: Julia Wingate Bacom, "Our Way of Life Is Ended Right Now," in Louis Fairchild, ed., *They Called It the War Effort: Oral Histories from Orange, Texas* (Austin, Tex.: Eakin Press, 1993).

2.18. ARMY NURSE LUCY WILSON SERVES IN THE PACIFIC THEATER

Lucy Wilson was born in Big Sandy in East Texas and grew up on a farm. She trained as a nurse at Parkland Hospital in Dallas. Wilson was twenty-three and working for the Red Cross in Tyler when she responded in December 1940 to a letter inviting nurses to enlist in the Army Nurse Corps. She chose William Beaumont General Hospital in El Paso—"the farthest place from home so I could travel a little farther"—for one year of active duty. In the summer of 1941 Wilson was offered overseas duty and was posted to the Philippines. On the day her enlistment was to expire, the Japanese bombed Pearl Harbor, Hawaii, and within hours attacked Guam and the Philippines. Before American troops abandoned Manila in late December, the nurses were evacuated to the Bataan Peninsula to set up field hospitals. On April 8–9, 1942, in advance of the surrender of Bataan, they were evacuated again, to the island of Corregidor, where they nursed patients in the Malinta Tunnel Hospital. Wilson was among the twenty-one nurses evacuated to Australia before the Japanese captured Corregidor and took the U.S. forces, including the remaining nurses, prisoner. Their escape and the plight of all the "Angels of Bataan and Corregidor" was dramatized in the 1943 film *So Proudly We Hail*.

Shortly before 6 a.m. on 7 December 1941—but for us, across the international date line, it was 8 December—the day I was originally to have been discharged from the Army—Pearl Harbor was bombed. I took my morning report to the Nursing Office about 6:30. On the way over, a soldier stopped me and said the Japs were bombing Pearl Harbor. The men were always kidding with me so I didn't pay him any attention. When I got back to the ward, one of the soldiers had his radio on and then we knew it was a fact.

By the time I was to get off duty we were informed to go be issued a helmet and gas mask and go through a tent where gas was released to test out the mask. We were to carry these with us at all times. It took nearly all day and I got very little sleep before going on duty at 7 p.m.

Earlier in the month they had decided if we were not busy we could take off four hours from 10 p.m. to 2 a.m. to take a nap, with our clothes on, in a room on the ward which had a bed with mosquito netting; and if the corpsman needed us he could wake us up.

I had barely gotten to sleep when the loudest noise I had ever heard in my life began. I tore down the mosquito net getting out of bed. I was so scared I was nauseated. The Japs were bombing Nichols Field near Fort McKinley. I kept looking at the ceiling and walls to see why they didn't come tumbling down. After a few seconds I realized I would be receiving new patients and I had better get prepared. Thanks to my training in the Emergency Room at Parkland Hospital, I got all my shock blocks out which were used to elevate the foot of the bed when patients were in shock. I knew I would need all the beds I could muster so I went through both wards and everyone that had been operated on more than four days ago I made get out of bed! In those days a patient stayed in bed for two weeks, even if it was a simple appendectomy.

At that time you had to boil water in a tablespoon and sterilize needles and syringes in order to give morphine injections. So I immediately boiled a 50 cc syringe and enough water to fill it and added fifty ¼-grain morphine tablets and dropped them in the syringe and all the hypo needles I had. I had hardly finished that when the wounded started arriving. I gave each patient a shot as he came in and put an X on his forehead with a Q-tip of gentian violet so I would not give him more than one dose, changed needles, and gave a shot to the next patient . . . all this before a doctor had time to get there. I had a ward full of patients before they arrived—and began making decisions on who would go to surgery first.

All that week we were very busy with so many badly wounded patients. After I got most of the patients asleep I tried to get other work done. My corpsman would check patients, but he was wearing shoes that squeaked very loud with each step he took, till I was afraid no one would be able to sleep. It was a long time later that I heard the Japanese Navy and Air Force had struck in the early morning hours of 8 December 1941 at 0140 in British Malaya, 0305 in Thailand, 0610 in Singapore (it fell 15 February), 0805 at Guam (which surrendered on the 10th), 0900 in Hong Kong (which fell on Christmas Day). Wake surrendered on the 22nd. The fall of Wake and Guam made it more difficult for us.

On 24 December we got a call telling us to take what we could carry in our hands and a bus would pick us up. It took us to Limay on the beach on Bataan. Of course I took only white uniforms with me in one piece of Hartman airplane luggage. All day we were jumping out of the bus into muddy ditches when Jap planes were flying over. We had nothing to eat all day and arrived at Limay near midnight; and some-one opened some cans of beans and remarked it was Christmas Day! We set up a hospital there.

On 26 December, Manila was declared an Open City.[8]

Our white uniforms were so visible from the air that they issued size 42 olive drab coveralls to us. The seat came about to my knees as I weighed under 100 pounds. It was difficult to walk in the sand with nurses oxfords on, too. Sometimes it would be 9 a.m., before I would get off duty and then someone would wake me up at noon to fold gauze for dressings. Finally, one day one of the other nurses told them that I was on night duty and to leave me alone—they did.

On 23 January 1942, I was transferred to Hospital #2 under the trees on Bataan. Gunny sacks or tow sacks were tacked to some trees to encircle the nurses quarters which consisted of beds under mosquito nets only. We bathed in the stream that went through the area. Here I was put in the Operating Room which was in a tent. Sometimes when bombs and shells landed we wondered if the tent wasn't going to fall down, it shook so bad. This meant that sometimes we would work night and day for 48 hours without stopping. Sometimes we would eat with our gloves on so we wouldn't have to scrub as long when we went back to OR. We only ate twice a day and that consisted mostly of rice with weevils in it stored since 1918, and anything else that could be scrounged up. We had a monkey that played around with us and would empty our ink wells; he disappeared—I'm sure we ate him as well as all the cavalry horses (which were delicious), and water buffalo. Sometimes the Philippinos would go out fishing and when one or two-inch fish were cooked with their heads on with their eyes still in, I simply could not eat them.

They moved the Operating Room from the tent into a building farther away from the nurses' area and built a bamboo shed near the Operating Room for the OR nurses to sleep in. It was about a foot off the ground to keep snakes out and the bamboo floor had cracks about an inch or so wide. Sometimes a small earthquake would cause a leg of the bed to slip into the cracks and wake me up. Bamboo was used for everything—even for the glasses we had to drink out of.

Eating everything we could get our hands on, we all had diarrhea. One day, I ran behind a bush and hurriedly took down my coveralls and started to vomit at the same time I was having diarrhea. I heard a noise and looked around to see a huge iguana lizard looking at me. I nearly fell over into the excreta!

By April, hunger and disease were greater enemies than the Japanese. There was a lack of air observation, fire control, communications equipment, and motor transportation; and we learned from listening to patients that 20% of the ammunition were duds, since it was so old, some of it having been stored since 1918. . . .

In the last days, many left sick-beds to fight. Many were too weak to carry machine guns through the jungle and steep ravines.

During those last days, many shells were passing over our heads both ways, from Corregidor and from front lines in Bataan; and if any had fallen short of their target they would have landed on the hospital. Hospital No. 1 was bombed by Japanese, even though it was marked by a Red Cross. We also treated Japanese prisoners in the hospital.

The amazing thing was there were very few mental breakdowns. I actually saw only one man who lost control of himself and that was in the early days of the war. There was no rear area—this was it, and everyone fought to the last ditch.

Late in the evening of 8 April, word came up to the OR that General Wainwright wanted all the nurses moved to Corregidor before the surrender, the next morning at 6 a.m. Since the OR was quite a distance away from where the regular Nurses Quarters were located, by the time we received the word, took off our gloves and gowns in the middle of operations, and walked down there, most of the nurses were already gone. Walking out in the middle of an operation with hundreds lined up under the trees waiting for surgery was devastating to me. This I have to live with for the rest of my life.

Source: Lucy Wilson Jopling, *Warrior in White* (San Antonio: Watercress Press, 1990).

2.19. NELL STEVENSON JOINS THE WOMEN AIRFORCE SERVICE PILOTS

Nell Stevenson was born in Floydada in 1921, grew up in Canyon, and graduated from West Texas University at the age of nineteen. One of the 1,074 women who completed WASP training at Avenger Field in Sweetwater, she served at Biggs Army Air Field in El Paso, Mather Army Air Base in Sacramento, California, and Deming Army Air Field. After the war she worked briefly at ferrying surplus planes for the government and then moved to Arizona, where she became one of the first female stockbrokers in Phoenix.

I graduated when I was nineteen in 1941, early part of 1941. During my senior year we had the Civilian Pilot Training Program there, and they would only accept one female in the program and the spot was already taken, so I didn't get the chance to go into that, but I'd always been interested in flying. When I was small, every time the barnstormers would come through in West Texas my dad would take me out to whatever pasture they were landing in and we would see them come in. Anyway, I moved to Amarillo after I graduated and took a job with *The Amarillo Times,* one of the newspapers there, in their advertising department. Sold advertising. . . . I had gotten my degree in economics and in journalism also and worked on the college paper and the college annual. So, I got a job in advertising and was able to join a flight club in Amarillo. There were several of us went together, we took $150 to join the club. We had a Taylorcraft and so I started flying. It only cost $1.50 an hour, but since I was only making $12.50 a week that didn't go too far. But we would—the ones of us that wanted to fly—we would skip dinner, lunch or anything to save enough money to fly. . . .

I was in Amarillo when Pearl Harbor happened. It was that spring then that I saw that they were looking for women to train to fly and there was an article about [WASP director] Jacqueline Cochran and so forth. When I went in, you had to be twenty-one. . . . You had to have a private pilot's license and seventy-five hours of flying time, so by that time I had gotten my private and was working on the hours. At that time they were doing interviews in Fort Worth, so I got in touch—sent a letter down there [and] I got a reply to come to Fort Worth for my interview and bring all my credentials.

. . . And I was interviewed by Jacqueline Cochran. She was very interested in the fact that I already had a college degree. . . . So I reported to Sweetwater in May of 1943, and it was a wonderful adventure. We worked all the time; we flew. One week we would fly in the mornings and have ground-school in the afternoons. Link trainers in the evenings. The next week it would be just the opposite. But we were up and marching to breakfast by five o'clock in the morning. After breakfast, down to the flight-line or to ground-school and lights out were ten o'clock at night. We were busy all that whole time. Sometimes it was seven days a week because we got our primary, basic and advanced and the number of hours we needed—the same as the men got in nine months, we did in six months.

. . . [T]here were twenty out of our class that were chosen to go to Mather Field at Sacramento, California for B-25 Transition School. . . . At the end of that time there were ten of us sent to Biggs Field at El Paso and the other ten were sent to March Air Force Base at Riverside, California. At Biggs Air Force Base we were in the 6th Tow Target Squadron, which was attached to the 3rd Air Force. We flew every kind of mission in training—ground to air: mostly the boys at Fort Bliss, which were stationed at El Paso, right across the road from where the Biggs Field is.

At Biggs Field we would fly strafing missions; we flew tow target missions where we would tow the target behind our airplane. We towed targets in B-25s and B-26s, we strafed in P-47s and the Navy SBD, A-24 and A-25. . . .

We didn't shoot at people, but we strafed them. We would go right down and go right over the top of the convoys going out into the desert. . . . They were supposed to hit the dirt and protect themselves as if they were being shot at. Now we also did gas missions, which we really had real gas in the tanks and we did gas the troops, and they had to put on their gasmasks and everything. And we did that in the single engine planes too. And we would go over like in a strafing mission, but as we got over the troops we hit the button and turned the gas on. . . .

[W]hen we were towing targets they shot at the targets, and they shot real bullets at the targets. And sometimes they hit the targets, and sometimes they came pretty close to the airplanes. . . .

We also towed targets at night, and they were supposed to catch the target in their search light and shoot at the target. Sometimes they would catch the plane in the search light and you would see a flak breaking pretty close to you, and when that happened we would usually abort the mission and roll in our target and go back to base, and tell them we'd come back when they learned to shoot at the right thing.

Source: Nell "Mickey" Stevenson Jennings Bright interview, WASP Oral History Project, Texas Woman's University.

Part Three

CONFORMITY, CIVIL RIGHTS, AND SOCIAL PROTEST, 1945–1965

In the two decades after World War II, Texas underwent profound economic and social change. Foremost was the transition from an agricultural to an industrial economy. By 1950 the state ranked twelfth in the nation in manufacturing, with petroleum refining and chemical industries leading the way, while in the 1960s electronics (most famously Texas Instruments and Electronic Data Systems) outpaced all other sectors. The mechanization of agriculture transformed farming into agribusiness and led to the collapse of sharecropping—the 1960 census listed no croppers at all—and the near disappearance of tenant farm families. Seventy-five percent of Texans lived in urban areas by 1960, and Latinos, at 15 percent of the population, had surpassed African Americans (12 percent) to become the largest minority group.

The old racial and political order, however, died hard. As southerners, Texans experienced two decades of turbulent and transformational politics. Separate African American and Hispanic civil rights movements pulled down the walls of legal segregation, with assistance from the U.S. Supreme Court, and struggled against white resistance to make integration a reality. Disgruntled anti-Roosevelt conservatives decamped from the Democratic Party to support the Republicans, foretelling the eventual end of one-party rule. And like the rest of the country, Texas was caught up in the Cold War with a new antagonist, the USSR, and the fear that Communist "subversives" in government and the public schools were secretly working for the destruction of capitalism.

Historian Nancy MacLean suggests that a useful way to approach the history of American women in the second half of the twentieth century is through socioeconomic class, specifically by examining the relationship of various groups to the family wage system.[1] The idea that a male breadwinner should be paid sufficiently to provide for a dependent wife and children—a family wage—traces back to the trade unionists of the nineteenth century. During the Progressive Era, middle-class reformers of both sexes advocated it as a way to end child labor and permit working-class mothers to stay home with their children instead of toiling in sweatshops. Improved wages made this ideal possible for larger numbers of households in the early decades of the twentieth century, although low-skilled workers, and especially workers of color, continued to be excluded.

The family wage system peaked in the 1950s and 1960s, when robust economic growth produced a rise in living standards that enabled more white families than ever before to live comfortably on the income of a male breadwinner. It was the longest-lasting, most broadly enjoyed reign of prosperity that any generation of Americans had ever experienced. Average real income increased as much between 1947 and 1960 as in the previous fifty years, and white-collar jobs for the first time outnumbered blue. The GI Bill, which offered veterans guaranteed low-interest home loans, spurred an exodus of white families to the suburbs, where the postwar building boom barely kept up with demand. Sixty-two percent of Americans could claim home ownership by 1960 (up from 44 percent in 1940), and an expansion in consumer credit helped fill the new houses with electric appliances and a mesmerizing new invention, television, which was in 65 percent of American homes by 1955. MacLean suggests that women's experience of this period is significantly linked with their relationship to the family wage system. For white middle-class women, the most financially comfortable and home-focused, the 1950s were the low point of organized feminism. By contrast, women of color and working-class women, who were excluded from the security of the family wage, became the most publicly active, organizing civil rights and labor protests, often with men of their own class. These women's lives and experiences diverged less from those of the men of their own group than was the case for middle-class women. This section examines each group in turn.

GENDER ROLES AND THE DOMESTIC IDEAL

Postwar affluence and widespread home ownership helped promote a preoccupation with domesticity and the nuclear family. The cultural ideal for women was marriage and full-time suburban motherhood, reflected in popular television shows such as *The Adventures of Ozzie and Harriet* and *Leave It to Beaver*. The demographic trend of the 1930s and early 1940s toward later marriage and smaller families abruptly reversed. Nationally, the proportion of the population that remained single plunged from 31 percent in 1940 to 21 percent by 1960. Couples married younger: in 1950 the median age of marriage in Texas dropped to 22.8 for men and 20.3 for women, virtually the same as the national average. Although the birthrate declined in the state's small rural towns, it rose among the suburban white middle class, part of a national spike in births between 1947 and 1964 known as the baby boom. White women in Texas bore an average of 3.3 children.

After years of steady increase, the proportion of white women in college dropped, as more opted for early marriage and motherhood. At the same time, more men enrolled than ever before, thanks to the GI Bill, which paid tuition for veterans and a simultaneous living allowance for dependents. In the mid-1930s the proportion of women in Texas state-supported colleges had been nearly equal to that of men (46 percent), and they earned *more* baccalaureate degrees. In the following decades the percentage of women steadily declined, falling to 36 percent in 1951–1952. The sex discrepancy was even more revealing in absolute numbers: there were four thousand fewer female college students than fifteen years earlier. Nor were women earning degrees in proportion to their enrollment; a national study revealed that two-thirds dropped out before graduation, usually to get married. Among African American women, who had never been able to rely on the family wage system, no such decline occurred, and they continued to earn more degrees than men. In 1951–1952 women were 59 percent of the enrollment at Prairie View College and 55 percent at Texas Southern University.

Multiple factors shaped the postwar embrace of domesticity. After the privations of the Depression and the disruptions of war, many young people craved the emotional reassurance of early marriage and stable family life. Dating patterns changed similarly. Going steady, which mimicked the committed coupledom of marriage, displaced the custom of seeking popularity by having as many dates as possible. Political tensions helped fuel conservatism and a desire for security. As the United States and the USSR faced each other in a nuclear standoff or Cold War, and Communism spread to China and across Eastern Europe, a strong family order offered an antidote to uncertainty and a base for social stability. The return to rigid gender roles was also a reaction against women's wartime freedoms, which had generated fears of sexual promiscuity and experimentation. The cultural message to women, once again, was that they made their greatest contribution to society as homemakers and mothers. One Texas student remembered her college years in this way: "In the back of my mind there was always the assumption, even when I was getting my graduate degree in education, that any work I did was temporary, something to do until I assumed my principal role in life, which was to be the perfect wife and mother, supported by my husband."[2]

Low expectations for girls led some young women to drift into marriage without much thought (see Document 3.2). Others were motivated by sexual desire and the strong social taboos that still existed against premarital sexuality for girls, even though sex researcher Alfred Kinsey's famous *Sexual Behavior in the Human Female* (1953) reported that half the women surveyed had admitted to sexual intercourse with one partner before marriage. The commitment implied in going steady gave dating couples more leeway for erotic exploration and put enormous sexual pressure on girls. A double standard allowed boys to push for concessions and required girls to set the limit. Necking and petting had become conventional, but girls who yielded to the point of intercourse risked their reputations—and worse, since few unmarried couples had access to contraception. Pregnancy was a social disgrace; girls disappeared from school and usually surrendered their babies for adoption. Marriage was a young woman's only safe and sanctioned outlet for sexuality. "Sex tripped us up," recalled a former University of Texas student, who dropped out after her freshman year to marry. "There was no way in that time and where I lived that you could have sex without fear of being pregnant. In essence, I got married in order to have a sex life. I thought that was why everyone got married."[3]

In an era when only low-wage jobs and a limited range of careers were open to women, marriage and motherhood offered autonomy as well as social approval. Teaching, nursing, and social work, the most common "female" professions, required long hours for low pay and offered little opportunity for advancement. National surveys showed that a majority of adults regarded homemaking as a full-time occupation, and women consistently expressed a desire for children and pleasure in motherhood. But in 1963 *The Feminine Mystique*, a best seller by New York journalist Betty Friedan, tapped into a hidden vein of unhappiness with the domestic ideal. Surveying a group of white, suburban, college-educated wives, Friedan found them frustrated and dissatisfied. The mystique of feminine fulfillment through marriage and motherhood repressed and stunted women, she argued, and denied them full use of their talents and potential.

Historians have since shown that Friedan overgeneralized, equating her sample with American women at large, and that she inaccurately blamed mass-circulation magazines for trumpeting marriage and motherhood as the only roles to which women should aspire. But for many women the restlessness and frustration were real enough. Future governor Ann Richards described her experience as a young wife and mother in Dallas during the late 1950s and early 1960s: "We fell into a routine. All week long, David would get off from work and go have a couple of beers with the guys and get home around seven or eight o'clock at night. I would cook dinner, iron shirts, look after the children. It started to dawn on me that this is what life was going to be like for a long time. I was mostly involved with my babies. . . . Cecile would be carrying on or Dan would be crying, and my life would be this endless test of, Can I get everything done? . . . When I felt myself beginning to get frantic and overwhelmed, I would throw the kids in the car and take the mile drive over to [my friend's house]. 'Virginia,' I'd babble, 'I am just losing my mind.'"[4]

Like so many young women of her generation, Ann Willis had married her steady boyfriend, David Richards, at age nineteen, while they were students at Baylor University. After graduation she taught junior high school while David earned a law degree. She was eager to start a family—the first of the couple's four children arrived in 1957. While David built a successful labor law practice, Ann's life was "birthday parties for little kids, Easter egg hunts, Indian Guide meetings, Girl Scouts": "I was always painting a room or re-covering a chair, or out in the garage trying to create a playroom for the kids." Richards enjoyed her family, but what Betty Friedan called "the problem that has no name" hovered at the back of her mind. "There were moments," Richards wrote in her autobiography, "when I felt that there was something more to life and I just didn't know what it was."[5]

WOMEN AT WORK

The cultural emphasis on domesticity notwithstanding, the number of employed women climbed steadily in the postwar decades. In 1940, women had been 23 percent of the Texas labor force; by 1960 the figure had risen to 33 percent. More married women worked for wages than ever before—nearly one-third by 1960. Postwar inflation pushed them into the labor market, where they found jobs in the clerical and service sector, which expanded faster than the population of young single women, whom employers had traditionally preferred. The corollary to young marriage and early childbearing was an increasing number of middle-aged mothers who joined the workforce after their children were grown or in school.

Census figures showed upward occupational mobility for second- and third-generation Hispanic women in the United States. By 1950 the largest number—24 percent—worked in clerical jobs. Twenty-two percent were factory workers, and 15 percent had service sector, or "pink collar," jobs such as beauticians, telephone operators, and food service workers. Only 19 percent were in domestic service. For African American women, the opposite was true. Nearly 52 percent still labored in domestic service, while another 22 percent did service sector work. Only 7 percent held factory jobs, and less than 2 percent were clerical workers, invariably in black-owned businesses. Unyielding racism kept them out of white-collar jobs. In 1955 the American Friends Service Committee sponsored a year-long attempt to place eight stellar graduates of Prairie View College as secretaries in the white Dallas business community, without success. The Texas Employment Commission sorted job applicants by race, and in the late 1950s and early 1960s only a handful of black women were able to secure secretarial positions in white institutions.

Female membership in labor unions had expanded significantly during World War II, and while postwar layoffs from manufacturing decreased those numbers, women in many of the pink-collar trades were stronger and more numerous than before the war. In the 1940s and 1950s they pursued what some historians have called labor feminism, a struggle not only to eliminate the wage gap between women and men but to win contract provisions such as maternity leave that protected female employment rights. In 1947 the National Federation of Telephone Workers (NFTW), including the Southwestern Telephone Workers Union, to which Texas women belonged, struck AT&T for wage equity. In Texas, telephone workers' salaries were so low that when the Fair Labor Standards Act established a minimum wage of twenty-five cents an hour during the Depression, exchanges in eighty-six Texas towns had to raise starting pay in order to meet it. Operators in those communities had been starting at as little as $9 weekly, and the maximum salary was $15, which took ten to thirteen years to achieve, even though an operator needed no more than a year to become fully skilled. No matter how many decades she worked after reaching the maximum, her salary would not rise. Metropolitan wages were only a little better. In 1935 the maximum in Fort Worth had reached $22 for a six-day week. Two years later Southwestern Bell cut the work week to five days and changed the maximum to $20, which left women with less take-home pay.[6]

The NFTW strikers (who included both operators and linemen) demanded a wage increase of $12 a week and picketed with signs that proclaimed "The Voice with a Smile Will Be Gone for a While." The first nationwide telephone strike, it was also the largest labor action of 1947 and the biggest walkout of women in U.S. history—two-thirds of the 345,000 strikers were female. In Dallas the Southwestern Telephone Workers Union strikers were led by Nelle Wooding, who was chair of traffic (switchboard operation) for the state's northeastern division and president of the Dallas local (see Document 3.1). She claimed proudly that no more than fifteen of the one thousand workers in Dallas crossed the picket line. One widowed striker sold the French doors on her house when she ran out of money to feed her children. Hers was a common dilemma: the NFTW had no strike fund, and low salaries had prevented most of the women from accumulating savings. The union was unable to completely disrupt service and was further handicapped by a decentralized structure in which each regional affiliate was autonomous. After six weeks the NFTW allowed the affiliates to settle individually; none got an increase of more than $5 a week.

In the aftermath, the NFTW reorganized into a stronger, centralized union, the Communications Workers of America (CWA) and in 1948 affiliated with the CIO. In the 1950s, Texas CWA operators forced Southwestern Bell to air-condition its buildings by staging wildcat strikes after bargaining and grievance procedures failed. On sweltering days, sitting only inches apart at the switchboards and "reaching and stretching and all that an operator has to do, some of them would faint, and the ones that didn't wished they could, probably," Nelle Wooding explained. "So the girls just got enough of it and they'd walk off the job." To get them back, the company positioned fans over tubs of ice. "But anybody working in an air-conditioned telephone building today can thank the operators . . . because they got it. They walked off the job in every major town and lots of small ones."[7]

In the meatpacking industry, where women made up 20 percent of the workforce, they sought not only higher wages but also recognition of gender issues. In Fort Worth, the largest meatpacking center south of Kansas City, the CIO was rebuffed at Swift Company but succeeded in organizing the Armour plant for the United Packinghouse Workers of America (UPWA) in 1943. The union contract abolished the eight-cent-an-hour wage differential between whites and blacks but not the ten-cent gap between men and women, who during World War II had been able to move into previously male jobs such as boning. While the UPWA insisted on equal pay for women when they did identical jobs, it took no action on the traditional sexual division of labor. After the war, women experienced the usual layoffs and resegregation into female jobs such as packaging bacon and making sausage. But the union strictly enforced seniority accumulated during the war, which enabled women to return to work when employment levels began to rise again. Hattie Jones considered it unfair that women were forced out of knife jobs and into the frozen food department created after the war, but acknowledged, "I don't think we would have got to work any if it hadn't been for the union. They did give us a square deal: they let us go back to work in there, hold our seniority."[8]

The Fort Worth Armour Local 54 workforce was 55 percent white, 40 percent black, and 5 percent Mexican, and where a woman worked was a matter of skin color as well as sex. The sliced bacon and canning divisions, where the work was safe and relatively clean, were white women's domain, while women of color did dirtier and more strenuous jobs. Mary Salinas, a Tejana who helped found the local, worked in the beef cut, where the temperature was never above 40 degrees, "so we froze all night long." She and other women who wanted to make boner's wages eventually secured jobs in the sheep cut, but the company paid them only piece rates—three cents an animal. Male-dominated and wedded to the family wage ideology, which viewed women as dependents and temporary workers, the UPWA did not make women's issues a priority. "We had separate seniority lists, we had separate everything," Salinas recounted years later, and the UPWA district director "was for the men, period." In addition to lower wages, women received only half as much vacation time as men, but their most pressing complaint was lack of maternity leave. Women who did not return to work within a month of giving birth were fired. Armour terminated anyone who missed four days of work within a six-month period. Salinas was fired while recovering from a hysterectomy: "The company said I didn't have no business being in the hospital." She was taken back only because the women in her department put up a fight.[9]

While few women held high rank in UPWA's leadership, there were many at the shop floor level within the local unions, a consequence of the sex segregation of jobs. Mary Salinas served as a steward and as a member of the education and negotiating committees, and her experience was not unusual. When she was elected president of the local in 1954, however, she was the only woman at the head of a UPWA union. By then, it was official policy for women to be represented on all of the union's committees and at conferences and conventions. During the 1950s women began convening biennial national conferences that strengthened their influence. "We would have coffee and we would talk and exchange ideas about what could be done in the plant or what they would like to see put in the next contract," Salinas remembered. Pressure from women activists at contract meetings secured maternity leave (unpaid) and, by 1956, elimination of the wage differential between men and women. "We got a lot of things that were needed," Salinas concluded, "but I'm not saying that it was enough."

The UPWA stressed interracial solidarity and had a nondiscrimination clause in its contracts from 1941 on, but district officials in the South resisted challenging the status quo. Throughout the 1940s, blacks and whites at the Armour plant in Fort Worth maintained a delicately balanced accommodation. Blacks did not push too hard on racial issues, and whites accepted a limited degree of social interaction. The union hall was integrated and held mixed social events, ignoring Jim Crow custom. But the plant maintained distinct racial boundaries: some departments were integrated, and others were all-white. There were separate water fountains, toilets, and locker rooms and a partition down the middle of the cafeteria. When civil rights coincided with union goals, white workers demonstrated support, as when seven black butchers were unfairly dismissed for absenteeism. The entire plant, including the white women in the sliced bacon division, walked out, heeding the union's claim that whatever management did to blacks it would do to whites next.

The racial equilibrium was upset after a protracted and unsuccessful wage strike in 1948 that severely weakened the UPWA. To rebuild, and in response to pressure from the black-majority Chicago locals, the union undertook an active civil rights agenda. It commissioned Fisk University's Race Relations Institute to conduct a survey of racial attitudes among packinghouse workers in five cities, including Fort Worth. Surprisingly, the interviewers found that three-quarters of the white workers in Fort Worth approved of the union's nondiscrimination policy, and 60 percent had no objection to working along-side blacks in the same job classification. But only 20 percent were willing to work with blacks in higher job classifications, and just 10 percent were willing to work under a black foreman. These attitudes foretold trouble as the union stepped up its civil rights initiatives. It directed the locals to establish antidis-crimination committees in the plants, and the new master contract negotiated with Armour in 1952 included a requirement to desegregate all plant facilities. In Fort Worth two black women were transferred to the sliced bacon division, and the white women retaliated with a sit-down strike.

Management gave in (and the local made no protest), but turmoil over removing the "white only" and "colored" signs and the cafeteria partition went on for the next two years, with racist whites forming a "local rights committee" and blacks pressing back. The UPWA kept the pressure on Armour by threatening to strike its other plants if the company failed to abide by its contract, and it encouraged blacks and Hispanics to take a more active role in union politics. Mary Salinas was prominent in the antidiscrimination fac-tion, working for social as well as economic justice; it was strong enough in 1953 to defeat an all-white slate of candidates running on a white supremacist platform. "The names I was called because I was for the Negro people," re-membered Salinas, who admired black workers' staunch unionism. "You can socialize with them, you can eat with them, work with them, and I'm sure we're going to either hell or heaven with them, so I can't see why we put up all these fights."

After some foot-dragging, Armour proceeded with desegregation, and disaffected white workers ceased participating actively in the union, opening the way for more minorities in leadership, including Mary Salinas's election to two terms as president. Salinas and others in the new leadership helped break down the remaining self-segregation in the cafeteria. "After we got our trays we made sure that some of us would sit on the opposite side, where the wall had existed at one time. We were called a lot of names due to that but we didn't care." In 1954 a black woman again integrated sliced bacon, and the white women walked out. They got no sympathy from Salinas, who told them flatly that desegregation was in the contract and that they could accept it or quit. One by one, they went back to work.

An exception to the strengthening of female unionism was the International Ladies' Garment Workers' Union, which declined markedly in the 1940s and 1950s. Membership in San Antonio's three locals dropped from one thousand in 1940 to six hundred in 1950, and the union lost contracts in several children's wear firms. Houston, which had five ILGWU shops in the late 1930s, lost four between 1954 and 1966. Part of the problem was the state's distance from the ILGWU's New York base: Texas accounted for only 2 percent of the U.S. dress manufacturing market, and the national union could not afford to finance expensive strikes in such a remote location. Its white, male-dominated hierarchy also refused to hire Mexicana organizers, even as the percentage of Hispanic women workers steadily increased. Equally important was the state's unyielding hostility to unions, which organized labor's support for Roosevelt and the New Deal had only exacerbated. After the war, conservatives in the Texas Legislature passed a spate of anti-labor statutes, which manufacturers used to eliminate unions. The U.S. Congress, under Republican control, added to the burden with the Taft-Hartley Act, which outlawed closed shops—meaning that employers could not be required to hire union members only. In 1957 only 24 of Texas's 315 apparel manufacturing plants were unionized, and wages were among the lowest in the nation.

Against this background, ILGWU Local 180 struck Tex-Son Company, a San Antonio children's wear factory, in 1959. Although the strikers asked for a small wage increase and an additional holiday, the strike was primarily a protest against the company's practice of subcontracting work to a nonunion facility in Mississippi. It was one of the earliest efforts to resist outsourcing, which reduced hours and take-home pay. The local made a large reproduction of a check for $9.12 made out to Helen Martinez, a mother of four children (who joined her on the picket line) and asked how anyone could feed a family on such a pittance. Tex-Son was also the first ILGWU strike led by Mexican Americans. Sophie Gonzales was the organizer in charge, Gregoria Montalba was president of the local, and ten of the fourteen members of the negotiating committee were Mexican American women.

Violence between strikers and scabs was quickly and ruthlessly suppressed; the police manhandled and bloodied the picketers, and the press portrayed the strikers as rioters. In the aftermath the ILGWU structured its publicity around the culturally popular themes of motherhood and domesticity. It produced a five-minute film, *Mother Is on Strike*, to show at fundraisers and launched a family-themed regional boycott, "Don't Buy Tex-Son." Strikers stationed in front of retailers distributed handbills that entreated, "For OUR Children's Sake Please Don't Buy Tex-Son Products for YOUR Customers' Children." Their children handed out "Don't Buy Tex-Son" balloons to shoppers' children in front of department stores and bilingual fliers to their mothers: "My Mama sews in a factory making clothes for kids. But now she is on strike because she needs more money for my sisters and my brother and me, and her boss won't let her have it."[10]

Labor unions around the state raised money for the strikers, and more than one thousand marchers turned out for a union solidarity parade. As the strike entered its eighth month, Gregoria Montalba issued a letter to nonstriking women who had stayed on the job, pointing out that the company was rewarding their "loyalty" with short hours and layoffs once again. She listed the cities to which work was being sent and urged them to investigate and "THINK IT OVER." But too many unemployed Tejanas were always available to take jobs as scabs, and in the fall of 1961, two and one-half years after the walkout, the ILGWU concluded that the strike was a futile expense. Without the national union's support, the local was forced to concede, and the ILGWU expired in San Antonio.[11]

CIVIL RIGHTS, BROWN: "THEY TREATED US LIKE DUMB MEXICANS"

The most momentous social change in the two decades following World War II was the successful challenge to the always vulnerable foundations of Jim Crow. Economic development eroded the need for a stable, low-wage rural labor force kept impoverished and tractable through racial repression. As farmers and growers turned to mechanization, African Americans and Mexicans migrated to the cities, where employers depended less on labor repression. Though still second-class citizens, they found autonomy and wider economic and educational opportunities that enabled an independent middle class to emerge and press for social justice. The shared experience of discrimination did not, however, unite black and brown in a common struggle for civil rights. Mexican Americans disassociated themselves from black activists and insisted that they were white citizens of Spanish or Latin American descent, not a separate race. The U.S. Census classified Hispanics as white, and segregation was by custom only. Anglos had traditionally accorded some of the privileges of whiteness to the prosperous, English-speaking, educated (and usually light-skinned) Hispanic elite; they could hold political office, send their children to white schools, and marry their daughters to Anglo men (although usually not their sons to Anglo women). For roughly four decades, beginning in 1930, the legal strategy of Tejano civil rights activists was to challenge any limitations to the Mexican American claim to whiteness.

The discrimination that most rankled was in education, where Mexican American children lagged far behind. In 1950, according to the census, the median schooling for Spanish-surnamed adults was 3.5 years; for whites it was 10.3. The problem had deep roots in poverty and especially devastating consequences for girls, for whom the alternative to school was often very early marriage and teenage motherhood. Many children had to do migrant agricultural labor with their families, which meant missing months of each school year (see Document 3.3). Others started school with limited or no English-language ability, which local officials used as justification for isolating them in separate classes or relegating them to inferior "Mexican" ward schools. It was common practice to keep Mexican American children from advancing beyond the elementary level, either by making them repeat grades until they dropped out in frustration, or by not permitting them to transfer to Anglo secondary schools.

Parents protested without success until after World War II, when Manuela González of Pearland tried to enroll her daughter in the Anglo school instead of the rundown, one-room Mexican one on the edge of town, where a single teacher coped with fifty-one students in grades one through five. When González was rebuffed, she turned to LULAC, which appealed to the school board to no effect. LULAC then mobilized the Mexican American families in an eight-month-long school boycott that brought integration by degrees. The board unbent slightly and moved the shabby Mexican school next to the white one; Anglo parents complained that it was an eyesore. Finally the board moved it to a corner of the grounds, turned it into a depository building, and let the Mexican American children attend classes with the Anglo students.

While the Pearland school board was grappling with its dilemma, a circuit court in California ruled that, in the absence of a law requiring separation, the state could not segregate Mexican American children, who were considered Caucasian. Texas likewise had no law requiring Mexican American segregation, and the California decision encouraged LULAC to file suit on behalf of Minerva Delgado and twenty other parents. The resulting decision, *Delgado v. Bastrop ISD* (1948), was a substantial victory. The district court agreed that schools could not segregate Mexican American children, but it allowed separate first grade classes for those not proficient in English. The majority of school districts, however, ignored the ruling, forcing Hispanic parents and LULAC to file fifteen more suits in the 1950s. The last one, again with a female lead plaintiff, was *Herminca Hernandez et al. v. Driscoll Consolidated ISD* (1957). Nearly three-fourths of the Driscoll students were Mexican-origin, many from migrant families that spoke little or no English; the school district kept them all in first and second grade for two years each before moving them to third grade with Anglo students. Once again, a federal district court ruled that Mexican American children could not be separated as a group, only by individual performance on standardized language tests. And once again, the verdict had little effect beyond the injunction issued against Driscoll.

Historian Guadalupe San Miguel calls the 1950s "the era of subterfuge" in school segregation against Mexican Americans.[12] State education officials showed little disposition to intervene in local districts, which were so inventive in sidestepping the law that LULAC gave up on further litigation—it could not sue all 1,427 Texas school districts into compliance. The organization instead turned its efforts to preparing five- and six-year-olds to enter school with a basic English vocabulary. The Little Schools of the 400 program taught children four hundred English words the summer before they entered first grade. Although the brainchild of LULAC's Felix Tijerina, the Little Schools were designed and taught by women. When Tijerina could not find funding for his original concept of a radio classroom, Isabel Verver, a Ganado high school senior who vividly remembered the frustration of segregated classes and the struggle to learn English, persuaded him to let her organize a local class for preschoolers. Elizabeth Burrus, an experienced bilingual teacher, originated the list of four hundred words and designed a curriculum around them. The results of Verver's Little School more than justified the premise. At the close of the 1957–1958 school year, only one of the sixty students she had taught could not advance to second grade; ordinarily, 80 percent of children whose first language was Spanish had failed first grade at least once. The program spread to Houston, and Tijerina persuaded the legislature to authorize a state-financed program based on the Little Schools model. Participation in the summer-long preschools was made optional, however, and despite the success of the programs, no more than 12 percent of school districts ever participated.

Beatrice Moreno Longoria of Corpus Christi had a different kind of discrimination problem. She wanted to bury her husband, Felix, a decorated serviceman killed in the Pacific, in his hometown of Three Rivers when the War Department shipped his body home in 1949. She made a long bus trip to arrange it with the town's single funeral home, only to be told that she couldn't use its chapel for the wake because the white community of Three Rivers would disapprove. It was the second time within months that the Moreno family had confronted racial insult. Beatrice's sister Sara belonged to a Tejana social club that had tried to use a skating rink at a state park in Mathis, and Sara had been the only one allowed to buy a ticket—the other members looked too "Mexican." As club president, Sara had reported the incident to Dr. Hector Garcia, the group's sponsor and the president of the American GI Forum, a veterans' rights association. Garcia had initiated a protest through channels that got the skating rink's policy overturned. Sara and Beatrice took the burial problem to Dr. Garcia too; he notified the press, President Harry Truman, and prominent state and federal officials. The Longoria case drew national media attention, and Senator Lyndon Johnson intervened and offered burial in Arlington National Cemetery. The Three Rivers mortician relented, but Beatrice and the Mexican American community accepted Johnson's offer, a war hero's funeral for Felix and an affirmation of dignity and sacrifice for Beatrice.

Victories for civil rights in court, while essential to ending state-sponsored discrimination, did not protect against bigotry. Like Beatrice Longoria, other individual Tejanas chipped away at the foundations of discrimination each time they pushed back at someone in authority who didn't want to deal with "Mexicans" (see Document 3.4). Martha Cotera prevailed against school guidance counselors who automatically tracked Tejana students into vocational courses instead of academics. She went to summer sessions throughout high school in order to get the business courses out of the way and be allowed to do college preparatory work during the regular school year. But she was stymied when she moved to Austin in 1963 with her graduate-student husband and encountered an ironic twist on prejudice: landlords would rent to Mexican nationals (foreign students were presumed to be upper class and wealthy) but not to Mexican Americans. Cotera and her husband finally secured an apartment only after a landlord inspected their household furnishings, which fortunately included Martha's extensive book collection and plenty of expensive wedding gifts. "So he looked at them and he said, 'Well, I guess you're okay. You're educated Mexicans.' And it was really embarrassing, but by that time we were so desperate we took that, and just moved into the apartment."[13]

CIVIL RIGHTS, BLACK: "YOU'RE NOT DIRT, NO MATTER WHERE THEY MAKE YOU SIT"

In Texas cities the civil rights struggle unfolded without the white violence that wracked states such as Alabama and Mississippi and filled the national evening newscasts. Governor Allan Shivers, although a staunch segregationist, did not stand at the entrance of the state university to bar black students, as did Alabama's George Wallace, and Texas's large urban school districts desegregated without the vicious resistance that brought federal troops to Little Rock, Arkansas. The only newsworthy conflict took place in the small town of

Mansfield, where a white mob and the Texas Rangers, dispatched by Shivers, blocked black students from registering at the high school. Several factors made Texas different. It was a "rim" state, on the periphery of the South, where the percentage of African Americans in the population (13 percent in 1950) had been shrinking for decades. White supremacy was deeply entrenched, and politicians defended it reflexively—the legislature passed bills that denied funds to school districts that integrated without an affirmative vote by the residents, and it authorized closing the public schools in the event that federal troops were sent to integrate them. Nevertheless, negotiated desegregation was more common than intransigent resistance. Urban leaders wanted to avoid headlines and notoriety that would hurt the business climate and hobble economic growth.

School desegregation was more difficult for African Americans than for Mexican Americans because state law, which required separate schools for "Negroes," stood in the way, and white anxiety over "race mixing" ran much deeper. Between 1946 and 1950 the NAACP filed eleven discrimination suits challenging egregious violations of the "separate but equal" policy—schools without heat, water, and lights. All were equalization suits: NAACP lawyers did not challenge the separate-school law (although they considered it unconstitutional); they asked only that the districts be restrained from giving black students inferior schools. The hope was that since few districts could afford truly equal dual school systems, financial necessity would force integration. In reality the schools "complied" by improving but not equalizing the inferior black facilities. In a challenge to higher education, however, the NAACP won a landmark case. Since Prairie View State Normal and Industrial College did not have graduate programs, thus forcing African Americans to go out of state to pursue advanced degrees, the state university system was vulnerable to challenge. Lulu B. White of the Houston NAACP began searching for a plaintiff. After hearing her address a meeting in Houston and ask for a volunteer, Heman Sweatt, a postal worker and an aspiring law student, came forward. White and other supporters accompanied him to Austin to submit an application to the University of Texas School of Law, which rejected it. In *Sweatt v. Painter* (1950) the U.S. Supreme Court ordered the law school to integrate, and the barrier to graduate education was broken.

Undergraduate education at the University of Texas remained closed to African Americans until the Kansas school desegregation case, *Brown v. Board of Education of Topeka* (1954), in which the Supreme Court ruled that racially separate schools were unconstitutional. In 1956 the University of Texas became the first state university in the South to desegregate, but it was desegregation without integration. Black women were restricted to two residence halls and one that the university leased from Huston-Tillotson College, a black institution two miles away. One of the university residences was a ramshackle firetrap with stained, peeling wallpaper, bare light bulbs, battered furniture, and a cricket-infested bathroom. (University housing officials responded to the cricket complaint by stuffing newspapers under the doors.) The kitchen was too small to permit more than one student to cook at a time, and there was no dining room—the women frequently ate standing up. When a co-op dormitory was built for black women in 1958, Ku Klux Klan–affiliated students sent an ugly note, and someone drew a threatening graffito on the sidewalk.

The rationale for segregated dormitories was, as usual, keeping white women "safe." Isolating black women was an oblique way of channeling their visitors—black males—away from dorms where they might encounter white women. To make absolutely certain, African Americans of both sexes were barred from visiting white residence halls, a policy that was subsequently modified: blacks could visit whites of the same sex in their rooms but were barred from the dining and socializing areas. The slightest social contact between a white coed and a black male could set off alarm bells. The housemother of Mariann Garner's dormitory was scandalized when Garner's African American science lab partner walked her back one night after a session: "She called my mama, *collect,* mind you, to tell on me!"[14]

White anxiety over intimate interracial contact became national news in 1957 over a black woman's role in a University of Texas opera production. Barbara Smith was part of the first cohort of black students to enroll in 1956, transferring from Prairie View College in order to study with a noted music professor. A faculty committee in UT's College of Fine Arts chose Smith, who had a glorious soprano voice, to play the female lead opposite a white male in the school's production of *Dido and Aeneas.* The prospect of an interracial pair depicting tragic lovers provoked a racist outcry from members of the public and the state legislature, and the university's president stepped in and ordered Smith removed from the production. Enduring personal threats and unwanted media attention, Smith never let her dignity or composure slip. She told the campus paper that "after the first shock and hurt had passed, I began to realize that the ultimate success of integration at the University was much more important than my appearance in the opera." Decades later, however, she said frankly that the controversy "took a big chunk of my soul," adding, "Inside I cried for years."[15] Smith declined singer Harry Belafonte's offer to pay for her education at another university; she graduated and had a distinguished performing career.

African Americans remained second-class citizens on the University of

Texas campus for years. White women's dormitories were not integrated until 1964, after a series of protests by black students and liberal whites. Even then, housing officials made sure that the black coeds roomed together. When Linda Lewis, valedictorian of George Washington Carver High School in Waco, arrived in Austin in 1965, she found that the "fully integrated" residence hall advertised in the university's brochure was in fact some two hundred white women and six black ones—one African American pair on each floor. Although the era of hostility had passed, Lewis and her roommate endured a barrage of well-intentioned "dumb white folks' questions," ranging from curiosity about their hair to their thoughts on Martin Luther King. Even when white students were friendly, black women's experience was inevitably stressful; involuntarily serving as cultural envoys, they were never fully at ease on an integrated campus. Lewis and her friends took periodic "sanity breaks" to spend time with black people only, often by going over to Huston-Tillotson College to socialize and learn the latest dances. Criticism from their own community inflicted additional stress; some local African Americans accused them of elitism for choosing a white university over a black college.[16]

Young white women were drawn into civil rights through the student Christian movement, which at the University of Texas was centered in the YMCA/YWCA and the Christian Faith and Life Community. The ecumenical, interracial University Y, stressing the values of Christian liberalism and brotherhood, showed students the connection between religion and social justice. The Christian Faith and Life Community, where many Y members lived, was the only integrated housing on campus when it was founded. At this privately run religious study center, students learned Christian existentialism, a search for meaning that rejected absolutes and aspired to "intentional living," which led to activism.

For young women who felt moved to reject the social traditions of their upbringing and side with the liberal, integrationist minority, the experience could be either liberating or guilt-ridden. To Sandra "Casey" Cason Hayden, brought up by a liberal single mother, finding the student Christian movement was the beginning of an exciting journey of self-discovery (see Document 3.5). Hayden chaired the University Y's Race Relations Committee and taught at a church school in Harlem the summer following her graduation in 1959. Returning to UT as a graduate student, she coauthored civil rights pamphlets for the National Student Association (NSA) and attended its conference at the University of Minnesota in the summer of 1960. There she challenged the white members to endorse the sit-ins that African American students were beginning in the South. At the University of Texas that fall she helped found Students for Direct Action, which organized a year-long series of interracial desegregation protests at movie theaters near campus and called for nationwide demonstrations against segregated theaters. In her capacity as chair of the student government's Human Relations Council, Hayden successfully urged the NSA executive committee to pass a resolution commending the Austin movie theater stand-ins. Historian Doug Rossinow judges Hayden "the most important Y activist in helping move a group of white UT students into civil rights action between 1958 and 1961."[17]

Women brought up in conservative families and trained to observe strict racial and gender boundaries joined the civil rights movement with conflicting emotions. The kind of strength and support that black women drew from family and community was seldom a resource for their white allies, who risked losing the respect of relatives and friends. White women's presence in civil rights meetings and demonstrations was subversive in a way that white men's was not; proximity to black men violated rigid social taboos and unspoken sexual ones. Casey Hayden's roommate, Dorothy Dawson Burlage, always felt that she was repudiating the norms of southern ladyhood and shaming her family by working for racial equality (see Document 3.6); the internal struggle between conscience and convention stayed with her throughout her years as an activist. Some women who were alienated from their conservative relatives regarded comrades in the movement at the YWCA as a surrogate "family of choice" (see Document 3.7).

In Houston, African American students at Texas State University for Negroes (now Texas Southern University) coordinated a series of desegregation actions in 1960 and 1961. The legislature had hurriedly established TSU in response to Heman Sweatt's lawsuit, buying the campus of a black junior college and adding upper-division courses and a law school in the hope of avoiding integration at the University of Texas. Dubbed "Separate But Equal U" by scornful student radicals, TSU spawned a cadre of student protesters who eventually took the name "Progressive Youth Association." The nucleus of the group was a handful of students, including Holly Hogrobrooks, Jessie Purvis, and Deanna Lott, who began meeting after black students in Greensboro, North Carolina, staged a sit-in to desegregate the local Woolworth's lunch counter and made national headlines. The TSU cadre was galvanized into action when Hogrobrooks brought in a newspaper clipping in which Senator Lyndon Johnson confidently asserted that the complacent Texas "nigras" would never do anything so radical.

On March 4, 1960, a mixed group of students, male and female, sat down at the lunch counter of a nearby Weingarten's supermarket and politely asked to be served; it was the first sit-in west of the Mississippi River. The manager promptly closed the counter, and although the students were apprehensive about violence, none of the whites seemed to know what to do. "Spectators stood around," Hogrobrooks remembered. "Within fifteen minutes the law enforcement officers got there and they stood around. Everybody stood around!"[18] Everyone except the black female shoppers, who abandoned their carts in the checkout lines in a show of support.

Over the next few days the TSU students extended the sit-ins to lunch counters at Mading's Drug Store, Henke and Pillot Supermarket, Walgreens, and Woolworth. In contrast to the police and citizen violence that students encountered in places like Nashville, Tennessee, and Orangeburg, South Carolina, there were no arrests: businesses closed their counters rather than provoke a confrontation, and the police kept a low profile. The Progressive Youth Association moved on to the cafeterias at city hall and the Greyhound Bus Terminal, a one-day boycott of downtown stores, and stand-ins at movie theaters. The first mass arrests took place at the Union Station cafeteria; when Holly Hogrobrooks demanded to know the charges, she was told that the students were "loitering."

The zenith of the movement came in the summer of 1961, after the Congress of Racial Equality (CORE) launched a series of freedom rides to test the Supreme Court ruling (*Boynton v. Virginia*) that prohibited interstate bus and rail lines from segregating their cafeterias and waiting rooms. In August, seven Progressive Youth Association students, including Hogrobrooks and membership chair Marion Moody, joined a group of freedom riders who had traveled from Los Angeles to integrate the Union Station cafeteria. Since she expected to be arrested and it was CORE policy to refuse bail, Hogrobrooks wore multiple layers of clothing, despite the heat, in anticipation of a long stay. The toughest adult black women in the cell block asserted themselves as protectors of the female students. The "lawmaker," according to Hogrobrooks, was an older woman named Olivia, who "did not take nothin' offa nobody, including matrons."[19] The students were found guilty of unlawful assembly and fined, but the decision was reversed on appeal, which stopped the city from arresting peaceful protesters.

While jail was the ultimate test of courage, every act of peaceful protest required women to dig down into reserves of strength and dignity. For Althea Simmons, a new graduate of Howard University School of Law, being ignored was worse than confrontation. "The most dehumanizing incident of my life," she wrote thirty years after the fact, "occurred in the 1950s while we were trying to desegregate the eating facilities in Dallas. My sister, who was one of the first black students in law school at SMU [Southern Methodist University], and a white male law student and I sat at the lunch counter at the bus station downtown. Nobody shouted at us, nobody said anything to us, nobody wiped the counter where we were. They just ignored us. We sat there for about five or six hours. Nobody made any kind of gesture that could be perceived as being hostile. We just didn't exist. Even now it's painful because I am a person and for all practical purposes I didn't exist."[20]

Not all civil rights actions were orchestrated group protests. Buying a house in a white neighborhood was an individual assertion of equality to which white supremacists responded with anger and violence (see Documents 3.8 and 3.9). Individual women successfully defied "white only" signs with quietly determined one-woman sit-ins (see Document 3.10). Singly, in one-on-one confrontations with department store sales clerks, black women claimed the same right to try on hats, clothes, and shoes that white shoppers took for granted. Unlike lunch counter sit-ins and movie theater stand-ins, department store "try-ons," as they might be called, were female-only protests that took place out of television camera range and received no publicity. Lulu B. White, executive secretary of the Houston NAACP, marched into department stores and tried on hats before the clerks could stop her. Told that she couldn't do that, she would reply, "I have," and walk out; other women would follow her example the next day. Christia Adair, White's administrative assistant who succeeded her in 1950, bought a girdle she didn't need and insisted on having it fitted as a civil rights protest (see Document 3.11). African American women also exerted pocketbook power. In 1961 three hundred professional women in Dallas, calling themselves Interested Women, closed charge accounts and threatened a boycott during the Easter shopping season in order to force stores to stop discriminating.

A great deal of women's activity within the formal civil rights movement likewise took place out of public view. Men—ministers, NAACP lawyers, and newspaper editors—were the movement's leaders; women were its organizers. Usually working without official titles and almost always without salaries, black women have been termed "bridge leaders" because they linked local communities to the regional and national movement. Black women's influence, like white women's, was greatest at the grassroots level, where they had extensive social networks. Their church societies, women's clubs, and civic groups recruited members for the NAACP, mobilized volunteers, raised money, organized rallies, and sought plaintiffs for lawsuits. Two of Texas's most important bridge leaders, Lulu B. White of Houston and Juanita Craft of Dallas, began as volunteers for their local NAACP branches in the 1930s and earned recognition for undertaking extraordinary campaigns to build membership. In 1946 both women were advanced to state service: White, who had built the Houston branch to the second largest in the nation, was elected state director of branches, and Craft was appointed state organizer. Together and separately, they crisscrossed the state, speaking, raising money, organizing new branches, and energizing weak older ones.

Juanita Craft's work in Dallas illustrates the impact of a prominent bridge leader. In addition to her job as state organizer, Craft directed the NAACP's Dallas Youth Council. It was an unpaid, unprestigious position—youth councils were mainly social organizations—that she turned into an important job by leading the students in confrontations with Jim Crow. In 1955 the Youth Council initiated the first protest demonstration in Dallas, picketing the Melba Theater's "Negro Night," when blacks were allowed to sit in the balcony. A few months later Craft's teenagers staged a massive campaign—more than 1,300 people took part—against "Negro Achievement Day" at the Texas State Fair, the only day that African Americans had unrestricted access to the fairgrounds. Mounting picket lines at every entrance, they carried signs mocking "Negro Appeasement Day" and urged blacks to stay away.

In 1960 the Youth Council began lunch counter sit-ins, which led the city to set up a biracial Committee of Fourteen to explore negotiated desegregation. While it debated, Craft mobilized the young people for stand-ins at two segregated theaters. The operation, conducted jointly with white students, was "beautiful," she recalled later, with amusement: "The whites would get in line to get served, then a Negro showed up, and they said, 'We can't sell you a ticket.' He put his money back in his pocket and said thank you and would go out back and get in the foot of the line. This is what we would do all day. One woman, it got on her nerves so bad at one of the windows selling tickets down there, she just stuck her head out and started screaming 'I cannot take this any longer.' It really affected people."[21] By the summer of 1961 more than forty businesses announced plans to desegregate, and Craft had been selected to serve on the Committee of Fourteen.

While desegregation of public facilities proceeded peacefully and with relatively little acrimony, largely due to the efforts of business leaders who wanted to avoid image-damaging violence, what happened at the public schools was a very different matter. The prospect of white and black children (especially white girls and black boys) sitting next to each other in the classroom raised the inflammatory issue of "race mixing." School boards commonly resisted complying with the *Brown* decision, forcing the NAACP to sue repeatedly. Houston, the largest segregated school district in the nation, did nothing until the NAACP filed a class action lawsuit in 1956 with nine-year-old Delores Ross and fourteen-year-old Beneva Williams as lead plaintiffs. Both had tried unsuccessfully to enroll in nearby white schools; instead Ross had to walk fourteen blocks and cross under a railroad overpass to reach a black elementary school, and Williams was forced to walk twenty-one blocks to a black junior high. "We wanted to be like everyone else, to walk out our back door and go to school," an adult Ross told a reporter years later.[22] Instead, their families got threatening phone calls.

NAACP attorneys won *Ross v. Houston Independent School District* in 1957, but victory did not produce integration. The conservative federal judge ruled that the girls had been denied their rights under *Brown*, but he did not order the district to admit them or set any timetable for desegregation. While HISD ignored the *Brown* and *Ross* rulings, Hattie Mae White made history by winning election to the school board in 1958; she was the first African American since Reconstruction to gain significant public office in Houston. A summa cum laude graduate of Prairie View A&M, White was a former teacher, the mother of five children, and a member of numerous community organizations, including the Houston Association for Better Schools. She had made an impressive presentation to the school board two years earlier documenting the unequal education of black children, after which people of both races began urging her to run. When she narrowly defeated the conservative white incumbent, the windshield of her car was sprayed with bullets and a cross was set aflame in her yard. At HISD's televised weekly meetings White argued vigorously against the foot-dragging of the conservative majority and its voluntary integration plan, designed to keep out as many black students as possible. HISD did not desegregate until 1960, when black children were permitted to transfer to white elementary schools in token numbers and not without incident. Georgia Massie was turned away for days when she tried to enroll her son in Kashmere Gardens Elementary; she persisted despite threatening phone calls and cursing onlookers. "It wasn't that you walked in easily," she recalled. "I just had decided I just wasn't going to give up."[23]

Despite winning their lawsuit, neither Delores Ross nor Beneva Williams ever went to an integrated school. Ten years after *Brown* only 5 percent of black children attended school with whites. Among them were the daughters of Annie Rainwater of Carrollton. There a group of black parents led by Rainwater, a widowed mother of six, forced the Carrollton–Farmers Branch Independent School District to stop busing their children out of the community to "Negro" high schools in Dallas and Denton. Annie Rainwater's daughter Nancy was one of two dozen students forced to make a daily fifty-mile round-trip to Denton along rural roads in a rickety bus, which broke down one day and stranded the panicked group. After petitioning the school board without success, Rainwater filed suit on behalf of Nancy and her younger sister, Betty Jean, and refused to back down when the family was threatened. In 1964 federal judge Sarah T. Hughes ruled in favor of the Rainwaters and ordered the district to submit a plan for desegregation. Both sisters graduated from high school in Carrollton.

Even when desegregation was peaceful, it was never easy for African American students. Vivian Howard, one of five black students who enrolled in John H. Reagan High School in Austin when it opened in 1965, remembered that the white students "did not call me names but they did not welcome me," and the teachers "did not acknowledge us being there."[24] Like the earlier lunch counter protesters, the transfer students were simply ignored. Alice Darden Davis, a later crossover to Reagan, summarized the feeling of isolation: "I remember raising my hand to answer a question and the entire room stopping and turning, looking around at you . . . then they would just turn back around and continue with wherever they stopped before you spoke." Like many former crossover students who shared their memories years later, Howard and Davis stressed the negative aspects of integration as well as the positive. They especially regretted the loss of community and social life they had enjoyed at Austin's black high school, L. C. Anderson, where the teachers knew their students' families and emphasized self-esteem and striving along with academics. "They had a real personal interest in you," Davis recalled. Students who desegregated all-white schools had to do without mentors and close-knit groups of friends. "I was there," Davis said of her years at Reagan High, "but it was as if you weren't there."[25]

RED SCARE POLITICS AND THE MINUTE WOMEN

In the late 1940s and early 1950s frightening events overseas and Republican resentment of the long reign in Washington, D.C., of Democrats, who had substantially expanded national government, converged in militant and sometimes hysterical anti-Communism. A nuclear-armed Soviet Union extending military dominance across Eastern Europe challenged American power in the world and generated irrational fear of Communist infiltration at home. Republican critics of President Harry Truman's administration blamed supposed pro-Communist sympathizers in the State Department for America's failure to prevent the "fall" of China to Communist revolutionaries. Senator Joseph McCarthy's accusations, beginning in 1950, that Communists had burrowed into the federal government, spawned a cultural panic and irresponsible, unfounded accusations that ruined careers but never unearthed any subversives.

To conservative southern Democrats and the small but growing number of southern Republicans, the partial welfare state shaped under Franklin D.

Roosevelt's New Deal and continued under Truman's Fair Deal was itself evidence of creeping socialism. Communist conspiracy theories appealed especially to anti–New Deal, anti-labor ideologues who regarded the political Left as a threat to small government, racial conservatism, and "American" values. Among the most fervent McCarthyites were the Minute Women of the USA, founded and controlled by Suzanne Stevenson of Connecticut. Texas had one of the strongest Minute Women contingents in the country, with chapters in Houston, Dallas, San Antonio, and Wichita Falls by 1951. The Minute Women were officially nonpartisan and proudly and profoundly conservative. Members committed themselves to voting in every election and to purging federal and state government and local schools of Communist influence. The guiding principles that Stevenson drew up for the organization included, in addition to "belief in God and country," such bedrock conservative values as states' rights, lower taxes, and the "right to work," which in practice meant racial segregation, abolishing the income tax, and suppressing labor unions.

Minute Women tended to be relatively affluent, the wives of professionals and businessmen, and sometimes members of other patriotic organizations and of parent-teacher associations. In this respect they were not unlike traditional women's clubs, but in structure and operation the Minute Women of the USA were the complete opposite of a traditional female voluntary association. Officers were not elected; instead, a council selected by Suzanne Stevenson chose all regional, state, and local chairwomen. The chapter chairwoman and her executive committee set meeting agendas, and no one was allowed to make a motion from the floor. (Stevenson justified this undemocratic structure as a precaution to keep Communists from infiltrating.) Unlike other women's associations, the Minute Women did not operate as a pressure group; members acted individually as watchdogs and protesters.

The Houston chapter, with five hundred members by 1952, was the largest and most active in the state. Established in 1951 by Eleanor Watt and Helen Darden Thomas, it was the city's most aggressive anti-Communist organization and one of the nation's leading and longest-lived Minute Women chapters. It was Helen Thomas who suggested to Suzanne Stevenson that states' rights should be added to the Minute Women's credo—many of the chapter's members had joined because they feared integration and "race mixing." Thomas was also the Houston chapter's primary information gatherer, digging through government documents and organizational membership lists for "subversives" for the group to accuse and attack. Thomas had a right-wing heritage; she was the daughter of Ida Muse Darden, who after years as a lobbyist and publicist for conservative causes, had recently established a right-wing monthly newspaper, *Southern Conservative*. Stevenson called Darden's caustic prose "brilliant," and Darden, who had been on the attack against progressives and feminists all her life, lauded the Minute Women as "a new and responsible type of womanhood that has stepped forward with a firm determination to retrieve feminine leadership from their bumbling, fumbling, and addle-brained sisters."[26]

Although the Houston Minute Women gathered an enormous membership, President Virginia Biggers and a core of about fifteen activists did most of the planning, and some two dozen others reliably shouldered the work of telephoning and letter writing that pressured local organizations into canceling visiting speakers with progressive or leftist views. Advocates of internationalism, the United Nations (supposedly Russian-dominated), and racial understanding were especially likely to be targeted. Helen Thomas even drafted a pamphlet denouncing the Quakers, whose American Friends Service Committee organized an annual Institute of International Relations in Houston; it closed after audience heckling by the Minute Women's allies in the American Legion. The women's most intense preoccupation was the public school system, a potential conduit of Communism to the young. Suspicious of progressive education, they criticized innovations such as social studies and pressed for a curriculum of "basics," including the teaching of heritage and patriotism. They examined textbooks for socialist influence, disrupted HISD board meetings, demanded investigations of teachers, and forced the firing of the deputy superintendent. Two Minute Women won election to the school board.

In addition to suppressing free speech, the Minute Women censored books. San Antonio had a large and active chapter, which included the mayor's wife. The group's president compiled a list of some six hundred books on a wide range of subjects that she claimed were written by Communist sympathizers—including Albert Einstein's *Relativity* and Louis Untermeyer's *Treasury of Great Poems*. She demanded that the volumes be stamped with a warning of the authors' Communist-front affiliations, a suggestion that the San Antonio City Council seriously debated. The state textbook committee succumbed to Minute Women pressure and recommended eliminating the United Nations' Universal Declaration of Human Rights and all discussion of it from world history textbooks. (The State Board of Education retained the declaration but removed the commentary.) The Minute Women's membership and influence declined by the mid-1950s as Senator McCarthy overreached and his reputation plummeted, but the organization persisted for the remainder of the decade.

WOMEN AND THE RISE OF THE REPUBLICAN PARTY

Although state politics continued to be dominated by the Democratic Party until the end of the 1970s, a viable GOP slowly emerged in the postwar decades. Texas Democrats were split into two factions: those who supported the national party's positions, and disgruntled conservatives who loathed the New Deal and FDR's embrace of bigger government, organized labor, and minorities. Some conservatives, such as Oveta Culp Hobby, the *Houston Post* publisher who chaired National Citizens for Eisenhower, stayed in the Democratic Party but supported Republican presidential candidates. (Ike rewarded Hobby by appointing her secretary of health, education, and welfare.) The most disaffected Democrats, who felt more affinity with the Republicans' opposition to taxes, the welfare state, and civil rights legislation, switched parties. As one woman summarized the attraction of Republicanism, "good government is less government—letting people find their own way and decide for themselves."[27] (Switching parties apparently came easier for women, who did not have to worry about alienating business contacts. In the 1952 election 59 percent of southern white women—but only 41 percent of southern white men—voted for Eisenhower.) Economic development also helped Republican prospects; the urban professional and managerial class and their wives, especially newcomers to the state, tended to lean toward the GOP.

Republican women did much of the work of building the GOP's voting strength at the grassroots. Middle-and upper-class housewives and mothers, they were motivated by Cold War anti-Communism and the conviction that women should be on the front lines in defending their communities. A Dallas activist who transferred her allegiance to the GOP summed up the rationale that moved many conservative women: "I thought, I don't want my kids to grow up in a socialist nation."[28] Such women found a home in the National Federation of Women's Republican Clubs, later renamed the Federation of Republican Women, which grew substantially in the postwar decades by reaching out to new constituencies—conservative "housewife activists" and southern women. Before the 1950s there were only a handful of Women's Republican Clubs in the South, but in the next half dozen years the numbers increased so substantially that statewide federations began to form. The clubs targeted "white, middle-class, civic-minded, patriotic, Protestant women," according to historian Catherine Rymph.[29] The national leadership encouraged Republican women to view political activism as a moral crusade, stressing Communism as a threat to religion (Communists were atheists) and a menace to democracy.

Women's Republican Clubs did the day-to-day menial labor essential to building the Texas GOP at the local level—one historian has called them the party's "organizational sinew."[30] Middle-class homemakers had the time to devote to party work and the willingness to undertake it as an investment in their families' futures. Women volunteers compiled the voter lists and did the precinct surveys, telephoning, and door-to-door canvassing. As new suburbs went up, Republican clubwomen were sometimes at work before the builders finished. In Dallas, Babs Johnson, with a child or two along in the car, was part of the corps: "We went up and down blocks to houses as they were built. We wrote down the house number, the streets. We covered our entire precinct that way so that the precinct chairman had a card file. When a person moved into that new house, we were assigned to call on the residents, find out their political persuasion, and ask for telephone numbers, because they weren't in the telephone books yet. Then, of course, our whole plan was to be able to persuade them to vote when the time came."[31]

In areas without precinct or county chairmen, the local Women's Republican Club was the de facto party organization (and often the impetus for establishing a county party). Women recruited other women through neighborliness and hospitality. "We were in a newly developed neighborhood in southwest Houston," Barbara Nowlin explained. "I had two small children. I held them by the hand, and we went door-to-door. I told the women in the neighborhood that I would like to start a Republican Women's Club. I invited them to come to my house on a particular night. The first meeting we had in the neighborhood thirty people attended. Soon it was fifty people, sixty people, and it just kept growing."[32] Suburban socializing built party networks and supplied Republican candidates with forums in which to meet voters. One of the first beneficiaries of women's labor was Bruce Alger, whose election to Congress in 1954 has been credited in large part to the Dallas Women's Republican Clubs. In addition to inviting neighbors for "Coffee with Bruce Alger" parties, the women passed out literature, yard signs, and bumper stickers in door-to-door canvases and manned phone banks at the candidate's headquarters. Alger, the first Texas Republican sent to Washington since the 1920s, considered the Republican clubwomen his most effective workers.

By 1955, with 64 clubs in nineteen congressional districts, Texas GOP women had met the National Federation of Women's Republican Clubs' criteria (at least one club in 75 percent of a state's congressional districts) for establishing a state federation. By the end of the year there were more than 2,000 members; a decade later membership reached 5,800 in 128 clubs.

Wherever the GOP ran candidates, women did the grassroots electioneering; candidates needed them in order to win. When John Tower, by the narrowest of margins, won a special election in 1961 to become the state's first Republican U.S. senator since Reconstruction, he credited women's work as crucial to his victory. Barbara Man, president of the Texas Federation of Republican Women in 1961–1962, was a mainstay. In addition to coffees and daily campaign work, Republican clubwomen got out the vote. Ruth Mankin described the election-night effort for Tower in her Houston precinct, the largest Republican-dominated one in the state: "We got in our cars and went door-to-door to all of the known Republican voters. We got people away from the bridge table. We got people out of the bath. We said you have got to come."[33] Similar efforts by women in North Dallas helped give Tower his 10,000-vote margin of victory. When he ran for reelection in 1966, he had in place a "Womanpower for Tower" organization that other GOP candidates subsequently adopted.

Doing the Republican Party's mundane "housekeeping" chores earned women male praise but not authority in the party hierarchy; women were county vice-chairs in charge of women's activities, not chairpersons. Barry Goldwater, however, acknowledged clubwomen's importance and made the most of their willingness to work, which enabled some to build recognition on the women's side of the party. Barbara Man was prominent in the Draft Goldwater movement and subsequently became southern regional director of his presidential campaign, responsible for eleven states. Rita Bass (Clements) directed the national door-to-door canvas for Goldwater, encouraging the state organizations to adopt the plan that the Texas Federation of Republican Women had developed for the Tower campaign. Man, Bass, and other TFRW leaders also received appointments as Republican national committeewomen for Texas. Personal satisfaction was the average clubwoman's reward. Winning elections was more important than achieving rank. "Our club did well and did what we wanted to achieve," Babs Johnson remembered. "We didn't really care who was at the top calling signals."[34]

LEGAL RIGHTS

Although no organized feminist movement existed in the two decades after World War II, individuals and groups chipped away at sex discrimination. The most blatant denial of political equality was the exclusion of women from jury service, which the former suffragists had tried without success to remedy as soon as they had the ballot. A sustained push for a constitutional amendment had begun in the late 1930s, led by Judge Sarah T. Hughes and the Texas chapter of the Federation of Business and Professional Women's Clubs (TBPW), a voluntary association founded after World War I. Hughes, who was acutely conscious of the irony that she could preside over a courtroom but not sit in a jury box, made jury service for women a personal crusade. The TBPW, affirming Hughes's contention that exclusion rendered women only half citizens, sponsored a jury service resolution in every session of the state legislature from 1939 until 1953.

In every essential feature the jury service campaign mirrored the suffrage battle decades earlier. Opponents made the same arguments that the anti-suffragists had used in the 1910s: women were too emotional to deliberate; they would neglect their homes and children; most didn't want to serve; some courtroom testimony was unfit for female ears. (The last objection was a variation on the old theme that politics was too dirty for women and the polls were no place for ladies.) Like the Texas Equal Suffrage Association, the TBPW did not succeed until it mobilized a broad coalition of women's groups behind the goal. In 1949, after a decade of trying, the TBPW lobbied a jury service amendment through the legislature, only to see it voted down in the required popular referendum. In the wake of this defeat, it revived a strategy used by earlier generations of reformers—the women's voluntary association coalition. The Texas Citizens' Committee on Jury Service for Women—composed of the TBPW, the League of Women Voters, the Federation of Women's Clubs, the Congress of Mothers and Parent-Teacher Associations, and the American Association of University Women—mounted the same kind of campaign that had won so many victories for organized women in the Progressive Era: public education on the issue, combined with intense legislative lobbying. They pushed a new bill through the 1953 legislative session and then spearheaded a successful drive to promote the amendment to the public, which approved it by a comfortable margin in 1954.

Texas was one of the last states to concede jury duty for women and joined the majority that made it mandatory for women on the same terms as men, rather than optional. (Twenty states had voluntary laws, permitting but not requiring women to serve.) The defeated opposition denounced the jury service law in language that echoed the diatribes of suffrage opponents thirty-five years earlier. Letters to the *Dallas Morning News* lamented that the government was on a "downhill cycle" toward "a modern Dark Age," and pronounced the amendment "the worst ever put into our State Constitution." With gloomy satisfaction one male opponent predicted that "the women who voted for it will get a real dose of it the first time they are tied up a week or two on a criminal case."[35] Like the suffrage amendment before it, the jury service law disproportionately benefited middle-class white women; the jury pool was drawn from women who paid poll and property taxes.

In another significant challenge to sex discrimination, women renewed their long-standing demand for admission to Texas A&M College. Early in the century a small number of women had been "unofficial" students, taking courses but not eligible to pursue a degree. In 1925, after Mary Evelyn Crawford, to her own surprise, somehow managed to complete all the requirements for a B.A. and was awarded a diploma, the board of directors made exclusion of women an official policy. Thereafter, women were permitted to attend only summer sessions (a legislative requirement) until 1933–1934, when a one-year exemption was granted for the daughters of faculty, who were suffering from Depression-induced salary cuts and wanted relief from the financial burden of sending female children away to college. Seeing an opportunity, a group of local women immediately filed suit to gain admission but lost. They did not appeal, and the pressure to overturn the discriminatory policy subsided for twenty years.

By the 1950s it was evident that excluding women was hindering A&M's growth. In rejecting female students, the college also lost males who preferred coeducational institutions or were married and chose universities that would also admit their wives. The faculty favored admitting women, but the president, the board of directors, and most of the student body were opposed. In 1958, after a *Bryan Eagle* editorial in favor of coeducation was picked up by newspapers across the state, local women again protested their exclusion. Myrna Gray, a local nurse two semesters short of a degree in biology, and community college students Lena Ann Bristol and Barbara Gilkey Tittle, applied for admission and were refused. Because all three were married and Bristol and Tittle had children, attending college outside Bryan–College Station was a hardship—Bristol was commuting 130 miles to Sam Houston State three times a week. Bristol and Tittle filed suit, claiming denial of equal protection of the law, a violation of the Fourteenth Amendment, and won in district court. The judge, an A&M graduate, was hanged in effigy and received so many threatening telephone calls that he requested police protection for his home.

The decision was reversed on appeal, and the women lost further appeals to the Texas and U.S. Supreme Courts. In 1959 three other women, two of whom desired to major in fields offered only at A&M, filed a class action suit, which also went all the way to the U.S. Supreme Court—in vain. Within a few years, however, stagnant enrollment and concern for the college's future prompted internal action. Under a new president, A&M undertook an evaluation and a long-range planning study that undermined sex discrimination by degrees. In 1963 women were admitted to the graduate and veterinary medicine programs and, on a limited basis, to undergraduate study. The Corps of Cadets vehemently opposed women on campus, and the Committee for an All-Male Military Texas A&M staged a protest at the state capitol, chanting "We want Aggies, not Maggies." By the spring of 1965, however, 321 women were enrolled (up from 15 in 1963). That year the board of directors authorized the president to use his discretion in admitting women. By the end of the decade, they were being admitted on an equal basis with men, although the university did not adopt an official coeducation policy until 1971. The Corps of Cadets continued to exclude women until 1974.

Although permitted to enroll, women were not made welcome. The university did not provide housing, health services, or even an adequate number of restrooms for female students. Dispersed throughout College Station and excluded from most campus activities, women remained few in number—it took a decade for them to reach 25 percent of the student body. Although nearly two-thirds of male students polled in 1965 approved coeducation, intransigent opponents organized protests and hanged a woman in effigy. One of the first class of women remembered getting threatening phone calls and letters. Those who in 1969 filled out a survey describing their campus experience still noted being treated as outsiders. Coeducation at A&M generated more protest and hostility than racial integration, which had met little resistance.

While it is easy to portray the post–World War II years as an era of conservatism and confinement—a time when home-focused wives did housework wearing makeup and high heels—the reality is more complex. The white, middle-class, suburban women of 1950s television were only one segment of the population and not even the broadest one. For every Ann Richards wondering what she was missing while she ironed shirts and refereed children's squabbles, there was a Mary Salinas organizing blue-collar women to demand wage and gender equity and a Juanita Craft crusading to end racial discrimination. The sitcom image of domestic womanhood notwithstanding, these two decades were a time of significant social change. Increasing numbers of white, married women worked for wages. Minority women challenged the racial status quo with demonstrations and lawsuits, while conservative white women emerged as grassroots activists and built the foundation for a two-party Texas. Voluntarist women brought an end to all-male juries, and college women sued for admission to Texas A&M. Within this varied activism a new consciousness gradually emerged. Women in the workplace began to question the sex segregation of jobs and to file wage-discrimination complaints, political activists to consider running for office themselves, and wives to wonder why they needed a husband's signature to apply for a credit card. By the late 1960s a resurgent feminist movement would address these issues and many more.

SUGGESTED REFERENCES

LABOR

While there is no history of Texas telephone workers, John N. Schacht's *The Making of Telephone Unionism, 1920–1947* (New Brunswick, N.J.: Rutgers University Press, 1985), is a thorough treatment of the 1947 strike; both Schacht and Thomas R. Brooks, *Communications Workers of America: The Story of a Union* (New York: Mason/Charter, 1977), quote Nelle Wooding's oral history. On meatpackers, see Roger Horowitz, *"Negro and White, Unite and Fight!" A Social History of Industrial Meatpacking, 1930–90* (Urbana: University of Illinois Press, 1997). More detail on Texas is available in Rick Halpern, "Interracial Unionism in the Southwest: Fort Worth's Packinghouse Workers, 1937–1954," in *Organized Labor in the Twentieth-Century South*, ed. Robert Zieger (Nashville: University of Tennessee Press, 1991), and Moses Adedeji, "The Stormy Past: A History of the United Packinghouse Workers of America–CIO, Fort Worth, Texas" (M.A. thesis, University of Texas at Arlington, 1975). Dennis A. Deslippe, *"Rights, Not Roses": Unions and the Rise of Working-Class Feminism, 1945–80* (Urbana: University of Illinois Press, 2000), is a study of labor feminism that includes packinghouse workers. The most detailed analysis of the Tex-Son strike is Toni Marie Nelson Herrera, "Constructed and Contested Meanings of the Tex-Son Strike in San Antonio, Texas, 1959: Representing Mexican Women Workers" (M.A. thesis, University of Texas at Austin, 1997). See also George N. Green, "ILGWU in Texas, 1930–1970," *Journal of Mexican American History* 1 (1971), and Irene Ledesma, "Texas Newspapers and Chicana Workers' Activism," *Journal of Western History* 26:3 (1995).

CIVIL RIGHTS

Guadalupe San Miguel Jr.'s *"Let All of Them Take Heed": Mexican Americans and the Campaign for Educational Equality in Texas, 1910–1981* (Austin: University of Texas Press, 1987), is definitive on the Hispanic struggle for integrated schools, as is Patrick J. Carroll, *Felix Longoria's Wake: Bereavement, Racism, and the Rise of Mexican American Activism* (Austin: University of Texas Press, 2003), on Beatrice Longoria's struggle to have her husband buried with honor. Cynthia E. Orozco, *No Mexicans, Women, or Dogs Allowed: The Rise of the Mexican American Civil Rights Movement* (Austin: University of Texas Press, 2009), is definitive on LULAC and women. Michael Lowery Gillette,

"The NAACP in Texas, 1937–1957" (Ph.D. diss., University of Texas at Austin, 1984), documents the work of Lulu B. White, Juanita Craft, and Christia Adair in building the organization. For overviews of the period, see Stefanie Decker, "African American Women in the Civil Rights Era, 1954–1974," in *Black Women in Texas History*, ed. Bruce A. Glasrud and Merline Pitre (College Station: Texas A&M University Press, 2008), and Ruthe Winegarten, *Black Texas Women: 150 Years of Trial and Triumph* (Austin: University of Texas Press, 1994). Biographical treatments include Merline Pitre, *In Struggle against Jim Crow: Lulu B. White and the NAACP, 1900–1957* (College Station: Texas A&M University Press, 1999), and Pitre, "Lulu B. White and the Civil Rights Movement in Houston, Texas, 1939–1957," in *Invisible Texans: Women and Minorities in Texas History*, ed. Donald Willett and Stephen Curley (Boston: McGraw Hill, 2005); Stephanie Lee Gillam, "Mama, Activist, and Friend: African American Women in the Civil Rights Movement in Dallas, Texas" (M.A. thesis, Texas Christian University, 1995); Rachel Northington Burrow, "Juanita Craft" (M.A. thesis, Southern Methodist University, 1994); and Burrow, "Juanita Craft: Desegregating the State Fair of Texas," *Legacies* 16:1 (Spring 2005). Lewis L. Gould and Melissa R. Sneed, "Without Pride or Apology: The University of Texas at Austin, Racial Integration, and the Barbara Smith Case," *Southwestern Historical Quarterly* 103:1 (July 1999), and Dwanna Goldstone, *Integrating the 40 Acres: The Fifty-Year Struggle for Racial Equality at the University of Texas* (Athens: University of Georgia Press, 2000), cover the barring of Smith from a student opera production. On Casey Hayden, see Doug Rossinow, *The Politics of Authenticity: Liberalism, Christianity, and the New Left in America* (New York: Columbia University Press, 1998), which focuses on Austin, and Martin Kuhlman, "Direct Action at the University of Texas during the Civil Rights Movement, 1960–65," in *The African American Experience in Texas: An Anthology*, ed. Bruce A. Glasrud and James M. Smallwood (Lubbock: Texas Tech University Press, 2007). Anna Victoria Wilson and William E. Seagall, *Oh! Do I Remember: Experiences of Teachers during the Desegregation of Austin's Schools, 1964–1971* (Albany: State University of New York Press, 2001), includes oral histories from women teachers.

CONSERVATISM

The role of the Minute Women in McCarthy-era politics is thoroughly discussed in Don Carleton, *Red Scare! Right-wing Hysteria, Fifties Fanaticism, and Their Legacy in Texas* (Austin: Texas Monthly Press, 1985). On Ida Darden, see Elna C. Green, "From Antisuffragism to Anti-Communism: The Conservative Career of Ida M. Darden," *Journal of Southern History* 65:2 (May 1999). Kristi Throne Strickland, "The Significance and Impact of Women on the Rise of the Republican Party in Twentieth-Century Texas" (Ph.D. diss., University of North Texas, 2000), documents the Texas Federation of Women's Republican Clubs.

LEGAL RIGHTS

Sarah T. Hughes supplies a firsthand account of the effort to secure the right of jury service for women in "Now I Can Throw Away That Speech," *Independent Woman* 34 (February 1955). On the fight for coeducation at Texas A&M, see Heidi Ann Knippa, "Salvation of a University: The Admission of Women to Texas A&M" (M.A. thesis, University of Texas at Austin, 1995), and Christopher Bean, "'We Want Aggies, Not Maggies': James Earl Rudder and the Coeducation of Texas A&M University," *East Texas Historical Journal* 44:2 (2006).

DOCUMENTS

3.1. NELLE WOODING LEADS THE 1947 TELEPHONE
WORKERS STRIKE IN DALLAS

Nelle Wooding spent forty-seven years as a telephone worker, beginning as a student operator in Dallas in 1914 and retiring in 1961 as a field representative for the Communications Workers of America, CIO. In 1937 she helped organize the Dallas local of the Southwestern Federation of Telephone Workers and was elected president. When the National Federation of Telephone Workers called a strike in 1947, Wooding, as chair of the northeastern division of Texas, led the walkout in Dallas. Although the telephone workers were ultimately forced to settle for a much smaller wage increase than they had demanded, the strike had other benefits. "It helped the union to grow up," Wooding asserted in her oral memoir. "It helped us to gain prestige in the eyes of both the company and the other unions. They saw that we'd had our baptism in fire, and we had more respect from them."

In 1947 we went out. And very naively, we in traffic [switchboard operation] thought they could not get along without us. We had dial service locally in Dallas at that time, a hundred percent, but toll was still manual, and that was, of course, the revenue bearing place and much the largest office. . . . So that toll traffic chairman and myself, I well remember standing out on Akard Street in front of the downtown building consoling each other, and we said, "Well, it couldn't last over forty-eight hours. They just couldn't possibly operate that board without us." But they did. Of course, they brought in people. As I said, our girls, bless their hearts, didn't go in. We were pretty nearly a hundred percent organized.

The people who worked on the switchboards—of course, they had as many management men as they could get, but that was limited. But as the work decreased in commercial and accounting, their departments were not well organized and many of those people did work, but as their work drained off because of the business shortage, they were told they'd either have to go down and work on the switchboards or be dismissed. Well, most of them went down and worked on switchboards. They didn't know anything about it. They had to be taught. They couldn't half do it, but they at least filled up a chair.

We stayed out for six weeks. We had no defense fund. We scrounged around every way under the sun. I don't remember now where we got the money. Finally somebody went to the AFL [American Federation of Labor] locals and they contributed some. . . .

The employees who had some other wage earner in their family and were not as hard up as some of the people—every day we had food at least at noon. They would bake cakes and pies, and cook hams and roast chickens, and make salad and all this and that, and people that were hurting most were the young girls who were living away from home and had to pay room and board. And that one meal a day at the union headquarters was about all the meal they had. We didn't have much money to give them. We tried to take care of real hardship cases. After we'd been out on strike several weeks, we did see one girl go in, one of my girls, so we called her that night, and her story was really pathetic. She was a widow. She lived with her sister. She and her sister both worked for the company and were both out on strike. The one in my local had two children. They had cut her water off. They'd cut her lights off, because she hadn't been able to pay her bill. She said, "I *had* to go to work to feed my children." So we didn't have any bitterness toward her, but we got enough money to get her utilities paid and see that she had food, and she came out again. She only worked about two days. You don't resent people when they're in that kind of trouble, and they'll respond when you help them. We just didn't have the means to help people like we wanted to, so there was a tremendous amount of individual sacrifice and effort made. And that's why I think it's commendable and really quite remarkable that such a large majority of them did honor the picket lines for the six weeks.

During the 1947 strike they used in toll, among other people, the engineers and various management people who were technically familiar with the equipment. But it takes experience to get the speed and skill of operating the switchboard. And we had many businessmen as customers. . . . The businessman would get the long distance operator on the line and say, "Operator, I want to call a list," and he'd give the names of anywhere from one to a dozen people in various towns that he wanted to talk with. They didn't usually give the number in those days; the operator had to call the distant town and get the number. So when the strike was over and one of our good members went back to work, she got a customer that she had often served. When he recognized her voice he said, "Operator, I do thank God you're back." He said, "I have certainly missed you. I have not gotten good service while you were gone," because those group calls just baffled those inexperienced engineers. They were technicians, but they weren't switchboard operators.

It was on a Saturday [that the strike ended], and very few people except the traffic would be working, so most of them just went on fishing for the rest of the day—whatever you wanted to do. But the traffic people, which was in my local, of course, went back to work. I said—or maybe it was their idea—they said, "We went out together. Let's go in together." And I said, "All right." So we were all out there at that one big place. We had to get cabs and this and that, those that didn't have private cars, and get back to the main telephone building over here on Akard—it's still there. And we just waited outside until they had all come. The general traffic superintendent was quite disturbed about the whole business and he came down and very haughtily said to me, "Well, are you people going in or not?" I said, "We're going in when we all get here." I said, "We went out together. We'll go in together." And we did. And we had passed the word around so when we went into the building, we began singing "Solidarity Forever" at the top of our voices. Well, the management was disgusted beyond words. The operating room was on the sixth floor; we had to take the elevators. And there was some little elevator girl who worked during the strike, and I'll never forget the look on that girl's face. There's only one working on Saturday. When she opened the door, and there was this mob of people singing "Solidarity Forever" she was frightened to death. I guess she thought we were going to mob her or something. We didn't, but we went up.

We stayed in the hall upstairs. We didn't go in the operating room until everybody got up there. Then when they were finally there and the chief operator, bless her heart, and she was our friend and she was just as nervous—her hands were just trembling—she was trying to assign the girls' positions. "You go here and you go there." Well, the board was manned with people that had worked and I said, "You get those girls off the board and mine will go in." I said, "There's a lot of strong feelings against those people who have taken their jobs for six weeks. I can't be responsible if you force those girls to go in there." And see, on each operating position, there's a double set of jacks. The girls have to wear headsets and they've got a cord that they plug in. The operators that were there were already plugged in. The girl relieving her would have to plug in right beside her. Of course, probably nothing too serious would have happened, but some of them were very upset. I said, "You get those scabs out of here, and those operators will go back to work." . . .

Of course, I wasn't going to work. I was a clerk and I didn't have to work that day. . . . So, I didn't have to go back to the board and I took my stand at the door by the set rack. The girls that had been on the board during the strike came out, wrapped their headsets, put them up, and went out the door. And I stood there with my arms folded just, I guess, glaring at every one of them. I didn't say a word. I just gave them good, hard looks so I'd recognize them if nothing else. So one of them, I understand, went out and cried and said I looked at her so mean. But that didn't hurt my conscience a bit.

Source: Nelle Wooding, Communications Workers of America, interview by John Schacht, 1978, University of Iowa Oral History Project, Archives of Labor and Urban Affairs, Wayne State University.

3.2. CEIL CLEVELAND BECOMES A TEENAGE BRIDE IN THE FIFTIES

Ceil Cleveland grew up in the small plains town of Archer City, which Larry McMurtry called Thalia when he used it as a setting for his novel *The Last Picture Show*. Many people thought Cleveland was the model for Jacy Farrow, the high school queen who was one of the novel's principal characters. College failed to hold Cleveland's interest: feeling purposeless and dissatisfied, she dropped out of North Texas State College (now the University of North Texas) at the end of her freshman year. She drifted into marriage with a man she had casually dated, because the culture expected nothing more of women, and at eighteen she couldn't imagine an alternative. Like nearly half of American women in the 1950s, she married while still a teenager and became part of the one-third who had their first child before the age of twenty.

One night on a date with the teacher, after seeing a picture show about the circus with Gina Lollobrigida flying on a high trapeze looking so free and happy in her little pink tights and curly black hair, which just made me feel sad and empty, we were driving home, and Greg said, "Look, the moon is on fire!"

I told him, "Don't be silly; it's just an old shed burning," and we alerted the firehouse. Standing by the car watching the fire, Greg told me that he liked to think the moon was really on fire, and that he wanted me to marry him—a declaration that astonished me, for I had no idea of marrying anyone for years, let alone someone in Thalia. But he was several years older than I, so I sputtered, "Not now, I mean I don't know, I mean I don't know what I mean . . ." I was so miserable what I basically wanted to do was cry, or just plain whine.

But Greg said sternly: "What kind of answer is that? I thought I'd get a better reply out of the only girl I ever asked to marry me!"

I felt just awful to have hurt his feelings, and the tone of his voice sounded a lot like Daddy's, so I muttered that I'd think about it. From then on, Greg considered it settled and went off and bought a ring. When he gave it to me a few weeks later during dinner at a steak house in Wichita, I put it on, upholding in that act my unbroken record of doing exactly what every man, from father to teacher, had told me to do. . . .

The next few months were surreal. I'd never thought it would come to this. I thought Mother would beg me not to marry, or that Daddy would forbid it. All the protective mechanisms I'd depended on for eighteen years were crumbling. Mother and Daddy had never let me take such a drastic step by myself before. I called my grandmother as a last resort, hoping she would tell me not to do this. She said, helpfully: "Marriage is very difficult, dear, but then, so are all relationships. However, in whatever circumstance one finds oneself, one must learn to be content."

Confused, I threw myself into plans for dresses, and cakes, and teas, and parties. At a shower, someone brought me a white organdy apron with purple flowers on it placed in the outline of a woman's pelvis and ovaries. Everyone laughed, but I was horrified. I hated aprons, and, for some unaccountable reason, this one in particular made me shudder.

It was not until many years later that my mother confided in a letter to me that she shared my repugnance for aprons, since they were, she wrote, "the symbol of the kitchen's defining women's lives." She'd never said so before, "because I guess I was afraid it would sound 'unpatriotic.'" . . .

The week before my wedding I would awaken in the middle of the night and murmur, "Why am I doing this? What will happen to me now? What will I do after this?" I had no idea. Picture shows always *ended* with weddings. They never *started* there except for one—*The Father of the Bride*—and that was a picture show about the *father*, not the *bride*.

When I went to my mother asking "What do brides do for the rest of their lives?" she gave a short laugh and said, "You'll find out soon enough," but even then I noticed a sadness in her eyes. I remembered some questions that Jo March had asked her mother in *Little Women*. I looked them up and tried them. "Mother, do you feel, like Mrs. March says, that you are angry every day of your life, but you try hard not to show it?" She looked thoughtful: "No, I am not angry every day. I have everything a woman could want. I just learned many years ago what was appropriate for a woman to want. I love my children very much, so I've chosen to decide not to want any more than that."

. . . I half wish my mother, for all her smarts, had been less supportive and more brusque, like the mother of a Thalia girl you may have read about who told her daughter pretty much the truth: Life is monotonous, and marriage often makes it more so; living in the Texas plains is too damn hard, where the land has so much power over you; there's nothing to do there but spend money, so you have to be rich even to go insane in Thalia; and a girl ought to go out and have a little fun and find out that boys aren't the magic creatures they're cracked up to be *before* she settles down with one of them.

But that would have made mine a different kind of mother. So I, like millions of girls before me, was offered up in an ancient tribal rite, by good women, kind women, loving women, even by women who didn't much believe in those rites anymore but found the truth too harsh and could not imagine any other way for a woman to live.

Source: Ceil Cleveland, *Whatever Happened to Jacy Farrow?* (Denton: University of North Texas Press, 1997).

3.3. MARÍA ELENA LUCAS WORKS AS A MIGRANT LABORER WITH HER FAMILY

María Elena Lucas was born in Brownsville in 1941, the eldest of seventeen children in a family that struggled to put food on the table. Every year they trekked to the Midwest to work in the vegetable fields. In an era when restaurants and gas station restrooms displayed "No Mexicans" signs, they were both necessary and unwelcome. Trapped in a cycle of poverty and migration, the children of such families more often than not had to give up on school. María Elena dropped out after a few grades and married at fourteen. She had seven children, laboring in the fields while pregnant and nursing, and later worked as an organizer for the Farm Labor Organizing Committee. In addition to the oral history excerpted below, there is also an autobiography, *Forged under the Sun/Forjada bajo el sol: The Life of María Elena Lucas*, edited by Fran Leeper Buss (University of Michigan Press, 1993).

We were a big family; my mother had seventeen babies and I was the oldest, so I began working right away. One of the first things I remember was the shrimp basin, standing up on a big wooden crate, competing with grown-ups on how to learn to do the job. About every day I would go with my daddy and mom to the water port, and the big boats that carry shrimp would come to the docks. I think it must have been before I even went to school, when I was under five. I was very little so they would have to put a big wooden box for me to stand on, and they taught me how to take the head off the shrimp. The head would go to the bucket; the body would go out to the stream of water. I would do this mostly during the night. This way I could help to provide food.

After that my daddy started taking us up North, to work the crops. We went mostly to Michigan, Wisconsin, Ohio, but we went also to Arkansas, to Indiana, and as far as Montana. Around Idaho, South Dakota, North Dakota, we were working in sugar beets and potatoes. . . .

Life was hard because Mom kept having kids all the time. It was bad because I was the oldest so I had to take care of them. I would have to do the watching mostly, and the dishwashing, washing clothes, and cleaning house, and taking care of children, and going to school. Going to school wasn't easy because I had to walk about six miles from where we lived clear across town, and we had no shoes and no sweaters during the wintertime when it was getting cold. My brother was the same. All the older ones had to go through the same thing; they were also raised the same way. I remember that all the time we would hit the garbage cans, raid the garbage cans in the neighborhoods and just pick up anything we could.

. . . But it was difficult 'cause every time we went up North, it got harder. I guess you've been told before about the discrimination. You weren't allowed to go into a place or to restrooms. . . . I didn't understand why I was told to go where the blacks were. I didn't understand why we had to sleep in a tent sometimes and cook outside. I didn't understand a lot of things, when I could see that a lot of other people had places to eat. It was especially hard to sleep outdoors with army blankets. My daddy would sleep inside the car, just sitting down to keep an eye on us. Sometimes he would just lay across the hood with a pillow while Mom and all of us kids would sleep on the side of the road, 'cause if we went to a public park we would get run out of there. We would stop in a little stream to wash our dishes and to wash up.

. . . We worked all the time when we were doing the crops. We would work the fields and get to the house and do the housework. We lived in cabins often about the size of a small room. Sometimes there was bunk beds and some of us slept in them and the rest on the floor, and sometimes there was a little table, a stove, and a bench. I remember that we used chicken coops, with three walls and then an open place. Then I remember also just being out in the open in Texas when we were working in straw you make brooms out of.

. . . My neck would hurt a lot and I was just a little girl. I can imagine how Mommy felt, being so many years older and pregnant so much and doing stoop labor. We would hoe with hoes with that short handle, so we were bent over all the time. The reason they used a short handle was to make sure that we were doing the job. If they looked out across the field and saw that we were standing straight up, they thought that meant we weren't working. . . .

When we were working up North we had cans of Carnation and Pet milk. We'd empty those out and make a slit in the can to save dimes in. Every week my daddy would give us the change in dimes. He'd say, "This is for when we get to Texas to buy you clothing and the supplies for school." So we would put our dimes in there. But when we got to Texas there was never enough. We could only get one pencil and one writing notebook and then a pair of shoes and two pairs of socks, and I don't remember getting any dresses, but maybe panties. Then my shoes wore out and I would go to school barefooted. My mom was always trying to get clothes, used clothes. Sometimes when I was barefoot, I wouldn't go to school.

. . . Also, school was hard 'cause I always would be taken out of school to work the fields three months before school was out, and I remember going back to school three months late all the time, so I didn't get much school and I was very, very dumb. I just never could learn and I only went to sixth grade. I grew and then, when I was fourteen, I met my first husband. I met him overnight in the government housing project where we were living. He was living right next door. There was a big screen on the outside with movies, and I was sitting down on his porch with his sister and she went in and he came out. He just sat next to me, and, all of a sudden, told me, "Will you marry me?"

And I said, "Yes." That's how it was. Then he kissed me and said, "Are you sure you'll marry me?" and I said, "Yes," again. So I think it must have been about three days later that he went to Ohio. I had an aunt and I told her that he was going to write me, and she would go and get the mail so my daddy wouldn't get to it, because if he would get to it that was the end of me probably. In every letter my future husband would ask me, "Will you still marry me?" And I answered back and I said, "Yes." So when he got back, I guess about a month later, I married him. It was sad, because what I was trying to do was get away. That was what I was trying to do. I don't think that I even loved him when I married him. I was only fourteen and it was just out of desperation.

Source: Fran Leeper Buss, *Dignity: Lower Income Women Tell of Their Lives and Struggles* (Ann Arbor: University of Michigan Press, 1985).

3.4. AURORA OROZCO FIGHTS FOR HER FAMILY'S RIGHTS IN CUERO

Aurora Orozco was born in Mexico in 1917 and grew up in Mercedes, a town in the Rio Grande Valley, where Anglos were a minority. When she moved to Cuero in DeWitt County after her marriage, she encountered an Anglo-dominated triracial society. In the entry below, she confronts a bank manager for the rights "*de mi familia*" (of my family)—a significant phrase, for Mexican culture restricted women's public voices to the defense of family and community. While raising six children, Orozco helped found several Hispanic civic associations, including a LULAC chapter.

When we came to Cuero during the 1950s, we noticed that the Jim Crow laws were present everywhere. The Mexican neighborhood was about two blocks from downtown. Most of the houses where poor whites lived were run-down. My husband's boss had to recommend us so we could rent a run-down house. There were signs that said "No Blacks, no Mexicans" in doctors' offices, restaurants, hospitals, and swimming pools. Like colored people, Mexicans had their place. In the hospital, the basement was for blacks and Mexicans. In restaurants, Mexicans were forced to eat in the kitchen. There were Catholic and Baptist churches for Mexicans on the west side of town.

We noticed that most Mexicans who lived in Cuero felt inferior to the Anglos because they didn't have any rights. They had to go to their boss and ask for a recommendation so they could rent or buy a house, furniture, or a car. The merchants perceived that all Mexicans were dirty, drunks, and thieves. There was an apartment house near where I lived. I decided to go and try to rent an apartment, but the owner told me they didn't rent to Mexicans. . . .

I remember that after a few weeks in Cuero, we decided to go to the movie theater. We went in and sat on the right side and enjoyed the movie. When we came home, a friend asked, "Where did you sit?" I told her, and she said, "It's a wonder that you were not asked to move." I asked why. "Because that side is for whites, the left side is for Mexicans, and the balcony is for blacks," she said. I told her, "I wouldn't move. My money is as good as any white person's."

You had to fight for your rights in Cuero, Texas. I decided to fight for the rights "*de mi familia*" when I went to the Buchel Bank to ask for a loan of $125.00. My husband's boss had already spoken to the banker, Mr. Henderson, so I went to his office and talked to him. He didn't seem very friendly. When I finished speaking, he waited a while, then said, "I don't want to lend you any money. You Mexicans and blacks never pay it back. If you ask a black or Mexican the whereabouts of these people, they never know. You all are deadbeats, drunks, and thieves." I felt insulted, so I stood up and said, "You cannot say that about my race, you don't know. We have all kinds of people, just like in your race. We are not all the same. It's a shame you advertise in the newspaper about your loans. Why don't you say it's not for Mexicans and blacks?" He stood up and said, "No one has spoken to me like that." I answered, "Maybe I am the one who had to tell you." I left and walked to the shop where my husband worked. At that moment, the phone was ringing. Mr. Bohne, my husband's boss, answered and said, "It's Mr. Henderson. He wants you to return to the bank." Mr. Bohne asked what happened. I told him the story, and he told me that everyone complained about Mr. Henderson. So I went back to the bank and Mr. Henderson let me have $125.00. I repaid the loan, and after that he was very friendly. I still have an account with the bank.

My husband didn't get mad. I was the one who spoke better English and took care of business matters. After the incident at the bank, some people asked me if I wasn't scared. I said, "No, it's for the Mexicans in Cuero. We have to fight for our rights."

Source: Aurora E. Orozco, "Mexican Blood Runs through My Veins," in D. Letticia Galindo and Maria Dolores Gonzales, eds., *Speaking Chicana: Voice, Power, and Identity* (Tucson: University of Arizona Press, 1999).

3.5. CASEY HAYDEN BECOMES A CAMPUS CIVIL RIGHTS ACTIVIST

Sandra Cason, known as Casey, grew up in Victoria and graduated from the University of Texas at Austin, where she was a leader in the campus civil rights movement. Her speech at the National Student Association's conference in Minneapolis in 1960, urging support for the southern sit-ins, drew Tom Hayden into the civil rights movement, and after their marriage in Austin in 1961, both became active in Students for a Democratic Society (SDS). Casey Hayden's most passionate commitment was to the Student Nonviolent Coordinating Committee (SNCC), which formed to organize the thousands of African American students who began staging sit-ins across the South in 1960 to desegregate public eating places. Hayden became one of the most prominent white women in the organization. In 1964 she and fellow SNCC member Mary King wrote "Sex and Caste: A Kind of Memo," a discussion paper that noted the parallels between the repression of African Americans and the subordination of women; it has since come to be regarded as one of the first manifestos of the 1960s feminist movement. In the selection below, Hayden describes how she discovered the civil rights movement through the Student YWCA and the Christian Faith and Life Community at the University of Texas.

The unfolding of my childhood toward the Southern Freedom Movement commences at the University of Texas in Austin, which I entered as a junior in 1957. . . . I found the YWCA early on, looking for community in this big, urban university setting. Here I met black students and entered campus politics, becoming a regional and national officer, chairing a large study group on "Peace and Disarmament" at the Y's national meeting in 1959. The other study groups were "The World of Work," "Race Relations," and "The Changing Roles of Men and Women." Here I learned the term "Student Christian Movement," sometimes shortened to "student movement," long before there was one.

 . . . Through the Y, I was grounded in a democratic manner of work, exposed to and educated about race, and a participant in direct action—though not in civil disobedience—by the time the sit-ins exploded the racial status quo of the country in 1960. The staff person at the Y, Rosalie Oakes, was my role model then, the first of the many women of the Y who inspired me in the years that followed. She was smart, well-informed, understanding, gentle, tough, and skillful, as were they all.

Through the YWCA I went to New York City the summer of 1959, after my senior year, to teach vacation Bible school at the East Harlem Protestant Parish (EHPP), the second of the institutions that funneled me into radical politics. This parish, meeting in a collection of storefronts and an old church building, was formed by middle-class ministers moving into a community of color and poverty. Letty Russell, one of the ministers there, was the first female I'd known in that position. Preaching on Sundays, she enlarged my sense of possibilities. I lived on East 103rd street, reputedly the worst block in the city, where I waded through broken glass over the tops of my shoes, a blonde in pastel ruffled cotton frocks. Rats in the walls kept me awake at night. The EHPP was my introduction to voluntary poverty.

When the sit-ins broke out across the South in the spring of 1960, I was back in Austin in graduate school. The national president of the student YWCA was a black student at Bishop College in Marshall, Texas, where police had used tear gas to break up a march. We brought her to speak at the Y just after she had been released from jail. She was a small person, and as she talked she was very quiet and dark. I remember sweating and crying in the packed little auditorium. After that I went to the meetings of the Austin Movement with the black women who lived across the hall from me in the only integrated housing on campus, the Christian Faith and Life Community (CF&LC), known by us as simply as "the Community"—the third of the life-changing religious organizations of my college years. Here I roomed with Dorothy Dawson, my oldest friend.

Calling itself a lay training center, the Community was established and staffed by ministers who had been through World War II, an event that, speaking conservatively, had challenged their beliefs. I learned at the Community to reject the absolute constructs and abstractions of civilization, following the lead of the existentialists. I learned to believe my own experience and join others to create meaning through intentional living. Intentional living was supported by honesty and, through covenant, a promise to be present and accountable to each other. At the CF&LC I experienced the creation of empowering community, and, within it an image of myself, in terms of which I then lived. Later, I understood the movement on this model. Our image of ourselves in the Southern Freedom Movement was that of the Beloved Community, created by the activity, the experience, of nonviolent direct action against injustice.

In the Community, as in the Y, all leadership slots were dual, co-chaired by a man and a woman. My politics and expectations were shaped by nonsexist institutions, where I met the black students who now came forward to claim their own lives and destiny. It was critical to my future that I had a few black friends and was loyal to them. I read Thoreau on civil disobedience during this time, read it deeply. My clearest memory of this spring of 1960 is picketing on Congress Avenue in a yellow dress and high-heeled white pumps.

Later I came to the movement's center, the Student Nonviolent Coordinating Committee (SNCC), which was composed of representatives of each local sit-in group. I reached SNCC through the Southern Student Human Relations Seminar, sponsored by the United States National Student Association (NSA). Connie Curry came through Austin recruiting for her seminar and telling the story of the Nashville sit-ins.[1] When we sat together in a little restaurant on the Drag and allowed that story to open our hearts, a new life began for me.

Source: Casey Hayden, "Fields of Blue," in Constance Curry et al., *Deep in Our Hearts: Nine White Women in the Civil Rights Movement* (Athens: University of Georgia Press, 2000).

3.6. DOROTHY DAWSON CROSSES THE COLOR LINE IN A CHEVROLET BEL AIR

Dorothy Dawson Burlage was born in San Antonio to a conservative family with deep roots in East Texas. As a child she learned the rules that decreed social distance between whites and blacks. The most rigid, "no physical contact was allowed between black men and white girls," precluded even trailing after the handyman on "adventures" at the family's country home unless her brother was along. Reared to be a proper southern lady, deferential and polite, she was also trained not to discuss race, religion, or politics in public. When Dawson transferred from Mary Baldwin College, an elite Virginia institution for southern girls, to the University of Texas, which was in the throes of desegregating, her life permanently changed direction. Discovering the student Christian movement, she learned to speak out against segregation, but not without feeling guilty for rejecting her upbringing and embarrassing her family.

In the fall of 1956, I transferred to the University of Texas (UT) in Austin, a liberal oasis in the state. It was expected that I, like other college girls, would find a mate and settle down in Texas, but during my years at UT I became an activist about segregation, a development that initiated a transformation in my identity as a southern woman. I had been raised with the expectation that I would be a southern lady—well mannered, never involved in political discussion or controversy, with all opinions and personal matters kept private, and dependent on men. I was not to be "forward" or even speak very loud. I could be strong, but only as long as it was not apparent. The fact that my mother had a job was of course inconsistent with her southern model, and in that sense she displayed an alternative to what she taught me. As I got older and felt morally compelled to speak out about civil rights, my outspokenness conflicted with my training to be a southern lady, creating an internal struggle that began in college and continued during my years in the movement.

At the university, many influences and mentors, mostly religious, helped me clarify my ideas and encouraged me to be more outspoken. The YWCA, an interracial, ecumenical Christian organization, was a major force in the struggle for racial justice. It was the gathering place for intellectuals and activists, and an alternative sorority life for me. I joined in 1956, and for the first time I felt a clear and strong connection between religion and social justice. The YWCA was the first interracial organization in which I was intensely active, providing an opportunity to work closely with black students and participate in discussions about racial issues.

I also attended lectures at the Christian Faith and Life Community, known simply as "the Community," an interracial off-campus residence privately owned and not affiliated directly with the university. It had one dorm for women and one down the street for men. I remember hearing that because it was desegregated, a cross had been burned in the front yard, and there had been death threats by mail and telephone.

Many of my friends who were active in the Y lived at the Community; they suggested that I move there. On the day I moved in, my life took a dramatic and an irreversible turn, when all the contradictions of my southern upbringing and my emerging social consciousness came together during a ten-minute car ride. I got in my pink and gray Chevrolet Bel Air to drive from the Community's women's dorm to the men's, where the lectures were held. I offered a ride to a white student who then saw two black students coming out of the building, so he offered them a ride as well. One of the black men got in the front seat of the car. In a split second, I felt my world turn upside down. For the first time in my life, I experienced being in a situation of apparent social intimacy with a black man—not just in a meeting or a class, but in my mother's car, breaking my mother's rules and violating nineteen years of her training. Although I felt physically sick with fear that I had crossed the color line and worried about possible retribution for breaking this southern tradition, the very intensity of my reaction taught me how deep had been my socialization into the racist system and how irrational it was to have such a reaction. I did not want white children to be raised the way I had been. From that moment on, I was even more determined to fight segregation.

. . . A catalyzing event for me at UT involved the policy regarding black and white participation in student theater and musical productions. In the spring of 1957, contrary to accepted practice, Barbara Smith, a black student, was chosen to play a leading role opposite a white male lead. Some members of the Texas legislature were upset and put pressure on the university. She was removed from the production, and in response, professors and students mobilized to defend her right to appear. At stake was not only segregation, but academic freedom. My conscience compelled me to support her rights, so I helped with petitions and joined the protest in front of Hogg Auditorium. I thought that Smith had been treated unfairly and that it was right to protest, but in those years the "public display" of such opinions was not behavior considered appropriate for a lady and so it was not at all easy for me to do. Most of what I remember about the experience was my fear, which was palpable. Usually my commitment to the cause of fighting segregation would be stronger than my southern lady persona and I could act on behalf of principle—but not always. The upbringing of southern white women with my class background was more repressive than most of us can comprehend these many years later.

. . . My decision to live in a desegregated residence was embarrassing to my mother, so she did not tell my grandmother that my dorm was interracial. My grandmother had the address and, without any forewarning, drove to Austin from San Antonio to see for herself where I was living, bringing Lola Mae, the black woman who worked for her, along for the trip. As they drove up, the sight of black students coming out of the dorm made it clear that I was living in an interracial residence. I cannot remember who was the most shocked and distressed by that encounter—my grandmother, Lola Mae, or I. I do remember that my grandmother stiffened her back and squared her jaw and that she communicated her intense disapproval when her blue eyes turned cold as steel. Lola, who was typically reserved and quiet around my grandmother, though they had known each other for years, did not say a word, but looked shocked and worried. I think my grandmother said something like, "Lord have mercy!" Within minutes she drove off, leaving me feeling like a leper, rejected by the matriarch of the family. The incident was never discussed, and race and politics remained painful topics in my family.

This split over beliefs about segregation was the beginning of a twenty-five-year period in which I would see little of my family. The rift was extremely painful for me, but I was adamant in my belief that the South must change. My beliefs were not based on a missionary spirit of "saving" blacks, but on my conviction that segregation was a toxic presence in the South for all of us.

Source: Dorothy Dawson Burlage, "Truths of the Heart," in Constance Curry et al., *Deep in Our Hearts: Nine White Women in the Civil Rights Movement* (Athens: University of Georgia Press, 2000).

3.7. FRANCES KENDALL BREAKS WITH HER FAMILY OVER SEGREGATION

Like so many of the young white college women who participated in the civil rights movement, Frances Kendall of Waco came to it via the National Student YWCA. Kendall attended the Y's annual National Student Assembly and in 1966 was elected to its National Student Committee, which met several times a year in New York City. One of the committee's projects was creating antiracism pilot programs for campus YWCAs. "Racism and white privilege were part of my everyday conversation," she writes. "And I began my personal exploration about what it meant to be white and Southern that lasted for more than ten years." Appalled and alienated by her relatives' casual racism, Kendall found a surrogate family in the YWCA.

I was born in 1947 and grew up in legally segregated Waco, Texas. My life as an upper-middle-class white child was not terribly unusual for the time, except that my father had died when I was four years old so my family configuration was not what was viewed as normal. Raised in an extremely patriotic, conservative, Texas Republican family, I was explicitly taught many lessons: America is the greatest country in the world and it is un-American to question anything it does; the race and class systems in the United States make good sense and should be defended at any cost; white people are better than black people—well, really black people are something less than human and so don't deserve the consideration that white people do; and segregation is God's way of designing the world. I fervently believed that the United

States was "the land of the free and the home of the brave" and that everything I had been taught was right.

Then, for grades nine through twelve, I went to National Cathedral School, an Episcopal girls' school in Washington, D.C., and the lens through which I viewed life changed dramatically. I was in class with black girls who were smarter than I was and whose families were wealthier than mine. . . . I heard weekly sermons at the National Cathedral on social ills in the country and particularly in the South. I was told that, to be truly Christian, I had to fight for social and racial justice, precisely the opposite of what I had been taught in my Episcopal church in Waco. I no longer knew where to place my allegiances. I was coming to understand that much of what I had been taught by my family and culture was not true, but I wasn't quite sure what or whom to believe. . . .

My visits at home were rife with verbal violence. By that time my mother and I had had many fights about why she hadn't stood up to the racism in our family. . . . I was besieged by hideous racist jokes from my brothers-in-law and male cousins. The more I fought back, of course, the greater pleasure they took in recounting the stories. While the women usually didn't tell the jokes, they didn't stop them, either. Our family was spoken of as upstanding leaders in the community, and yet I knew they were also old members of the Ku Klux Klan. They had joined in the 1920s, my mother told me, "to protect their women and children." How could I trust a mother who seemed to me such a coward? What did it say about me that this was the blood from which I had come? . . . It was in that state of disillusion and confusion that I went to college and became involved in the Y.

The Y provided a place to unpack and deconstruct—to take the lessons I had been taught about what was right and what was wrong, what was important and what was trivial, and rethink them, and to do that with the help, support, and pushing of people who were involved in the same struggle. Each of us had different questions to ask. Mine were centered primarily around issues of race, family, country and loyalty, and what it meant to be Christian—the easy ones.

In regard to race, I had been taught that things were as they were supposed to be, and that, as white people, we only had what we deserved, and so there was no reason to feel guilty about my family's socioeconomic status or the benefits given to us because of our skin color. My family had been in the cotton business for decades; the manual labor on which the company's success was built was done by African Americans. Yet I was taught that black people were not as smart, good, worthy. They weren't "people like us" and therefore didn't deserve the same treatment or opportunities. Black people were there to serve us. It was their job to care for us as we went about our lives. In one hand I held these messages; in the other I carried my experiences of people like Dorothy Height and Valerie Russell.[2]

Miss Height, a true giant in the fight for civil rights, ran the National YWCA Center for Racial Justice. I was regularly in her presence, hearing her speak and watching her work. Val worked with the Student Y as the editor of its newsletter, *Interact.* I am still able to recall instantly her deeply resonant voice, her wisdom, and her laughter. We sang freedom songs deep into more nights than I could count; they gave us hope and nourished our souls. Daily I grew in the knowledge that I had not been taught the truth. What I had been taught was "right" was in direct opposition to what I saw and experienced.

I was extremely confused about what "family" was. I had been born into a family that was fine, upstanding, Christian—one filled with civic leaders. Yet I felt shame rather than pride about my history. On the one hand, I remember being crystal clear about my intentions and the path I was compelled to follow. It was for me, as for many others, a moral imperative. On the other hand, I was bewildered and heart-sickened by my family's response to racial struggles and to my participation in them. How was it possible that those who were supposed to love me most, to be closest to me, felt so alien? Not only were they different, but, to me—they were morally wrong. I constantly questioned myself: if I had come from them, was I one of them? At some level I feared that, "come the revolution," I wouldn't have the guts to stand where I so vociferously said I would, that all my work to be different from my family would dissolve, that they had instilled their values too early for me to change. In spite of my fears, I pushed on, learning more about myself as a white person, asking harder and harder questions, being expected by my "family of choice" to see the world differently than I had been raised to. As I made choices to separate myself from my family, I moved toward the Y, finding acceptance there precisely because of the person I was becoming rather than in spite of it.

Source: Sara M. Evans, ed., *Journeys That Opened Up the World: Women, Student Christian Movements, and Social Justice, 1955–1975* (New Brunswick, N.J.: Rutgers University Press, 2003).

3.8. AFRICAN AMERICAN WOMEN IN DALLAS DEFEND THEIR NEW HOMES IN A HOSTILE WHITE NEIGHBORHOOD

Finding decent housing in segregated southern cities was an ongoing problem for African American families. In Dallas the black community was squeezed into a run-down section of the city's west side, where 90 percent of the dwellings had no indoor toilets and 85 percent lacked running water. In 1950-1951, middle-class families trying to escape these slum conditions bought homes in the Exline Park neighborhood along Oakland Boulevard, a section of South Dallas where an expanding African American neighborhood bordered on a white one. Angry whites responded with a dozen bombings. Police arrested ten suspects, but only one was tried and a jury acquitted him.

Juanita Craft, a Dallas civil rights leader and NAACP state organizer, describes black women's defense of their homes in two of the bombings. Expecting no help from the police, women as well as men armed themselves and fought back. The widow on Crozier Street to whom Craft refers is apparently Birdie Mae Sharpe, who on July 12, 1951, fired several shots at the retreating car of white racists who threw a bomb over her fence.[3]

1949 is when the Negroes started moving to South Dallas. And if you went down there and signed the paper and everything, that house would be bombed or burned that night. . . . [I]t was led by ministers, white ministers, and I don't know who else. But they would get in the streets and go to people's houses at night if people moved in and try to frighten them. And we have one old lady down here on Oakland now. She's about eighty-five years old. Her husband was a physician. And, of course, she was left alone quite a bit. So she decided to put a tub of water in her house, and sure enough, the mob went to her house one night and she walked out and said, "I want to see the leader!" Nobody would admit that they were the leader. About two nights later, they threw a bomb at her house, and she grabbed the bomb and threw it in a tub of water. That's the way she saved her house. Her husband's dead, but she's still living there over there on Electra Street[;] and on Hatcher Street, on Marburg and on Southland, nice little homes, they were just bombed and burned, just like nobody's business, when they found a Negro had bought them. We hired guards because the police weren't doing anything. We hired guards to go in there and stay at night. That's the only way you're going to keep it, you know, if you kept it over two or three nights.

The last one happened in 1951, and this was a lot of fun for me. It happened here on the corner of Southland and Crozier. This woman was a widow, and she had bought her home and fixed it up very nice inside, and she kept a gun lying on her back porch on a table, and that particular night she just happened to look up and saw this bomb coming over the fence. The fuse was lighted, and she ran and grabbed the gun and shot in the direction that it came from several times. What we couldn't understand was that the police was always near. In a short time, the police came in from the driveway, came running in after they heard the shots, you see. One policeman saw the bomb. He made a dive for cover, and the other made a dive for the bomb. He yelled to her, "Get me some water!" She got a bucket and went in the house and got a bucket of water out of the sink and carried it back to him. He doused the bomb. But the point was that their fish pond was there two feet away from where the bomb fell, and nobody thought about putting the bomb in the fish pond! So I teased her, I said, "So you wanted some clean water for your bomb!" Well, that's the last bombing we've had.

. . . However, before that time [1951], we'd gotten an ordinance passed that should have stopped it. I drove into one of these problems over on Howell Street. Corey Landers and I had been out in the rurals, and we were coming back and we saw a crowd of people in the street and we didn't know what it was. But this woman was a member of my church, a woman by the name of Walker, and she was moving into the house, and all these white women and their children and everything got buckets of rocks. You see, two would have a bucket filled with rocks, and they were just throwing at the house, trying to break the windows out, and things of that sort. The police just standing there trying to reason with them. You don't reason with people like that, you take them on to jail. But, you see, when we drove up, we didn't know what it was. We didn't know what we had driven into. We sat there and watched. Finally, Mrs. Walker, she was kind of a heavy woman like my size, and she came out of that house with a broom, and one of them hollered, "She's got a gun. Let's run!" So they started running away from it. And the City bought these houses that these people had bought.

Source: Juanita Craft, oral history interview by David Striklin and Gail Tomlinson, 1979, Juanita Craft Papers, Dallas Public Library.

3.9. IDA M. DARDEN, "WHAT ABOUT THE 'CIVIL RIGHTS' OF WHITE MEN?"

Ida Muse Darden of Fort Worth and Houston was a business lobbyist and self-taught journalist who spent decades championing conservative causes, beginning in the 1910s when she served as publicity director for the Texas Association Opposed to Woman Suffrage. From 1950 to 1961 she published a right-wing monthly newspaper, the *Southern Conservative,* in which she advocated states' rights and anti-Communism and denounced New Deal "socialism," congressional taxing power, labor unions, and the civil rights movement. In this column from October 1959, defending residential segregation, Darden followed common conservative practice and blended segregationist ideology with anti-Communism. By this logic, conservatives argued that civil rights advocates were subversives who aimed to stir up racial and class hatred and political chaos that would enable Communism to triumph over democracy. The U.S. Commission on Civil Rights, to which Darden refers in the opening paragraph, was created by the Civil Rights Act of 1957. The bipartisan, six-member commission included three southerners; it held hearings on implementing school desegregation in Nashville and on housing discrimination in Atlanta, Chicago, and New York.

The President's Civil Rights Commission, backed by weak-minded reformers, is reported to be going to push hard during the next two years for racial mixing in the housing area.

Instead of a chicken in every pot or two cars in every garage, the new objective is a black family in every white neighborhood.

When a colored man buys a house next door to a white man and moves in, the value of the white man's property is automatically reduced seventy-five per cent.

In such a transaction, the colored man is exercising what Liberal politicians, do-gooders and Communists call his "Civil Rights," but what about the white man?

Perhaps he has spent the greater part of his adult life in paying for his home with the honest belief that the value of his property would increase as the city in which it is located grows and expands.

At the time of the purchase, he takes into consideration, of course, that his home may be destroyed by fire, flood, tornado or other act of God and tries to protect himself with such insurance as is available and which he can afford, against these disasters.

But there is no insurance policy covering the loss when the Congress of the United States yields to pressure of powerful minority groups and pro-Communist forces and sets up a politically dominated Commission authorized to recommend action that wipes out seventy-five per cent of the value of a citizen's property which he bought and paid for in good faith.

Nobody but an imbecile or a degenerate will argue that there is any justice or "Christian tolerance" involved in any such proceeding.

In pressing for this arrangement, the Commission will be merely emphasizing the conception prevailing in American Communist circles that black men have "Civil Rights" but that white men have none.

Source: Ida M. Darden, *The Best of the Southern Conservative* (Houston: Ida M. Darden, 1963).

3.10. SUNNY NASH, "MY GRANDMOTHER'S SIT-IN"

Sunny Nash, born in 1949, grew up in Candy Hill, the "colored" section of Bryan. As a child she played in its unpaved streets, attended a segregated school, and, when she went downtown with her mother for a hamburger, had to eat outside the café's back door and do without a drink because African Americans were not allowed to use the restrooms. After a career as a singer, Nash became a journalist and chronicled her childhood in a series of sketches that depicted life in Candy Hill and the strength of her mother and her grandmother, Bigmama.

Aunt Effie's daughter, Ready Mae, had lost control of her car and run into a neighbor's porch. I'd overheard my mother, who had visited Ready Mae a few days before, telling my grandmother that Ready Mae was bandaged from head to foot and there were tubes going everywhere. I dreaded seeing that. My grandmother asked my mother if Ready Mae's eyes looked sealed. My mother said yes. My grandmother wanted to know if Ready Mae's body had swelled. My mother said yes. My grandmother inquired about Ready Mae's ability to breathe for herself. My mother said no. What a shame, they agreed, because Ready Mae had a husband and a house full of small children expecting her to get well one day and come home.

"Ready Mae is my niece and she's dying," Bigmama said to me calmly. "I'm going to pay my respects. I want you to go, too." . . . I followed my grandmother up the sidewalk. She pushed the door open, and we went into the hospital. Disinfectant, rubbing alcohol, and flowers hit my nostrils, reminding me of another place I hated just as much—a funeral home.

In the lobby, a couple of nurses behind the front desk ignored my grandmother's inquiry while they helped others who arrived after we did. My grandmother did not persist. Although I knew her temper to be short and hot, she never displayed a lack of restraint. Burning up inside, she walked away from the desk, stopped in front of a row of wooden benches and looked up at the hand-painted sign that read, "Colored." Like a smoking gun, she stood there staring at the sign; studying it. That was curious to me. She knew how to read. Why was she staring at the word, *colored,* like she'd never seen it before? After all, *colored* and *white only* were the first words southerners learned to read, and the only words all illiterate southerners recognized.

I'd been reading *colored* since I was three. When Bigmama taught me to recognize the word, I was so young I don't remember yet having seen my own reflection in a mirror. When I was drawing on the floor one day, she knelt, picked up a crayon, and, on a piece of my paper, wrote a word in large black letters. She called out each letter as if trying to make me aware of our vulgar circumstance without soiling me in the process.

"I'm sorry I have to teach you this ugly word, *colored,*" she said. "I don't want to! I have to! I wish I didn't! But if I don't make you understand, you'll have one hurt after another all of your life, or you'll go out and get yourself killed."

I stared at the letters she wrote.

"This is where we have to sit when we go out, Baby."

I was too young to understand.

"This word is wrapped in a hundred years of dirty politics."

I didn't understand that, either.

"It's their way of trying to keep you in a low place and make you feel like dirt, so you'll stay down on the ground." She dropped the crayon. "But you just remember, Baby, you're not dirt, no matter where they make you sit. Your place is as high up as you push it."

I stared at the letters and never forgot their arrangement.

Bigmama turned from the scribbled hospital sign that read, "Colored," and walked to the spacious other side of the waiting area. What was she doing? Without so much as a glance up at the "White Only" sign, she eased herself down into an upholstered chair. Throat clearing did not disturb her composure and quiet dignity. She crossed one slender ankle in front of the other and tucked her feet under the chair so only the toes of her black leather shoes peeked out. Her white gloved hands removed a silk floral scarf from her head, which she folded neatly and placed in her black leather purse. The heavy gold clasp aroused an echo in the hushed room. Looking my way, she patted a chair beside her. Timidly, I walked over, sat down, and stared at her stony expression, looking straight ahead.

My grandmother was born in 1890 and—like my mother, who was born in 1928, and me, born in 1949—had known only segregation. After sixty-five years of compliance, my grandmother had had enough. "*Brown v. the Board of Education of Topeka, Kansas,* says I can sit where I want," she said. . . . "The Supreme Court ruled it. I want to know if it's true." She explained that a little girl named Linda Brown had sued the school district for forcing her to attend inferior schools. Because she was not a white student, the law disqualified her from attending the district's better schools, limiting her access to an education equal to the one the district provided for white students.

"If that little girl can go all the way to Washington, D.C., and do all of that," Bigmama said, "then, surely, an old woman won't let a Black Code keep her from taking a comfortable chair. Black Codes have been on the books since they brought slaves to this country," she said. "And those codes are not just for Negroes. The codes keep black folk, black Mexicans, and prairie Indians in their place. Don't expect those laws to disappear overnight. New laws won't affect where you go to school or anything else you do for a very long time. Changes like that could take forever."

Afraid that my grandmother and I would be arrested or worse, my blood ran cold sitting under that "White Only" sign. I was proud and ashamed at the same time but too terrified to look up and see other people watching us. "I was about your age when the Supreme Court used the railroad to legalize what they called 'separate but equal,'" Bigmama said. "It was 1896. *Plessy v. Ferguson* made things separate, but it sure didn't make them equal."

Bigmama shifted in her chair and looked at me, whispering, "All Mr. Plessy wanted was a first-class train ticket. Well, he could spend first-class money on a first-class ticket, but Jim Crow said he couldn't put his black behind in a first-class seat."

"Who's Jim Crow?"

"A minstrel-show figure with a shiny black painted face and big white lips," she said, glancing up at the sign. "Two nations under God, one 'white only' and the other one 'colored.' They wrote laws to keep us from using their restrooms, drinking from their water fountains, trying on clothes in a store, eating with them, going to school with them, marrying them, and being buried under the same dirt with them."

"Was Jim Crow before or after the South lost their war?" I asked softly, hardly breathing.

"The North may have won the Civil War in the history books, but the South didn't lose," whispered Bigmama, smiling with a frown between her eyes as she often did. "The North gave the South everything the South was fighting to keep; because the North, the South, the West, and the East all wanted the same thing—us in a low place."

My grandmother stood up, smoothed her coat, and politely nodded to the other stunned hospital guests. "I'm going now," she said. "I never stay long where I'm not wanted. You don't have to go in Ready Mae's room if you don't want to. You can stay here."

I sprang out of that chair, not sure where I would feel more out of place—seeing Cousin Ready Mae in her condition or sitting alone under a sign that read, "White Only."

Source: Sunny Nash, *Bigmama Didn't Shop at Woolworth's* (College Station: Texas A&M University Press, 1996).

3.11. CHRISTIA ADAIR DEFIES JIM CROW BY TRYING ON A GIRDLE

The female world of shopping posed complex challenges to the unwritten rules of domination and subordination that sustained segregation. There were no "white" or "colored" sections in department stores, and racial rules were reversed: white women had to render service to black women. Saleswomen kept black customers in their "place" by waiting on them without deference or courtesy. Store management did the same by denying them customary services. Practices varied; some stores refused to let African Americans try on clothing at all, while others made them use the janitor's closet or an alteration room. Some millinery departments permitted black women to try on hats if the saleswomen first lined them with paper; others categorically refused. Black women pushed back, frequently refusing to buy items they couldn't try on. In this oral history excerpt Christia Adair, who became executive secretary of the Houston NAACP in 1950, explains how she desegregated the dressing rooms at one of the city's major department stores.

When you're in an NAACP office, as an administrator, people bring you every kind of problem.

And so the women began telling me that they couldn't try on hats—I knew it because I couldn't—they couldn't try on girdles; they couldn't do this. But I wouldn't ever be satisfied, I'd go try it out myself to see if this is really fact. Always carry somebody along to hear them say, "No, you cannot." And so there were times that I would go in, pick out a hat and the sales lady would put it on her head and say, "I think it's pretty; don't you like that?" I'd say, "Well, I like it on you but I don't know if I'd like it on me or not. I don't think the same hat that would become you would become me." And so they would always have their foot on the chair so you couldn't sit down in front of the mirror to try on a hat. You had to pick it up. Of course, I never bought anything that I couldn't try on. I haven't been a bully in my lifetime, but I never compromised.

. . . But anyway, I didn't buy anything. I'd do without it first. But then some prominent women came and told me they would have to go into an alteration room to fit a girdle if they wanted to buy it at a popular store in town, Sakowitz store was the store then. And I went. I never did particularly need a girdle, especially back there because I was pretty thin, skinny, didn't have time nor money to eat with. But anyway, I went to buy a girdle. And I picked out a girdle. Then I went to have the girdle fitted. And when they headed me toward the alteration room, I said, "I don't need to have anything done to it, I just want to try it on." They said, "Well, you go on in." I said, "Well, I don't want to try it on in the alteration room. I want to try it on in the fitting room." And they tried to shove me some place. I said, "Look, I tell you. Let me see the manager of this department." And so they had no alternative but to produce the manager, and the manager didn't want anybody to know that he was supporting that kind of attitude, so he put the woman on the spot and just passed the buck to her and said to her, "Show the customer to the fitting room."

So she showed me to the fitting room and was about to leave, so I said, "But you have to stay with me because I don't know how to fit a . . . I don't know how it's supposed to fit." And so she had to stand there and touch my Negro hide. And she sort of fumbled with me, my body, and I know she felt like her little hands were being contaminated, but that's what had to happen. And I sat and I laid and I did everything, moved it and the girdle did not fit and it was not what I wanted. Of course she had to go back and bring in one or two more to be sure I was getting the right fit. And then when I got all fitted and I had gone as far as I thought it was necessary to get justice out of the thing, and went to the counter, the girdle was $29. And I didn't need any kind of girdle, but I couldn't fail. I had to pay for it because that would be carrying it too far, but that was the kind of experience you had to suffer for the cause if you wanted to master the situation. And I did.

Source: Christia Adair interview, April 25, 1977, Black Women Oral History Project, Arthur and Elizabeth Schlesinger Library on the History of Women in America, Radcliffe College.

When the Governor's Commission on the Status of Women issued its report in 1967, it had no difficulty documenting inequality between the sexes. Women's rate of college attendance was well below men's (34 percent versus 48 percent), and they earned only 10 percent of doctoral degrees. Thirty-two percent of women were in the workforce, where they earned less than men even when doing the same work; female accounting clerks in Dallas, Houston, and Fort Worth, for example, were paid $23 to $27 a week less than their male counterparts. Professional women had no advantage, most egregiously illustrated by the example of a woman in publishing, with a college degree and twenty-five years' experience, who earned less than nondegreed men with only two to three years' experience. Nor were women fairly represented in supervisory positions even in professions that they dominated, such as teaching. Dallas, the report noted, had 172 public schools but only 26 female principals, all at the elementary level.

Appointed by conservative governor John Connally and chaired by W. S. Birdwell of the Texas Employment Commission, the Governor's Commission on the Status of Women had been formed to explore two seemingly conflicting aspects of the female experience: how could women continue to fulfill traditional roles as wives and mothers while contributing to the workforce, which also needed their talents and labor? Although charged with recommending ways to combat discrimination against women, the Governor's Commission suggested little of real substance. It managed to grasp that "at least half of all women who work do so out of economic necessity and to raise their families' living standards above the level of poverty or deprivation," but, in an obtuse follow-up, the commission advised women not to complain about unequal treatment: "Overly enthusiastic 'soap boxing oratory' can do the feminine cause more harm than good."[1]

The commission's only useful recommendation was the suggestion that the Texas Civil Rights Act of 1967, which forbade employment discrimination based on race, color, religion, or nationality be amended to prohibit sex discrimination as well. (This followed the example of Title VII of the federal Civil Rights Act of 1964, discussed below.) But on the issue of compensation the Governor's Commission waffled, asserting that "in this world we, each of us, achieve as individuals, not as members of a group," and that legislation "will not accomplish for any person what only he (or in this case *she*) can accomplish for herself." It declined to recommend a state law requiring equal pay for equal work, even though Congress had already passed a federal one, the Equal Pay Act of 1963. Rationalizing that if employers had to pay both sexes equal wages, fewer women would be hired, the commission blamed women themselves for employment inequality: "It is recognized that the working pattern of women is different from that of men. A young woman takes a job until she is married or until she has a baby and then retires from the work force until she has completed her family or never to return. It is a fact of life that an employer's expectation of reaping a substantial dividend from hiring and training a young man is much more apt to be realized than his similar expectation in the case of hiring a young woman."[2]

By 1967 every state had a commission on the status of women, and not all were as useless as the one in Texas. State commissions were modeled after John F. Kennedy's Presidential Commission on the Status of Women, chaired by Eleanor Roosevelt. The brainchild of the head of the U.S. Women's Bureau in the Department of Labor, the President's Commission had been appointed to recommend ways to overcome discrimination by private and government employers and to help support women's role as earners who were also wives and mothers. Although the President's Commission disbanded in 1963 after issuing a politically cautious report that brought no insights to the sex-role obstructions, most of the state commissions continued to function.[3] They met together in an annual conference and constituted a national network of women well-informed about sex discrimination and women's issues, even though they had little power to act. From this group emerged a handful of activists who founded the National Organization for Women (NOW) and ignited a new feminist movement.

TITLE VII AND CIVIL RIGHTS FOR WOMEN

Congress inadvertently provided the catalyst for NOW when it passed the Civil Rights Act of 1964 in response to African American demands for an end to racial discrimination. Title VII of the act prohibited employment discrimination on the basis of race, religion, nationality, or sex—the last was added by a southern congressman in hopes of torpedoing the bill (or, if it passed, of ensuring white women the same advantage as blacks). Title VII created the

Equal Employment Opportunity Commission (EEOC) to investigate claims of discrimination, and complaints from women denied jobs, raises, and promotions poured in. One group of Texas women soon discovered that the EEOC could not help them; employees of state government agencies were outside its jurisdiction. Thus the University of Texas and the state comptroller's office could continue to reject female applicants for computer operator positions with the excuse that they didn't like to hire women for night work. Only a loophole allowed an employee of the Texas Employment Commission to file a sex discrimination suit after the agency forced her to take early maternity leave and then fired her for being out more than six weeks — EEOC jurisdiction extended to all employment agencies, even state ones.[4]

The primary obstacle to relief under the EEOC, however, was the attitude of the director and most of the members, who regarded the sex provision of Title VII as a joke. In 1965 it ruled that sex-segregated job advertisements (Help Wanted—Male, Help Wanted—Female) were not discriminatory, prompting jocular press stories about the possibility otherwise of male secretaries and Playboy Club bunnies or—just as unimaginable—female airline pilots. Women's advocates were exasperated and angry. At the third Conference of State Commissions on the Status of Women, which met in Washington, D.C., in the summer of 1966, a handful of the delegates and some activist women in the federal government decided to form the National Organization for Women. The group held an organizing convention a few months later and elected *Feminine Mystique* author Betty Friedan as president. As she later noted, a law never meant to be enforced against sex discrimination in employment was the spark that ignited an organized women's movement.

Modeled on the NAACP, NOW was a civil rights organization created to pressure the government to enforce economic and legal equality for women. Title VII, as one historian has pointed out, had given women "a wedge with which to open up the whole gender system to question" and turn private grievances into political issues.[5] NOW's organizers rejected any idea of sex roles as "natural" and unchangeable. The organization's statement of purpose called for an equal partnership of the sexes and equitable sharing of domestic and child-rearing responsibilities, so that women were not forced to choose between family life and paid work. Like the presidential and state commissions on women, it stressed equal employment opportunity for women and what the federal government could do by way of remedy. In addition to requesting broader enforcement powers for the EEOC, NOW called on the government to emulate other industrialized countries and support women's needs with child care centers, pregnancy leave, and training programs for mothers returning to the labor force after raising families. It criticized "the assumption that these problems are the unique responsibility of each individual woman, rather than a basic social dilemma which society must solve."[6]

As its first official act NOW challenged the EEOC's obstinacy on sex-specific job advertisements. Prior to Title VII, women's marginalized job status had been considered just a "fact of life," as the Texas Governor's Commission on the Status of Women had unhelpfully concluded. Women's complaints to the EEOC forced the recognition of a new concept, "sex segregation" in employment, which the ads both reflected and reinforced. As part of its campaign, NOW mobilized women to picket local EEOC offices, and in 1968 the commission reversed its earlier ruling and barred sex-segregated job advertising. By that time NOW had also successfully lobbied President Lyndon Johnson to modify his 1965 executive order barring discrimination by businesses that received government contracts, so that it included discrimination based on sex as well as on race.

Like the NAACP and LULAC, NOW was founded as a lobbying and litigating organization; its goal was to eliminate legal sex discrimination. Because it pursued equality through government action and the courts—it established the NOW Legal Defense Fund to support women who filed sex discrimination suits—historians have termed its philosophy "liberal feminism." It manifested in Texas when NOW called a national Women's Strike for Equality Day (slogan: "Don't Iron While the Strike Is Hot!") on August 26, 1970, the fiftieth anniversary of the ratification of the woman suffrage amendment. More than two hundred Austin feminists observed the day with a demonstration on the capitol grounds. They discussed job discrimination, day care, and abortion and concluded with an evening of music, skits, and rap sessions. In Houston the local NOW chapter sponsored a rally with pickets in front of the Federal Building that drew three hundred women. The feminists passed out leaflets demanding an end to sex discrimination in employment, repeal of antiabortion laws, and the establishment of day care centers for working mothers. After speeches by NOW members, the pickets moved to Foley's Department Store and defiantly ordered lunch at the Men's Grill, which was off-limits to women.[7]

Houston's NOW chapter, which had formed early in 1970, was the only one in Texas until San Antonio's was chartered in 1971; feminists in Austin and Dallas organized the following year. Like chapters in other states, the Texas locals adhered to national NOW policy but chose their own projects. In an era when nearly all television and radio newscasters were men—supposedly news delivered by a woman wouldn't be taken seriously—getting the stations to hire women was a priority. In Houston in 1973 nearly half of the radio and television stations had no female on-air professionals; a survey four years later found that 100 percent of the city's television news anchors and 87 percent of reporters were male. Houston NOW threatened to challenge the stations' broadcasting license renewals, and San Antonio NOW filed sex discrimination charges with the EEOC against two of the Alamo City's radio stations. Dallas County NOW formed a media task force that successfully pressured three local television stations to hire and promote more on-air women.[8]

Houston NOW established an Equal Employment Opportunity Task Force, whose targets included government contractors who failed to follow non-discrimination guidelines and the *Houston Chronicle*'s sex-segregated help-wanted ads, a violation of Title VII. The Houston chapter also filed a class action complaint with the EEOC against the city's police department for setting requirements designed to disqualify female applicants. San Antonio NOW cooperated with the National Council of Negro Women to document housing discrimination against women. Austin NOW created the city's Rape Crisis Center—the chapter's Rape Task Force developed the proposal, persuaded the Austin City Council to appropriate funds, and trained the volunteers.[9]

The Texas State NOW formed in 1973 at the suggestion of the national organization's southern regional director. Martha Dickey, president of Dallas NOW, was elected the first state coordinator; two years later she became the first national NOW officer from Texas when she was elected national finance vice president. By 1976, Texas State NOW had twenty-nine local chapters, with memberships that varied from a dozen or fewer to more than one hundred in Houston and Dallas. Following the lead of the national organization, Texas State NOW did much of its work through task forces. Some, like the Rape and Violence Against Women Task Force, aimed to change social policy and did. In an era when rape was popularly perceived as the victim's fault, the combined efforts of NOW chapters nationwide created rape victim support systems and resulted in new police and court procedures: the rape kit for collecting medical evidence, and an end to the practice of grilling the rape victim about her past sexual history during trial. Women abused by their husbands bore a similar stigma of having in some way "provoked" attack. Wife beating was the subject of jokes, and "domestic violence" did not exist as a concept until NOW feminists publicized the problems of perfunctory police response and the need for shelters for battered women and their children.

The Education Task Force's goal was eradicating "sexism" (another new word) in textbooks, a collaborative effort between local NOW members, who reviewed texts up for adoption and testified before the Texas Education Agency, and the task force chair, who used the data to compile an annual list of the most unacceptable textbooks for Texas schools. In response to pressure from Texas State NOW, the TEA in 1973 for the first time included sex roles in its guidelines for textbook publishers. NOW pointed out that 40 percent of women were in the workforce, and publishers were told to depict women in varied roles and nontraditional jobs. Antifeminists representing a variety of conservative and right-wing groups mobilized as a counterforce and within a few years persuaded the agency to backtrack and mandate the portrayal of traditional roles for men and women as well as changing ones. Conservative women outmaneuvered NOW because they were more experienced in working the system—since the 1950s they had been monitoring textbooks for "pro-socialist" content—and were more politically astute. Representing themselves (inaccurately) as simple housewives, they approached state education officials as individuals and proper ladies seeking help, while NOW's Education Task Force was perceived as demanding and essentially unappeasable.[10]

Other task forces monitored and lobbied for legislation. A major concern of the Older Women's Task Force was the financial insecurity of displaced homemakers, divorced and widowed women who had been full-time wives and mothers and found themselves in need of employment, without work experience, and ineligible for Social Security because their children were over eighteen. After the opening of the 1977 legislative session, Texas State NOW's coordinator, Barbara Duke, delivered a public Women's State of the State message in Austin, calling for financial recognition of women's contribution to marriage, including unemployment and disability benefits for homemakers. The Displaced Homemaker Act, which passed easily because no one wanted to vote against motherhood, provided nothing so radical, but it set up two pilot centers to provide services for divorced and widowed women who lacked workplace experience or skills.[11] Society "honored" women who devoted themselves to homemaking only with empty rhetoric, feminists argued; in reality, the housewife's role was demeaned and devalued (see Document 4.2).

The displaced homemakers bill was only one of several measures for mothers and children for which Texas State NOW lobbied. Belying the popular perception of the organization as focused on upwardly mobile professional women, NOW put child support enforcement, day care, and family violence on its legislative agenda. A priority of the Child Support Task Force was amending the state's weak child support law: 90 percent of single-parent families were headed by women, and 80 percent of them were unable to collect all of their court-ordered support. The neediest were forced onto public assistance; studies revealed that 71 percent of Texas welfare recipients qualified for benefits because one parent, usually the father, was absent and not paying child support. Jailing the delinquent parent—if he could be found—did nothing to help the struggling family. In 1983 NOW helped lobby a constitutional amendment through the legislature that permitted garnishment of wages for nonsupport.[12]

On one issue, support for lesbian civil rights, Texas State NOW, by virtue of its late founding, escaped the divisiveness that wracked the national organization. After the emergence of the national gay pride movement in 1969, many closeted lesbians in NOW, who had kept their identity secret for fear of losing their jobs or custody of their children, began to come out and demand support for lesbian rights. A gay/straight rift opened. Many heterosexual feminists contended that lesbianism was not a feminist issue and posed a danger to NOW's public credibility. Betty Friedan, fearing—rightly—that opponents would attach the lesbian label to all feminists, famously denounced it as a "lavender menace." Some chapters purged lesbian members, who in turn denounced them as heterosexist. The issue divided the national leadership for years and some heterosexual women were never reconciled, but by the time Texas State NOW was founded, the national organization had voted to support lesbian rights. In 1975, two years after its birth, Texas State NOW voted to create a Lesbian Rights Task Force. It also approved a resolution supporting the right of divorced lesbians to custody of their children and in subsequent years offered practical advice on winning such cases. In the 1980s the Lesbian Rights Task Force ranked third in funding among Texas State NOW's task forces, and President Gloria K. Sprinkle affirmed that lesbian rights were a civil rights issue.[13]

Texas State NOW's strength peaked in the mid-1980s at nearly five thousand members. NOW feminists tended to be white, middle-class, and educated; the failure to attract significant numbers of minority women was a continuing concern. State representative Wilhelmina Delco, the first African American elected to the legislature from Travis County, explained part of the difficulty in a 1973 speech to Austin NOW: "One major reason is the media image of 'women's lib' as a movement of bored, middle-class housewives looking for the excitement of the working world; black women traditionally are (very poorly paid) working women envious of the very idea of being able to stay home full-time."[14] Nor was it easy for black women to feel sisterhood with liberal white women in whose homes so many were employed to do the "dirty work."

Austin NOW was unable to come up with a minority outreach strategy, but in 1989 a group of Dallas women established a truly multicultural chapter that was a model for the nation. Karen Ashmore, a full-time white fund-raiser for a private black grade school, belonged to a NOW chapter that was 98 percent white, with one African American and one Latina, when she and several other white members decided to form a rainbow chapter. It held meetings in a minority neighborhood in a black church and publicized them in the minority media. The working-class women who began to attend made their priorities clear: not reproductive freedom (although they supported it) but basic survival issues such as discrimination, homelessness, child care, and police brutality. As a consequence Dallas Rainbow NOW projects included sponsoring a legal aid clinic on discrimination and moving people into abandoned housing. It helped establish the Ida Delaney Justice Committee, after Delaney, an African American, was shot and killed by an off-duty white policeman whom she cut off in traffic as she drove to work. NOW members were a visible presence in the courtroom: "We made sure the judge and jury understood that we wanted justice." The police officer was the first ever convicted by a Dallas jury for killing a civilian. Within fifteen months of its founding Dallas Rainbow NOW was 45 percent white, 45 percent African American, and 10 percent Latina.[15]

THE NEW LEFT AND WOMEN'S LIBERATION

In the spring of 1969 fifteen University of Texas students, inspired by the feminist protest at the Miss America pageant at Atlantic City, New Jersey, the previous September, picketed the Neiman Marcus fashion show sponsored by the university's Home Economics Department. With their faces garishly made up to resemble dolls and wearing paper dresses decorated with magazine advertisements for beauty products and padded bras, they protested the manipulation of women into roles as sex objects by the fashion and advertising industries. When Miss America made a visit to campus a few months later, they dressed up as lipstick tubes and permanent-wave boxes to dramatize their opposition to the system's use of women's bodies to make money. "Miss America is a body, not a person," wrote one protester. "Sure Toni [Home Permanents] offers her a scholarship, look what they're getting for their money—a beautiful little Barbie doll that endorses Toni home permanents whenever you pull her string to make her talk."[16] Women's liberation had arrived in Austin.

Like NOW feminists, women's liberationists were predominantly white and middle-class; unlike them, they were young, proudly radical, and disdainful of female beauty culture. (The protesters at the Miss America pageant in Atlantic City flung girdles, bras, hair curlers, high-heeled shoes, and other "instruments of torture" into a "freedom trash can.") Wearing jeans and long hair instead of sweater sets and bouffant hairdos, women's liberationists were especially visible on college campuses, where they emerged from New Left causes. Always a tiny minority, the student radicals were alienated from the "uptight" lifestyle and conservative values of the 1950s and affronted by the nation's political leadership in the 1960s. Inspired by the civil rights demonstrations and the black freedom movement, the New Left protested racism, economic inequality, and, most vociferously, the escalation of the Vietnam War and everything that supported it—the military draft, campus ROTC, and university contracts with the U.S. Department of Defense. In the fall of 1966 ten young women, one of them eight months pregnant and another carrying a month-old baby, staged a sit-in at the Selective Service office in Austin. Most of the women were University of Texas students, and several of them were members of Students for a Democratic Society and staff writers for Austin's newly founded underground newspaper, the *Rag*, where the plan for the sit-in had been hatched. The group presented a written statement protesting the draft as "an affront to democracy and to the freedom of the individual" and then sat for four-and-a-half hours inside the office's main entrance, attracting a crowd of journalists and some watchful police officers.[17]

Students for a Democratic Society (SDS) was the loudest campus voice of the New Left. Susan Torian Olan, a member of the Austin chapter (the South's largest), described it as "a gut punch against mainstream U.S. politics and culture." University of Texas SDS printed and distributed leaflets against the Vietnam War and imperialism, sat in to protest U.S. Marine Corps recruiters on campus, organized a demonstration against Vice President Hubert Humphrey's visit to Austin, and sponsored a campus visit by Student Nonviolent Coordinating Committee leader Stokely Carmichael. SDS's Gentle Thursday became part of 1960s legend; after skipping classes to sit on the grass and listen to music, the group moved to the ROTC building and chalked the airplane in front of it with peace slogans and flower designs.[18]

Inadvertently, SDS and other New Left organizations helped lay the groundwork for the emergence of women's liberation, as female members came to resent male authoritarianism and sexism. Sharon Shelton-Colangelo described the moment when feminist consciousness dawned for her. In the early days the *Rag* put a photo of a woman staffer typing in the nude on the centerfold or, when sales were down, on the front page. "During one of our low sales periods," Shelton-Colangelo recalled, "we were discussing who would be the nude that would be on the front page, and someone said, 'What about you, Sharon? You haven't been the nude.' Well, I hadn't been the nude, but something inside me rebelled against the idea of taking off my clothes to sell *The Rag*. It wasn't that I was a prude. I had certainly gone skinny dipping, and I talked about the sexual revolution as much as anyone. But I did not want to pose for *The Rag*, and after countering accusations that I was being provincial (after all, I was from Wichita Falls), I heard myself saying, 'Why not have a male? Why not a male nude?' A male nude? Everyone laughed. That wouldn't sell *Rags*. What a ludicrous thought! But even as we all laughed (me included) I did exchange some meaningful glances with some of the other women present. Why was it our bodies that sold *Rags*? How was this different from what happened in the larger society? It wasn't much later that we had a women's meeting in SDS, an announcement which initially, by the way, drew similar laughter."[19]

Several SDS women, including Mariann Visard (later Wizard) and Alice Embree (both veterans of the Selective Service Office sit-in), and Susan Olan, were among the handful of students who began gathering early in 1969 at the University Y to air gender issues; others, such as sisters Judy and Linda Smith, former Peace Corps volunteers, were active in other New Left causes. Meeting in a discussion or "rap" group for consciousness raising, they shared personal experiences and worked toward an understanding of how social norms devalued women and suppressed their potential. Judy Smith and half a dozen or so members of this women's liberation group worked on the *Rag* and contributed articles on feminist issues. In addition to agitprop demonstrations, UT women's liberationists opened a birth control counseling service; the contraceptive pill, which had been introduced in 1960, was not readily available to college women unless they were married. Single women who requested contraception from the university health center were likely to get "long lectures on 'fooling around before marriage,'" one reported, and "Planned Parenthood, while more sympathetic, won't help students—too much pressure from university officials."[20] Subsequently, women not affiliated with the New Left who worked at the University of Texas Press began weekly consciousness-raising sessions that grew into the Austin Women's Organization; in 1972 it opened the Austin Women's Center.[21]

Women's liberation had no organizational structure; it was a cultural movement of local groups that formed spontaneously. In contrast to NOW, which focused on equal opportunity and legal rights, women's liberation wanted to change consciousness and culture (see Document 4.1). Such self-proclaimed "radical feminism" identified male dominance—patriarchy—and the rigid gender roles into which the sexes were socialized as the source of women's oppression. "We in Women's Liberation are very different than the feminists [of the nineteenth century]," Judy Smith explained. "We realize that the role of women must be totally questioned—not just on the political and economic levels—and redefined according to the choices we make about our own lives. We deny any inherent difference between men and women and regard everyone as human beings with the same potential." To the bewilderment of their male counterparts in the New Left, women's liberationists declared that they were fed up with sexist language. "A Woman Is Not a Chick," Sue Hester announced in a *Rag* article. Nor was she a "broad" or a "girl." "Perhaps if the demeaning names are dropped," Hester suggested, "women and men can gradually cease playing the silly, negative sex role games we were all conditioned to play and start relating to each other as EQUAL human beings."[22]

Women's liberationists also opened the subject of sexuality to analysis from a female point of view. One *Rag* contributor mocked the objectification of women's sexuality, the "diamond and emerald encrusted vagina to be given as a prize to the worthy," and the tradition that women should be the "docile" partners in sexual relationships.[23] In rap groups women shared their sexual embarrassments and frustrations, especially faked orgasms and ignorance about their bodies. They discovered that everyone else had the same problems and that they weren't alone in wanting sensitivity and satisfaction from male partners even though they didn't know how to ask for it. The Austin Women's Center sponsored several sexuality workshops, including one on the female body and sexual response that included a self-help presentation on breast and cervical examinations.

The idea that women were entitled to assert their sexual desires opened wide-ranging discussions of sexual lifestyles and the possibility of rejecting "compulsory heterosexuality." "If the women's movement is basically about alternatives to current rigid sex roles," an Austin liberationist argued, ". . . then women and men must be able to freely choose whether to relate heterosexually, homosexually, or bisexually." Frieda Werden found "just what I'd long been looking for" when she met an open lesbian couple. Despite years of sexual experience with men, including marriage, she had felt unsatisfied. For "nouveau lesbian" converts like Werden, "discovering lesbianism really meant discovering sex for the first time." After she came out in her rap group ("with encouragement and approval from the straight women"), Werden abandoned heterosexuality permanently. In 1974 she co-organized the Austin Women's Center's first sexuality workshop, with a panel of speakers representing the variety of sexual lifestyles: monogamous heterosexual marriage, heterosexual cohabitation, heterosexual open marriage, celibacy, lesbianism, lesbian-oriented bisexuality, and bisexuality. Werden called the first lesbian meeting at the women's center and helped found the Austin Lesbian Organization.[24]

CHICANA FEMINISM

Chicanas confronted the double discrimination of sexism in the Chicano movement and racism in the feminist movement, and their quests for women's rights and civil rights intertwined. Their inclusive style of political activism differed from that of both Anglo women and Chicano men; it was "a leadership that empowers *others*, not a hierarchical kind of leadership," Rosie Castro explained. By that she distinguished Chicanas' community-based activism from NOW's emphasis on individualism and personal fulfillment. But the statement was also a complaint, made in 1989 at a reunion of Chicano activists, that histories of the Chicano movement neglected the contributions of women, who had done much of the grassroots work. María Elena Martínez summed up the frustration of fighting on two fronts at once: "The white women, they automatically assumed that only white women were going to lead. And within the Chicano movement, that [*sic*] was just automatically assumed that . . . the men were going to lead."²⁵

Chicana feminism emerged most visibly within the Chicano student movement and its political organization, the Mexican American Youth Organization (MAYO), founded in San Antonio in 1967. The organizers, José Angel Gutiérrez and four other young men, criticized their elders in LULAC and the American GI Forum as assimilationist, apolitical, and ineffective in promoting Hispanic civil rights. Calling themselves Chicanos rather than Mexican Americans, MAYO members rejected LULAC's long crusade for whiteness and proclaimed their brown mestizo heritage. As cultural nationalists, Chicanos considered themselves a *raza* (people) dispossessed of their homeland in the Southwest, originally part of Mexico, by Anglo oppressors. As a *movimiento*, inspired by the Black Power movement, they sought economic and social justice for struggling Hispanics and a political base from which to contest local elections.

MAYO staged protest demonstrations and supported striking farmworkers, but its most widespread activity was organizing high school student walkouts to protest discrimination and inferior education. The most celebrated took place in Crystal City, Zavala County, in 1969, and young women were leaders of the protest. While the students had a plethora of complaints, flagrant racism in the selection of cheerleaders and the homecoming queen were pivotal. Although Mexican students outnumbered Anglos by four to one, the cheerleading squad was always composed of three Anglos and one Mexicana. After Diana Palacios was twice denied a place on the squad, she and Severita Lara, one of the most assertive Mexicanas, who repeatedly defied the ban on speaking Spanish, circulated a petition demanding equal representation for Chicanas, which the school board rejected. The administration, responding to a request by Anglo alumni, also instituted a new requirement that candidates for homecoming queen have at least one parent who was a graduate of the high school, thus eliminating all but half a dozen of the nearly three hundred

Chicana students. In protest, Palacios and Lara collected signatures from dozens of girls and presented the petition to the principal, who did nothing.

Organized and guided by MAYO's José Angel Gutiérrez and his wife, Luz Bazán Gutiérrez, the students prepared for a walkout. Severita Lara, Diana Serna, and Mario Treviño were chosen to lead it, with Lara as primary spokesperson. The list of demands included control over student elections, bilingual education, instruction in the Hispanic heritage of Texas, a Mexican-origin guidance counselor, and bicultural, bilingual teachers, administrators, and staff. After both the principal and the school board rejected Lara's presentation of the list, and she was briefly suspended without due process, several hundred students walked out on December 9, 1969. Fully supported by the Chicano parents—especially the mothers, whom the Gutiérrezes had carefully cultivated—the boycott spread to the junior high and elementary schools. It prompted a Texas Education Association investigation and, after Lara, Serna, and Treviño went to Washington, D.C., to tell their story, visits from the Justice Department and the Department of Heath, Education, and Welfare. The walkout lasted nearly a month, until the school board capitulated to nearly all the students' demands. The walkout "gave us self-esteem," Lara told a reporter years later. "I was proud I was Chicano. I was no longer embarrassed to eat my taco and my tortillas."[26]

Within days after the Crystal City walkout ended, the Gutiérrezes and other MAYO activists founded La Raza Unida (People United) Party (LRUP). A Chicano third party, it aimed to achieve community control by getting Mexicanos elected to local offices, including the school board. In preparation for the school walkout, José and Luz Gutiérrez had organized the Crystal City adults into Ciudadanos Unidos (United Citizens), to support the students with rallies and protests; it became the new party's base and the machine that selected candidates for the ticket. Knowing that the older males would resist equal standing for the women, the Gutiérrezes initially organized men and women separately. After the walkout ended, Luz and the other women, including Diana Serna's mother, Olivia, invaded the men's meeting (chaired by Olivia's husband) and announced, "We don't want to be the tamale makers and . . . the busy bees. We really want to be part of the decision making process."[27] Thereafter Ciudadanos Unidos was gender integrated, and as historian Armando Navarro has noted, "Women often were the CU's backbone when it came to work."[28] None, however, held the presidency, and it was several years before women were elected to the board of directors.

When LRUP was formally organized on January 17, 1970, Luz Gutiérrez was elected party chair for Zavala County. Female leadership and support were essential to LRUP's five years of community control there. A cadre of politically active housewives, including Enriqueta Palacios, whose daughter Diana had been at the center of the cheerleading dispute, and Virginia Muzquiz, who had been the first Mexicana to run for the state legislature (unsuccessfully, in 1964), did crucial work in getting out the vote. In addition, Muzquiz, whose knowledge of the Texas Election Code was encyclopedic, held a school for poll workers and watchers before each election, drilling them so that they could stand up to any Anglo election judge who tried to bend the law.

In contrast to the major parties, LRUP offered Chicanas the opportunity to run for office—out of pragmatism. As Martha Cotera later explained: "Guys wanted us to run for office . . . because they were running out of guys. . . . [A] lot of the time men couldn't run because of their jobs; they were vulnerable to being dismissed. So we needed wives to run, we needed women to run that weren't as vulnerable or maybe didn't even have jobs."[29] Elena Dias was elected to the Zavala County Commissioners Court in 1972. By then LRUP had spread across South Texas and into the Southwest and California; 36 percent of county chairpersons and 20 percent of precinct chairs were women. Viviana Santiago and Mercedes Casarez won seats on the Crystal City school board in 1973 and 1974, respectively. In 1974, when LRUP swept the Zavala County offices, Rosa Marta was elected district clerk, Virginia Muzquiz, county clerk, Carmen Flores, county treasurer, and Irene Cuellar, Precinct 3 justice of the peace. No women, however, were put forward as candidates for mayor and the city council.

As LRUP organized beyond Zavala County, women held informal caucuses to express concern about the party's need to address women's issues and the lack of female speakers and workshop leaders. (When Martha Cotera presented a list of demands for inclusion at an LRUP meeting, a young male shouted, "Why don't you go home and do the dishes, where you belong?") At the state organizing convention in 1971, women comprised slightly less than one-third of the delegates, and only two women were appointed to the platform committee. One of them, Evey Chapa, a feminist who became state committeewoman, was probably responsible for the platform's statement about female equality. A relatively mild discussion, it noted that "the minority woman does not have the luxury of dealing exclusively with feminism and fighting male chauvinism, as racism plays an even bigger role in suppressing peoples in the state of Texas." It affirmed the family as the basis of the party and took no separate stand on women's rights beyond endorsing the Equal Rights Amendment and the repeal of legislation that discriminated against women. The platform also specified that all resolutions referring to equal rights include women, and it encouraged women to join the party and participate in all decision-making positions.[30]

Early in 1973, Chapa, Martha Cotera, and other women who felt that "words are not enough" began meeting to discuss women's role in the movement and formulate plans for a party women's caucus, Mujeres por la Raza Unida. Mujeres held its first conference at the statewide LRUP meeting that summer; Virginia Muzquiz, who had succeeded Luz Gutiérrez as party chair in Zavala County, was the featured speaker. Nearly two hundred Chicanas attended the workshops on state and local political structure and political organizing. The mission of Mujeres por la Raza Unida was to attract more women to the party, secure more leadership positions for women, and encourage them to run for political office. Mujeres worked through small regional conferences and local chapters; a statewide caucus formed in 1975 with Angelita Mendoza as secretary. In 1975 the women challenged the men for the party's top post—María Elena Martínez ran for LRUP chair. After Mujeres formed, Martínez recalled, "there was the whole question of why women automatically assumed that we had to run for vice chair and not chair? So from the very beginning of the [women's caucus] meeting, when the discussion started focusing on who would be running for vice chair . . . I said, 'And why are we not running for chair? . . . We work [for] the party and we've organized the party. I do not understand why we have to automatically assume that we can only be vice chairs.'"[31] Martínez lost in 1974 but won two years later; she was the party's last head.

Chicanas grappled with Chicanismo and the feminist movement simultaneously. The first National Chicana Conference, also known as La Conferencia de Mujeres por la Raza, met in Houston in 1971. Organized by Elma Barrera, the city's first Hispanic television reporter, and the Magnolia Park YWCA, the conference brought together approximately six hundred women from two dozen states. The majority were young, and the agenda was radical; in addition to long-standing grievances of inferior education and employment discrimination, the participants debated issues of sex, marriage, contraception, and even religious oppression. "I have been told that the Chicana's struggle is not the same as the white woman's struggle," Barrera announced. "I have been told that the problems are different and that . . . fighting for our rights as women and as human beings is anti-Chicano and anti-male. But let me tell you what being a Chicana means in Houston, Texas. It means learning how to best please the men in the Church and the men at home, not in that order." Among the conference resolutions was a demand for "free legal abortions and birth control for the Chicano community, controlled by Chicanas" and a recommendation that every Chicano community establish twenty-four-hour day care facilities that would "reflect the concept of La Raza as the united family."[32] By the end of the conference a dissident faction had emerged. Contending that the focus should be more strongly on racism and that the meeting should have been held in the barrio rather than in a "gringa" institution, the dissidents walked out.

Chicana feminists kept aloof from the Anglo feminist movement, both to protect themselves from criticism by their men and because they resented the attitudes of their Anglo counterparts. Prominent LRUP activists such as Rosie Castro, a teacher who ran in 1971 for the San Antonio City Council on the Committee for a Better Barrio slate, and Martha Cotera, an Austin librarian and information specialist who assisted in the Crystal City revolt, were plain-spoken critics of mainstream Anglo feminists. "Unfortunately, the only effect Anglo feminism has had on the Chicana has been negative," Cotera wrote in the early 1970s. "Suddenly mujeres involved in the struggle for social justice, who have always advocated more and stronger family participation in all po-litical activities, are suspected of assimilating into the feminist ideology of an alien culture that actively seeks our continued domination." Because Chicano males were quick to label La Raza feminists *agringadas* (assimilationists) and *vendidas* (sellouts), Cotera became a lay authority on Mexicana history, with the goal of binding feminism to La Raza's cultural nationalism. In *Diosa y Hembra: The History and Heritage of Chicanas in the U.S.* (1976) and other writ-ings, she set out the facts of Hispanic women's long tradition of community activism, aiming to make it "OK to be Chicano and OK to be a feminist."[33]

Middle-class Anglo feminists seemed not to understand—or from Chi-canas' perspective, not to care—that Chicanas confronted racial and class barriers that were as much of an obstacle as sex discrimination, if not more so. Rosie Castro explained: "Our people cannot come out of oppression un-less we do it together. . . . [I]t's a race question. . . . All [Anglo feminists] wanted was to co-opt the Chicanas to support the White women's agenda."[34] Chicana feminists perceived NOW feminists as not only racist but also classist and paternalistic (or maternalistic). They held conferences with registration fees that kept poor women from attending, and they expected the Chicanas who could afford to participate to be deferential; those who sought real input were called divisive. "Many Anglo women, including feminists, simply cannot accept the fact that there are minority women with brains and status," Cotera wrote with asperity.[35]

An especially pointed criticism was that Chicanas needed to focus on eco-nomic survival, while the goal of NOW feminists was personal advancement. From Cotera's perspective, the NOW feminists were not interested in radi-cal change, just "anything that would benefit their careers. Anything that would give them more money and better jobs and access to credit." When convenient, Chicanas worked with Anglo feminists because, as Cotera astutely noted, "whatever they get, we're gonna get," but Chicanas preferred to address women's issues within the context of the Chicana community and in their own cultural voice. Their concern was always to ensure "that our feminist expression will be our own and coherent with our Raza's goals."[36]

REPRODUCTIVE FREEDOM

Feminism made its greatest impact on political debate with the divisive issues of abortion and the Equal Rights Amendment and provoked a backlash that stimulated the growth of a powerful new conservative movement. NOW included an abortion demand in the Bill of Rights adopted at its second convention in 1967 only after vociferous debate. Younger women led the push. "Kids from Michigan, Ohio, and Texas kept standing up and shouting 'We've got to have an abortion plank,'" one of the state presidents recalled.[37] The decision caused a schism; professional women who wanted NOW to focus on education and employment discrimination left the organization and formed the Women's Equity Action League (WEAL).

By that time the American Law Institute had been advocating less restrictive abortion laws for several years, as had some physicians and welfare rights groups. Beginning in the late 1960s a handful of states loosened their laws, allowing for abortion in cases of rape, incest, or fetal deformity or to safeguard a woman's physical or mental health. Texas remained in the restrictive category, permitting abortion only if the pregnancy was life-threatening. The Texas statute did not prevent abortions; it simply forced women with means to get a legal abortion out of state. Planned Parenthood of San Antonio had so many requests for abortion referrals that it secured group airfare rates for patients to fly to California. In addition to denying women personal autonomy and discriminating against those too poor to travel, the Texas statute spawned a dangerous underground of unregulated abortion providers and put sympathetic doctors at risk of criminal prosecution if they performed the procedure. Women who attempted self-induced abortion ended up in hospital emergency rooms, often with permanent womb damage. When feminists took up the abortion issue, they rejected reform of existing laws and called for complete repeal.

The beginnings of *Roe v. Wade*, the 1973 Supreme Court decision that struck down the Texas abortion law, trace back to the tiny Birth Control Information Center that Judy Smith, Victoria Foe, Bea Vogel Durden, and other women's liberationists at the University of Texas established next to the *Rag* office in 1969. In addition to contraceptive advice, the volunteers quietly gave referrals to safe and sanitary abortion clinics in Mexico. Not knowing what kind of legal trouble they might be courting, and worried that they might be prosecuted as accomplices to an illegal act, they sought advice from Sarah Weddington, a recent graduate of the UT law school. Weddington could not find a clear answer in the statutes, and after a bill to reform the state's abortion law failed in the legislature, she agreed to challenge its constitutionality in court. She solicited assistance from former classmate Linda Coffee in Dallas; Coffee located a pregnant plaintiff, Norma McCorvey, who was listed as Jane Roe in the lawsuit Weddington and Coffee filed in federal court. In 1970 a three-judge panel agreed that the Texas law was an unconstitutional violation of the right to privacy under the Ninth Amendment but declined to issue an injunction ordering the state to stop enforcing it.

While Weddington and Coffee were prosecuting *Roe,* middle-class women in Dallas established an abortion reform advocacy group. The Dallas Committee to Study Abortion formed in 1969 after the Women's Auxiliary of the Unitarian Church, which had been discussing the issue, invited Virginia Whitehill as a guest speaker. Whitehill, who thought she was probably the only woman in Dallas who belonged to both NOW and the Junior League, emphasized the disproportionate burden of the law on poor women, and her listeners decided to organize. The Dallas Committee mailed out literature and lobbied in Austin; Whitehill became its chief fund-raiser and traveling speechmaker. After the *Roe* verdict, additional abortion rights groups emerged in Houston, Galveston, and Austin. At the instigation of the Dallas Committee, an umbrella group called the Texas Abortion Coalition (TAC) formed at the end of 1970, with Sarah Weddington as acting chair. Adopting the slogan "Abortion Is a Personal Decision," the TAC planned a statewide campaign for a repeal law. Weddington drafted a model bill, which the legislature rejected in 1971, and she argued the appeal of *Roe v. Wade* before the U.S. Supreme Court. Its ruling, on January 22, 1973, upheld a pregnant woman's right to privacy.

Opponents of abortion immediately organized in protest. At the beginning the Catholic Church led the movement; it had formed the Right to Life Committee as soon as the states began to consider abortion reform. After *Roe* the organization formally separated from the church (although it continued to work closely with it) and welcomed abortion opponents of all denominations. A state affiliate, Texas Right to Life, was in place before *Roe* reached the Supreme Court and afterward followed the national committee in conducting a media campaign centered on images of late-term fetuses and depicting abortion as murder. Feminists responded with a symbolic wire coat hanger and emphasized the number of women who died from illegal abortions. When antiabortionists adopted the label "pro-life," feminists became "pro-choice," and in many cities the two sides held competing vigils every January 22. The *San Antonio Express* in 1977 depicted the irreconcilable divisiveness: a photo of three women, one of them a nun, singing the national anthem at a Right to Life memorial service, sat above a headline, "San Antonio Memorial Service Held for 'Butcher Abortionist Victims,'" describing the local NOW chapter's counter demonstration.[38]

THE EQUAL RIGHTS AMENDMENT: FOR AND AGAINST

While *Roe* was working its way through the courts, two long campaigns for equal legal rights finally bore fruit. In 1971 the legislature passed the Texas Equal Legal Rights Amendment (ELRA) to the state constitution, and the voters approved it overwhelmingly the following year. The thirteen words— "equality under the law shall not be denied or abridged because of sex"—had failed in six previous legislative sessions, beginning in 1959. Like the campaign to admit women to jury service, the ELRA was a legislative project of the Texas Business and Professional Women's Clubs. Hermine Tobolowsky, a Dallas attorney, first approached the legislature in 1957 and made equal legal rights a personal crusade after she became TBPW president in 1959. For years she toured the state giving speeches, wrote articles and pamphlets, and lobbied. Beginning in 1965 another Dallas attorney, Louise Raggio, chair of the Family Law Section of the American Bar Association, put together a task force that wrote the Marital Property Act, a comprehensive revision of the statutes that, in effect, gave married women equal legal rights. Each woman believed that her own bill made the other's unnecessary. The Marital Property Act did have far-reaching effects,[39] but the TBPW stubbornly persisted. For Tobolowsky, who had been insulted by the chief justice of the Texas Supreme Court when she applied for a clerkship—"no woman has sense enough," he snapped—getting an ELRA on the books was as much a matter of principle as law.

In 1972, Congress at last passed the federal Equal Rights Amendment (ERA), first proposed by Alice Paul of the National Woman's Party in 1923 and introduced annually thereafter. Texas suffragists had opposed the ERA, fearing it would invalidate hard-won state laws protecting women factory workers, and the old Progressive Era women's coalition lobbied against it for decades. But by the 1970s nearly one-half of American women were in the labor force, and the growing number of professional women found laws that limited female working hours to be a career-building hindrance. Union women were likewise beginning to modify their opposition, and some, having discovered that protective legislation restricted them from earning overtime pay and receiving promotions, had begun to challenge the laws in court. By the time Congress acted, Left-liberal women were solidly behind the ERA, and ratification by three-fourths of the states seemed easily within reach. The Texas Legislature approved the amendment quickly—the *Texas Observer* noted that "it raised about as much interest as a sewer bond referendum"— and nearly unanimously, well aware of the advantage of a yes vote in an election year.

Texas was one of twenty-two states that ratified the ERA in 1972, before Phyllis Schlafly of Illinois had fully launched a campaign to derail it. Schlafly, a right-wing Republican activist whose book *A Choice, Not an Echo* had helped Barry Goldwater win the GOP presidential nomination in 1964, published a monthly newsletter and held an annual political leadership conference in St. Louis to teach conservative women strategies for defeating liberal candidates in local elections. Her opening salvo, "What's Wrong with 'Equal Rights' for Women" in the February 1972 *Phyllis Schlafly Report*, laid out the arguments that antifeminists would articulate for the next decade: the ERA would force women to work outside the home, abolish alimony and child support, and make women subject to the military draft. "The women libbers don't understand that most women want to be a wife, mother, and homemaker and are happy in that role," she insisted.[40] Schlafly, who could afford full-time household help while she traveled around the country denouncing the ERA, implicitly championed the family wage ideology and the financial benefits it offered women like herself. Wanting equality instead of dependence on a male earner was "anti-family" in her view. By fall Schlafly and her supporters had STOP ERA "STOP" (stood for "Stop Taking Our Privileges") up and running, with the goal of defeating the amendment in the states where it was pending and persuading those that had already ratified (such as Texas) to rescind their approval. In 1975 she appointed state STOP ERA directors and expanded her political reach by founding the Eagle Forum, which she called "the alternative to women's lib."

Initially, Schlafly relied on conservative women active in Republican politics to build the anti-ERA movement; as a Catholic she had no entrée into the network of fundamentalist Protestant churchwomen. They were recruited by Lottie Beth Hobbs and Becky Tilotta of Fort Worth, who formed Women Who Want to be Women (WWWW) in 1974. Both were prominent in the Church of Christ, which like all fundamentalist denominations interpreted the Bible literally and believed that gender roles were divinely ordained.

Hobbs, a graduate of Abilene Christian College, supported herself by writing and distributing religious-inspirational books, which she used in teaching women's Bible classes (the Church of Christ did not permit women to teach mixed groups). After reading a leaflet advocating the ERA, Hobbs checked out some books on feminism from the public library and was shocked: "They were so awful that I put them under the bed so my nieces and nephews wouldn't see them!" Tilotta, a former dean of women at Oklahoma Christian College (supported by the Churches of Christ) and an attendee of Phyllis Schlafly's annual leadership seminars, considered feminism apocalyptically dangerous. The women of NOW were "pushing to tear down the home. Lesbianism and homosexuality are their goals . . . to get that legalized so that these gay people can adopt children," Tilotta asserted. "It's the most damnable thing that has ever hit our nation, some of the things they stand for. I think we've got to speak out against this evil. God has destroyed whole nations because of this."[41]

Tilotta and Hobbs expressed the indignation of fundamentalist Christians who were appalled by the new morality of the sexual revolution and convinced that feminism, uncloseted homosexuality, sex education in the public schools, and the ERA all stemmed from the same source. The WWWW spoke for the religious Right; the secular Right organized through the Committee to Restore Women's Rights (CRWR) and Happiness of Womanhood (HOW), both led by women who belonged to the ultraconservative, Communist-hunting John Birch Society. Dianne Edmondson, a transplant from Oklahoma, where she had helped defeat ERA ratification, headed CRWR in Texas and claimed the organization had forty chapters. Two political scientists at the University of Houston conducted a study of anti-ERA women who lobbied at the capitol and found that nearly all were white. As a group, they were predominantly middle-aged and middle- to upper-middle-class; almost three-fourths were housewives. More than half had attended college, and almost two-thirds had grown up in small towns or rural areas. Nearly all were church members; two-thirds were fundamentalists, predominantly from the Churches of Christ.[42]

Churchwomen from nonfundamentalist denominations were more likely to support the ERA; Church Women United, the National Council of Churches, the United Methodist Church Women's Division, and the United Presbyterian Church all endorsed it. With the exception of the PTA, so did most of the voluntary associations of the old Progressive Era women's coalition. The countervailing force to the WWWW and the CRWR was Texans for ERA, formed late in 1974 by a coalition of NOW, the League of Women Voters, the American Association of University Women, WEAL, and the Texas Women's

Political Caucus. Texans for ERA was coordinated by Barbara Vackar, but its primary spokeswoman was Hermine Tobolowsky. The pro and anti factions faced each other in the 1975 and 1977 legislative sessions, as the antis, with WWWW in the lead, pressed for recision of the state's ratification. Dubbed "pink ladies" by the press because they wore pink dresses and skirts, the antis arrived in church groups by the busload and distributed loaves of homemade bread to legislators on opening day to reinforce the homemaker image. Phyllis Schlafly made an appearance in 1975.

Like the anti-suffragists in the Progressive Era, the ERA opponents were masters at generating misinformation that kept the liberal opposition scrambling to control the damage. WWWW printed leaflets with alarmist titles such as "Warning! ERA is Dangerous to Women!!" and "Legalize Homosexuality?" but the most widely disseminated one was "Ladies! Have You Heard?"—known as "the pink sheet" (see Document 4.3). Written by Lottie Beth Hobbs, it was, in the liberal *Texas Observer*'s judgment, "an efficiently dishonest piece of propaganda."[43] According to Hobbs, the words "equality of rights under the law shall not be denied or abridged by the United States or by any state on account of sex" would force wives to provide half of the financial support of their families, subject women to military draft, decriminalize rape, legalize homosexual marriage, and require unisex military barracks and public restrooms. Texans for ERA countered with a rebuttal, "the blue sheet," by Hermine Tobolowsky (see Document 4.4). In response to a legislator's request for a legal opinion, the attorney general's office also disputed the pink sheet's claims.

Like the suffragists battling the "Negro bogey" in the 1910s, the pro-ERA forces were never able to slay the "unisex bathroom" specter. Even though the state ERA, whose wording was nearly identical to the federal one, had not produced any de-sexing calamities, the antis were vocal enough to bring some legislators to their side. The WWWW so successfully linked ERA opposition to biblical morality that Texans for ERA finally had to issue a response in religious terms: "In the Judeo-Christian tradition the message of Genesis is that God is indeed the Creator. Both men and women were made equal in God's sight. Any discrimination on the basis of sex is contrary to the will of God."[44] Ultimately the feminists were able to beat back recision, but their efforts probably mattered less than the support already demonstrated by the four-to-one margin of approval of the state ELRA by electorate, which gave legislators political cover to avoid a vote. Texas was one of only three southern states to ratify the ERA, and the only one that did not rescind its approval.

SPLINTERED SISTERHOOD: THE 1977 HOUSTON WOMEN'S CONFERENCE

The reemergence of large numbers of middle-class white women into public activism, as historian Nancy MacLean has observed, coincided with the gradual disintegration of the family wage system over the last quarter of the twentieth century. By the 1970s the booming economy of the long post–World War II era that had supported the suburban stay-at-home motherhood ideal was over. Two decades of slow growth and stagnant wages that undercut men's ability to support families as sole breadwinners lay ahead. At the same time, the social structures that had braced the family wage system—women's lack of access to good jobs and reliable means to control fertility, plus the stigmatization of divorce and homosexuality—were eroding. Some women sought to dismantle a system that now hindered more than helped them. Others, alarmed by the increasing number of cohabiting couples, single-parent households, and open lesbian partnerships, rallied to defend it. Both sides had a national stage in Houston on November 18–21, 1977.

The National Women's Conference was funded by Congress and established as a follow-up to a 1975 United Nations conference in Mexico City marking the "International Year of the Woman." It was the first national women's conference in the United States since the women's rights meeting in Seneca Falls, New York, in 1848. Two thousand women and girls participated in a relay to carry a torch from Seneca Falls to Houston, a media event that lasted fifty-one days; a thousand more joined the relay runners for the final mile. The conference drew two thousand delegates, representing fifty states and six territories, and nearly as many members of the press, as well as thousands of observers. The enabling legislation passed by Congress required that each state's delegation reflect the racial-ethnic diversity of its population. The delegates' mission was to debate and vote on the recommendations, called the National Plan of Action, drafted by the National Commission on the Observance of International Women's Year. Appointed by President Gerald Ford in 1975, the commission had been charged with recommending policies to make "A More Perfect Union" for American women.

The national conference was preceded by state pre-conferences, also funded by Congress, to discuss women's issues and elect delegates to Houston. The Texas meeting, held June 24–26 on the University of Texas campus in Austin, attracted more than 2,500 participants. The state coordinating committee strove so conscientiously for racial and ethnic balance that minority women were disproportionately represented: 17 percent of workshop and reaction session chairpersons were African American and an equal percentage were Chicana. An outreach committee made a special effort to draw in women who were poor, rural, older, or students. Owanah Anderson, a Choctaw-Chickasaw Indian from Wichita Falls, chaired the state meeting; vice chairs were Wilhelmina Delco, an African American, and Diana Camacho, a Chicana. The delegate-nominating committee offered a slate of candidates with heavy minority representation; only 52 percent were Caucasian.[45]

The inclusive numbers notwithstanding, the gathering fractured along the usual fault lines while still in the planning stages. There was no lesbian representation on the coordinating committee, and a subsequent request to rectify the omission was voted down on procedural grounds; lesbians considered, but decided against, a boycott and demonstrations.[46] Chicanas, even though they had eight members on the committee, were alert to the likelihood that Anglo women would want to make all the decisions. When they perceived that prominent Anglo feminists—committee member Diana Camacho dubbed them "Big Mamas"—intended to plan the conference with little input from the coordinating committee, Hispanic women took independent action (see Document 4.6). Martha Cotera organized a Chicana Advisory Committee for International Women's Year Concerns and contributed most of its operating funds (for which she was later denied reimbursement by the conference organizers).[47] Determined that Chicanas would not "come into the Conference as 'observers' [or] 'subsidized women,'" the Chicana Advisory Committee demanded opportunities for volunteer input at the coordinating committee meetings and protested the conference registration fee as a deterrent to participation by poor women.[48] Working separately, the Chicana group put in place its own committees for media and public relations, resolutions, caucuses, and entertainment (which included a Spanish-language presentation of Henrik Ibsen's feminist play, *A Doll's House*). Nearly four hundred Hispanic women attended.

Antifeminists were the least represented group; the only conservative woman on the coordinating committee was Genne Ridgeway, a homemaker who served on the board of Texas Right to Life. Phyllis Schlafly's Eagle Forum made a nationwide attempt to pack the state conventions and elect a majority of delegates, and the Texas Eagle Forum acted accordingly. Its president announced in the state newsletter, quoting Schlafly, "We must take over the state meeting . . . and make sure it projects a pro-family, pro-homemaker, pro-morality, and pro-life image."[49] In more than a dozen states conservatives did overwhelm the conventions, but Texas feminists had obtained a copy of Schlafly's letter and were prepared. Conservatives were unable to prevent passage of a resolution supporting the ERA—thanks to the presence of Chicana feminists, according to some sources.[50] The convention also narrowly approved civil rights for lesbians, whom one opponent described as "an abomination to God." A pro-life resolution, passed by the Mothers and Children Workshop, was derailed by the resolutions committee, which did not forward it to be voted on. There was no mention of abortion, pro or con, in the conference recommendations. Of the fifty-eight delegates elected to represent the state in Houston, only six opposed the ERA and abortion rights. Disgruntled conservatives subsequently held a press conference in Dallas to announce that they had filed a request for investigation of the balloting with IWY officials. "The militant libbers and lesbians were in control, not the grassroots Texas woman as it was billed," a spokeswoman contended. "There was no shred of morality from the platform."[51]

When the National Women's Conference convened in November, the feminist-antifeminist divide became newspaper and television fodder. Three First Ladies—Lady Bird Johnson, Betty Ford, and Rosalyn Carter—spoke, and political and feminist celebrities were highly visible. New York congresswoman Bella Abzug presided, and Liz Carpenter, an IWY commissioner from Texas and former press secretary to Lady Bird Johnson, gave a welcoming address. Texas congresswoman Barbara Jordan delivered the keynote speech. Thousands of women attended as observers, and for some the experience was an epiphany (see Document 4.7). While the debates were loud, antifeminists made up only about 20 percent of the delegates. The pro–Plan of Action majority was strong enough to pass even the three most controversial planks: support for the ERA (seconded by Ann Richards), reproductive freedom (seconded by Sarah Weddington), and lesbian civil rights, which Betty Friedan, to everyone's surprise, finally endorsed. Other recommendations in the plan addressed domestic violence, homemakers, minority women, child care, rape, education, and health. Only the proposal for a cabinet-level women's department in the federal government was turned down. The antifeminist minority, calling itself the Pro-Family Delegation, compiled a dissenting report and released it to the news media.

The main antifeminist event, billed as the Pro-Family Rally, was held across town while the National Women's Conference was in progress. Lottie Beth Hobbs, president of the Pro-Family Forum (the new name for the WWWW, which began cooperating with Phyllis Schlafly's Eagle Forum in 1975), planned and organized the rally and convinced Schlafly that it should be held in the Astroarena (capacity 12,000) as a show of strength. Hobbs also coauthored a petition opposing "ERA, Abortion, Federally-controlled Early Childhood Development Programs, and the Teaching or Glorification of Homosexuality, Lesbianism, or Prostitution," to be signed and sent to Congress as a counterweight to the NWC's Plan of Action. The Pro-Family Rally outdrew the NWC, overflowing the Astroarena, and when Hobbs opened the gathering, she shared the stage with piles of boxes containing three hundred thousand signed copies of the pro-family petitions. The predominantly white crowd represented a variety of conservative organizations and women like Sarah Welch, spokeswoman for a group from Katy, who contended that the feminist movement "plainly shows contempt for the homemaker and the leadership of men in the family."[52] The speakers included right-wing congressman Robert Dornan of California and Texas state representative Clay Smothers, who had led the unsuccessful effort to rescind the state's ratification of the ERA, but the main attraction was Phyllis Schlafly, whose speech was titled "ERA: An Attack on the Family." A grassroots uprising of social conservatives had put gender issues at the center of national political discourse, and "family values," first voiced by antifeminist women, became the rallying cry of the New Right.

AFTERMATH: WOMEN AND THE NEW RIGHT

The Houston conferences were watershed events, but not in the way the IWY organizers had intended. Although feminists demonstrated their strength in passing the Plan of Action, President Jimmy Carter never implemented its recommendations. Antifeminists not only succeeded in mounting an impressive display of power at their counterdemonstration but also forged a "pro-family" image with broad appeal. The National Women's Conference, while inspirational for feminists, dismayed many other women and helped the antis recruit new followers. One such woman told a sociologist that she had decided to go to Houston as an observer after attending the Texas women's preconference and being shocked by the presence of "lesbians with Levis on and hair on their legs." A Democratic Party activist, she did not belong to either the Eagle Forum or the WWWW, and she endorsed equal rights and even abortion "for medical and psychological reasons." But she was morally offended by "abortion on demand" and "homosexuals coming out of the closet . . . where they belong"; lesbianism, she said firmly, was "a serious threat to the family."[53]

The National Women's Conference gave antifeminists the "proof" they needed that all feminists were either lesbians or lesbian sympathizers. Within three months the Texas Eagle Forum issued a pamphlet entitled *Christian Be Watchful: Hidden Dangers in the New Coalition of Feminism, Humanism, Socialism, and Lesbianism,* calling attention to Betty Friedan's endorsement of lesbian rights and to the lesbian attendees' celebration of the passage of the sexual preference plank by releasing balloons that proclaimed, "We are everywhere." *Christian Be Watchful* went through four printings between February and December 1978, and large lots were sent on request to Eagle Forums in states where the ERA was pending so that "Eagles" could distribute copies to legislators. By then, conservative women had all but succeeded in killing the amendment; although Congress extended the deadline for ratification, ERAmerica, the coalition cochaired by Liz Carpenter, won no more victories. When the time expired in 1982, feminists still had only thirty-five of the required thirty-eight states.

By then, Ronald Reagan, the choice of social conservatives, was in the White House. When he won the Republican nomination in 1980, the party platform did not endorse the ERA and supported a constitutional ban on abortion. Republican feminists who were committed to the party's core values of free market economics, strong national defense, and limited government, but who also supported the ERA and held moderate views on abortion, found themselves a marginalized minority. One such woman was Anne Armstrong of Kenedy County, counselor to Presidents Nixon and Ford, who had worked for the ERA but also cochaired Reagan's 1980 campaign. She took the lead in forming the Texas Women's Alliance in 1984 as a vehicle for party women not aligned with the New Right. Although officially open (by invitation only) to conservative women of both parties, the TWA was an elite group of predominantly Republican business and professional women. Its purpose was to research issues, make policy recommendations in areas such as international trade, tax reform, higher education, and the state budget and, in Armstrong's words, "change the perception that women are solely concerned with what are perceived to be women's issues."[54] It functioned as a working group for well-connected traditional conservatives who had, or aspired to have, party influence or to hold public office.

By contrast, New Right women in Texas worked through a variety of grassroots organizations, including Concerned Women for America, the Texas Christian Coalition, the American Family Association, the Texas Eagle Forum, and the Pro-Family Forum. The Texas Eagle Forum, founded in 1977, was headed first by LaNeil Wright Spivey and after 1993 by Cathie Adams. Both women were from Dallas and appointed by Phyllis Schlafly. Spivey's background was in evangelical church work, while Adams's was in political activism. Drawn into Republican politics by her opposition to abortion, Adams was a frequent delegate to the state and national GOP conventions. Under Spivey and Adams the Texas Eagle Forum built a network of active local chapters that focused on fostering conservatism at the grassroots. Volunteers lobbied in Austin, and the organization published legislative scorecards on its policy items to serve as voter aids. The Eagle Forum joined other New Right groups in backing Christian conservatives to run against moderate Republicans for the State Board of Education and crusaded to open curriculum changes and textbook selection to public scrutiny; they demanded abstinence-only sex education and the teaching of creationism alongside evolution. One local Eagle Forum president, Alice Patterson, became state field director for the Texas branch of Pat Robertson's Christian Coalition in 1991 and in four years built membership from under nine thousand to nearly seventy thousand.

Moderate Republican women who were pro-choice, citing the party's bedrock principle of government noninterference with individual liberty, found the ascension of the New Right alarming. "Pat Robertson, well he scared the hell out of me . . . with his narrow-mindedness, his bigotry, his 'our kind of people' kind of thing," one complained. "The party has hardened toward the religious right, and their only issue, as far as I can see is abortion, which I just can't see as anybody's business. They are chasing off moderate Republicans."[55] The Texas Federation of Republican Women resisted New Right influence longer than the state party, which by the mid-1990s was dominated at every level by Christian conservatives. In reaction, Democrat Cecile Richards in 1995 founded the Texas Freedom Alliance, subsequently renamed the Texas Freedom Network, as a moderate-liberal opposition to the religious Right. The following year it organized the Texas Faith Network, a coalition of mainstream ministers, as an alternative voice to the conservative clergy. By the time Samantha Smoot succeeded Richards as executive director in 1998, the Texas Freedom Network claimed seven thousand members. Concentrating especially on public relations work, the TFN functioned as a grassroots-level resource on the Christian Right, investigating its funding sources and mobilizing opposition to initiatives such as private school vouchers and textbook censorship.

Opposition to abortion was a core issue for the New Right. While political pressure from conservative activists failed to overturn *Roe*, it chipped away at the foundations. Legislatures in Texas and other states enacted restrictions such as consent requirements and regulation of abortion providers, while the Hyde Amendment, which Congress passed in 1976, banned federal funding for abortions except in cases of rape, incest, or life-threatening pregnancy. Pro-choice forces pushed back, organizing and lobbying. Texas State NOW gave its Reproductive Rights Task Force funding priority, and in 1978 the Dallas Committee to Study Abortion morphed into the Texas Abortion Rights Action League (TARAL).[56] TARAL's Education Fund established the Rosie Jiménez Project to raise money and make referrals for women unable to afford abortion clinic fees. Rosie Jiménez had died in McAllen in 1977 from an illegal abortion, the first victim of the Hyde Amendment, which severely curtailed access for poor women. The year before the Hyde Amendment went into effect four thousand indigent Texas women had abortions paid for by Medicaid; in 1981 only nine did.

Fundamentalist Christians believed that the nation risked God's punishment by sanctioning abortion, and their surge into the antiabortion movement inflamed the rhetoric of resistance. In the 1980s the focus turned to grassroots direct action—mass protests and blockades, violence, and bombings—to intimidate pregnant women and shut down clinics. A Fort Worth clinic was burned to the ground, and one in Mesquite suffered an arson attack. Protesters from the Pro-Life Action Network, a national organization led by James Scheidler, stormed a Planned Parenthood clinic in Houston and tried to invade the operating rooms; when prevented, they occupied the waiting room and chained the front door shut. In Dallas a group of Ku Klux Klansmen and one unmasked woman demonstrated in front of a clinic. Pro-life protesters "stand in the alley and scream at patients," the director of Waco's Planned Parenthood reported; they "accuse the staff of murder" and shout that their "souls will burn in hell."[57] Clinics mobilized volunteers to escort women through hordes of protesters who chanted "baby killers" and "God knows your name, we know your name," but the harassment was emotionally draining for both patients and staff. "It is effective, and it is intimidating, and it is scary," the director of Planned Parenthood of Bryan told an interviewer. "The girls cry when [other employees] get something in the mail, and you know it affects their families and their home lives."[58] Within three years of the Bryan clinic's opening, all of the original employees except the director had left.

A landmark legal ruling grew out of a massive protest in 1992 when Randall Terry, director of the national organization Operation Rescue, vowed to close every abortion clinic in Houston while the Republican National Convention met in the city. Four thousand trained volunteers defended clinics when Operation Rescue protesters tore up copies of a judge's restraining order requiring them to keep a prescribed distance from the clinics and then rushed the entrances. In *Operation Rescue v. Planned Parenthood* (1994) a Texas jury assessed punitive damages of more than $1 million against four male defendants from Operation Rescue and Rescue America. It was the largest civil award ever imposed against the antiabortion movement, and that same year Congress passed legislation criminalizing clinic blockades. Clinic violence peaked in Texas in 1992 but pro-life lobbying intensified. As Republicans gained control of the state Senate and approached a majority in the House, pro-life victories mounted. In 1999, Texas tied with Michigan for first place in passing anti-choice legislation.[59]

CRACKING THE GLASS CEILING:
WOMEN IN ELECTORAL POLITICS

When the Texas Women's Political Caucus (TWPC) formed in 1971 as an affiliate of the newly established National Women's Political Caucus, only two women sat in the state legislature: Senator Barbara Jordan (see Document 4.8), elected in 1966, and Representative Frances "Sissy" Farenthold, elected in 1968. Jordan, an imposing African American with a mesmerizing baritone voice, had become an insider in the small club of senators by refusing to be defined by gender or race; she went on to a career in Congress and iconic status in the Democratic Party. Farenthold, a conspicuous island in a sea of 149 men, had an experience more typical of female invaders of male territory. Capitol guards, assuming that all women were secretaries, tried to prevent her from parking in the reserved lot and from entering the legislative chambers. "I was not a token, I was a joke," she later recalled. "There was a sort of pethood ordained for you if you accepted it."[60] Farenthold did not. She refused to let the House proclaim her its valentine on February 14 and protested when she was barred from a lunchtime committee meeting at the male-only Citadel Club in the Driskill Hotel. A former director of the Nueces County Legal Aid program, Farenthold had run for office hoping to change state policies that stood in the way of relief for poor clients, but she was pegged as a "lost causes" liberal, and most of her bills failed.

The TWPC organized with the goal of making women political players instead of anomalies. "A white male geriatric club is not a democracy," its first chairman, Helen Cassidy, observed dryly. Functioning as the political arm of the women's movement, it aimed to increase the number of women in elected and appointive offices and to work with both major parties to promote women's issues. Founder Chris Miller, who owned a public relations agency in Fort Worth, decided to form a state caucus after attending a NOW convention in California, at which Betty Friedan announced that every state needed a chapter of the National Women's Political Caucus. Miller made up her mind to act during the flight back to Texas. The TWPC spun off local caucuses (eighteen by 1975) that recruited and trained women to run for office and taught basic campaigning and fund-raising skills.

As political candidates, women faced multiple disadvantages. They had heavier family responsibilities, were less likely to work in professions such as law and business that provided both gravitas and financial security, and had more difficulty raising campaign funds. The parties did not recruit them, and women were less likely to consider themselves qualified to run. Those who persevered still confronted what has been called the "no-win" conundrum: women who conformed to traditional norms of femininity were considered not capable, while those who did not forfeited respect. Married women were rebuked for neglecting their children (by women as well as men), and single women were accused of being lesbians. During Irma Rangel's first campaign in 1976 a small group of male supporters summoned her to a private meeting and voiced the lesbianism concern. Rangel, whose fiancé had been killed in the military many years earlier, denied the charge and told the men that she did not intend to sleep with any of them to prove it; "I wasn't that desperate to get elected," she noted.[61]

During the TWPC's first election year, 1972, unusually fractious politics encouraged women to make high-profile races. La Raza Unida for the first time fielded a statewide ticket, and women's contributions to the party enabled Alma Canales to claim the lieutenant governor's place on it. Sissy Farenthold had made a name for herself in the previous year's legislative session as a prominent member of the "Dirty Thirty" mavericks who exposed the role that members of the House, including the speaker, had played in the Sharpstown stock fraud scandal, accepting bribes in return for legislation to benefit a Houston bank. She ran as a reformer for governor and came in second in a primary field of seven Democrats, forcing Dolph Briscoe into a runoff, which he won. Although Farenthold and Canales were defeated, 1972 was a breakthrough year for women's legislative races. Helped by voter disgust with the legislative scandal, five women, including TWPC founders Chris Miller and Sarah Weddington, won seats in the House, and one woman was elected to the Senate. Eddie Bernice Johnson and Senfronia Thompson were the first African American women to serve in the House, and Kay Bailey (later Hutchison) the first Republican woman. Betty Andujar became the first Republican elected to the Senate since Reconstruction. Barbara Jordan moved on to Congress, the first Texas woman elected in her own right to the U.S. House of Representatives.

At the same time, women pressed for more influence within the party structures. Democratic women were helped by a sweeping revision of rules for delegate selection that the national party mandated in 1970. The new rules required state delegations to national Democratic conventions to include women, minorities, and youth "in reasonable proportion to their numbers in the population." The demise of the old boss-run system opened opportunities for liberal women like Houston's Billie Carr, the state's best-known Democratic organizer. A protégé of Frankie Carter Randolph, who had bankrolled the launch of the *Texas Observer*, Carr won a seat on the Democratic National Committee in 1972 and became the whip of its progressive caucus. The National Women's Political Caucus pressured both parties, putting them on notice to expect challenges at the 1972 presidential nominating conventions if women were not fairly represented in the state delegations. The TWPC and other state caucuses held workshops to teach women how to run as delegates, and the result was a spike in female representation. Women made up 40 percent of delegates at the 1972 Democratic National Convention and 30 percent at the Republican Convention, up from 13 percent and 17 percent, respectively, in 1968.

Raza Unida women who belonged to the TWPC withdrew in 1973; they felt that the Anglo members neither understood the concerns of Chicanas nor solicited their input. They especially resented the TWPC's halfhearted support of Alma Canales's candidacy for lieutenant governor the previous year; it had endorsed but not worked for her.[62] Chicanas channeled their political energy into Mujeres por la Raza Unida. Nevertheless, the TWPC helped put the first Latina in the legislature. In 1975 it began targeting legislative districts with open seats or vulnerable incumbents and raising money for female challengers. Democrat Irma Rangel, a Kingsville attorney, was one of the first beneficiaries, winning her race in 1976. Thereafter the number of female legislators rose steadily; it doubled between 1972 and 1978 and doubled again between 1978 and 1990. In 1986 Judith Zaffirini of Laredo became the first Latina elected to the Senate; Leticia Van de Putte of San Antonio won a special election in 1999 to become the second. By the 1990s Latinas were represented in the House in more than token numbers, a consequence of the growing pool of college-educated Hispanic women. Although in 1998 thirty-three women sat in the legislature — a slight decline from the previous session — they made up less than 20 percent of the total, putting Texas in the bottom half of the states in terms of female representation. Nor had women moved into the leadership. No woman had chaired any of the half dozen most powerful, or "mega," committees, and only one, Wilhelmina Delco, was ever appointed speaker pro tempore of the House.

Women did, however, influence legislation. Women of both parties, but especially Democratic women, were far more likely than men to sponsor legislation to assist children and families and to advance the status of women. When professional women began winning seats in the early 1970s, they immediately joined forces to end credit discrimination. With the memory of being told that she needed her husband's signature to apply for a credit card (although she was putting him through law school) still rankling, Sarah Weddington sponsored the Equal Credit Act, which enabled married women to

get credit cards in their own names. Her office sent out a questionnaire asking women about their experiences in applying for credit and got back stories
of blatant discrimination; one woman reported being turned down because
women were "irresponsible," and she might "take a mortgage and run off
to California after a man."[63] Weddington and Kay Bailey, a co-sponsor of
the credit bill, pushed through legislation reforming the rape statutes. Eddie
Bernice Johnson sponsored the bill that protected pregnant teachers from
being fired. Senfronia Thompson succeeded, after twelve years, in passing a
bill providing for limited alimony (Texas was the only state without it).

Below the level of the statehouse, women made the transition from civic
volunteer to city council, and from campaign coordinator to candidate.
Housewife volunteers could become mayors, as Lila Cockrell proved in San
Antonio in 1975, setting a precedent eventually followed in the rest of the
state's largest cities and countless small towns. Less commonly, they could
become county commissioners, as Ann Richards did in 1978 to the dismay of
the road crew in her Travis County precinct (see Document 4.9). Richards
moved up to become state treasurer in 1982, the first woman elected to statewide office since Miriam Ferguson's second gubernatorial victory fifty years
earlier.

In 1990 Richards became the first woman elected to the governor's office
in her own right. Although she had easily won two terms as state treasurer,
the gubernatorial race was a bloody, gender-polarized struggle. As a liberal
Democrat in a state becoming more Republican every election cycle, she was
fortunate in her opponent, Clayton Williams, whose macho cowboy persona
and sexist gaffes alienated women of both parties. The most offensive remark
was tossed off to a reporter during a rainy tour of the candidate's ranch: "The
weather's like rape. If it's inevitable, you might as well lie back and enjoy it."
"If that man wouldn't turn somebody into a raging feminist, I don't know
who would," complained a Republican who volunteered for Richards, and
many other GOP women cast ballots for her.[64] Exit polls revealed a marked
gender gap: 61 percent of women voted for Richards, including 21 percent of
Republican women, while a solid majority of men supported Williams.

Richards's breakthrough victory helped free the women who came after
her from having to justify their right to run. Democrats Eddie Bernice Johnson and Sheila Jackson-Lee, both African Americans, and Republican Kay
Granger were elected to the U.S. House of Representatives in the 1990s; they
were the first women in the Texas congressional delegation since Barbara Jordan left office in 1978. Kay Bailey Hutchison, after helping found the Texas
Women's Alliance, began a steady ascent to the political summit. In 1990
she won the state treasurer's position that Richards had vacated, becoming

the first Republican woman elected to statewide office. Three years later she became the first Texas woman to win a seat in the U.S. Senate, easily defeating a male opponent in a special election in which her sex was not an issue. In 1994 she won a full term with 60 percent of the vote, while Richards was defeated for a second term by George W. Bush and his formidable communications director, Karen Hughes, the former executive director of the state Republican Party. Together they skillfully won back the GOP women who had defected in 1990 by portraying Bush as a moderate and Richards as too liberal and too feminist for Texas. A record number of women ran for the legislature that year, and Republican women made proportionally greater gains than Republican men. By the end of the decade, GOP women had almost closed the gap with Democratic women in the legislature. Nearly all of the Republican women were Anglo; most Latinas and African Americans remained attached to the Democratic Party (see Document 4.10).

TITLE IX AND GENDER EQUITY IN SPORTS

While women were challenging their marginalization in electoral politics, a similar process was under way in athletics. When Jody Conradt was hired as a physical education instructor at Sam Houston College (now Sam Houston State University) in 1970, she taught seven courses and coached three women's teams, each of which had a budget of $400. The players were issued skirts instead of shorts and paid for their own road trips. "You had to travel in students' cars," Conradt recalled, "so one of the prerequisites for making the team was 'Do you have a car?' Then you'd worry about if they could play or not."[65] By the time she arrived at the University of Texas in 1976 to coach women's basketball, women's sports had their own governing body, the Association for Intercollegiate Athletics for Women (AIAW), but the basketball players were still wearing bows on their uniforms and playing half-court ball. Only one female athlete in fifteen at UT received a scholarship (compared to two out of three for men), and Conradt was paid less than an assistant football coach. Female athletes could not eat at the training table, and they had to stay in cheaper accommodations when their teams traveled. A decade later, however, the Lady Longhorns were outdrawing the men's team. They finished an undefeated season in 1986 by winning the NCAA championship, the AIAW having been elbowed aside and eliminated. UT's Clarissa Davis was the tournament's Most Valuable Player, and Conradt, already twice named Southwest Conference Coach of the Year, was invited to take the team to the White House.

The difference between 1970 and 1986 was Title IX of the Education Amendments Act of 1972, which outlawed sex discrimination in any educational program or activity receiving federal funds. The drafters did not foresee the impact on athletics; they aimed to eliminate inequities in higher education, such as quotas for women in graduate and professional schools. Unexpectedly, the feminist movement and pent-up demand combined with Title IX to make a sports revolution. Title IX guidelines for athletic programs do not require equal division of funds or equal numbers of female and male players, only that women have opportunities to participate in rough proportion to their enrollment. Before Title IX, female students commonly got only crumbs from athletic budgets. In 1973 the 153 women athletes at Texas A&M University shared a bookstore stipend of $350, bought their own equipment, and took turns doing the team laundry. Thirty-five years later there were eleven women's varsity teams with a combined budget of $25.2 million, and women's basketball alone was allotted $2.8 million.

Title IX was implemented slowly—final guidelines were not issued until 1979—and women had to combat male resistance to make even moderate gains. In the fight over funds, male athletic directors conceded as little as possible. The women's athletic program at the University of Texas became one of the best in the nation because it was one of the very few funded separately and administered by a female director, Donna Lopiano (1975–1992), who built it from scratch. Jody Conradt, one of Lopiano's first hires, jettisoned "girls' rules" and coached the Lady Longhorns to play "real" basketball—full court, fast-paced, and aggressive—that packed the stands and raised more than enough revenue to cover expenses. At the same time, she tried to avoid what women physical educators had always deplored about male sport: a win-at-all-costs mentality, corruption, and exploitation of student athletes. Conradt built teams with depth rather than star power, and she and Lopiano publicized the Lady Longhorns' 94 percent graduation rate.

The most talented female athletes achieved celebrity status. The Lady Raiders of Texas Tech, coached by Marsha Sharp, emerged in the early 1990s as a team powerful enough to defeat the Lady Longhorns in Southwest Conference championships because of Sheryl Swopes's remarkable gifts. Swopes led Tech to its first national championship in 1993, scoring forty-seven points, more than any other player, male or female, in a collegiate championship. Described as "the female Michael Jordan," she was the first woman to have an athletic shoe, Nike's Air Swopes, named for her. Swopes signed with the Women's National Basketball Association when it formed in 1997 and helped lead the Houston Comets to four consecutive championships.

Expanded opportunity did not free women from the persistent stereotype that sport is "unfeminine." It was an easy reach to label female athletes "masculine," often a code word for lesbian, and lesbian players could make an entire program controversial, as happened to the Lady Longhorns after the *Austin American-Statesman* in 1993 printed a series of articles asserting that the lesbian presence on the team hurt recruiting. And while Title IX greatly increased the number of female players, it contracted opportunities for female coaches and administrators. Women coached 90 percent of women's college teams in 1972 but only 44 percent by the end of the century, as salaries rose and became more attractive to men. The percentage of women running collegiate athletic programs plunged even more steeply, largely because most institutions merged men's and women's programs (although Title IX did not require any such change), leaving men in charge. Most disheartening to female administrators, the wealthy and powerful NCAA flexed its muscle against the AIAW and killed it off in 1981 by holding competing championships for women. Donna Lopiano, who was AIAW president at the time, surmised that "we became too powerful, too threatening for the status quo in intercollegiate athletics to allow us to continue to do our thing."[66] With the demise of the AIAW, women lost both an advocacy group and their alternative philosophy of sport as physical education rather than lucrative entertainment. Women coaches had wanted equality and difference; ultimately, in order to be competitive, they accepted the male model.

Despite the advances it made possible, Title IX did not bring equity—almost no schools met the criteria. In the 1990s half of undergraduates were women, but they made up only one-third of athletes at Division I schools and received only one-fifth of recruiting monies. At Baylor University, for example, the budget for the women's basketball program was less than one-half of the men's. The men's program had three assistant coaches, and the team traveled in chartered buses; the women had one assistant coach and traveled in vans. Baylor, Southern Methodist University, and Texas Tech were all involved in Title IX disputes in the 1990s. Surprisingly, so was the University of Texas, which had the best women's program in the country and had won national championships in track, volleyball, and swimming, as well as basketball. In 1992 seven female undergraduates filed a class action suit, claiming that by not offering more varsity sports for women, UT was in noncompliance. The case was a landmark in that women were on the offensive, seeking to add new sports rather than protecting existing ones from funding cuts or elimination. In an out-of-court settlement, UT agreed to add women's softball and soccer teams, increase scholarships, and work toward a goal of 44 percent female representation in varsity sports.

In the public school system, pressure to meet Title IX guidelines came from parents and feminist groups. Texas State NOW urged its local chapters to investigate their school districts and talk to principals. Athletic opportunities for girls varied widely by district; some offered a sport or two, while in others girls had no outlet other than cheerleading. The Texas division of the Women's Equity Action League (WEAL), which had formed in Dallas in 1971, filed the state's first Title IX complaint with the U.S. Department of Health, Education, and Welfare in 1973. It accused the Waco and Dallas school districts of sex discrimination in employment, course assignments, and, most egregiously, athletics. In Waco, boys' sports were allotted $250,000 annually, while girls received $970 and played no sports except tennis. In Dallas, 871 girls participated in three sports—tennis, swimming, and bowling—while 8,809 boys played ten sports. In neither district were women coaches accorded the same extra pay and decreased teaching loads that male coaches received. Two decades later such blatant inequality had been eliminated, but a survey of school districts found that it was common for boys' programs to be considerably better equipped and to have the most favored practice times. The authors judged Title IX's impact on the public schools "minimal" and attributed the failure to administrators' vague understanding of the law and of what constitutes discrimination.[67]

WOMEN IN THE WORKFORCE

Women's participation in the labor market rose impressively in the last quarter of the century. In 1970 slightly less than 41 percent of Texas women were in the civilian labor force; by 1999 the figure was 60 percent, and they made up 45 percent of the state's workers. The most dramatic increase took place in the 1970s, when the number of wage-earning women increased by 38 percent. Working mothers became the norm: the 1980 census reported that 60 percent of those with school-age children and nearly half of those with children under five were in the workforce. Although the wage gap between the sexes had narrowed, in part due to declining earnings for blue-collar men, it remained glaring. In 1999 white women earned less than three-quarters of the wage of white men, while for African American women the ratio was 61 percent and for Hispanic women 46 percent. Women made some inroads into the skilled trades, but the majority continued to work in the less well-paid, female-dominated sectors of the labor force.

Low rates of unionization also held down Texas women's earnings. Nationally, one woman in eight belonged to a union; in Texas, only one in twelve did. Only one-fourth of the state's textile and apparel plants, where women were

80 percent of the workforce, recognized a union; employers had shifted from the Dallas–Fort Worth area to the southern and border counties to exploit the Latina labor supply. Employee demand for union representation by the Amalgamated Clothing Workers of America prompted a massive strike from 1972 to 1974 against Farah Manufacturing Company, one of the largest producers of men's slacks in the country. Farah operated nine plants in the Southwest, including one in San Antonio and five in El Paso, where it was the largest private employer. The workforce was 85 percent female and overwhelmingly Chicana.

In addition to meager wages, the Farah workers endured onerous daily production quotas, such as sewing three thousand belts—six per minute—onto pairs of slacks. Gender grievances were abundant: women were never advanced to supervisory positions; Anglo overseers gave preferential treatment to younger women willing to go out with them; and there were no maternity benefits. Some pregnant women lied about their due dates in order to keep working as long as possible, and those who did not return to work quickly after giving birth lost their seniority and had to return to starting pay. Some four thousand women struck, but the decision was not easy for many (see Document 4.5). "I had to think about it before I walked out," Virgie Delgado recalled, "because there are 9 kids in my family, and me and my sisters work at Farah to support our family. I had to go home and tell my mom what I was going to do. She said to do what I thought was right."[68] Wives and husbands did not always agree, one spouse joining the walkout and the other refusing.

The Farah strike took place while the Chicano movement was gaining strength across the Southwest, and the strikers articulated their grievances as a struggle for *dignidad* and respect. The Amalgamated Clothing Workers of America astutely portrayed the dispute as part of the Mexican American movement for social justice. Posters and buttons depicted a Chicana raising a clenched fist and the logo "Viva la Huelga! (Long Live the Strike!) Boycott Farah Pants." The national boycott called by the ACWA was supported by trade unions and enough Left-liberal sympathizers to cause a $20 million drop in Farah's sales. Citizens Committees for Justice for Farah Workers raised money for the strikers and picketed stores that stocked the company's suits and slacks. Although the strike was settled to the workers' benefit in 1974, and Farah was sharply rebuked by the National Labor Relations Board, the aftermath was disappointing. Many strikers were fired within a few months. The company claimed, disingenuously, that the women had failed to meet the piecework quotas, and the (male) union representatives declined to file grievances on their behalf. Twenty-two months of protest and picketing, however, had changed some of the women permanently. "For years I wouldn't do anything without asking my husband's permission," one told an interviewer. "I see myself now and I think, good grief, having to ask to buy a pair of underwear! Of course I don't do this anymore. [The time of the strike] was when it started changing. All of it. I was able to begin to stand up for myself, and I began to feel that I should be accepted for the person I am."[69]

In the decade following the Farah strike, conditions worsened for textile workers. As major manufacturers transferred operations to Mexico and Asia to take advantage of cheaper labor costs, small marginal shops that paid subminimum wages and ignored health and safety standards moved in. La Mujer Obrera (the Woman Worker) formed in El Paso in 1982 to represent Latinas in the depressed garment industry. A group of Farah workers unhappy with the Amalgamated Clothing Workers of America for ignoring gender issues founded La Mujer Obrera, which trained women to confront workplace abuses such as work speedups. In 1991 it led, in conjunction with the International Ladies' Garment Workers' Union, a nine-month strike against four El Paso operators that helped publicize nonpayment of wages, a common sweatshop practice. Employers claimed not to be able to pay workers until a manufacturer had paid them for a contract; after the employees had worked several weeks for reduced or no wages, the dishonest owners shut down, relocated, and reopened under a different name. After the strike, El Paso's state representatives pushed a bill through the legislature that made nonpayment of wages a felony. Overall, however, the decline in the state's manufacturing base left Latinas facing higher unemployment and declining wages.

Working-class African American women were disproportionately clustered in low-wage, nonunion service jobs, held back by the kind of prejudice Linda Baxter encountered when she sought employment at Stephen F. Austin State University. Baxter applied for jobs at the university library, post office, and shuttle bus service but was offered a position only in the cafeteria, where 95 percent of the workers were black women. In 1975 the cafeteria workers won a class action civil rights lawsuit, *Annie Mae Carpenter et al. v. Stephen F. Austin State University*, charging that the university hired African Americans only in bottom-tier jobs in food service and housekeeping and underpaid them. Despite the verdict, SFASU refused to pay restitution. A decade later both sides were back in court, after the cafeteria workers joined the Texas State Employees Union and the university retaliated by forming a private food service corporation. In defiance of a court ruling that the workers be allowed to keep their jobs under privatization, more than half were fired; they began two years of picketing and protest that culminated in December 1987 with a massive "Jobs with Justice" rally that drew workers from more than a dozen unions in four states, and speakers representing the Texas Coalition of

Labor Union Women, NOW, and the Southern Christian Leadership Conference, among others. Pressured by prominent local citizens to end the demonstrations, university officials finally capitulated. The workers, most of them black women, won a wage increase and benefits and eventually $800,000 in back pay from the *Annie Mae Carpenter* suit.

In the professions, women made enormous gains, in part because of their sharply rising college attendance. By 1989 women were 51 percent of undergraduates at the state's public universities. In 1990 they made up 40 percent of Texas law school graduates; by the end of the decade they received nearly 40 percent of dentistry and medical degrees. Women physicians, however, tended to cluster in primary care, obstetrics, and pediatrics, fields that did not require extended training and presented fewer obstacles to combining career and family. Because they were less likely to pursue subspecialties, women earned less, on average, than male physicians. In academia, women increased their numbers but remained well short of equity. The Texas Higher Education Coordinating Board reported in 1989 that women were 27 percent of full-time faculty at public universities and 43 percent at community colleges (where salaries were lower). In both categories more than 80 percent of them were white. Few women reached top administrative positions, but Lorene Rogers, a biochemist who served as president of the University of Texas at Austin from 1975 until 1979, became the first woman to head a major American university.

Women who tried to enter the clergy met stiff resistance; many denominations regarded their ordination as contrary to biblical teaching. The Episcopal Church reversed its opposition in 1976, after years of pressure from the Episcopal Women's Conference, headed by Helen Havens of Houston, and from the National Coalition for Women's Ordination that grew out of it. In 1977 Havens and Sandra Michells of El Paso became the first women in Texas ordained as Episcopal priests. The state's largest Protestant denomination, Southern Baptists, remained overwhelmingly opposed to women in the pulpit, although individual churches ordained a handful of women seeking positions as military and hospital chaplains and campus ministers. Martha Gilmore, one of the first Baptist ministers, precipitated a controversy when she sought ordination by her home church, Dallas's Cliff Temple Baptist, in 1977. A process that took only days for male candidates dragged on for two months in Gilmore's case. Opposition from a prominent clergyman leaked into the press, and religious conservatives voiced opposition on local radio talk shows: "These people calling in about this horrible woman that was going to be ordained! It was just a nightmare," Gilmore recalled.[70] After her ordination Gilmore was not invited to preach or take any other significant responsibility in the church; a few years later she transferred her membership to the United Methodist Church.

FAMILY AND PERSONAL LIFE AT THE END OF THE CENTURY

The enormous increase in women's labor force participation and the self-sufficiency it brought them changed personal lives and altered family structures. Age at marriage rose, as did the divorce rate and the percentage of never-married women. Cohabitation increased, and rates of marriage dropped, especially among African American women. Women had fewer children and bore them later, and the number of adult women who had children outside marriage rose. Among married couples with children, the dual-income household displaced reliance on a male breadwinner and the family wage system. A wife's paycheck might even come from a branch of the gender-integrated armed services, especially among minority women. María Jiménez of San Antonio chose the army because she didn't want a nine-to-five routine or the pay discrimination that Latinas encountered in the private sector: "Here, in the military, I'm a female, I do this job, I have a counterpart, same rate, same time and service as I am, he's a male. We get paid the same."[71] Immigrant communities, such as the tens of thousands of Vietnamese who arrived in the last quarter of the century, maintained traditional family structures but grappled with changing gender relations as economic necessity forced wives to become paid workers and entrepreneurs (see Document 4.11).

Lesbians who were mothers of children born during heterosexual marriages formed new, blended families with same-sex partners. Afraid of losing jobs, housing, and child custody, many lesbian couples avoided detection by posing as roommates. This subterfuge eventually failed Mary Jo Risher of Garland, a nurse and former PTA president, whose ex-husband sued for custody of their son when he discovered that she was gay and living with her partner, Ann Foreman, and Foreman's daughter. In 1975, Dallas County Domestic Relations Court transferred custody of the boy to his father. The jury trial, and the issue of whether lesbians were "unfit" to be mothers, was covered by media across the country. The Texas Fifth District Court dismissed Mary Jo Risher's appeal in 1977; her story was the basis for a book, *By Her Own Admission* (1977), and a television movie, *A Question of Love* (1978).

At the same time, lesbians and gays were bringing their underground culture into the open and forming communities that demanded civil rights and an end to the criminalization of private sexual behavior. Lesbian attorney Bobby Nelson filed suits that forced the University of Texas to recognize the

Gay Liberation Front as a campus organization in 1974 and Texas A&M University to do the same for Gay Student Services in 1984. In 1988 the groups Among Friends and Lesbian Visionaries in Dallas created the Texas Lesbian Conference. Its annual three-day meeting, rotated between Dallas, Houston, San Antonio, and Austin, claims to be the only such state conference in the country. Several hundred women gather for speakers, performance artists, and workshops on topics such as women's health, lesbian sexuality, and political activism. The San Antonio Lesbian and Gay Assembly (SALGA), which functioned from 1989 to 1998, sponsored topical community conferences; its annual gay pride picnic drew thousands. Dulce Benavides cochaired SALGA, but Latinas also organized separately. Letitia Gomez joined the Gay Chicano Caucus of Houston while working in the city as a bilingual social worker and later organized lesbian Latinas while doing graduate work at Trinity University in the 1980s. Subsequently she became the first executive director of the Latino Lesbian and Gay Organization, headquartered in Washington, D.C., and dedicated to eradicating AIDS in the Latino/a gay community.[72]

The most remarked-upon change in family life was the growth of female-headed families, which rose significantly after 1970. Such households, especially when headed by minority women, were far more likely than two-parent families to live in poverty. In 1996 in Texas, 34 percent of female-headed families lived below the 100 percent poverty level; only 8.7 percent of married-couple families did. As political conservatives gained strength nationally in the 1980s and advocated dismantling the "welfare state," public assistance to single mothers became an inflammatory issue. Even though Texas ranked near the bottom of the states in the amount spent on public assistance, the legislature in 1995 passed a welfare reform bill, Achieving Change for Texans (ACT). Among other provisions, ACT imposed a time limit on benefits and a work requirement for mothers unless they had children under the age of five (subsequently revised to children under two). In 1996, Congress passed the Personal Responsibility and Work Opportunity Act, which ended Aid to Families with Dependent Children, instituted in the 1930s, and replaced it with Temporary Assistance for Needy Families (TANF), also a time-limited program.

TANF required recipients, almost always poor single mothers (and more than three-fourths of them Hispanic or black), to take any job available no matter how ill-paid; Texas was among the states that emphasized quick job placement rather than investing funds in education and training for potential welfare leavers. The new system moved large numbers of women off the welfare rolls and into the workforce but not out of poverty. Poor single mothers, who often had limited education, tended to cycle between welfare and work.

They were handicapped by low-wage, unstable jobs, inadequate and unreliable child care, and the state's weak safety net, which made it difficult to find subsidized housing and maintain health insurance. "Sarah," a nurse's assistant whose husband had left her and their children, moved back and forth between TANF and work and described life after welfare: "I'm not on any kind of assistance. So, right now, I have to volunteer for as many hours as I can get at my job. . . . I have to work at least 80 hours or plus, just to get a $500 [two-week] paycheck. I got $600 this payday; I had 114 hours. . . . So my typical day is no time with the kids . . . because, the thing I always say to them, you know, 'Momma's got to go to work.'"[73] Sarah, who subsisted with assistance from relatives and food banks, was one of a large cohort of Texas families that left TANF whom social scientists studied between 1998 and 2000; eighteen months after leaving public assistance, only 5 percent of them had moved out of poverty.

CONCLUSION: FACING FORWARD, LOOKING BACK

When Linda Dorsey of Stephenville graduated from high school in 1965 and wanted to attend North Texas State University, her widowed mother sent her to secretarial school instead. Money was tight and there was a younger brother to be educated as well; Dorsey's mother and her older sister, a secretarial school graduate who was working to help put her husband through the University of Texas, both agreed that it was more important for boys to go to college than girls. Law as well as culture treated women unequally. In 1965 it was legal for a woman to be paid less than a man for doing the same job, for employers to designate jobs as "male" and "female," for labor unions to keep separate seniority lists for men and women, and for banks to refuse credit to married women in their own names. Titles such as policeman, fireman, and anchorman meant exactly that—jobs for which women were by definition excluded. Assumptions about gender were so deeply embedded in the culture and internalized by both sexes that, as Dorsey wryly realized only later, women themselves enforced discrimination.

The feminist movement challenged and eliminated obvious legal inequalities and significantly changed assumptions about women's roles in society. Linda Dorsey's daughter became a university professor, her daughter-in-law an attorney. By the end of the century women made up nearly half of the state's labor force and were represented in virtually every field. Traditional family patterns had been eroded, not only by the new norm of the middle-class working mother, but also by the large number of single parents and the claims for recognition of lesbian and gay couples. The rapid changes in women's work and family lives disturbed and divided society and generated an antifeminist backlash that injected acrimonious debates about sex and gender into the political discourse. Feminists had to confront the unexpected and, to them, unfathomable reality that some women were perfectly satisfied with the existing gender system. Although both feminists and antifeminists were largely white and middle-class, their lifestyles had little in common and their views on family, ethics, and government power diverged sharply. New Right women mirrored their feminist opposites in forming effective organizations to protest and lobby. Each side regarded any ground gained by the other as a threat to its most deeply held values.

At the century's end this tension remained unresolved and seemingly irreconcilable. And while the dismantling of legal barriers created the appearance of equality, fundamental discrepancies persisted. Although a woman had held the state's highest elective office, men constituted more than 80 percent of the legislature and an even higher percentage of corporate executives. Women continued to bear the primary caretaker role in the family, even if they were also full-time breadwinners. Government policy exacerbated this difficulty for poor single mothers, as welfare reform forced them into low-wage jobs without providing adequate support services.

In 1967 the Governor's Commission on the Status of Women told women not to protest discrimination too vigorously and admonished that "in this world we, each of us, achieve as individuals, not as members of a group." Over the next three decades, groups not yet formed in 1967—Texas State NOW, the Texas Women's Political Caucus, Mujeres por la Raza Unida, La Mujer Obrera, Women Who Want to be Women, and the Eagle Forum—demonstrated the contrary: what women can achieve as individuals may well depend on their strength as a group. The unfinished portions of their agendas, liberal and conservative, continue to unite and divide Texas women in the twenty-first century.

SUGGESTED REFERENCES

FEMINIST MOVEMENTS

Except for women's liberation in Austin, there is little secondary literature. Doug Rossinow's *The Politics of Authenticity: Liberalism, Christianity, and the New Left in America* (New York: Columbia University Press, 1998), is Texas-focused and includes a chapter on women's liberation at the University of Texas, drawing on articles that campus feminists published in the underground newspaper the *Rag*. Frieda L. Werden's "Adventures of a Texas Feminist," in *No Apologies: Texas Radicals Celebrate the '60s*, ed. Daryl Janes (Austin: Eakin Press, 1992), is a first-person account. There are scattered issues of newsletters from short-lived women's liberation groups: *Second Coming* (University of Texas), *Sisters Unite* (University of Houston), *The Turn of the Screwed* (Dallas). A good run of *Houston Breakthrough* is archived at the University of Houston. The activities of the National Organization for Women are detailed in the state and chapter newsletters held at local university archives: *Texas NOW Times* (originally *Texas State National Organization for Women Newsletter*); *NOW Hear This* (Dallas County); *Austin NOW Times* (originally *Austin NOW Newsletter*); *Say it NOW* (San Antonio); *The Broadside* (Houston); *NOW News: Bay Area Chapter; Here and Now* (North Dallas NOW and Rainbow NOW); *NOW or Never* (Denton County). Essential texts in Chicana feminism are Mirta Vidal, *Chicanas Speak Out: Women, New Voice of La Raza* (New York: Pathfinder Press, 1971), which covers the National Chicana Conference; Martha P. Cotera, *Diosa y Hembra: The History and Heritage of Chicanas in the U.S.* (Austin: Information Systems Development, 1976); and Cotera, *The Chicana Feminist* (Austin: Information Systems Development, 1977), a collection of her essays. See also Mary Ann Villarreal, "The Synapses of Struggle: Martha Cotera and Tejana Activism," in *Las Obreras: Chicana Politics of Work and Family*, ed. Vicki Ruiz (Los Angeles: UCLA Chicano Studies Research Center, 2000), and Teresa Paloma Acosta and Ruthe Winegarten, *Las Tejanas: 300 Years of History* (Austin: University of Texas Press, 2003).

On the Texas Equal Legal Rights Amendment, see Judie Gammage, "Quest for Equality: An Historical Overview of Women's Rights Activism in Texas, 1890–1975" (Ph.D. diss., North Texas State University, 1982), and Rob Fink, "Hermine Tobolowsky, the Texas ELRA, and the Political Struggle for Women's Equal Rights," *Journal of the West* 42 (Summer 2003). Louise Ballerstedt Raggio, *Texas Tornado: The Life of a Crusader for Women's Rights* (New York: Citadel Press, 2003), recounts the history of the Marital Property Act from a participant's standpoint. Janet K. Boles, *The Politics of the Equal Rights Amendment: Conflict and the Decision Process* (New York: Longman, 1979), is based on research in Texas, Georgia, and Illinois. Also useful on the ratification effort in Texas are Charlotte Guinn Ross, "The Federal Equal Rights Amendment as an Issue in the Texas Legislature" (M.A. thesis, Texas Woman's University, 1979), and Gara Johnson-West, "The ERA in Texas: Success by Default, Not a Liberal Groundswell in a Sea of Conservatism" (M.A. thesis, Baylor University, 2001). David W. Brady and Kent L. Tedin provide a statistical portrait of the opposition in "Ladies in Pink: Religion and Political Ideology in the Anti-ERA Movement," *Social Science Quarterly* 56 (March 1976). Sarah Weddington offers a first-person account of *Roe v. Wade* in her *A Question of Choice* (New York: Penguin Books, 1992). Marian Faux's *Roe v. Wade: The Untold Story of the Landmark Supreme Court Decision That Made Abortion Legal* (New York: Macmillan, 1988), is especially useful in documenting the beginnings of the pro-choice movement in Texas.

POLITICS AND PUBLIC LIFE

For early biographical sketches and statistics, see *Texas Women in Politics*, ed. Elizabeth W. Fernea and Marilyn P. Duncan (Austin, Tex.: Foundation for Women's Resources, 1977). Works that focus on the legislature are Nancy Baker Jones and Ruthe Winegarten, *Capitol Women: Female Legislators, 1923–1999* (Austin: University of Texas Press, 2000), which combines biography with analysis, and Terry L. Gilmour, "A Difference: Women in the Texas Legislature" (Ph.D. diss., Texas Tech University, 1999). On Latinas, see Sonia R. García, Valerie Martinez-Ebers, Irasema Coronado, Sharon A. Navarro, and Patricia A. Jaramillo, *Políticas: Latina Public Officials in Texas* (Austin: University of Texas Press, 2008); José Angel Gutiérrez, Michelle Melendez, and Sonia A. Noyola, *Chicanas in Charge: Texas Women in the Electoral Arena* (Lanham, Md.: AltaMira Press, 2006); and Sharon A. Navarro, *Latina Legislator: Letitia Van de Putte and the Road to Leadership* (College Station: Texas A&M University Press, 2008). There is no scholarly biography of Barbara Jordan, but see Shelby Hearon and Barbara Jordan, *Barbara Jordan: A Self-Portrait* (New York: Doubleday, 1979), and Mary Ellen Curtin, "Barbara Jordan: The Politics of Insertion and Accommodation," *Critical Review of International Social and Political Philosophy* 7 (Winter 2004). Ann Richards's first gubernatorial campaign is covered in Sue Tolleson-Rinehart and Jeanie R. Stanley, *Claytie and the Lady: Ann Richards, Gender, and Politics in Texas* (Austin: University of Texas Press, 1994), and Celia Morris, *Storming the Statehouse: Running for Governor with Ann Richards and Dianne Feinstein* (New York: Scribner's, 1992).

WORK

Laurie Coyle, Gail Hershatter, and Emily Honig, *Women at Farah: An Unfinished Story* (El Paso: REFORMA, 1979), is a short history based on oral history interviews; Emily Honig, "Women at Farah Revisited: Political Mobilization and Its Aftermath among Chicana Workers in El Paso, Texas, 1972–1992," *Feminist Studies* 22 (Summer 1996), reinterviews the strikers two decades later. See also Jennifer Rebecca Mata, "Creating a Critical Chicana Narrative: Writing the Chicanas at Farah into Labor History" (Ph.D. diss., Washington State University, 2004), and Irene Ledesma, "Unlikely Strikers: Mexican American Women in Strike Activity in Texas, 1919–1974" (Ph.D. diss., Ohio State University, 1992). Benjamin Marquez, "Organizing Mexican-American Women in the Garment Industry: La Mujer Obrera," *Women and Politics* 15:1 (1995), is the most detailed account of La Mujer Obrera.

DOCUMENTS

4.1. BEA VOGEL DURDEN EXPLAINS WOMEN'S LIBERATION IN THE *RAG*

The *Rag*, published from 1966 to 1977, was Austin's underground newspaper, started by a small group of University of Texas students after the campus paper, the *Daily Texan*, took a pronounced turn to the right. Produced by volunteers who determined the content by consensus, it was the voice of the 1960s counterculture; the University of Texas board of regents sued unsuccessfully to prevent its distribution on campus. *Rag* staffers included activists in university women's liberation, who regularly contributed articles on women's issues and the emerging feminist movement. Bea Vogel Durden, the author of this piece, was in a situation common to professional women in the 1960s. With a Ph.D. in biology from Yale and two small children, she came to UT when her husband was offered a job on the faculty, but the university declined to provide a position for her as well. In addition to founding the American Arachnological Society, Vogel Durden volunteered with the birth control information service operated by the university women's liberation group and contributed articles on contraception to the *Rag*.

Women's Liberation groups are spontaneously and independently appearing in many cities across the country. Women's Liberation has been meeting in Austin regularly since February [1969], and yet few people know what it is really about.

To dispel a few misconceptions, it would be easier to say what Women's Liberation is *not*, and then a little about what it *is*. Women's Liberation is not "hate men" or "compete with men" or "be as good as men." Women's Liberation is not sexual promiscuity or sexual chastity.

Women's Liberation is basically an attempt to improve women's self-image and an attempt to give women a positive sense of identity. It is freeing ourselves from a role imposed on us by our society or any particular sub-culture. Women's Liberation is an attempt to relate to other women in non-competitive terms, and to relate to men on terms other than sexual.

Our meetings may start out by asking each other "what do you think is wrong with your life?" There are usually a variety of answers, but many women are surprised to find that instead of being maladjusted individuals, they are trying to play parts that they don't feel. Their problems are not those of a solitary person, but those of our sex. This is the first step in thinking objectively about the problems, and trying to work out solutions.

The problems are complex, but among them are economic problems: good jobs are not always open to women, women are paid less than men for the same kind of work, women are promoted less frequently than men, and are less likely to be "at the top." Professional problems: women are sometimes discriminated against by graduate departments, often given less interesting offers than men because "you'll just get married in a couple of years and leave," and more important, are *trained from the cradle to have different goals.* . . .

The most dehumanizing problems a woman faces are the psychological ones. Girls are brought up not thinking of themselves as people, but only as they relate to men. The only really acceptable role for a woman is marriage and children. The most successful professional woman is still looked down on unless she also has been able to marry and raise children. . . .

Women are generally treated by men as sex objects. Girls have to be attractive, glamorous or beautiful depending on their natural endowments, so that the "right man" will marry them. Development of character ranks second, way below this, and intelligence ranks hardly at all in the development of a girl. Girls are supposed to be protected from the harsh realities of the world. They usually do not have as much freedom as their brothers during adolescence, leave home to live at a university dormitory which is often stricter about her life than her home was, and ideally she marries soon after college. The girl has never had a chance to be independent or develop her resourcefulness or maturity. . . .

There are two objections generally raised to Women's Liberation. The first is that women don't want to be liberated. Currently most women probably don't. We are conditioned not to stand out, or deviate, to dissent. However, if even 25 or 30% of American women were "liberated" there would be a sudden shift in attitude. This argument has been used against many successful reforms at their beginnings.

The second objection is that there are inherent, that is, inborn differences in man and woman. It is said that it is a woman's nature to be less creative. In the Arts, women are less mechanical than men; women are less intelligent and more emotional, etc., etc., etc. When the facts are examined, psychological tests of personality, it is very difficult to tell which traits are inherent differences and which are the result of social environment. . . .

We really don't know what the inherent personality traits are in men and women.

We do know that both women and men are oppressed by the sexual role society expects them to play and inhibition of individual interests and tendencies often leads to frustration and loss of effectiveness.

We hope that Women's Liberation in Austin is the beginning of self-awareness in women and eventually men.

Source: Bea Vogel Durden, "Women's Liberation in Austin," *Rag,* June 26, 1969.

4.2. NIKKI VAN HIGHTOWER, "FEMINISTS: TRUE CHAMPIONS OF THE HOMEMAKER"

Nikki Van Hightower, born in Billings, Montana, in 1939, came to Texas as a college student and earned her B.A. and M.A. degrees at the University of Houston. After completing a Ph.D. in political science at New York University, she returned to Houston, and in 1976 Mayor Fred Hofheinz appointed her as women's advocate for the city. Van Hightower's zeal in monitoring the affirmative action program, exposing sex- and race-based salary discrimination, and advocating pregnancy benefits for female employees irritated the Houston City Council. So did her pronouncement in her first Women's State of the City address that the 1970s were an era of tokenism for women. The council reduced her salary to $1 a year in an effort to get her to quit; the mayor reinstated her under a new title, affirmative action specialist. (His successor fired her.) Van Hightower originated the idea for the Houston Area Women's Center, established in 1977 to provide a crisis shelter for abused women and serve as a community center offering a range of services and support. She was the first president of its board of directors and served as executive director from 1979 to 1986. In 1986 Van Hightower won election as Harris County treasurer; in 1990 she lost a race for Texas state treasurer to Kay Bailey Hutchison. Van Hightower then returned to academia, teaching in the Department of Political Science and the Health Science Center at Texas A&M University.

In the speech below, given at the 1977 convention of the Texas Women's Political Caucus in El Paso, Van Hightower rebuts the common antifeminist accusation that feminists were hostile to homemakers.

The federal government's *Dictionary of Occupational Titles,* considered the world's most comprehensive source of job information, describes and rates the level of complexity of the tasks involved in 30,000 job titles. Foster mother received one of the lowest possible ratings, slightly below horsepusher, who is someone who feeds, waters and otherwise tends horses in route by train. Other low ratings include the following:

Child-care attendant, which is rated the same as parking lot attendant.

Nursery school teacher is rated far lower than marine mammal handler.

Practical nurse is rated slightly lower than poultry offal man, who is someone who shovels ice into chicken offal containers.

Homemaker, which is cross referenced with general maid, is rated slightly lower than dog pound attendant.

It is through derogatory statements, and insulting ratings, such as these that women in the roles of homemaker and mother are effectively degraded in this country. But I have not heard our anti-rights people speaking up on this issue. I suppose they are reluctant to do so, because if they did, they would come off sounding just like feminists, because feminists have been complaining about the low value our society places on traditional women's work for years. In fact, this was a major impetus for the development of the present movement. And it was because we brought this matter into the open, that we were then blamed for creating the low status of home-maker. . . .

One would think that if the anti-rights people truly cared about the woman homemaker, they would have been the ones lobbying for legislative changes that would acknowledge the equal contribution of homemakers to that of the employed spouse.

To the contrary, it has been the feminists who have carried the load for social security coverage for homemakers: the elimination of taxation on all transfers of property between a husband and wife at death: changes in welfare requirements, so that a family is not automatically disqualified for welfare if a father is present in the home: and displaced homemaker centers to assist in the transition from working inside the home to working outside the home.

We have lobbied for day care assistance, not to force women to leave their homes, but to support the family when both parents were in the workforce.

We have struggled for the right of married women not to be denied economic opportunities such as credit and property ownership.

In the courts we have challenged the right of employers to deny women equal access with men to benefits of leave and health insurance because their temporary disability was due to pregnancy.

And where have these home-loving women been through all of this? In most cases they were working against these changes. They were out politiking around the country preaching that women should be in the home unconcerned about their rights.

But do these anti-rights people really believe that women should stay in the home? If they did, there seems to me to be several things they could be doing that would be much more effective than disrupting the work of feminists.

First of all, they could practice what they preach and stay home. Since there aren't that many of them, it wouldn't get all that many women off the streets, but it would be a start.

Next, all of them with maids to do their housework could start cleaning their own homes and donate their pay to their housekeepers so that they could stay in their own homes. Their husbands could do the same for their secretaries.

They could insist on having males to wash their hair and do their nails in the beauty parlors. They could demand to be waited on only by males in the department stores and restaurants, and, of course, be willing to pay the extra price tag that males would demand for their services.

They could lobby for the expansion of welfare benefits so that all women with children could remain in the home, rather than cleaning houses, waiting on tables, and washing hair.

Do you really think they want these women to stay in the home? I don't think so.

Clearly the ideology of the feminist movement has touched an exposed nerve ending. It has tapped a level of fear in some women that most of us never anticipated. . . .

The reason they are so adamantly anti-feminist is that we threaten their personal security which has been achieved through accepting female inferiority relative to males. It follows that the only way they can secure their position is to limit the choice of all women.

The bargain they struck was that they would accept inferior status in society as women, (which they euphemistically call being different), provide sexual favors and domestic service in exchange for the support and protection of men. . . .

The feminists have upset the complicated balance of their relationships. We say women have a right to freedom and dignity, and to full humanity. They say—get lost! We are not giving up our meagre toe hold on comfort and control for some amorphous and hopeless cause. Women are not equal, they can never be equal. . . .

It takes a good deal of faith to be a feminist—faith in ourselves and the other members of our sex that we are worthwhile human beings . . . that we will rise to each occasion, and overcome the obstacles that have been placed in our paths because we are women.

Source: Nikki R. Van Hightower Papers, box 8, folder 9, Special Collections, University of Houston Libraries.

4.3. LOTTIE BETH HOBBS, "LADIES! HAVE YOU HEARD?"

Lottie Beth Hobbs of Fort Worth, founder of Women Who Want to be Women, prepared the alarmist flyer below in order to rally opposition to the Equal Rights Amendment. In an oral history in 1998 she recalled its origins:

> In 1974 or 1975, I wrote the text and took it to my printer and told him to print up ten thousand copies in various colors. I asked him if he could think of some way to dress it up a little. So he looked at it, found pictures of two ladies in his clip-art collection, and drew the phone line around the page connecting them. . . . My sister-in-law came up with the title. She said that when ladies were in the beauty shop or somewhere, the way to get their attention was to say "Have you heard?" So we gave it the title "Ladies! Have You Heard?"[1]

The flyer became known as "the pink sheet" after Hobbs decided to use "feminine" pink paper for subsequent printings. Distributed on church literature tables, hung on doorknobs, and reprinted in small-town newspapers, it helped recruit thousands of conservative women into Women Who Want to be Women. The pink sheet was widely copied both inside and outside the state—a Georgia woman told Hobbs that it defeated ratification there. Some of the paragraphs were drawn nearly verbatim from issues of the *Phyllis Schlafly Report*, which had quoted selectively and sometimes misleadingly from law journals. The *Yale Law Review* was actually pro-ERA, but the out-of-context quotations gave the opposite impression.

DO YOU KNOW WHO IS PLANNING YOUR FUTURE FOR YOU?
ARE YOU SURE THEY ARE PLANNING WHAT YOU REALLY
WANT? IF NOT, IT'S TIME TO WAKE UP AND SPEAK UP!
THE HOUR IS LATE!

ARE YOU SURE YOU WANT TO BE "LIBERATED?"

God created you and gave you a beautiful and exalted place to fill. No women in
history have ever enjoyed such privileges, luxuries, and freedom as American women.
Yet, a tiny minority of dissatisfied, highly vocal, militant women insist that you are
being exploited as a "domestic drudge" and a "pretty toy." And they are determined
to "liberate" you—whether you want it or not!

What is "liberation?" Ask women in Cuba. Castro "liberated" Cuba! Remember?

WHAT IS THE EQUAL RIGHTS AMENDMENT?

On March 22, 1972, the U.S. Congress passed the Equal Rights Amendment
(ERA) and sent it to the states for ratification. If it is ratified by 38 states, it will become law, enforced by the federal government, superseding all state laws on related
subjects.

The Amendment reads: "Equality of rights under the law shall not be denied or
abridged by the United States or by any state on account of sex." Simple, isn't it?
Deceptively simple. Sounds good, doesn't it?
BUT HAVE YOU LOOKED AT THE HOOK INSIDE THE BAIT?

THE MOST DRASTIC MEASURE

Senator Sam Ervin called the ERA "the most drastic measure in Senate history."
Why? Because it strikes at the very foundation of family life, and the home is the
foundation of our nation. Can you possibly avoid being drastically affected by the
ERA? NOT A CHANCE!

Actually, it is a loss of Rights Amendment. How will it affect YOU?

DO YOU WANT TO LOSE YOUR RIGHT NOT TO WORK?

If you are married, you may choose to work outside your home. But you may
choose to stay at home, to rear your children, to be supported by your husband. The
ERA will abolish this right. It will invalidate all laws which require the husband to
support his family and will make the wife equally responsible for support. You can
be forced to supply half the family support, or all of it if you are a better wage earner
(pp. 944–945, *Yale Law Journal*, which was inserted in the Congressional Record by
Senator Birch Bayh, leading proponent of ERA).

What about your children? You can be forced to put them in a federal day care center, if one is available. And to see that one is available is a major goal of the National Organization for Women (NOW)—leaders in the movement to ratify the Equal Rights Amendment.

Under the ERA, if a wife fails to support her husband, he can use it as grounds for divorce (*Yale Law Journal,* p. 951).

This can work a special hardship on senior women who have spent their lives rearing their families and are not prepared to enter the job market.

WILL THE ERA HELP DIVORCED WOMEN?

Divorced women will lose the customary right of child custody, child support, and/or alimony, and can be forced to pay child support and alimony, if her husband wins custody of the children (*Yale Law Journal,* p. 952).

WHAT ABOUT OTHER EFFECTS ON FAMILY LIFE?

Wife and children will not be required to wear the name of husband and father. They can choose any name they wish. Can you imagine the resulting confusion? According to leading law counsels, the ERA will permit homosexuals to "marry" and adopt children.

DO YOU WANT TO LOSE YOUR RIGHT TO PRIVACY?

The aim of NOW and other pro-ERA groups is to totally "desexigrate" everything. Professor Paul Freund, Harvard Law School, testified that ERA: "would require that there be no segregation of the sexes in prison, reform schools, public restrooms, and other public facilities."

This includes all public schools, college dormitories, and hospital rooms.

DO YOU WANT YOUR HUSBAND TO SLEEP IN BARRACKS WITH WOMEN?

If your husband is in the armed forces, or a fireman, what can you expect under the ERA? It will be illegal to have separate facilities—so your husband will be sharing sleeping quarters, restrooms, showers and/or foxholes with women.

DO YOU WANT TO LOSE YOUR RIGHT NOT TO BE DRAFTED?

Some women are crying for "equal rights" in the armed forces. But do you want them to abolish your right NOT to be drafted? ERA will do this. All women will register at age eighteen, subject to all military duties including combat.

If you have small children, "whichever parent was called first might be eligible for service; the remaining parent, male or female, would be deferred" (*Yale Law*

Journal, p. 973). Do you want this for your daughters? Men, do you want your wives and daughters living in barracks with men? Going into combat with them?

DO YOU WANT PROTECTIVE LAWS AGAINST SEX CRIMES?

The ERA will abolish "seduction laws, statutory rape laws, laws prohibiting obscene language in the presence of women, prostitution and 'manifest danger' laws" and all laws against forcing women into prostitution (*Yale Law Journal,* pp. 954, 964).

WILL ERA PROVIDE BETTER PAY FOR WOMEN?

Not at all. Proponents of ERA incessantly sing the tune: "We want equal pay for equal work." They do not tell you that this is already guaranteed under:

(1) The Civil Rights Act of 1964, Subchapter VI: Equal Employment Opportunities (42 U.S. Code 2000e-2).

(2) The Equal Opportunities Act of 1972 (Public Law 92–261).

So the "equal pay for equal work" argument is deceptive—merely a smokescreen to hide the real intent of the ERA.

WILL THE ERA HELP WORKING WOMEN?

As noted above, it will NOT provide higher pay or increased job opportunities. It will NOT cause a husband to do more work around the house. It WILL, however, very adversely affect women in industry, by invalidating ALL PROTECTIVE LAWS FOR WOMEN—laws regulating weight lifting restrictions, rest periods, excessive working hours, and maternity leaves.

The ERA will do nothing for teachers. Their protection is already guaranteed by law. It WILL, however, adversely affect education by eliminating all single sex schools—military schools, seminaries, or women's colleges.

HOW WILL THE ERA AFFECT CHURCHES?

The National Organization for Women (NOW) is demanding that women "be ordained in religious bodies where that right is still denied." To refuse to do this will be illegal under ERA. One goal of NOW is to abolish the tax-exempt status of all churches.

If the Equal Rights Amendment is ratified, all Christian colleges which receive one dollar of federal money will no longer be permitted to have sexually segregated dormitories, showers, or restrooms.

A WOMAN'S UTOPIA?

At women's lib rallies, Russia is proudly cited as a country where women have equal rights. Harry Trimborn, staff writer, *Los Angeles Times*, visited Moscow and described just how "great" it is (*L.A. Times*, Dec. 23, 1970): "The women do the work and the men tell them how to do it. Like sweeping the streets, bricklaying, loading cargo ships, collecting garbage, building dams, digging ditches and mining coal . . . then she must spend at least 50% of her off-work time shopping and cooking. She can expect little help from her husband."

A Russian woman must put her baby in a state-operated child care unit. She (as well as men) can be jailed for refusing to engage in "socially useful labor" or for leading a "parasitic way of life."

This is a living picture of "liberation!"

CAN A STATE REVOKE ITS RATIFICATION OF ERA?

Absolutely! When 38 states ratify the ERA, it will become the 27th Amendment to the U.S. Constitution. At one time, 33 had ratified. Nebraska and Tennessee have rescinded their ratification.

"Clearly a state can change its mind either way before the amendment is officially declared to be ratified" (Prof. Charles L. Black, Jr., of Yale University Law School, *Congressional Record*, May 8, 1973, p. 8522).

WHAT CAN YOU DO ABOUT IT?

1. Find out where your state now stands on the Equal Rights Amendment.

2. Find out who your State Legislators are (you can call your local Democratic or Republican Headquarters). Write them. Ask them to oppose ERA. Tell them that NOW does not speak for you nor for most women. Ask your friends to write.

3. If possible, visit your representatives personally.

4. Work to inform as many people as possible (copies of this article available, 50 for $2.00; 100 for $3.50. Add .50 for postage.)

(NOTE: Proponents and opponents alike recognize the *Yale Law Journal*, Vol. 80, No. 5, April, 1971, herein used as documentation, to be an accurate analysis of the meaning and effects of the Equal Rights Amendment. Congresswoman Martha Griffiths, leading proponent, gave a copy to each member of Congress.)

TOO LONG WE HAVE BEEN THE SILENT MAJORITY. IT'S TIME TO SPEAK UP! LET YOUR VOICE BE STRONG AND CLEAR!

Source: Charlotte Guinn Ross, "The Federal Equal Rights Amendment as an Issue in the Texas Legislature, 1971–1975," M.A. thesis, Texas Woman's University, 1979.

4.4. HERMINE D. TOBOLOWSKY, "ANSWERS TO THE MIS-STATEMENTS IN 'LADIES! HAVE YOU HEARD?'"

Dallas attorney Hermine Tobolowsky wrote this response to "Ladies! Have You Heard?" (see Doc. 4.3) on behalf of Texans for ERA. A point-by-point rebuttal of Hobbs's contentions, it was printed on blue paper to contrast with the signature pink of Women Who Want to be Women. Tobolowsky was well known for her long advocacy of the state's Equal Legal Rights Amendment, which passed the legislature in 1971. She also wrote the text for a short brochure, distributed by Texans for ERA, answering the most commonly asked questions about the amendment.

Under the question, ARE YOU SURE YOU WANT TO BE LIBERATED? the statement is made that a "tiny minority of dissatisfied, highly vocal, militant women" want to "liberate" American women. Apparently, they are referring to the supporters of the Equal Rights Amendment. The enclosed list shows that most of the representative groups supporting ERA are nationally recognized groups including such responsible groups as the American Bar Association and the National Federation of B&PW, AAUW, etc., groups that certainly do not fit the picture described in the opening paragraph of the 2 pages of misinformation printed under the name of "Women Who Want to be Women."

Under the heading "THE MOST DRASTIC MEASURE" the claim is made that ERA strikes at the foundation of family life. Another mis-statement! It actually strengthens the family by establishing a real partnership in law as well as in fact in the marriage relationship and strengthening the bonds between men and women. It will give women the opportunity to protect themselves from selfish husbands who might try to convey away all of the family property in those states which still leave all of the family assets in the hands of the husband. It will force Congress to change Social Security laws to eliminate the discrimination that prevents a husband from drawing on his wife's Social Security account even though the married woman pays the same Social Security as her male counterpart, it will eliminate too many unjust laws to attempt to enumerate them here.

Under the heading of "DO YOU WANT TO LOSE YOUR RIGHT NOT TO WORK?" the claim is made that ERA will abolish the right of a woman not to work. There is no State in the Union with a law forcing any man to work nor is there any such Federal law, hence the Equal Rights Amendment could not possibly force women to work—that would be inequality. The *Yale Law Journal* is misquoted; what it actually says is quoted in an article on the Texas Equal Rights Amendment in the *Texas Tech Law Journal*, Volume 5, No. 2, page 637 as follows:

"In this regard, the *Yale Law Journal* states: 'The Equal Rights Amendment would bar a state from imposing greater liability for support on a husband than on a wife merely because of his sex. However, a court could equalize the civil law by extending the duty of support to women. . . . If husband and wife had equal resources and earning capacity, neither would have a claim of support against the other. HOW-

EVER, IF ONE SPOUSE WERE A WAGE EARNER AND THE OTHER PERFORMED
UNCOMPENSATED DOMESTIC LABOR FOR THE FAMILY, THE WAGE EARNING
SPOUSE WOULD OWE A DUTY TO THE SPOUSE WHO WORKED IN THE HOME."

Thus ERA will not change the way people live their lives. Husbands doubtless will
continue to be the primary breadwinners in the majority of families.

There is absolutely nothing in ERA to require parents to put their children in
federal day care centers. ERA affects only laws that apply differently to men and
women. Many states, including Texas, presently have laws requiring a wife to support a husband who needs support if she can do so—no law forces either a husband
or a wife to support the other if he or she does not have the means to do so. In sum-
mary, NO law now requires either men or women to work and ERA would not change
this—if there were any such law forcing anyone to work, we would not have so many
on welfare.

Under "WILL THE ERA HELP DIVORCED WOMEN?" the claim is made that
women will lose the customary right of child custody, support and alimony and be
forced to pay child support and alimony.

No State in the Union gives a woman the right of child custody by law—all
states provide that custody shall be decided on the basis of what is best for the child
and hence custody laws do not favor one sex over the other and will not be changed
by ERA. While men are the ones usually required to pay child support, women also
have a moral and legal obligation to support their children—it is usually the men
who pay because they have the finances to do so, but women can be ordered to pay
and in some cases are presently required to pay child support. This would not be
changed by ERA. Besides, any decent mother or father will support his or her children to the best of his or her ability. There is not and never has been any alimony in
Texas and most other states have also abolished alimony. If a state does have alimony, I see no reason why a husband should not have a claim if his wife is financially
able to pay just as the wife should have a claim against a husband.

The heading "WHAT ABOUT EFFECTS ON FAMILY LIFE?" makes the claim that
if ERA passes, wife and children will not be required to wear the name of husband
and father and it will create confusion. In some countries, wife and children do not
take the name of husband and father and there are some decisions in this country to
the effect that they do not have to do so, but ERA will not prohibit continuation of
the usual practice of the wife assuming the name of her husband and the children
going thereby. Nor will ERA have the effect of permitting homosexuals to "marry"
and adopt children—I know of no lawyers who think it will have that effect nor does
the w.w.w. sheet identify the "leading law counsels" who so state. Remember the
American Bar Association supports ERA.

Under the heading "DO YOU WANT TO LOSE YOUR RIGHT TO PRIVACY?" the
statement is made that there could be no segregation of the sexes in "prison, reform
schools, public restrooms, etc." This ignores the fact that the Supreme Court has
repeatedly held that there is a Constitutional Right to privacy and that ERA does
not repeal other Constitutional Rights—it only repeals discriminatory statutes. The

Constitutional Right to privacy also applies to segregation of military barracks. (See Supreme Court case *Griswold vs. Connecticut.*)

Under the heading "DO YOU WANT TO LOSE YOUR RIGHT NOT TO BE DRAFTED?" the public is misinformed that women have a present right not to be drafted. On the contrary, there is no right not to be drafted by either men or women. By the end of World War II there were a number of bills introduced in Congress to draft women and had the war lasted another 6 months, women would have been drafted. Texas passed a bill in 1957 to draft women into the militia in time of war. This does not mean that women with small children will be drafted—you will recall that under the present draft law, men with small children were deferred.

Under the heading "DO YOU WANT PROTECTIVE LAWS AGAINST SEX CRIMES?" the w.w.w.w. sheets indicate that ERA will abolish laws against sex crimes. This is totally untrue. No criminal sex laws apply only to one sex. They prohibit a criminal act and ERA does not require that criminal acts go unpunished. They are designed to punish the criminal because he or she has performed a criminal act not because of the sex of the offender.

Under the heading "WILL ERA HELP WORKING WOMEN?" the w.w.w.w. sheet indicates that ERA will adversely affect women in industry because it will invalidate all protective laws for women, such as weight lifting restrictions, etc. ERA does not require the repeal of any protective law—only that its "benefits" be extended to both sexes. Since men die at a younger age than women and suffer more from stress diseases, such as heart, ulcers, they obviously need protective laws just as much as women.

Under the present practice, so-called "protective" laws have been used as an excuse not to promote women, not to hire them in the more lucrative jobs. However, there have been several Federal Court decisions holding that "protective" laws which apply to women only violate the Equal Employment Opportunities Act and are thus invalid. As a result, many states have already repealed such laws or extended their benefits to men to bring them in line with the federal law. In other states, including Texas, the Attorney General has ruled such laws invalid if they apply to women only. ERA will not prohibit one sex schools if the schools are private and privately financed, but it will prohibit public one sex schools and since they are supported by taxpayers, men and women, this is as it should be.

The Constitution protects separation of Church and State and guarantees religious freedom, hence the claim by w.w.w.w. that ERA will interfere with church internal policy is incorrect.

As may be seen from the enclosed sheet of supporters of ERA, the attempt to link ERA supporters with communist Russia is a smear tactic. Actually, other than w.w.w.w. the only opposition I know of to ERA, organized opposition that is, comes from the Communist Party, the Ku Klux Klan, and the John Birch Society.

There is federal court authority to the effect that once a state has ratified a constitutional amendment, it cannot legally revoke that ratification.

As to the claim of w.w.w.w. to represent the "SILENT MAJORITY," I call attention to the fact that the Texas Equal Legal Rights Amendment passed by a 4 to 1 majority when the people had a chance to vote on it and that in every state where the people have had a chance to vote, it has passed overwhelmingly. I think they might more properly be dubbed the "squawking minority."

Source: Marjorie Schuchat Papers, Woman's Collection, Blagg-Huey Library, Texas Woman's University.

4.5. JUANA TARANGO GOES ON STRIKE AT FARAH MANUFACTURING

Juana Tarango was a young mother with three children under the age of five when she began sewing garments at Farah's Third Street plant in El Paso. Her husband worked for the city, but "we couldn't save anything and I didn't want to live in a rented place all my life." Meeting even ordinary expenses on one salary was difficult; if a child got sick "that would really throw us off because that meant we had to pay for a doctor and we would be really short of cash." Juana's job at Farah enabled the family to buy a house eventually, but juggling employment and motherhood was a perpetual challenge. If she needed to meet with one of her children's teachers, she was required to bring her supervisor at Farah a signed note documenting the appointment; when the children were sick, she relied on her mother or sister-in-law to take them to the doctor. In the document below, Tarango describes the perils of union organizing and her decision to join the walkout in 1972. Although the terms of the strike settlement in 1974 required that the workers be reinstated, Tarango was fired a year later. Farah inflated production quotas and cited failure to meet them as justification for terminating many former strikers.

Everybody was afraid to talk about the union. Everybody was afraid. If they heard you talk about it, some of the women thought that we were foolish. There was a lot of people in there that thought that the union wouldn't do us much good. So they said, "Look, if the union comes in here, a lot of benefits will be taken away from us, like the doctors will be taken away from us, the buses" [—things that] Farah used to bribe the people with. Like for Christmas he would give the people presents, and he would raffle off furniture and washing machines. A lot of the people really thought that he was being very nice. When really they weren't thinking that that money was THEIR money that he was giving away.

When I was pregnant with my youngest I was working there. My husband was also working there, but what he was making wasn't enough. When you have a house payment and the kids are small, and you have all these things you have to pay [for], it's really something. But we fought it out, and we made it. I worked, I think, up to the eighth month. And let me tell you, it was pretty bad. Because they take no consideration, even if you're pregnant, you still have to do the same thing, and there's no change, nothing at all. They don't even take you down [from the machine] to rest your legs. If you're sewing, you're sewing. If you're standing up, you have to stand up all day. Then after the baby's born you just take a month off and that's it. You have to go back to work. If you didn't go back to work exactly a month after, you would just lose your whole seniority. . . .

That's why we decided we needed a union, and we should organize. . . .

There was a lot of people that were fired even before the walkout. Just because they heard them talk about union and they would get fired before they could get anybody to organize or get anybody to sign cards or anything.

And me, I guess they thought that they kept me very happy. Like I said, I always did my work, I tried very hard in doing my work, and they didn't think, I guess, that I would finally walk out, 'cause I never complained, I never said anything.

The day that we walked out, the supervisor saw that I had the little plaque on, and he went over and he looked sort of startled. He said, "You?!" I said, "Yes." He said, "What have we done to you?" I said, "Oh, I couldn't—I wouldn't know where to begin." "We haven't done anything to you." I say, "But you have done a lot to all the people around me, and I've seen it going on." And he says, "Oh no. What have we done? Tell me, begin telling me. You have all these benefits, and what more do you want," trying to bribe me. And I says, "Oh, no. I have seen people that you don't even give them a chance to go to the bathroom. . . ."

And that man just said, "Well," he said, "we're not really that bad." And I said, "No, I've seen a lot of goings-on. Nobody's going to talk me out of it." It even made me cry just to think of the things that had happened, and he still had the nerve to come and ask me what it was that I had seen. And I told him also. I said, "Look, there's a lot of intelligent workers here. And I think that they could be brought up to be supervisors. And I don't see any of them, that you give any promotions or anything like that to *our* people. When I see that you bring in *your* people—you know, their race, or friends or relatives of them—that didn't know anything about work at the plants or anything like that." . . .

I walked out [on strike] at lunchtime. There was supposed to be four of us . . . and we decided it had to be right after lunch. . . . One of them was right next to me, and I told her, "Come on, it's time to go [walk out]." She said, "Wait, I'm going to wait for my sister, she's way back there." And then this other lady, she was back there too, and she told me, "Now, it's time." I said, "ok, let's go." And that other girl said, "No, I'm going to wait for my sister," and she never came out [on strike]. She stayed in there.

. . . [The strikers] would go stand in front of the factory and yell, "Come on, come on, union!" The women [inside], some of them it would really make them very mad, because they thought that if all this keeps going on, well the plant's going to close, and Farah had them all terrorized, that he would just rather close the factories than give in to the union. So a lot of the women were afraid that if he closed the factory, well what would they do? Where would they go? Where would they get a job? Some of them were just afraid, and they thought that we were really going to cause a lot of trouble. They didn't realize that the one that was causing the trouble was the boss. The big boss.

Source: Juana Tarango, oral history interview by Gail Hershatter, August 1, 1977. Courtesy of Gail Hershatter.

4.6. DIANA CAMACHO, "CHICANAS CHANGE THE COURSE OF TEXAS IWY"

The United Nations declared 1975 as International Women's Year (IWY) and sponsored a huge international meeting in Mexico City to discuss ways to improve women's status worldwide. Participating nations were required to hold follow-up conferences, and the U.S. Congress therefore authorized funding for the National Women's Conference, held in Houston in November 1977, to promote equality between the sexes. The delegates were chosen in state women's conferences; the Texas meeting took place June 24–26 in Austin. Diana Camacho, secretary of the Mexican American Business and Professional Women's Club of Austin, was appointed to the Texas IWY Coordinating Committee, which was in charge of planning the Texas meeting. She was also one of the conference's two vice chairpersons. Here she describes her other, unofficial role as program planner for the Chicana Advisory Committee for IWY Concerns, an ad hoc group that operated independently of the coordinating committee. In this post-conference memo she angrily relates the attempt of Anglo feminists to preplan the state meeting's agenda and the Chicana Advisory Committee's successful work to make the program multicultural and the Texas conference welcoming to Hispanic women.

Chicanas Change Course of Texas IWY

This statement is not too bold. It is not strong enough, it requires elaboration, realization, full discussion. Yes, we changed the course of Texas IWY. Chicanas have been monitoring IWY for years—since Mexico City, even. We were there, not officially but with our own money we made the trip. Then recently, like September, 1976 we sent over 100 nominations, just from Austin, for Texas Coordinating Committee membership to National IWY Commission. We stayed on top of the nomination process. We wrote our congresspersons, called friends in Washington, held meetings, threatened and demanded representation, and we got some.

Through all this, Mexico City meeting to [the] present, remember the name Martha Cotera: the energy, anger, stamina. If anyone deserves an award for the one who put it together, kept it together, encouraged the disillusioned—give it to her. It's true one person did not do it all, but she was the constant current, the force. She tapped chicana talent, chicana resources, chicana energy and chicana anger. She pushed her activities across chicana party lines, across income levels, education levels and organizational jealousies. While doing this, she wrote a book: "Chicana Feminism."[2] What more can I say about her? Plenty.

Martha was not a member of Texas IWY Coordinating Committee—well, not officially anyway. The day before the Texas IWY Conference, one gringa said it was not fair that Martha seemed to be given the opportunity to speak her opinion more than most Committee Members. We pointed out that Martha attended more Coordinating Committee Meetings than most of its members; and so it went.

In January, 1977, the newly appointed Texas Coordinating Committee members received word we were to meet in two weeks. We were (get this) to bring copies of proposals for the Texas IWY Conference, but federal regs [regulations] were not available except for one copy at the State Library in Austin and copies committee members had. In two weeks we were to prepare conference proposals and bring 40 copies. Imagine. Then we found out about a meeting held in Austin, 6 to 8 weeks before, attended by Liz Carpenter, Jane Hickie, and Cathy Bonner.[3] They discussed and decided what proposal Cathy Bonner would submit and strategies for awarding it to her. She had a copy of the regs. As you can see she had 6 to 8 weeks, while we had less than two.

Chicanas who found out were pissed, we were mad!! How can I put it, "era rabia." We bootlegged a copy of names of Chicanas on the newly appointed committee. Using watts [i.e., WATS] lines and other forms of communication, Chicanas in Austin invited them to meet us at Villa Capri Restaurant for a pre-meeting meeting the morning of the first Texas IWY Coordinating Committee Meeting, February, 1977. At the Villa Capri Chicana Meeting, we strategized, decided on motions, and resolutions.

At the Coordinating Committee Meeting, two hours later, all hell broke loose.

Yes, we blew their "ladies tea party meeting," but from then on their respect for us was firmly established. Not that the rest of the months were easy, but they always knew we were not to be bought off, we had nothing to lose. Let me tell you, they knew and shall not now forget our presence.

I could elaborate on countless events to further substantiate evidence of the threat they felt. If I am asked, "Was that necessary?", then I would realize how little, you reader, know of Chicana Herstory at hands of the "white feminist." Be aware and try to mentally tabulate the amount of money we spent out of our pockets. For the Texas Conference in June, Chicanas had a huge organization. We had Housing Committee, Resolutions Committee, Media and PR Committee, Chicana Caucus Meetings Committee, Food and Entertainment Committee, Chicana Reception Booth Committee. How many participated you ask? I need more time to gather the info. The organizing Chicanas in Austin met every Monday for three months.

Recommendation: Funding sought for a state Chicana conference, yes, we need to get together again, and again. Do you recall Chicanas across every line such as geography, party lines, education, income ever coming together? No. We need to learn skills together, share information, experiences, get angry, laugh, and cry together. It is long overdue. We did it in June, 1977, we can do it again. Call it a Chicana Congress.

Source: Martha Cotera Papers, box 9, Benson Latin American Collection, University of Texas Libraries, University of Texas at Austin.

4.7. JACKIE WEGER, "HOUSTON WOMEN'S CONFERENCE, 1977"

Jackie Weger reared a family before earning a B.A. degree and teacher certification from the University of Houston-Victoria. A resident of Wharton, she has published sixteen novels and spends part of each year in Panama at a Catholic mission, teaching women in poverty how to earn money. One of thousands of women who attended the National Women's Conference as an observer, she wrote this reminiscence in 2005.

When I decided to attend the Woman's Conference in Houston, I did not have a clue that it was to be such an historic event. I was 37 years old, the mother of five children, and new to Houston. My experiences suggested conferences were a way to meet people—especially, like-minded women. However, nothing in my life prepared me for the epiphany I underwent that afternoon. The sight that greeted me when I rounded the corner of the Albert Thomas Convention Center boggled my mind. Billie Jean King, Bella Abzug, and Betty Friedan leading a march that seemed of thousands of women. What struck me was that these three women, Titans all, whose faces were so familiar across our country—Abzug with her signature hats, Friedan, often on television to discuss theories in her book, *The Feminine Mystique*, and Billie Jean King of tennis court fame—were all so *ordinary-looking*. Abzug was elegant, Freidan looked like some kid's little old grandmother, and Billie Jean King was all ropy muscles. None of these women were glamorous in the literal sense of that word. Yet, each was a successful woman, and they got that success with brains, backbone, and moxie. I decided right then that brains, backbone, and moxie was going to be my staff of life. It was a relief, really, to understand that I did not have to be utterly glamorous in order to be successful.

I had the sensation that the women attending the conference were those who did not tell themselves, *No!* I soon learned why not. There are dozens, if not hundreds, of people over the course of our lives that tell us women, No! Moreover, hundreds of those *No* folk were lined up outside the Convention Center. I fell in with the marchers behind the torchbearer and flag wavers, and boy! We had to negotiate a phalanx of protesters. There was a man with a bullhorn yelling at us to "go home where we belonged." There was even a Boy Scout troop waving protest posters as we crowded into the Convention Center. It was a bit scary. The little Boy Scouts looked somewhat lost, but the adult protesters were mean looking. Some of their caterwauling was utterly vile. However, the leaders of the march ignored them, so, for the most part, did the rest of us.

I came early to the feminist movement for the simplest and most practical reasons. I had five children, and women's groups and organizations were the only advocates addressing gender issues, especially those of a young mother such as myself. Buying a home was beyond our means, yet it was impossible to find decent rental housing that accepted more than one or two children. At that time in the midfifties and into the sixties, feminist groups were the only voices heard arguing that families with children should not be discriminated against in housing. Children cost money. I had to work—at least part-time. Yet, every job application asked how many children one had, if one had transportation—questions that are no longer on applications and are today, deemed discriminatory. Those of us women who really needed work to help support our families were often passed over because of *having* that family. The feminist agenda addressed these issues and many more. Birth control was an issue, too. I had my five children because I could not get access to conventional birth control—yet once I had them, I was at a severe disadvantage in housing and jobs.

The 1977 conference had an agenda—more issues than I can recall. Decent housing, equal pay for equal work, credit in our own names, women being considered first class citizens on a par with men. The conference was exciting beyond measure. I sat next to Margaret Mead in one of the seminars and later heard her speak. I shook the hand of Jean Stapleton of *All in the Family* fame. Unlike Archie, she is not a bigot. Phyllis Schlafly, an outspoken critic of gay men and lesbians, was a protester—yet the Conference voted to include gays and lesbians—human beings all. Phyllis was eventually silenced when her own son came out of the closet.

Hotel rooms were difficult to come by, so I slept two nights in my car. I would do it again many times over. In my college classes I often hear young women say, "I am not a feminist." I say, "Oh, but you are—if you've ever asked your husband to wash a dish or change a diaper—you are on a feminist track." If you have ever argued, or even complained that the men where you work get more pay for the same work you do—that is a gender issue. There are many more gender issues in our daily lives. I get to vote in every election because early feminists lobbied for it. I get to have credit, buy a car or a house in my own name because modern feminists fought for that right and won. I have the privilege of a university education at the mature age of sixty-five because feminists lobbied for and won against age discrimination. Perhaps every young woman will not consider herself a feminist—but sometime, somewhere, on one of the myriad issues we face in life—she will find herself on the side of feminists.

Source: Jackie Weger, copy in authors' possession.

4.8. BARBARA JORDAN CONFRONTS THE RACIAL FACTOR IN POLITICS

Barbara Jordan (1936–1996) grew up in Houston's African American Fifth Ward and earned a B.A. in political science from Texas Southern University. After receiving a law degree from Boston University, she set up a private practice in Houston and began volunteering with the liberal Harris County Democrats. Her remarkable gift for oratory quickly got her promoted from block work in black precincts to the speechmaking circuit. Jordan won a seat in the Texas Senate in 1966 and in 1972 was elected to the U.S. House of Representatives. She was the first Texas woman elected to Congress in her own right and the first African American ever elected from Texas. During the House Judiciary Committee's televised hearings on the Watergate scandal in 1974,

Jordan gave a somber and eloquent speech in defense of the Constitution that made her instantly famous. She retired from Congress after her third term and returned to Texas to teach at the Lyndon B. Johnson School of Public Affairs at the University of Texas at Austin.

Jordan owed her political career to the civil rights movement. Labor lawyer Chris Dixie, chair of the Harris County Democrats, recruited her to run for the state legislature in 1962 and 1964; both times she lost while others on the slate did well. Only after the abolition of the poll tax, the Voting Rights Act of 1965, and a series of Supreme Court rulings that forced reapportionment of legislative districts across the South, did African Americans begin to win political office. After Harris County reapportioned in 1965, creating the minority-heavy state senatorial District 11, Jordan won it easily. In this excerpt from her autobiography, she describes the frustration of losing her first two races for the lower house because too few white liberals supported her candidacy.

One day Chris Dixie said to me that I ought to run for the Texas House of Representatives when that election came up again in 1962. Dixie was the one I worked with most closely on this whole political scene, so when he broached that matter I paid attention.

I said: "Well, Chris, I make enough money to eat and buy my clothes, and gasoline for my little Simca, but I certainly don't make enough money to run a political race." I told him that. I said: "I don't have the money." But he said: "Don't worry about that. The filing fee is five hundred dollars and I'll lend you the money for a filing fee. You can pay me back."

. . . There were twelve state representatives coming from Harris County, all running at large, so that we all had to canvass the whole county. The Harris County Democrats advanced their slate of candidates for the state legislature, and I was one of these, and each of us had as an opponent a conservative, backed by other groups. My opponent in the race was Willis Whatley, a lawyer also.

We were all presented to a big gathering of Democrats from Harris County, twelve of us, including me and Bob Eckhardt. Each candidate was presented and said a few words, and I was the tenth candidate to get up and give a speech. . . .

At the conclusion of my speech the audience stood up and applauded. . . . They hadn't stood for the others. . . . And after that response the last two speakers, whoever they were, Places Eleven and Twelve, were just wiped out.

From that time on, as we moved along on the campaign trail, the standing joke was: "Let's get there early so we can get on the program before Barbara Jordan."

. . . On occasions when I would be at the same meetings with my opponent, Willis Whatley, I would listen to him and I would say to myself: "Anybody in his right mind will vote for me against this fellow." I would think: Because I've got a better case to present. I'd look at him and I'd just shake my head, thinking: You ought to just forget it, Willis, and go back to the practice of law.

So one fine day Election Day came. And I cast my vote at seven o'clock in the morning. The polling place was filled by seven o'clock there in Fifth Ward, and I got reports that it was that way at all the black boxes in the city . . .

As the first returns showed up on the television, I, of course, was behind. But Chris kept telling me: "Just wait until after ten o'clock when the black boxes come in." But they came in and I still hadn't won. Reality entered. I got forty-six thousand votes, and Willis Whatley got sixty-five thousand. And that was that.

. . . I did well in the black areas, but I didn't do well anywhere else. The feeling I had was that I had been used to get black people to vote. And that nobody else on the ticket brought that kind of strength to me in return. Those fine people, I thought, all the Harris County Democrats, they had me come to teas and coffees in their areas in the southwest part of town, and the people would come to hear me and be very polite. But they didn't give me their votes.

. . . After the primary I continued to go around and speak and meet people and testify before committees in the Texas Legislature on pending educational bills that would benefit blacks. All that whole bit in order to get my name well-known. One day I went to Austin to testify, and when I sat up in the House gallery and looked down at Willis Whatley at his desk, I thought, "I ought to be in his place. I deserve it."

Then it was time to run again in 1964, and I hoped things would be different. This time there was another seat where the incumbent was more vulnerable than Willis Whatley, so I thought: I'll try for that place instead. But John Ray Harrison—a white who had been a part of that original slate of twelve candidates, and I guess had also lost—wanted to run for that better seat.

One day he called me to his office and explained that it would make better sense for me to go again for the same place, Place Ten, against the same opponent that I had before. He made me feel that it was the thing to do, so I agreed to that. But I remember thinking after I left him that Harrison had sold me a bill of goods, and that I had made a mistake in not saying: "I'm going against this guy who is more vulnerable." I knew that, and I took a deep breath and said to myself: "Well, you made a mistake."

Willis Whatley, now the incumbent, had his big billboards all over the county, and his conservative groups behind him. So we had a repeat performance.

When I saw that the second race was an extension of the first, and that Whatley had won, and that John Ray Harrison had also won, but I had not, I didn't go to the campaign headquarters. Instead, I just got in my car and drove around most of election night. The question was: "Is a seat in the state legislature worth continuing to try for?" I got a few thousand more votes the second time out, but the basic facts were the same. I asked myself: "Am I just butting my head against something that's absolutely impossible to pull off?" I drove around in the car, listening to the returns while I asked myself: "Why are you doing this?"

After I got home and had gone to bed, my campaign manager and campaign coordinator came to my house asking: "Where have you been? The people are all waiting for you at headquarters." I said: "I've been driving around." And when Chris called to say, "Well, we've got the analysis for you," I snapped at him, "I've got the analysis for you: I didn't win." And went back to bed.

I had to decide by myself whether I was going to stick it out a little longer, and thinking that if I did I certainly couldn't do it in concert with anybody else. I couldn't let anyone else get in my head and make my decisions any more. I wasn't going to go to their teas if they were not voting for me at their polls.

Source: Barbara Jordan and Shelby Hearon, *Barbara Jordan: A Self-Portrait* (New York: Doubleday, 1979).

4.9. ANN RICHARDS MOVES FROM CAMPAIGN VOLUNTEER TO COUNTY COMMISSIONER

Ann Willis Richards (1933–2006) was one of the most politically gifted of the generation of women who began winning elective office in the 1970s. After years as a Democratic Party volunteer while raising a family in Dallas and Austin, she stopped running other people's campaigns and launched her own. She was the first woman elected Travis County commissioner (1978), the first woman elected state treasurer (1982, 1986), and the first woman elected governor in her own right (1990). Famous for her sense of humor, she became a national figure after she addressed the Democratic National Convention in 1988 and joked that President George H. W. Bush "was born with a silver foot in his mouth." In this early interview Richards explains the road she traveled from housewife-volunteer to the quintessentially male position of county commissioner.

I taught school I guess about a year and a half before I had my first baby and then I had one, and then I had two, and then I had three and then I had four and did all of the things that women are supposed to do—kept house and I read women's magazines that told me that I was a nurse and a chauffeur and a sex goddess and a child care keeper—all of the things you're supposed to do and it never occurred to me that I should of ever done anything else, because I was told all my life as a child there was no greater cause. . . . [B]ut they made a real mistake with us when they started giving us an education, because I think once you've got your mind expanded a little bit, you really can't tell yourself that folding towels and properly decorating a house is a full time job nor is it really that mentally rewarding. It just isn't, that's all. I occupied myself in a lot of political campaigns, in a sort of telephone answering, trying to get people to run for precinct chairman way—a lot of envelope stuffing stuff and I did that practically because it was a way out, a way of being involved a bit, taking some time away from the house and I loved politics because my husband did. . . . We [women] were not given positions of responsibility and we always felt sort of on the fringe of what was going on. Invariably, those of us who were around for a number of years and had some expertise were superseded by some young man that was ten years younger than we were and who was obviously on his way up.

So I got a telephone call from a friend of mine that said she had this young woman who wanted to run for office and would I look at her and talk with her. I said I wouldn't touch it with a ten foot pole, that I'd had my fill of politics and had not found it personally that satisfying and, besides that, the thought of a young woman wanting to run for the Legislature was, you know, a little crazy. She convinced me that I should go down and meet Sarah [Weddington]. We had lunch together. I was really impressed by her presence and I agreed, on the basis that she'd let me run the campaign and she would be the candidate and would do what I told her to do, that I would be willing to do it. It was kind of a magic marriage because Sarah was desperate for someone to tell her what to do, and I was desperate for somebody who would let me tell them what to do. . . . Well, that success was a truly heady victory, and I think the experience of working principally with women was so exciting to me and you have to realize that by this time I was, you know, thirty-seven-years old, not exactly what you would call the age of awareness but it was just terrific. So we won.

. . . [A] young man involved in that campaign named Charles Miles, who is a young aggressive black leader in East Austin[,] . . . called me to say that a friend of his was running for the Legislature, and she was a woman I had heard of but never met that was on the Austin School Board, Wilhelmina Delco. Wilhelmina was black and they were very much interested in seeing her get elected, but they didn't have the expertise to deal with it. Charles asked me to come over to East Austin to talk to Wilhelmina and to run the campaign, and I did and managed that campaign which gave me another level of credibility. It doesn't mean that you're any smarter than you ever were. It just means that someone says, well she was successful there so we'll let her do something else, and I worked on Gonzalo Barrientos' campaign. . . .

I became, I guess someone whose advice was sought in the area of politics. I did not run myself, I had no aspirations to be in office. In fact, I always thought David [my husband] would run for something. Then we had an officeholder in this County Commissioner's seat that a lot of us had talked about really needing a good opponent for various reasons. We started looking for someone to run, thinking principally David might be the one, but David would be a real good officeholder if a committee would form and pick him up on a litter and bring him in and crown him. But a friend called and it was one of the young activists from the campus and said "we've been thinking about it Ann, and the truth of the matter is that you are the one who should be the candidate." [I said,] "You're kidding, you know it was outrageous. You know a woman can't run for county commissioner. It's never been done—da dah, da dah, and I don't want to be in office anyway." Well, the long and short of it was that David was the one who said you cannot turn down the opportunity. . . .

So I still said Oh Gosh, I'm not sure I wanted to do it, and I made them put together the statistics I would have had put together for anyone who wanted to run to see if I could run, and we took the kids and went to the beach and pored over those statistics for three weeks and it was obvious I could run. A woman ran well in the City Council race in this area. It seemed like an area that was transitional enough to be progressive thinking and be willing to elect a woman, so the upshot was I finally said I would do it and set about doing it in a very methodical way. . . . I had women who were so anxious to try their skills as I had done when I ran Sarah's campaign, and I let them do it and they were absolutely magicians in putting it together. The question came up all the time about whether a woman could be a county commissioner, and the more I ran the more I was convinced that of course I could. Businessmen don't type their own letters, they hire people who are skilled in doing that. County commissioners in urban areas don't lay their own roads and don't run their own bulldozers. They hire people who know how to do that, and this is basically an administrative job.

Well, after I ran for county commissioner, you can imagine that the road crew of my precinct was in terror of what had happened to them. They are principally what we call cedar choppers. I mean they are all inbred. I mean, I've got five of one family, they are all brothers on the road crew. There are 31 of these men. My road foreman, of course, was not so happy, but after we met, he decided he could get along with me all right and he would stay on. The big day came for me to go out to the road office and meet the crew. The first thing they were worried about was if they were all going to keep their jobs. They'd all been told you know, that I would fire them and stuff, so—As we were walking into the barn there that houses all the machinery and trucks, there was a really sleazy, rotten-looking dog lying down on the pavement, and I commented on how moth-bitten this hound looked and said something about they ought to be able to do better than that. I went on upstairs to the little room up there where they have coffee. Well, I made a speech trying to assure them that I was an okay person and they all did have their jobs and they weren't all going to have to join a union tomorrow and weren't going to have to wear chains on their legs and, you know, trying in some way to disarm a very difficult situation. After I finished, there was dead silence. I said, "If you [have] any questions, I don't care what you ask me. Ask me now, 'cause let's get it all out in the open. We're going to be working together and we need to know each other. Not a word. So I said, "What about your dog, that rotten dog I saw downstairs. What's the dog's name?" Silence. No one said a word. Finally, an old man on the front row said, "Well, why don't you ask James?" That's the road foreman. "Why don't you ask James what the dog's name is?" And I said "James, what's your dog's name?" James shuffled from one foot to the other and this voice came from the back, "Well, you're just going to find out sooner or later. We call her Ann Richards." And then there was this young man on the front row said, "B-b-b-but we call her Miss Ann."

So that was the first real ice breaker, you know, with that crew. That fact that I took that well, that that dog was named after me. I'm sure they had cussed and kicked that dog during that campaign.

Source: Ann Richards, oral history interview by Lynn Cooksey, 1979, Austin History Center, Austin Public Library.

4.10. CAROLE WOODARD DISCOVERS THE ODDS
AGAINST AFRICAN AMERICAN REPUBLICANS

During the 1930s African Americans switched political allegiance en masse from the Republicans, the party of Lincoln, to the Democrats, the party of the New Deal. At the end of the twentieth century only 5 percent of African Americans in Texas were registered Republicans. More than 90 percent supported Democratic candidates, and even those at higher income levels tended to stay with the Democratic Party. Carole Woodard, one of the tiny Republican minority, found that party loyalty trumped racial solidarity when she ran for office in the early 1990s and spoke at a Juneteenth celebration.

I campaigned [for county clerk] with very little money. After everyone got me involved, I had very little support. I lost by about 1,000 votes. I ran against Patricia Ritchie, who worked as the assistant under the county clerk, who had been there for thirty years. She had been her assistant for all those years. I really thought that I was going to win. I campaigned with about $1,200. It was mainly with the work of my husband and my church that we were able to make our own signs. Steve Stockman ran for Congress, and he helped me. He included me in his mailers because I didn't have money to do my own. I carried all of north Galveston County. It was really the black people that did not vote for me. We were hoping that I could have gotten a small percentage of the swing votes from blacks, but I didn't get it because I was a Republican. That is what they told me in all of the churches I campaigned in. "We don't vote for Republicans." It didn't matter that I was the most qualified candidate, both in education and experience. What mattered was that I was a Republican, and they would not vote for a Republican whether they were qualified or not. The more vicious part of my campaign came from black Democrats. And I am black.

When I was running for county clerk, I went to a June 19th celebration. June 19th is a celebration that black people have in Texas because that's when the slaves were freed here. There are celebrations all over, and politicians use that time to make all of the picnics and the big gatherings where they talk to people about voting. All of the candidates go and try to reach blacks. A prominent black woman elected official stood up and said that the Democrats freed the slaves. I was appalled. I went there to speak, and they would not even let me speak. They let all of the black Democratic candidates speak, but they would not let me speak because I was a Republican. So I pushed my cards, and I spoke to people and said, "That is not true." Think about it—Abraham Lincoln was not a Democrat. Then when you brought it to their attention, it was like, that is right. He wasn't. But with her there saying what she did, they believed it. If you don't go back in your brain and pull up history, it is never even questioned. It is done so subtly. I was able to make it through the crowd. I stopped and talked to people and said, "With all due respect, she lied to you."

Source: Meg McKain Grier, *Grassroots Women: A Memoir of the Texas Republican Party* (Boerne, Tex.: Wingscape Press, 2001).

4.II. JENNIFER CHAU, "BEING VIETNAMESE AND TEXAN"

When South Vietnam was overrun by Communists from the north in 1975, thousands of South Vietnamese who had been associated with the American military presence fled to the United States. Jennifer Chau's father, an officer in the Army of the Republic of Vietnam, and mother were among them; both were members of the ethnic Chinese minority. Texas was second only to California in its population of Vietnamese refugees. Thousands settled in Houston and in Gulf Coast towns, where they worked as shrimpers and crabbers. They soon made up 5 percent of the population of Palacios, where Jennifer Chau grew up, and by 2000 there were more than 143,000 Vietnamese Texans, the largest Asian minority in the state.

The first wave of refugees, unlike the "boat people" who began arriving a few years later, were largely educated, professional people. In the United States they had to take whatever low-wage jobs they could find; frequently both parents had to work. In Houston, Vietnamese women became nail technicians and opened hundreds of discount nail salons; so many sought licensing as manicurists that the Texas Cosmetology Commission felt compelled to offer the exam in Vietnamese. Other women, like Chau's mother, opened restaurants that operated on family labor. As Chau explains in this memoir, written while she was a student at the University of Houston-Victoria, she grew up as a double minority. She was an Asian in America and a Buddhist in the majority-Catholic Vietnamese enclave in Palacios—and uncomfortable in both roles.

How I Came to Be:

My father was 21 when he came to the United States from South Vietnam in order to train at Fort Knox, Kentucky, in the US Army Armor School in 1974. When South Vietnam fell to the North Vietnam communists, my father had to choose to leave his family and friends in Vietnam and began a new life here in the States. My mother left a week before South Vietnam fell in April 1975. With a bag in hand and my grandmother's quick negotiations with an American, my mother and my grandmother got onto a plane in search of refuge. My parents met in Huntsville in 1976 and moved to Oklahoma in hopes of a new life. I was born in 1983 there in Oklahoma City, the second child of my parents, and no more than two years later, my parents moved to Houston. When the haunting echoes of a failed business and bankruptcy in my father's ears became too much, he decided for all of us, my mother, grandmother, and two sisters, to move to Palacios because a psychic predicted his success there. We began my journey living in government housing and I remember sleeping on a mattress on the floor with my older sister and my grandmother. My father took up crabbing as his job because all other options were lacking. In Palacios, if you were a Vietnamese, you were either a shrimper or a crabber. This all changed one day when my mother, a waitress at the wage of $2.15 an hour, filled out an application for my dad to the Texas Parks and Wildlife Department. From there, things were beginning to look up.

The Mirror:

When I was four years old, I remember distinctly climbing onto my mother's dresser/vanity to look into a mirror. The first thing that came to my mind was, I wasn't white. I had not actually understood that I was different, although I knew that I could speak another language. I remember telling the other kids that my mother was pregnant with me and right before she had me, my parents got into a car and drove to the United States. At that age, I didn't know what Vietnam really was, except that it was a place that made me different from the other kids. Therefore, I lied to make them think that I was an American, that I was not different, and them being the same age, they naturally believed me. I went through school with difficulties with English at first, and often went to an ESL [English as a second language] class in order to learn how to say difficult words like "vegetable." I don't have any problems with that word now, but I remember how much I struggled to get it. I also remember being yelled at by teachers when I spoke Vietnamese. I wasn't allowed to speak it in the classroom in earshot of the teacher, or it would be a "mark" or "sit out at recess" offense. To ensure that I didn't receive punishment, I stopped speaking Vietnamese all together. Since my grandmother moved to Houston to be with my grandfather who had just come over from Vietnam, and with both my parents being busy supporting the family, I soon spoke only English, and for a moment had lost the meaning of the Vietnamese language.

The Cafeteria:

Eating in the cafeteria was no small occurrence. While the other kids were eating normal things like hamburgers and pizza, my poor intestines had not yet developed around such "abnormal foods." I often searched the cafeteria for "normal" things like rice and gio (a boiled pork roll). When I didn't find any, I started bringing in my new (garage sale) "Little Mermaid" lunchbox. Complete with the com nam (rice cake), gio, and nuc mam (fish sauce), all I needed was my drink, which was cha (tea). Unlike south Texas sweet tea, this was jasmine tea that was diluted down with water. It was the only drink in my house besides water, because soft drinks and punch were a treat, and not readily available to me. So there I was, sitting in the cafeteria, and an Anglo girl sat across from me. She asked me what stank so much, but I was oblivious to the fact that nuc mam (fish sauce) was actually salted oils from a fish hanging in the sun for weeks. What smell? I offered her some of my tea, and she drank it expecting what she was used to. She ended up lowering the cup and sticking out her tongue with disgust. Needless to say, that was the last time I packed my Vietnamese lunch.

The summer before I entered into the 5th grade, I was best friends with a girl named Sherry. Sherry and I were at the pool one day when she asked me what my religion was. I told her I was Buddhist. She looked at me with this aghast look on her face and said, "You mean you don't believe in God?" Quick to cover my tracks, I answered, "Of course I do," and proceeded to explain a religion that I didn't know, but of course you couldn't have known that from the way I was telling it. Being Buddhist meant that I was different from 99% of the other Vietnamese in the town. In fact, at the time, I was one of very few families that did not live in the "Vietnamese Village," three streets filled with trailers of only Vietnamese people, complete with their own church. I say "their" because I was never privy to that group. I sought to be friends with white kids because the other Vietnamese kids found me strange. I didn't live where they lived, I didn't go to their church, I didn't dress like them, and I wasn't skinny like them. In a nutshell, I was an outsider, Vietnamese speaking or not. In fact, I remember this game of rubber band jump-rope that the Vietnamese kids would play, yet they would pick all the other kids (white, black, and Hispanic) before they chose me to play. I built up the courage to ask them one day, and being as passive as they were, they allowed me to. I was filled with joy and excitement till I saw the look of annoyance on their faces, and so I stopped and left, ashamed that I had even asked.

It's My Party:

When I was in the 8th grade, I had a best friend that was white. This was very normal for me, because my best friends growing up were always other outcast white girls, never popular girls of any other races, and definitely not Vietnamese girls. This year was different, however, and I was best friends with an Anglo girl one year younger than me. Her brother and I were in the same grade, and they were from a very well-to-do family. Their last name rang with power in the city, and anybody with the last name like theirs got somewhere regardless of talent or potential. Needless to say, it was a weird match but we saw past that and were inseparable. That is, until the other kids found out that we were best friends. . . . As I sit here writing, I have just finished sifting through old school notes passed to each other in the boredom of class or the excitement of gossip. I've come across 20 letters from my then best friend, "Lilly." We had been best friends for the first semester, and so naturally, when Christmas break came up, we were seething with excitement about her first sleepover birthday party. The list was prepared, the details were smoothed out, all that was left was final approval from her parents. The next letter states that she was sorry she had to uninvite me, because her parents "did not know me well enough." Surprisingly, her parents didn't know any of the minorities well enough, and her final birthday party list was filled with her Anglo cousins and friends. Another letter recounts her friends and cousins asking how she could be friends with me. I was, after all, unpopular Jennifer Chau, not good enough to hang with the top Anglo kids. Her answer was that if they didn't know me, they "shouldn't be talking." I guess that peer pressure can cave everything in. It wasn't because I didn't want to be friends with her, it was because she didn't want everybody else judging her because she was friends with me. Youth is funny in that when you sign every letter "best friends forever" it is just a phrase that is easily abandoned.

My Big Fat . . . Chinese Restaurant:

One of the bold ventures that brought my family to enjoy the somewhat financial stability that we have now, is that my mom opened a restaurant when I was six years old. It started in a 700 square foot building, aptly named "Eggroll Express." It later changed into a much larger building and was renamed "Yangchow Restaurant." I was so very proud that my parents had taken on this endeavor. But, the main thing that you have to remember being from a Vietnamese family, is that EVERYONE puts in effort. My grandmother's job was to make the eggrolls. My older sister, who was ten at the time, helped clean the tables and waitress. Even at six, I often stood on top of a chair, or stayed next to my mother's hip at the wok stove, taking in every moment. To get me out of the way, my mother would send me to "help" at the cash register. To everyone's surprise, or not, I was able to master the art of monetary exchange. Basically, I could tell you prior and after tax how much an order of fried rice and eggrolls cost before calculating it in the register. I continued helping at the cash register for the next 14 years, although as I grew older my job began to incorporate duties such as dish washer, the to-go window register, hostess, waitress, sous chef, and assistant manager. When I was finally able to drive, I still visited my mother's restaurant every day during lunch. At our high school, we had open campus, so this was acceptable. I worked every day at the restaurant during my lunch break, and on days that I didn't help, I had to have a very good excuse. I was expected to work during lunch, and after school until dinner. I had very few days off. Even after graduation when I was attending college, I was still expected to work at the restaurant any time that I wasn't in class. Especially when my mother became very ill, I was the person that was expected to step in and cook for the restaurant. I had been the only child that had stayed with my mother the entire time to work, help out, and watch her cook; and so naturally, it was I who took over the reins of the restaurant. And until the day that my mom sold the restaurant, I still worked there, even when I had already moved to Houston.

Source: Jennifer Chau. Copy in authors' possession.

NOTES

PART ONE TEXT

1. Gertrude Beasley, *My First Thirty Years* (1925; reprint, Book Club of Texas, 1989), 81–82, 161–163.

2. Nelle Wooding, interview by John Schacht, 1978, University of Iowa Oral History Project, Archives of Labor and Urban Affairs, Wayne State University, p. 2.

3. Ruthe Winegarten, *Black Texas Women: 150 Years of Trial and Triumph* (Austin: University of Texas Press, 1995), 167.

4. Mario T. García, "The Chicana in American History: The Mexican Women of El Paso, 1880–1920—A Case Study," *Pacific Historical Review* 49:2 (May 1980): 330.

5. Quoted in Stephen H. Norwood, *Labor's Flaming Youth: Telephone Operators and Worker Militancy, 1878–1923* (Urbana: University of Illinois Press, 1990), 133.

6. Irene Ledesma, "Unlikely Strikers: Mexican-American Women in Strike Activity in Texas, 1919–1974" (Ph.D. diss., Ohio State University, 1992), 86–87.

7. Calculated from *Report of the Commissioner of Education for the Year Ended 1899–1900*, vol. 2 (Washington, D.C.: U.S. Government Printing Office, 1901), 1920–1921, and *Report . . . for the Year Ended June 30, 1910*, vol. 2 (1911), 904.

8. *Report . . . for the Year Ended June 30, 1910*, 2:1261, 1272.

9. *The University of Texas Medical Branch at Galveston: A Seventy-five Year History by the Faculty and Staff* (Austin: University of Texas Press, 1967), Appendices P and R.

10. Pauline Periwinkle [Isadore Callaway], "Conclusion Drawn[:] Few Mothers Wise," *Dallas Morning News*, January 4, 1915.

11. Cheryl Ellis Viaini, "Galveston's Midwives in the Early Twentieth Century," *Houston Review* 19:1 (1997): 39–48.

12. "'Fewer and Better Children' Said Mrs. Decker," *Texas Club Woman*, October 20, 1906.

13. *Dallas Morning News*, February 11, 1907.

14. Mrs. Cree T. Work, "A Pure Food Law and Its Administration," *Holland's Magazine*, January 1907, 6, 31.

15. "Texas Fifth in Bales of Cotton Manufactured," *Dallas Morning News*, April 26, 1908.

16. Texas Legislature, House, *Journal of the House of Representatives of the Regular*

Session of the Thirty-fifth Legislature Convened January 9, 1917, and Adjourned March 21, 1917 (Austin: Von Boeckmann-Jones, 1917), 1280.

17. Ann R. Gabbert, "Prostitution and Moral Reform in the Borderlands: El Paso, 1890–1920," *Journal of the History of Sexuality* 12 (October 2003): 12.

18. Howard B. Woolston, *Prostitution in the United States prior to the Entrance of the United States in the World War* (Appleton-Century Co., 1921; reprint, Montclair, N.J.: Patterson Smith, 1969), 341–342.

19. Charles F. Robinson II, "Legislated Love in the Lone Star State: Texas and Miscegenation," *Southwestern Historical Quarterly* 108:1 (July 2004): 65–86.

20. Quoted in Deborah Gray White, *Too Heavy a Load: Black Women in Defense of Themselves, 1894–1994* (New York: W. W. Norton, 1999), 60.

21. Irene Castaneda, "Personal Chronicle of Crystal City," in *Mexican Women in the United States: Struggles Past and Present*, ed. Magdalena Mora and Adelaida R. Del Castillo (Los Angeles: Chicano Studies Research Center, UCLA, 1980), 186.

22. Gabriela González, "Two Flags Entwined: Transborder Activists and the Politics of Race, Ethnicity, Class, and Gender in South Texas, 1900–1950" (Ph.D. diss., Stanford University, 2005), 5.

23. Ricardo Flores Magón, "A la mujer," quoted in Martha P. Cotera, *Diosa y Hembra: The History and Heritage of Chicanas in the U.S.* (Austin: Information Systems Development, 1976), 67.

24. Juan Gomez-Quinones, *Sembradores: Ricardo Flores Magón y el Partido Liberal Mexicano: A Eulogy and Critique*, UCLA Chicano Studies Center Monograph 5 (Los Angeles: Aztlán Publications, 1973), 76–77 n. 60.

25. Quoted in Clara Lomas, "Transborder Discourse: The Articulation of Gender in the Borderlands in the Early Twentieth Century," *Frontiers* 24:2–3 (June–September 2003): 73.

26. *El Paso Times,* January 29, 1917.

27. Yolanda Chávez Leyva, "'There Is Great Good in Returning': A Testimonio from the Borderlands," *Frontiers* 24 (June–September 2003): 7.

28. "Woman's Vote Will Cover Texas," *Galveston News,* June 14, 1914.

29. Minnie Fisher Cunningham to Jessie Daniel Ames, August 19, 1916, Jane Y. McCallum Papers, part II, box 54, file 14a/1, Austin History Center, Austin Public Library, Austin, Tex.

30. Hortense Ward, "Shall Women Have Adequate Laws?" *Texas Magazine* 7 (January 1913): 239–242.

31. Carrie Chapman Catt to Edith Hinkle League, July 17, 1918, McCallum Papers, box 3, folder 4.

32. Jane Y. McCallum, "Activities of Women in Texas Politics," in *Citizens at Last: The Woman Suffrage Movement in Texas*, ed. Ruthe Winegarten and Judith N. McArthur (Austin: Ellen C. Temple, 1987), 221.

PART ONE DOCUMENTS

1. A row of one-story, one-room wooden shacks that opened directly onto the street.

2. Todd was finishing a speaking tour in New York; Texas was next on her itinerary.

3. The Texas Woman Suffrage Association changed its name to the Texas Equal Suffrage Association in 1916.

4. Cunningham always believed that the suffragists had been defeated through election fraud, but the TESA did not have the funds to launch an investigation.

5. Charlotte Rowe of New York was a speaker and an organizer for the National Association Opposed to Woman Suffrage.

PART TWO TEXT

1. Ada Morehead Holland, *Brush Country Woman* (College Station: Texas A&M University Press, 1988), 82.

2. Quoted in Elizabeth Maret, *Women of the Range: Women's Roles in the Beef Cattle Industry* (College Station: Texas A&M University Press, 1993), 30.

3. Ruth Allen, *The Labor of Women in the Production of Cotton* (University of Texas Bulletin 3134, September 1931), 71.

4. Thad Sitton, *Harder than Hardscrabble: Recollections of Life from the Edge of the Texas Hill Country* (Austin: University of Texas Press, 2003), 79.

5. Allen, *Labor of Women*, 45, 48, 182, 218.

6. Quoted in Robert A. Caro, *The Years of Lyndon Johnson: The Path to Power* (New York: Random House, 1981), 509.

7. Mary Edna Gearing, "The Conservation of Women on the Farm," in *Sixteenth Texas Farmers' Congress, 1913*, Texas Department of Agriculture Bulletin 33 (Austin: Von Boeckmann-Jones, 1913), 71.

8. Cunningham was the first Texas woman to seek the office, and she wrote an account of her campaign. See "Too Gallant a Walk," *Woman's Journal*, January 1929.

9. Jane Y. McCallum, "Activities of Women in Texas Politics," in *Citizens at Last: The Woman Suffrage Movement in Texas*, ed. Ruthe Winegarten and Judith N. McArthur (Austin: Ellen C. Temple, 1987), 228.

10. "Women Seek Party Rights," *Dallas Morning News*, September 9, 1926.

11. McCallum, "Activities of Women in Texas Politics," 222; Jane Y. McCallum to Mrs. Abe Blum, February 8, 1923, box 15, Jane Y. McCallum Papers, Austin History Center, Austin Public Library, Austin, Tex.

12. Mattie Lloyd Wooten, "The Status of Women in Texas" (Ph.D. diss., University of Texas, 1941), 190–192, 270–272, 277.

13. Diane Manning, *Hill Country Teacher: Oral Histories from the One-Room School and Beyond* (Boston: Twayne, 1990), 93.

14. Wooten, "Status of Women in Texas," 187–189. In 1929–1930 white male teach-

ers averaged $1,518.71 annually, while white women averaged $1,002.24 (*Texas Almanac*, 1931, 267).

15. Manning, *Hill Country Teacher*, 52.

16. Marion Elizabeth Watts, "A Study of the Problems of Women Teachers in South and Southeast Texas" (M.A. thesis, University of Texas, 1943), 156-157.

17. The salary differential between black male and female teachers was not as great as for whites, but the wages for both were abysmal. William Joseph Brophy, "The Black Texan, 1900-1950: A Quantitative History" (Ph.D. diss., Vanderbilt University, 1974), 35, calculates the ratio of black teachers' salaries to whites' at 58 percent in 1930 and 61 percent in 1940. In 1937-1938 the average annual salary for a black woman teacher was $616, while a man averaged $729 (Wooten, "Status of Women in Texas," 189).

18. Dorothy Redus Robinson, *The Bell Rings at Four: A Black Teacher's Chronicle of Change* (Austin: Madrona Press, 1978), 33.

19. Oral memoirs of Maggie Langham Washington, March 10, 1988-March 13, 1989, Baylor University Institute for Oral History, Waco, Tex.

20. Patsy Cravens, *Leavin' a Testimony: Portraits from Rural Texas* (Austin: University of Texas Press, 2006).

21. Ruthe Winegarten, *I Am Annie Mae: The Personal Story of a Texas Black Woman* (Austin: Rosegarden Press, 1983), 54.

22. William Henry Kellar, "Alive with a Vengeance: Houston's Black Teachers and Their Fight for Equal Pay," *Houston Review* 18:2 (1996): 89-103.

23. Neil Foley, *The White Scourge: Mexicans, Blacks, and Poor Whites in Texas Cotton Culture* (Berkeley: University of California Press, 1997), 41.

24. Aurora E. Orozco, "Mexican Blood Runs through My Veins," in *Speaking Chicana: Voice, Power, Identity*, ed. D. Leticia Galindo and María Dolores Gonzales (Tucson: University of Arizona Press, 1999), 110; Chad Richardson, *Batos, Bolillos, Pochos, and Pelados: Class and Culture on the South Texas Border* (Austin: University of Texas Press, 1999), 125.

25. Quoted in Emma Perez, *The Decolonial Imaginary: Writing Chicanas into History* (Bloomington: Indiana University Press, 1999), 85.

26. Cynthia E. Orozco, "The Origins of the League of United Latin American Citizens (LULAC) and the Mexican American Civil Rights Movement in Texas, with an Analysis of Women's Political Participation in a Gendered Context, 1910-1929" (Ph.D. diss., University of California at Los Angeles, 1992), 327.

27. "A Diary Setting Out Briefly the Life of May Eccles," vol. 8: February 5, 14, September 15, 1931; vol. 9: January 20, March 15, 1932, February 7, 1933, Daughters of the Republic of Texas Library at the Alamo, San Antonio.

28. Jeane Westin, *Making Do: How Women Survived the '30s* (Chicago: Follett, 1976), 205-206.

29. Mary Loretta Sullivan and Bertha Blair, *Women in Texas Industries: Hours, Wages, Working Conditions, and Home Work* (Washington, D.C.: U.S. Government Printing Office, 1936), 14.

30. John Thomas McGuire, "'The Most Unjust Piece of Legislation': Section 213 of the Economy Act of 1932 and Feminism during the New Deal," *Journal of Policy History* 20:4 (2008): 516–517. By October 1933 roughly 1,900 federal employees, three-fourths of them women, had been fired or resigned as a consequence of the Economy Act. Congress repealed Section 213 in 1937, but only a handful of women got their jobs back. The Railway Mail Service refused to rehire Gussie Howell or any other former female employees.

31. Quoted in Julia Kirk Blackwelder, *Women of the Depression: Caste and Culture in San Antonio, 1929–1939* (College Station: Texas A&M University Press, 1984), 126.

32. Dennis H. Cooke and E. R. Enlow, "Local Residents and Married Women as Teachers," *Review of Educational Research* 4:3 (June 1934): 288; John Edward Carrico, "A Study of the Employment of Married Women as Teachers in the Public Schools" (M.A. thesis, University of Texas, 1933), 14–15, 23; Hoy Chaddick, "The Problem of the Married Woman in the Public Schools" (M.A. thesis, University of Texas, 1939), 70.

33. Oral interview 722, Sra. X, 1979, Institute of Oral History, University of Texas at San Antonio.

34. Quoted in Rebecca Sharpless, "Women and Work during the Great Depression in Texas," in *Invisible Texans: Women and Minorities in Texas History*, ed. Donald Willett and Stephen Curley (New York: McGraw Hill, 2005), 153.

35. Irene Ledesma, "Unlikely Strikers: Mexican American Women in Strike Activity in Texas, 1919–1974" (Ph.D. diss., Ohio State University, 1992), 95.

36. Geoffrey Rips, "Living History: Emma Tenayuca Tells Her Story," *Texas Observer*, October 28, 1983, 11 (first quotation), 10 (second quotation).

37. Ruthe Winegarten, *Black Texas Women: A Sourcebook* (Austin: University of Texas Press, 1996), 175–176.

38. Mary Cimarolli, *The Bootlegger's Other Daughter* (College Station: Texas A&M University Press, 2003), 94.

39. This was a temporary subterfuge. A 1936 court decision, *U.S. v. One Package of Japanese Pessaries*, ruled that the distribution of contraceptives, when prescribed by a physician to save a life or promote well-being, was not a violation of the Comstock Act.

40. Dr. John Zell Gaston, "Abstract of Discussion" following "The Responsibility of the Medical Profession in the Movement for 'Birth Control,'" by George W. Kosmak, *Journal of the American Medical Association* 113:17 (October 21, 1939): 1559; Mrs. George Ripley, "Birth Control," *Latch String*, June 1936, 18 (quotation).

41. Westin, *Making Do*, 159–160.

42. Mary Potchernick Cook, "Angelina's Rosies: Women at War in World War II East Texas" (M.A. thesis, Stephen F. Austin University, 1998), 103.

43. Olivia Rawlston, interview by Glenn Scott, no. 1, Texas Labor Archives, University of Texas at Arlington, p. 5 (first quotation), p. 7 (second quotation).

44. Joyce Nozaki, interview by Joy Yukashi Nozaki Gee, Florin Japanese American Citizens League Oral History Project, California State University, Sacramento,

p. 71. Tapes of the Beatrice and Torata Akagi interview are at the Institute of Texan Cultures, San Antonio.

45. Quoted in Cindy Weigand, *Texas Women in World War II* (Lanham, Md.: Republic of Texas Press, 2003), 166–167.

46. Quoted in Susan Hartmann, *The Home Front and Beyond: American Women in the 1940s* (Boston: Twayne, 1982), 42.

47. Quoted in Weigand, *Texas Women in World War II*, 167.

48. Josephine Kelly Ledesma Walker, interview by Monica Rivera, U.S. Latino and Latina World War II Oral History Project, University of Texas at Austin, http://www.lib.utexas.edu/ww2latinos/.

49. Cook, "Angelina's Rosies," 125.

PART TWO DOCUMENTS

1. Robertson, a Baptist, infused his campaign with religious rhetoric, criticizing modern materialism and calling for renewed emphasis on Christianity, the Bible, and the Ten Commandments.

2. Although Prohibition had ended the commercial sale of liquor, it could be purchased by prescription from drugstores for "medicinal use," a loophole that was widely abused. KKK Grand Dragon Z. E. Marvin, Robertson's political benefactor, was reputed to do a high-volume prescription whiskey business through his drugstore chain.

3. At the Democratic presidential nominating convention in New York City the previous month, Ames had been part of the Texas delegation, of which at least half were Klansmen. The convention was polarized by the issue of Klan influence in the party, and a platform resolution to repudiate the KKK by name lost by a single vote. During the raucous balloting, the Texas delegation had been surrounded by a cordon of New York City policemen for its own protection.

4. Davis was the Democratic presidential nominee.

5. Oral memoirs of Martha Cotera, March 3–April 6, 1973, Mexican-American Project, Baylor University, Program for Oral History, Waco, Tex., 4.

6. Leona B. Hendrix was probably an area representative of the National Business and Professional Girls Council in Kansas City.

7. Quoted in Cynthia E. Orozco, "Alice Dickerson Montemayor's Feminist Challenge to LULAC in the 1930s," *IDRA Newsletter*, March 1996, 7.

8. All military troops were required to move out. U.S. forces retreated to Bataan and Corregidor.

PART THREE TEXT

1. Nancy MacLean, "Postwar Women's History: The 'Second Wave' or the End of the Family Wage?" in *A Companion to Post-1945 America*, ed. Jean-Christophe Agnew and Roy Rosenwig (Oxford: Blackwell, 2006).

2. Brett Harvey, *The Fifties: A Women's Oral History* (New York: Harper Collins, 1993), 50.

3. Ibid., 52.

4. Ann Richards, with Peter Kobler, *Straight from the Heart: My Life in Politics and Other Places* (New York: Simon and Schuster, 1989), 98–99.

5. Ibid., 118–119.

6. Blanche Wells, "History of CWA Local 6201, Fort Worth," MS, Texas Labor Archives, University of Texas at Arlington.

7. Nelle Wooding, interview by John Schacht, 1978, University of Iowa Oral History Project, Archives of Labor and Urban Affairs, Wayne State University, p. 26.

8. Roger Horowitz, *"Negro and White, Unite and Fight!" A Social History of Industrial Unionism in Meatpacking, 1930–90* (Urbana: University of Illinois Press, 1997), 166.

9. This and all subsequent quotations regarding the UPWA are from the Mary Salinas interview, United Packinghouse Workers of America Oral History Project, State Historical Society of Wisconsin, Madison. Excerpts from the Salinas tapes also appear in Rick Halpern and Roger Horowitz, eds., *Meatpackers: An Oral History of Black Packinghouse Workers and Their Struggle for Racial and Economic Equality* (New York: Twayne, 1996).

10. Irene Ledesma, "Texas Newspapers and Chicana Workers' Activism," *Journal of Western History* 26:3 (1995): 323 (first quotation); Vicki L. Ruiz, "Tex-Son Strike," in *Latinas in the United States: A Historical Encyclopedia,* ed. Vicki L. Ruiz and Virginia Sanchez-Karrol (Bloomington: Indiana University Press, 2006), 745 (second quotation).

11. Toni Marie Nelson Herrera, "Constructed and Contested Meanings of the Tex-Son Strike in San Antonio, Texas, 1959: Representing Mexican Women Workers" (M.A. thesis, University of Texas at Austin, 1997), 37.

12. Guadalupe San Miguel Jr., *"Let All of Them Take Heed": Mexican Americans and the Campaign for Educational Equality in Texas, 1910–1981* (Austin: University of Texas Press, 1987), 134.

13. Oral memoirs of Martha Cotera, March 3–April 6, 1973, Mexican-American Project, Baylor University Program for Oral History, Waco, Tex.

14. Mariann Garner-Wizard, "The Lie," in *No Apologies: Texas Radicals Celebrate the '60s,* ed. Daryl Janes (Austin: Eakin Press, 1992), 84.

15. Nancy McMeans, "Barbara Smith Came to UT for Education," *Daily Texan,* May 9, 1957; "Barbara Smith Conrad: Mezzo-soprano, Civil Rights Pioneer," http://txtell.lib.utexas.edu/stories/c0006-short.html.

16. Linda Lewis, "Young, Gifted, and Black," in Janes, *No Apologies,* 65–67.

17. Doug Rossinow, *The Politics of Authenticity: Liberalism, Christianity, and the New Left in America* (New York: Columbia University Press, 1998), 102. After Students for Direct Action called for nationwide demonstrations against segregated theaters, Hayden received a telegram of praise from Eleanor Roosevelt.

18. Thomas R. Cole, *No Color Is My Kind: The Life of Eldrewey Stearns and the Integration of Houston* (Austin: University of Texas Press, 1997), 29.

19. *Ibid.*, 75.

20. Barbara Simons, ed., *I Dream a World: Portraits of Black Women Who Changed America* (New York: Stewart, Tabori, and Chang, 1989), 35.

21. Juanita Craft, oral history interview by David Striklin and Gail Tomlinson, January 23, 1979, Craft Papers, Dallas Public Library, pp. 14–15.

22. "Girls Helped Spark Long Integration Battle at HISD," *Houston Chronicle,* May 17, 2004.

23. Ibid.

24. Vivian Howard, interview by Rosalee Martin, May 29, 2001, Texas Council for the Humanities, "Parallel and Crossover Lives: Texas Before and After Desegregation," http://www.humanitiestexas.org/programs/past/crossover/hustontillotson/.

25. Alice Darden Davis, interview by Rosalee Martin, May 25, 2001, Texas Council for the Humanities, "Parallel and Crossover Lives," http://www.humanitiestexas.org/programs/past/crossover/hustontillotson/davis.php.

26. Quoted in Elna C. Green, "From Antisuffragism to Anti-Communism: The Conservative Career of Ida M. Darden," *Journal of Southern History* 65:2 (May 1999): 311.

27. Meg McCain Grier, *Grassroots Women: A Memoir of the Texas Republican Party* (Boerne, Tex.: Wingscape Press, 2001), 26.

28. Grier, *Grassroots Women,* 29.

29. Catherine E. Rymph, *Republican Women: Feminism and Conservatism from Suffrage through the Rise of the New Right* (Chapel Hill: University of North Carolina Press, 2006), 112.

30. Roger M. Olien, *From Tokenism to Triumph: The Texas Republicans since 1920* (Dallas: Southern Methodist University Press, 1982), 143.

31. Grier, *Grassroots Women,* 210.

32. Ibid., 214.

33. Ibid., 50.

34. Ibid, 219.

35. Scrapbook prepared by Kate Adele Hill, Bryan–College Station Business and Professional Women's Club, Woman's Collection, Blagg-Huey Library, Texas Woman's University, pp. 2, 6.

PART THREE DOCUMENTS

1. Constance Curry directed the National Student Association's Southern Student Human Relations Project. It sponsored a three-week Southern Seminar every summer for selected white and black southern college students. The seminar's purpose was cross-racial communication; participants studied the social and political factors that shaped the South's oppressive, racially polarized culture. Hayden was one of sixteen students at the 1960 seminar, held at the University of Minnesota. Afterward, they attended the NSA Annual Congress, at which members of SNCC made a presentation on the black student sit-ins to desegregate lunch counters that had begun in

the spring and asked for NSA support. White southern students requested a plenary session panel to respond, and Curry made certain that Hayden was on it. The other three members—all men—argued against sit-ins; Hayden, speaking last, defended the ethical right of the oppressed individuals to peaceable protest. She received a standing ovation, and the NSA passed a resolution of support.

2. Dorothy Height was president of the National Council of Negro Women.

3. Ruthe Winegarten, *Black Texas Women: A Sourcebook* (Austin: University of Texas Press, 1996), 206–207; Juanita Craft to Walter White, August 4, 1951, box 1, folder 1, Craft Papers, Dallas Public Library.

PART FOUR TEXT

1. *Report of the Governor's Commission on the Status of Women, State of Texas* (n.p., 1967), 50.

2. Ibid., 54 (all quotations).

3. The Governor's Commission on the Status of Women in Texas disbanded in 1969 when John Connally left office. In 1970 Preston Smith appointed a Texas Status of Women Commission, which sponsored a statewide conference and then disbanded. Governor Dolph Briscoe established a Commission on the Status of Women in 1977, which Bill Clements abolished in 1979. In 1983 Mark White established the Governor's Commission for Women, with a small staff and a biennial budget, and every subsequent governor has continued it.

4. "And Now, Governor . . . ," *Texas Observer*, August 21, 1970, 7–8.

5. Nancy MacLean, *Freedom Is Not Enough: The Opening of the American Workplace* (New York: Russell Sage Foundation; Cambridge, Mass.: Harvard University Press, 2006), 123.

6. Quoted in Ruth Rosen, *The World Split Open: How the Modern Women's Movement Changed America* (New York: Penguin Books, 2000), 79.

7. *Rag*, September 8, 1970; *Houston Chronicle*, August 27, 1970.

8. Carol Kneeland and Jorjanna Price, "One Year Later It's Still a White Man's Career World," *Houston Journalism Review* (October 1973): 6–9; *Broadside* (Houston), December 1973, March 1974; *Say It NOW* (San Antonio), September 1974; *NOW Hear This* (Dallas), August 1977; *Houston Breakthrough*, February 1977.

9. *Broadside* (Houston), May 1972, August 1975; *Say It NOW* (San Antonio), March 1976; *Austin NOW Newsletter*, February, April, May, and June 1974.

10. Bonnie Cook Freeman, "Antifeminists and Women's Liberation: A Case Study of a Paradox," *Women and Politics* 3:1 (Spring 1983): 21–38.

11. *Texas State National Organization for Women Newsletter*, February and August 1977.

12. *Austin NOW Times*, March–April and October 1983.

13. "Lesbian Mothers and Child Custody," *Texas NOW Times*, April–May 1983; G. K. Sprinkle, "Politics and Lesbian Rights," *Texas NOW Times*, December 1983–January 1984.

14. *Austin NOW Newsletter,* May 1973.

15. Eleanor J. Bader, "NOW Confronts Racism," *New Directions for Women,* November–December 1990, 3, 11.

16. "Fashion Scene," *Rag,* May 12, 1969, 1, 14; "Women's Liberation," *Second Coming,* December 1, 1970, 6–7; "Miss Who?" *Rag,* November 3, 1969.

17. "All-Woman Sit-in at S.S. Office," *Rag,* October 31, 1966, 1, 3, 10–11; "Rag Recollections," *Austin Chronicle,* September 2, 2005, 2.

18. Susan Torian Olan, "Blood Debts," in *No Apologies: Texas Radicals Celebrate the '60s,* ed. Daryl Janes (Austin: Eakin Press, 1992), 20–22, 29–30 (quotation).

19. "Rag Recollections," 6.

20. Quoted in "Birth Control," *Rag,* November 3, 1969.

21. Frieda L. Werden, "Adventures of a Texas Feminist," in Janes, *No Apologies,* 199–202. Doug Rossinow, *The Politics of Authenticity: Liberalism, Christianity, and the New Left in America* (New York: Columbia University Press, 1998), Chap. 8, describes the emergence of women's liberation from the New Left at the University of Texas.

22. [Judy Smith], "Women's Psyches," *Rag,* July 31, 1969; Sue Hester, "A [Woman] Is Not a [Chick]," *Rag,* July 5, 1971.

23. Barbara Wuensch, "Women's Liberation," *Rag,* September 15, 1969.

24. *Second Coming,* 1:3 (June 25, 1971); Werden, "Adventures of a Texas Feminist," 206.

25. Vicki L. Ruiz, *From Out of the Shadows: Mexican Women in Twentieth-Century America* (New York: Oxford University Press, 1998), 100 (first quotation); María Elena Martínez, oral history interview by José Angel Gutiérrez, 1998, Special Collections, University of Texas at Arlington, 50 (second quotation).

26. "Crystal City Walkout Seen as Turning Point," *San Antonio Express-News,* December 6, 1994. See also Lara's letter expressing Chicano pride to the editor of the *Zavala County Sentinel,* November 27, 1969.

27. Ruiz, *From Out of the Shadows,* 116 (quotation); José Angel Gutiérrez, *The Making of a Chicano Militant: Lessons from Cristal* (Madison: University of Wisconsin Press, 1998), 193–194. In 1981 Olivia Serna was elected mayor of Crystal City.

28. Armando Navarro, *The Cristal Experiment: A Chicano Struggle for Community Control* (Madison: University of Wisconsin Press, 1998), 310.

29. Mary Ann Villarreal, "The Synapses of Struggle: Martha Cotera and Tejana Activism," in *Las Obreras: Chicana Politics of Work and Family,* ed. Vicki L. Ruiz (Los Angeles: UCLA Chicano Studies Research Center, 2000), 290.

30. The platform is reprinted in Alma M. García, ed., *Chicana Feminist Thought: The Basic Historical Writings* (New York: Routledge, 1997), 167–169. By contrast, see the platform of LRUP of Northern California, 165–167, which contains a truly radical set of demands for women's rights.

31. Martínez interview.

32. Mirta Vidal, *Chicanas Speak Out: Women, New Voice of La Raza* (New York: Pathfinder Press, 1971), 5, 12, 14.

33. Martha Cotera, "Mexicana Feminism," *La Mujer Mexicana* (1973?), box 4,

Martha Cotera Papers, Benson Latin American Collection, University of Texas Libraries, University of Texas at Austin (first quotation); Villarreal, "Synapses of Struggle," 291 (second quotation).

34. Rodolfo Rosales, *The Illusion of Inclusion: The Untold Political Story of San Antonio* (Austin: University of Texas Press, 2000), 116.

35. Martha P. Cotera, "Among the Feminists: Racist, Classist Issues," in her *The Chicana Feminist* (Austin: Information Systems Development, 1977), 40 (quotation); Marta Cotera, "Feminism: The Chicana and Anglo Versions; A Historical Analysis," in García, *Chicana Feminist Thought*, 229–230. (When her work appears in Chicano publications or anthologies, Cotera's given name is sometimes printed in the Spanish alternative.)

36. Villarreal, "Synapses of Struggle," 293; Cotera, "Mexicana Feminism."

37. Quoted in Lawrence Lader, *Abortion II: Making the Revolution* (Boston: Beacon Press, 1973), 37.

38. *San Antonio Express,* January 23, 1977, 2-A. See also *Texas State National Organization for Women Newsletter,* May 1977, which reprints the full text of the defensive speech "We Are Pro-Life," delivered by Pat Konstam at the NOW memorial service.

39. Before 1967 the husband controlled the couple's community property, and the wife could not give any of it to their children except by will. She could not transfer any property brought into the marriage without his signature, could not borrow money in her own name, and could not make a bond without her husband's signature. A married woman could not start a business until she had gone to court and petitioned to have coverture removed; if her husband refused to join the suit, it could not proceed.

40. Quoted in Donald T. Critchlow, *Phyllis Schlafly and Grassroots Conservatism: A Woman's Crusade* (Princeton, N.J.: Princeton University Press, 2005), 218.

41. Ruth Murray Brown, *For a "Christian America": A History of the Religious Right* (Amherst, N.Y.: Prometheus Books, 2002), 65 (Hobbs quotation); Kaye Northcutt, "Fighting the ERA: The Ladies Mobilize," *Texas Observer,* November 15, 1974, 3 (Tilotta quotation).

42. David W. Brady and Kent L. Tedin, "Ladies in Pink: Religion and Political Ideology in the Anti-ERA Movement," *Social Science Quarterly* 56:4 (March 1976): 564–575. Ruth Murray Brown, in *For a "Christian America,"* 69, notes that while only 2.5 percent of religiously affiliated Texans belonged to the Church of Christ, 59.7 percent of anti-ERA activists were members. Baptists and Methodists each accounted for 9.2 percent.

43. Northcutt, "Fighting the ERA," 3.

44. "Religion and Equality: God's Plan for Us," *Texans for ERA Newsletter,* April 4, 1977. Copy in Marjorie Schuchat Papers, Woman's Collection, Blagg-Huey Library, Texas Woman's University.

45. Fact Sheet and Minutes of the Executive Committee, May 15, 1977, both in box 4-7/21a, and Nominating Committee File, box 4-7/15, all in IWY Texas Coordinating Committee Records, Texas State Library and Archives, Austin.

46. Texas IWY Executive Committee Minutes, March 25, 1977, box 4-7/16, IWY

Texas Coordinating Committee Records. According to Martha Cotera, a lesbian boycott was avoided through the efforts of the Chicana Advisory Committee, "which worked closely with them, convinced them to come to the conference, and [to] make it a progressive agenda and outcome." Martha Cotera e-mail to Harold Smith, June 16, 2009.

47. Cotera recalls that the state coordinating committee promised to reimburse the Chicana Advisory Committee and that she spent $10,000 of her own money. When the Chicana committee submitted its receipts and accounts, it was told that the money left over from the $100,000 federal grant had been returned to Washington. Cotera to Smith, June 16, 2009.

48. Quoted in Advisory Committee for IWY Concerns to Chicana Members of the Texas State IWY Coordinating Committee, February 5, 1977, box 9, folder 3, Cotera Papers. The $5 conference registration fee could be waived if requested, but the Chicana Advisory Committee felt strongly that having to ask for a fee waiver humiliated poor women and would keep them from attending. Since the conference received a federal subsidy, Chicanas wanted registration to be free or nominal—not more than $1. Martha Cotera recalled that "we advised our entire contingent to get on [*sic*] the fee waiver line . . . in order not to create class distinctions." Cotera to Smith, June 16, 2009.

49. *Eagle Forum*, May 1977, copy in box 4-7/6, IWY Texas Coordinating Committee Records.

50. See the statement by Diana Camacho: "I have it in writing from Owanah Anderson, the presiding officer, 'Had the Chicanas not come—the Antis would have taken the delegates.' This was written begrudgingly." Camacho to Pat Vasquez, attached to "Chicanas Change the Course of Texas IWY," box 9, folder 3, Cotera Papers. Martha Cotera elaborates: "Our [Chicana] Committee assured that the Texas Conference would be a pro-ERA conference, which would not have been the case if we had not had over 400 Chicanas attend the conference . . . and of all the women, Martha Smiley was the only one that admitted we had made the one real important contribution (getting the conference to be an ERA conference) since most of the other women recruited were very conservative, and the Texas Women's Political Caucus did not have the impact it could have had in this case." Martha Cotera e-mail to Harold Smith, June 1, 2009.

51. Rita V. Gomez to Owanah Anderson, July 1, 1977, box 4-7/16, IWY Texas Coordinating Committee Records; "Anti-ERA Forces Demand Probe of Balloting at Austin Women's Meeting," *Houston Post*, July 2, 1977. By contrast, a lesbian attendee complained that the group was underrepresented: there were no lesbians on the coordinating committee, and of the thirty workshops only the one on alternative lifestyles had a lesbian participant. "A Lesbian's Thoughts on IWY," *Houston Breakthrough* 2:7 (July–August 1977): 18.

52. "Old Values Best, 'Silent Majority' Roars," *Houston Post*, November 11, 1977.

53. Brown, *For a "Christian America*," 116–117.

54. *Houston Post*, October 18, 1985, copy in box 6, folder 1, Texas Women's Alliance Records, University of Texas at San Antonio Archives.

55. Jane Guzman, oral history interview by Kristi Strickland, 76, Special Collections, University of North Texas.

56. According to Virginia Whitehill, TARAL had a previous incarnation as Texas Citizens for Abortion Education and Motherhood by Choice. Virginia Whitehill, telephone interview by Judith McArthur, September 14, 2007.

57. Denise A. Hulett, "Every Child a Wanted Child: The History of Planned Parenthood in Waco" (M.A. thesis, Baylor University, 2000), 101–102.

58. Alesha E. Doan, *Opposition and Intimidation: The Abortion Wars and Strategies of Political Harassment* (Ann Arbor: University of Michigan Press, 2007), 113.

59. *Fort Worth Star-Telegram*, January 15, 2000; "TARAL Education Fund Report," January 19, 2000, copy in box 5, folder 9, Virginia Whitehill Papers, Southern Methodist University. In 1999 there was no abortion provider in 93 percent of Texas counties, and the state's teenage pregnancy rate was the fifth highest in the nation.

60. Quoted in Nancy Baker Jones and Ruthe Winegarten, *Capitol Women: Texas Female Legislators, 1923–1999* (Austin: University of Texas Press, 2000), 153, 154.

61. Quoted in Sonia R. García, Valerie Martinez-Ebers, Irasema Coronado, Sharon A. Navarro, and Patricia A. Jaramillo, *Políticas: Latina Public Officials in Texas* (Austin: University of Texas Press, 2008), 39.

62. Although several secondary sources claim that the TWPC did not endorse Canales, see "Report of Workshop: Women's Political Caucus, Raza Unida Convention, December 29, 1973," box 5, folder 1, Raza Unida Party Papers, Benson Latin American Collection, University of Texas Libraries, University of Texas at Austin. A few months earlier at the National Women's Political Caucus convention in Houston, Chicanas demanded and received the right to organize separate caucuses. See Evey Chapa, "Report from the National Women's Political Caucus," in García, *Chicana Feminist Thought*, 174–177.

63. *Legislative Bulletin from the Office of Sarah Weddington*, April 27, 1973, box 17, Cotera Papers.

64. Beth Eakman, oral history interview, OH 1174, Special Collections, University of North Texas.

65. "No. 500: Conradt Hits Another Lofty Plateau in a Career Etched in Milestones," *Austin American-Statesman*, March 13, 1988.

66. Quoted in Mary Jo Festle, *Playing Nice: Politics and Apologies in Women's Sports* (New York: Columbia University Press, 1996), 211.

67. Women's Equity Action League Papers, box 12, folder 48, Schlesinger Library, Radcliffe Institute, Harvard University; U.S. Congress, House, *The Women's Educational Equity Act: Hearings before the Subcommittee on Equal Opportunities of the Committee on Education and Labor*, 93rd Cong., 1st Sess., on *H.R. 208* (Washington, D.C., Government Printing Office, 1973); Sandra Davis Maddox, "Title IX of the Educational Amendments of 1972: Level of Implementation in Texas Public Schools"

(Ph.D. diss., University of North Texas, 1995). Maddox found that only 51 percent of principals surveyed answered questions about Title IX correctly.

68. San Francisco Bay Area Farah Strike Support Committee, *Chicanos Strike at Farah* (San Francisco: United Front Press, 1974), 6.

69. Quoted in Laurie Coyle, Gail Hershatter, and Emily Honig, *Women at Farah: An Unfinished Story* (El Paso: REFORMA, 1979), 42.

70. Quoted in David Stricklin, *A Genealogy of Dissent: Southern Baptist Protest in the Twentieth Century* (Lexington: University Press of Kentucky, 1999), 128. Stricklin's interviews with Gilmore are available in the Texas Collection at Baylor University.

71. Marilyn P. Davis, *Mexican Voices, American Dreams: An Oral History of Mexican Immigration to the United States* (New York: Henry Holt, 1990), 358.

72. See newsletters in the Texas Lesbian Conference Records and the San Antonio Lesbian and Gay Assembly Records, both in the University of Texas at San Antonio Archives.

73. Laura Lien and Deanna T. Schexnayder, with Karen Nanges Douglas and Daniel G. Schroeder, *Life after Welfare: Reform and the Persistence of Poverty* (Austin: University of Texas Press, 2007), 1–2.

PART FOUR DOCUMENTS

1. Quoted in Ruth Murray Brown, *For a "Christian America": A History of the Religious Right* (Amherst, N.J.: Prometheus Books, 2002), 39, 41.

2. *The Chicana Feminist* (Austin: Information Systems Development, 1977). Martha Cotera was elected as one of the fifty-eight Texas delegates to the National Women's Conference.

3. Liz Carpenter, former press secretary to Lady Bird Johnson, was an IWY commissioner and co-chair of ERAmerica. Jane Hickie was chairperson of the board of the Austin Women's Center, a member of the steering committee of the National Women's Political Caucus, and a past president of the Texas Women's Political Caucus. Cathy Bonner was president of Bonner, Inc., an Austin public relations firm, and the legislative lobbyist for the Texas Women's Political Caucus. She and Hickie also served on the board of the Texas Foundation for Women's Resources.

INDEX

Note: The letter *d* following a page number denotes a primary document.